Uwe Schütte (Ed.)
German Pop Music

CW01091543

Companions to Contemporary German Culture

Edited by
Michael Eskin · Karen Leeder · Christopher Young

Volume 6

German Pop Music

A Companion

Edited by
Uwe Schütte

DE GRUYTER

ISBN 978-3-11-042571-0
e-ISBN (PDF) 978-3-11-042572-7
e-ISBN (EPUB) 978-3-11-042354-9
ISSN 2193-9659

Library of Congress Cataloging-in-Publication Data
A CIP catalog record for this book has been applied for at the Library of Congress.

Bibliographic information published by the Deutsche Nationalbibliothek
The Deutsche Nationalbibliothek lists this publication in the Deutsche Nationalbibliografie;
detailed bibliographic data are available on the Internet at http://dnb.dnb.de.

© 2017 Walter de Gruyter GmbH, Berlin/Boston
Cover image: Kraftwerk © Magdalena Blaszczuk
Printing and binding: Hubert & Co. GmbH & Co. KG, Göttingen
♾ Printed on acid-free paper
Printed in Germany

www.degruyter.com

Table of Contents

Uwe Schütte

Introduction – Pop Music as the Soundtrack of German Post-War History

In 2015, three German bands gave concerts in Berlin that warrant closer attention. In mid-January, Kraftwerk played eight concerts at the Neue Nationalgalerie, a hallmark of modernist architecture designed by Mies van der Rohe in 1968. The series sold out immediately and the intense coverage by the national media ran the gamut from derision to emphatic praise. The band, known for pioneering popular electronic music since its commercial breakthrough release, *Autobahn*, in 1974, devoted each evening to one of the eight albums that form the core of its musical output. Versions of their songs, some dating back forty years, were digitally reworked with the latest sound technology and accompanied by stunning 3D video projections.

The videos consciously renounced any attempt to appear up-to-date in their visual aesthetic. Instead, some playfully combined sparse modernist graphic elements derived from the Bauhaus movement with visual allusions to German expressionist cinema (particularly *Metropolis*, 1927), while others featured footage from the post-war period of the 1950s and 1960s showing economic prosperity, political optimism and a (self-)satisfied sense of national achievement in the aftermath of the Holocaust. Although the genocide was never hinted at, it loomed large over the seemingly-innocuous images of travel on an *Autobahn* or urban nights illuminated by joyful neon lights. Sound and vision, the spoken and the unspoken, combined to form an integrative, immersive experience that is unique in contemporary electronic music and confirmed Kraftwerk's standing as the most important and influential of all German bands.

Then, on a hot summer day in July, DAF, which stands for 'Deutsch-Amerikanische Freundschaft' [German-American Friendship], gave a sold-out concert in a repurposed former East Germany railway repair works. The duo – consisting of drummer Robert Görl and singer Gabi Delgado-Lopez – performed highlights from their 1981 *Gold und Liebe* [Gold and Love] album. Just three songs into the set, DAF launched into their best-known song, the controversial 'Der Mussolini'. Delgado-Lopez sang out 'Tanz den Kommunismus' [Dance communism] while lifting his clenched left fist, and then 'Tanz den Adolf Hitler' [Dance the Adolf Hitler] while raising his right arm in the Hitler salute, a gesture banned under German law. He then barked 'Und jetzt nach links' [And now to the left] while pacing to the left of the stage and 'Und jetzt nach rechts' [And now to the right] while marching in strides to the opposite side of the stage.

DOI 10.1515/9783110425727-001

As goes without saying, what we witnessed was not a political statement but rather a grotesque, subversive appropriation of the gestures of the two political ideologies that dominated German history in the twentieth century. Whenever Delgado-Lopez gave the Hitler salute, the crowd cheered wildly although none of them are likely to have been of a right-wing political persuasion. Nor could anyone suspect this of the band since both members are openly gay and Delgado-Lopez is the son of a Spanish *Gastarbeiter* [guest worker] who immigrated to Germany in the 1960s. Furthermore, their merchandize stall sold T-shirts depicting the Kalashnikov logo of the left-wing terrorist group, Red Army Faction (RAF), although the lettering had been changed to read 'DAF'.

Finally, in early December, Fehlfarben played a rapturous concert in a former cinema near the Spree River, which once formed the border between East and West Germany. A small but appreciative audience had gathered to hear the band play tracks from their recently released album, but it rapidly became clear that the crowd really wanted songs from their 1980 debut *Monarchie und Alltag* [Monarchy and Everyday Life], a quintessential record of punk rock aesthetic and sociocultural highlights. Fittingly, since Fehlfarben was formed when post-punk was emerging in Germany, this pivotal punk band never looked the part. They rejected safety needles, colourful hairstyles and torn clothes and wore conventional hair cuts and suits. Finally, their Teutonic iteration of 'No future!', the anarchic battle call of British punk, was the seemingly affirmative 'Keine Atempause, Geschichte wird gemacht – es geht voran' [No respite, history is being made – we're moving on].

This transformation of and reaction to an Anglo-American musical movement highlights how, like their Krautrock predecessors, Fehlfarben did not want to copy a foreign model or even to translate it into German. Rather, the band transcended German punk's international origins with a mixture of irony and seriousness. Their strategy of disguising criticism as affirmation confounded expectations and clichés and, since it required a certain level of attention to be understood, this strategy anticipated the contemporaneous neutralization of punk's rebellious spirit. In addition, Fehlfarben did not just sing of affirmative subversion but lived it too: Singer Peter Hein refused to quit his day job, preferring the financial security of a boring office job in the German division of an international company to the fickle life of a musician and the siren call of commercial success.

Accordingly, at the Fehlfarben concert in December, one could not fail to notice the large number of ordinary-looking people in their fifties and sixties, none of whom displayed the usual pop-cultural signs of social dissent, such as T-shirts with protest slogans or badges. Nevertheless, just like the band, one must assume they were non-conformists, treading a thin line between social adjustment and refusal to believe in the hollow promises of capitalism in the age of late globalization.

Each of these three bands express a different sense of German identity in their music, which is closely interconnected with contemporary German history, society and culture. Coincidentally, all three bands were formed in Düsseldorf, the capital of the [then West] German state of North Rhine-Westphalia. After the Second World War, this very modern city developed into the fashion and advertising capital of Germany. Thanks to its famous Academy of Art, which produced artists such as Joseph Beuys, Gerhard Richter, Markus Lüpertz and Jörg Immendorff, it was also considered the artistic capital of Germany. The surrounding Ruhr district, on the other hand, was heavily industrialized and had a large working-class population – socio-economic factors that had a significant impact on the bands discussed above.

The relationship between musical styles and regional surroundings has been an important factor in the development of German pop music. The federal system instituted after the war allowed different musical cultures to flourish in (and around) the country's larger cities. Indeed, unlike centralist countries such as the United Kingdom or France, local scenes in Hamburg, Cologne, Munich, Frankfurt and elsewhere did not need to compete directly with the capital. Although this situation naturally changed following the German reunification in 1990, the local identities of regional music scenes remain largely intact today and continue to contribute to the fascinating varieties of German popular music explored in this volume.

German Pop Music and Academia

Popular culture became a subject of academic study following the pioneering work of the Centre for Contemporary Cultural Studies, founded at the University of Birmingham in 1964. Since then, cultural studies has been an important part of the humanities predominantly under the leadership of Anglophone scholars. Initially, universities in Germany (and Austria) were less receptive to this new trend. However, it gained greater legitimacy and considerable momentum in Germany under the moniker *Kulturwissenschaften* due to increasing pressure on academics to embrace interdisciplinary research methods and explore popular culture.

The success of film studies in the past decade, in addition to the academic study of graphic novels, demonstrates an increased interest in pop-cultural products amongst German studies scholars working in the English-speaking world. Despite all of this, the study of popular music continues to play a somewhat underrated and neglected role. Whilst film courses are now part and parcel of many German degree programmes, pop music is mainly used in language teaching classes. Yet there is eminent potential for teaching German history, society and culture through the medium of pop music, as the present volume aims to demonstrate.

German pop music offers an important opportunity to reflect on questions of German national identity and the definition of Germanness. Pertinent examples chosen from the history of German pop music enable us to ask how the nation is imagined and constructed both *in* and *through* pop music, and how it challenges received notions of Germanness. Simon Frith, a leading scholar of popular music in the UK, asserts: 'As the nation always oscillates between different enunciative positions, and national identity is a constant process of re-articulations, the question is not (only) how popular music reflects the people or nation, but also how it *produces* them.'[1] As John Connell and Chris Gibson similarly report, popular music is 'an integral component of processes through which cultural identities are formed, both at personal and collective levels', for which reason 'music [...] is embedded in the creation of (and constant maintenance of) nationhood'.[2]

Frith explains that there 'is an important reason why German popular music has to be understood differently to popular music elsewhere: twentieth-century German history has posed German musicians and audiences particular problems of national identity'.[3] One of these problems was that popular music in post-war Germany had to address the fact that the Nazis had appropriated popular culture for their racist notion of *völkische Kultur*. Another was that popular music had to navigate between the overwhelming influence of Anglo-American culture and music, and the many problems of German post-war history: the trauma and guilt resulting from the unspeakable atrocities committed during the war, the pressures resulting from the material and ideological reconstruction efforts, the division of the nation in 1961 and its mismanaged reunification in 1989/90.

Following the financial crisis of 2007/08, the German economy has recovered more rapidly than those of English-speaking countries. At the time of writing, an unabashed neo-liberalism continues to undermine the foundations of the welfare state established in the 1970s. Concomitantly, large numbers of (East) Germans have been taking to the streets to demonstrate against massive immigra-

---

1 Simon Frith, 'Music and Identity', in *Questions of Cultural Identity*, ed. by Stuart Hall and Paul du Gay (London: Sage, 1996), pp. 108–127 (p. 109).
2 John Connell and Chris Gibson, *Sound Tracks: Popular Music, Identity, and Place* (London: Routledge, 2003), pp. 117–118.
3 Simon Frith, 'Editorial introduction', *Popular Music* 17/3 (1998), v–vi (p. v).

tion and a perceived deterioration of German values whilst despicable attacks on refugee camps occur at an alarming rate across the country.

The popular music discussed in the present volume has delivered, as it were, the soundtrack for the post-1945 period of German history sketched above. It has functioned as a fascinating cultural mirror, which also reflects the sociological changes and political developments in the Federal Republic. The development of popular music in East Germany, however, will not be discussed at length in this volume, due to the repressive cultural politics in the German Democratic Republic (GDR). Even though bands there often found cunning ways to escape state pressures by retreating into subculture niches, official control of the media and record companies restricted the development of interesting, innovative pop music. Furthermore, musical transfer across the wall was mostly a one-way affair, from West to East. West Germans, let alone the wider world, took little or no notice of East German pop music.[4]

A crucial terminological point must also be stressed: The term *pop music* will be understood to apply to all the music discussed in this volume, which includes heterogeneous styles from rock and mainstream pop to industrial and forms of electronic dance music. As Diedrich Diederichsen explains in his fundamental theoretical work *Über Pop-Musik* [On Pop Music] (2014), the cultural phenomenon of pop music transcends music per se: 'Pop music is actually a complex of images, performances, (mostly popular) music, lyrics and myths tied to real persons.'[5] Following Diederichsen, then, we should acknowledge that cover design, stage outfits and haircuts, interview statements or promotional photographs are as important as the music and lyrics themselves. In this sense, pop music is a multifaceted 'package' that is difficult to define. At best we can say that pop music is mainly, although not exclusively, directed at and consumed by young people and tied to progressive, leftist, non-conformist, emancipative notions.

In accordance with Diederichsen, we will recognize a clear dividing line when looking at the overall development of pop music (and pop culture in general). The first, heroic phase, which he calls 'Pop I', lasted roughly from the early 1960s until the mid-1980s and was primarily characterized by political dissidence and subversive transgression, sub-cultural resistance and opposition to

---

4 For a concise overview of pop music in East Germany, see Fritz Herbert, 'Über sieben Brücken musst Du gehen: Eine kurze Geschichte des DDR-Rock', in *Made in Germany: Die hundert besten deutschen Platten* (Höfen: Hannibal, 2001), pp. 97–101; and Michael Rauhut, 'Am Fenster: Rockmusik und Jugendkultur in der DDR', in *Rock! Jugendkultur und Musik in Deutschland*, ed. by Bundeszentrale für politische Bildung (Berlin: Links, 2005), pp. 71–78.
5 Diedrich Diederichsen, *Über Pop-Musik* (Cologne: KiWi, 2014), p. xi. All quotes in English are my translations, unless otherwise stated.

mainstream culture. This element of protest against dominant social and political systems disappeared completely in the politically affirmative 'Pop II' phase, which runs from roughly the early 1990s to the present.

The political affirmation of 'Pop II' is perhaps not surprising given that pop music reached the top ranks of political power in the 1990s: Bill Clinton famously played a song by Elvis on his saxophone on a US TV show, Tony Blair invited Britpop band Oasis to Downing Street and the conservative German chancellor Angela Merkel told *Myself*, a glossy women's magazine, that she likes the Beatles and Bruce Springsteen.[6] Regardless of whether her passion for pop music is authentic, Merkel's statement proves Diederichsen's point that popular music no longer has an automatic claim to signifying opposition to and critical distance from the ruling powers.

Pop music also no longer has an inherent claim to representing opposition to racist, chauvinistic, homophobic, nationalist and similar political persuasions. In the German context, this de-tabooization of nationalist discourse across the entire spectrum of German mainstream pop music in the wake of reunification is highly significant and is also accompanied by the rise of racist music, which operates both underground (due to criminal prosecution and state censorship) and, in a more veiled form, in the form of popular bands like Frei.Wild.[7]

By and large, the artists and bands discussed in this companion fall into the Pop I phase, even if their musical output coincides chronologically with the post-heroic phase of pop music. Since Germany has the third most important music market in the world,[8] bands can earn a living even if their criticisms of mainstream culture or their challenging aesthetic positions prevent them from achieving success in the charts.

This volume also distinguishes between the term 'pop music' in the sense outlined above and 'popular music' that only aims at commercial success. Hence, we do not explore types of German popular music with greater market shares than the music examined in this volume, e. g. the neo-*Schlager* of Helene Fischer, the so-called *volkstümliche Musik* popularized by TV programmes such

---

6 'Im Interview: Angela Merkel', *Myself*, 9 (2009), 54–57 (p. 55).

7 On right-wing rock in Germany, see Thomas Neumann, *Rechtsrock im Wandel: Eine Textanalyse von Rechtsrock-Bands* (Hamburg: Diplomica, 2009); and Martin Büsser, *Wie klingt die Neue Mitte? Rechte und reaktionäre Tendenzen in der Popmusik* (Mainz: Ventil, 2001). On nationalist discourse in mainstream pop music, see Frank A. Schneider, *Deutschpop halt's Maul! Für eine Ästhetik der Verkrampfung* (Mainz: Ventil, 2015).

8 According to statistics provided by the International Federation of the Phonographic Industry (IFPI), it is bigger than that of the UK and only surpassed by the markets in Japan and the United States.

as *Musikantenstadl* or *Der Blaue Bock*, the surprisingly successful pop update of medieval music played by bands like Corvus Corax, the various short-lived chart successes that talent shows such as *Deutschland sucht den Superstar* regularly push on the market, not to mention manufactured acts, such as boy bands that target female teenagers or classically-trained opera singers performing pop music aimed at an elderly audience.

Since this companion cannot address all German music, we have also limited ourselves to bands that use German lyrics. Interestingly, a great deal of the music that tops the charts is German in origin but the producers and artists concerned play down and even disguise this fact. Most notoriously, Frank Farian's bands Boney M. and Milli Vanilli featured only black singers and dancers, and the lyrics were in English with Farian himself providing the vocals.

Another relevant example is Modern Talking, a duo that achieved immense international success. Following a reunion in 1997, Thomas Anders and Dieter Bohlen disbanded for good in 2003. The techno pop act Scooter, on the other hand, is still going strong in commercial terms. This band was founded in 1993 in Frankfurt and has sold more than 30 million records and had more than 20 top ten hits, which included 'Hyper Hyper', 'Move Your Ass' and 'The Question Is What Is the Question'.

This survey also disregards Germans who have produced or recorded their music abroad. They include musicians such as the Hollywood film music composer Hans Zimmer or the deceased Velvet Underground *diseuse* Christa Päffgen a.k.a. Nico. German folk music and the various genres of German jazz also lie beyond our scope, although they occasionally overlap with pop music, such as in the case of Michael Wollny, who released free-floating piano versions of songs by Kraftwerk and The Flaming Lips. Indeed, a closer examination of the full spectrum of German pop(ular) music would require an entire encyclopaedia.

The Invasion of Anglo-American Pop Music After 1945

Popular culture peaked during the so-called Golden Twenties of the Weimar Republic but was disrupted by the historical disaster of National Socialism. The demise of the Nazi regime left a cultural vacuum that was quickly filled with Anglo-American music. Hence, the gradual development of post-war German pop music in its early stages must be considered against the backdrop of this decisive historical context.

The role played by radio stations aimed at the occupying military forces should not be underestimated. The broadcasts by the American Forces Network (AFN) and British Forces Broadcasting Services (BFBS) also acquainted young German listeners with pop-musical developments in Britain and the United States. Later, DJs such as John Peel from the BBC or the US top 40 chart show hosted by Casey Kasem were broadcast by the army stations which kept their German listeners up to date.

A first indication of rock 'n' roll's coming victory march was shown by the rapturous reception Bill Haley's 'Rock Around The Clock' found amongst the youth of Western Europe following screenings of the 1955 film *Blackboard Jungle*[9] and his 1958 concert tour, both of which caused outbreaks of violence that led to cinemas and concert venues being vandalized. These riots also left behind a shocked generation of parents who rightly sensed that this inflammatory new music from America would create a shared sense of rebellion amongst the post-war youth.[10]

Two events in particular promoted the infectious spread of pop music to post-war Germany. The first was Elvis Presley's spell as a GI in the provincial town of Bad Nauheim between October 1958 and February 1960. He was already a major star at the time and his presence created a considerable 'Elvis mania' amongst German teenagers which was fuelled by the media. The weekly magazine *Bravo*, which was founded in August 1956 and is still being published today, provided endless coverage of the star even though he never performed during his army service. While Haley's music demonstrated the unruly aspect of pop music, Elvis stood for the physical, sexualized side of rock 'n' roll. He was the very incarnation of rock 'n' roll on German soil and represented the disruptive spirit of this new music that was there to stay.

The second was the Beatles' two forays into Germany in 1960/61 and again in 1962, which inaugurated the era of beat music. They had long-term gigs at the legendary Star Club in the Reeperbahn area of Hamburg and their music inspired a number of German imitators, most notably The Lords and The Rattles, who only sang in English. Never surpassing the musical genius of their model, both of these bands nevertheless benefitted greatly from the craving of young people for this new type of music.

---

9 The German title was the more appropriate *Saat der Gewalt* [Seeds of Violence].

10 Between 1956 and 1958, there was a marked increase in youth riots that confirmed the seditious nature of rock 'n' roll. Statistics show a total of 93 riots with more than 50 participants, mostly males between the age of 14 and 25 and often of working and lower middle class origin. See Christian Peters, 'Halbstark mit Musik: Der Rock 'n' Roll erobert Deutschland', in *Bundeszentrale*, pp. 35–41 (p. 37).

The Rolling Stones were the next wave in this invasion of English-language music. Their eagerly anticipated first tour of Germany resulted in a riot at the Berlin Waldbühne venue on September 1965 and the authorities had to rescue the band by helicopter. However, this legendary outbreak of vandalism was due less to the incendiary sprit of rock than to fans' frustration at the band's lacklustre performance, which led to a violent eruption that was not yet connected with any form of social protest. This soon changed, however, as English-language rock music became the soundtrack of a cultural revolution and political rebellion in Germany.

The cultural critic Klaus Theweleit even saw the role of pop music as 'a kind of symbolic de-nazification'.[11] Conservative society revealingly responded by denouncing rock music with racists labels such as *Negermusik* ['negro' music], a term coined by the Nazis. A leading newspaper described Jimi Hendrix, for example, as someone who 'looked like he was coaxed out of the jungle with the help of a banana'.[12]

The music of the Rolling Stones also inspired many German imitators, all of whom sang in English only. Setting aside such inferior copycats, only a handful of musicians dared to use their mother tongue at that time. Amongst them was (the aptly named) Drafi Deutscher, whose 'Marmor, Stein und Eisen bricht' [Marble, Steel and Iron Breaks] turned into a major hit. However, Deutscher was an exception and proved unable to repeat his one and only success. Most vocalists singing in German – such as Peter Kraus, Conny Froboess or the German (would-be) 'Elvis' Ted Herold – only delivered toned-down, inoffensive versions of rock 'n' roll and beat songs that were exclusively for commercial purposes and lacked any sense of rebellion or nonconformity. Their 'music', however, was only a prelude of things to come.

Schlager – (Un-)Easy Listening in the Post-War Era

The gradual paradigm shift in the German post-war musical landscape unfolded against the background of *Schlager* music. *Schlager* are a German version of easy-listening music that played a vital role in the social psychology of the trau-

---

11 See Martin Büsser, *On The Wild Side: Die wahre Geschichte der Popmusik* (Mainz: Ventil, 2013), p. 21.
12 See Peter Wagner, *Pop 2000: 50 Jahre Popmusik und Jugendkultur in Deutschland* (Hamburg: Ideal, 1999), p. 54.

matized post-war generation. Apart from the inherent function of such music to distract the listener from personal, everyday worries and instil passivity, *Schlager* then also served as consolation and reassurance in a post-war period marked by hunger and great uncertainty. Many had lost family members on the battlefield or during the Allied air raids that greatly intensified during the last year of the war.

While the destroyed nation was being rebuilt from the rubble of the cities, *Schlager* evoked consoling images of a beautiful and romantic countryside and painted a distorted, idyllic picture of Germany that excluded any reference to the horrors of the war and the atrocities of the concentration camps. In a sense, one could even say that the *Schlager* dream world re-echoed the Nazi ideal of a racially cleansed Germany.

Schlager also provided a soundtrack to the renewed self-esteem that resulted from the phenomenal economic recovery from the early 1950s onwards. The ensuing culture of consumerism and foreign tourism cemented a mind-set that refused to look back at the horrendous crimes committed or the traumatic suffering of the German population. A popular song like the 'Lied vom Wirtschaftswunder' [Song of the Economic Miracle] (1958) by Wolfgang Neuss and Wolfgang Müller mirrored the desire to ignore the recent past, even though this *Schlager* alluded to it. No tongue in cheek, however, is detectable in 'Konjunktur Cha-Cha' [Economic Boom Cha-Cha] by the Hazi Osterwald Sextett. The song unabashedly praised financial greed and welcomed the capitalist market system as a new arena of a supposed natural struggle in which only the strong survived, a continuation of the Social Darwinist beliefs propagated by the Nazis.

Julio Mendívil charts the entire history of the *Schlager* from its beginnings to its rather sorry state in the present day. The focus of his chapter is on the period from the 1960s to the mid-1970s, which he describes as the golden era of the genre. He discusses the various stylistic adaptations *Schlager* underwent in reaction to new trends and developments as well as the impact of the media, in particular the TV programme *Die Hitparade*, on the genre. He puts special emphasis on the representation of the Other in this most conservative and highly parochial genre of popular German music.

The Musical Revolution of the late 1960s

During the second part of the 1960s, the dominance of Anglo-American pop music in Germany began to decline. Even though artists like Jimi Hendrix and Frank Zappa, or a band like The Doors, served as countercultural heroes of an increasingly politicized youth, a musical paradigm shift began to set in. One indicator was that musicians started to sing in their native tongue and chose German names for their bands. This was a revolutionary move during those rebellious times in which pop music continued to be a unifying force for the younger generation throughout the Western world. Bob Dylan, plugging in an electric guitar for the first time during his Newport Festival appearance in 1965, symbolically demonstrated that the times were indeed a-changin'.

As David Robb discusses in his chapter on protest music during the era of the so-called student revolution in the late 1960s, the German *Liedermacher* [song-maker] movement was thoroughly affected by the revolutionary spirit of the late 1960s. The *Liedermacher* had already successfully reclaimed the German tradition of (folk) song from the political abuse it had suffered under the Nazis. In tune with the rebellious zeitgeist, singers such as Franz Josef Degenhardt now increasingly began to turn their songs into mouthpieces for social critique and political agitation.

Liedermacher music covered a broad range from the conservative German Romantic folk singing of the Youth Movement up to contemporary folk music. Some of the *Liedermacher* creatively combined the cabaret musical tradition of the Weimar era with the new folk style, while others modelled their technique on the new American finger-picking style associated with US protest singers such as Pete Seeger and Woody Guthrie.

Although the political message of many *Liedermacher* was clearly radical, their music was sometimes merely a vehicle for the lyrics. Ton Steine Scherben, however, marked the emergence of the first German band to successfully marry revolutionary politics with the incendiary sound of rock music. Like the American agit-rock band MC5, founded in Detroit in 1965, Ton Steine Scherben's mission was not just to radicalize their audience but also to encourage them to take political action, and even to incite riots. As Robb details in his chapter, the band was successful in this aim, and thus occupies a special place in the history of German pop music.

What later came to be known under the problematic portmanteau term Krautrock unwittingly turned into Germany's most important contribution to international pop music. Indeed, the influence of Krautrock on British and American bands up to the present day can hardly be overestimated. As John Littlejohn illustrates in his chapter, it was a very heterogeneous, highly experimental movement that largely broke with Anglo-American pop music norms. A desire to question the cultural dominance of Anglo-American music and to create a new, untainted German identity led to this innovative form of music and also serves as a paradigm for the close connection between radical societal change and revolution in the arts. As Ralf Hütter, a founding member of Kraftwerk, explained:

We woke up in the late '60s and realized that Germany had become an American colony. [...] There was no German culture, no German music, nothing. It was like living in a vacuum. [...] Germany had lost its identity. We all felt very lost. To be able to feel any bonds at all, we had to go back to the Bauhaus school. [...] Our roots were in the culture that was stopped by Hitler; the school of Bauhaus, German Expressionism.[13]

Though other musicians took their inspiration from different sources and influences, the sense of a need for a new German cultural identity untainted by the fascist past connected a vast number of newly emerging bands in the late 1960s and early 1970s. Krautrock, as Henning Dedekind defines it in his seminal book, is 'less a clearly definable, uniform style but rather a shared mind-set: the will to question the traditional, to explore new territories and to develop one's own musical language'.[14]

Krautrock was no expression of a new kind of patriotism or national pride but rather an attempt to liberate oneself from the inferiority complex that resulted from the dominance of Anglo-American music. It was largely the creation of an educated middle class who chose experimental music over the secure careers that awaited them. Krautrock bands were profoundly influenced by Karlheinz Stockhausen, although his contribution lay less in his compositional techniques than in his 'radical dissolution of traditional musical structures in favour of concentrating on sound itself'.[15] Yet another vital source of inspiration was the concept art of Joseph Beuys. In analogy to his 'extended definition of art', Krautrock developed an 'extended definition of sound': 'Every noise is sound, and every sound is music. The liberation of sound turns into the central element of a rock music that has once and for all abolished the strict demarcation between note and noise.'[16]

Krautrock bands only rarely made direct political statements in their music. The politics of this movement were instead expressed through their non-conformist looks, the exploration of new ways of communal living in the rural setting of deserted farms and the use of drugs for both experimental and recreational purposes. Crucial to the alternative spirit of the times were also the organization of non-commercial activities like free festivals or the fairly success-

---

13 Interview with Michael Dee, quoted in Tim Barr, *Kraftwerk: From Dusseldorf to the Future With Love* (London: Ebury, 1998), p. 74.
14 Henning Dedekind, *Krautrock: Underground, LSD und kosmische Kuriere* (Höfen: Hannibal, 2008), p. 17.
15 Ibid., p. 52.
16 Ibid., p. 53.

ful attempt to build distribution networks independent of the major record companies. A new era had truly begun.

Deutschrock – German Pop Music in the 1970s

The main thrust of the Krautrock movement only lasted approximately five years and was essentially finished by the mid 1970s. The previously self-imposed ban on German-language lyrics was now lifted by a new bourgeoning music scene. Unlike their adventurous Krautrock brethren, the bands that soon attracted the label *Deutschrock* showed little ambition to venture beyond the established parameters of Anglo-American blues, rock and hard rock. Conventional song structure replaced 'cosmic' experiments and the music featured German lyrics so as to target a mainstream audience.

Some bands even changed their orientation from the 'cosmic' to the regional by singing with pronounced local accents. Bavarian acts like the Spider Murphy Gang or Haindling made a number of albums which employed elements of southern German dialect in their lyrics. While the former basically imitated American rock music models from the 1950s and 1960s, Haindling managed to create a unique mix of world music elements steeped in Bavarian folk music. Many of the bands that heavily used their local dialects came from Cologne, in particular Zeltinger Band, Bläck Föös (which means 'bare feet' in the Cologne dialect) and, notably, BAP.

BAP was founded in 1976 and is still a major force in *Deutschrock*, regularly playing sold-out shows in large venues and stadiums. Their back catalogue comprises 23 albums so far, out of which 11 hit the number one spot in Germany. Such success seems astonishing given the fact that the lyrics of the songs can only be fully understood in their home part of Germany since the Cologne dialect is so different from standard German that the songs are virtually incomprehensible in other parts of the country. However, BAP's popularity is due to their musical formula, which consists of a clever mix of styles easily identified with mainstream acts such as The Kinks, Bob Dylan, The Rolling Stones and, last but not least, Bruce Springsteen, who is apparently a close friend of BAP singer and band founder Wolfgang Niedecken.

Udo Lindenberg is undoubtedly the most notable figure in the development of *Deutschrock*, not least due to his role as a trailblazer for later artists. Lindenberg began his career in 1971 with an unsuccessful album in English, prompting him to switch to German for the follow-up *Daumen im Wind* [Thumbs in the Wind] in 1972. The next year brought his phenomenal breakthrough with *Andrea*

Doria featuring the hit 'Alles klar auf der Andrea Doria' [No Problems on the Andrea Doria].

The purposely shoddy delivery of his often witty (and occasionally poetic) German lyrics, combined with a penchant for every-day subject matters in his songs, secured him a large following. A considerable number of successful albums were released in the 1970s, often two per year, and Lindenberg has been able to sustain his momentum from the 1980s to the present by changing styles and collaborating with (international) stars such as Eric Burdon, David Bowie and Nena. Today, he occupies the position of 'elder statesman' of *Deutschrock*, and is best remembered for his 1986 hit 'Sonderzug nach Pankow' [Special Service to Pankow] in which he lampooned the East German *Politbüro* and its chairman Erich Honecker.

Alongside Lindenberg, Herbert Grönemeyer rose to considerable fame following the release of *4630 Bochum* (1984), his patriotic paean to the small industrial town in the Ruhr area he hailed from. Originally an actor who had starred in the war movie *Das Boot* [The Boat] (dir. Wolfgang Petersen, 1981), Grönemeyer decided to concentrate on a musical career. Although he was not as prolific as Lindenberg, his follow-up albums to *4360 Bochum* made him so popular in Germany that he chose to relocate to London in the late 1990s to escape public attention. Grönemeyer also made various attempts at establishing himself beyond Germany with English-language releases but met with limited success compared to his combined album sales in Germany of over 13 million, which makes him the all-time best-selling musical artist in Germany.

A number of lesser-known singer-songwriters such as Klaus Lage, Marius Müller-Westernhagen, Wolf Maahn, Heinz Rudolf Kunze, Konstantin Wecker and Reinhard Mey began to flourish in the shadow of these two towering figures during *Deutschrock*'s boom in the 1980s. Largely unaffected by the comings and goings of musical trends, most of these artists are still active and cater to loyal audiences that have aged with them.

The 1980s also saw the emergence of several internationally successful German hard rock and heavy metal bands that sang only in English, such as Helloween, Accept, U. D. O., Warlock and Kreator. The most notable and longest-standing German hard rock band is The Scorpions from Hanover. They were formed in 1965 by Rudolf Schenker and, despite many personnel changes over the course of five decades, continue to enjoy great success today. Their metal hymn 'Rock You Like A Hurricane', from the best-selling album *Love At First Sting* (1984), was an international hit. It was eclipsed, however, by their rather cheesy 'Winds of Change' single from 1991, which sold some 14 million copies and became the unofficial anthem of German reunification.

German pop music could be viewed as a genuinely bilingual enterprise since use of the English language has often enabled German (hard) rock bands to achieve massive international success. However, the lyrics of the Scorpions are often not only of poor linguistic quality but also on purpose in poor taste. There is ample evidence of the despicably sexist nature of macho penetration fantasies in their song 'Dynamite': 'Kick your ass to heaven / With rock'n'roll tonight / Shoot my heat into your body / Give ya all my size'. Sung in English, such lines do not sound as offensive and simplistic to Germans as they would in German, but underline the decision to focus on German-language bands in this volume.

Deutschrock also allowed women to carve out careers for themselves in the male-dominated realm of rock music. Ina Deter, for example, discarded her initial image as a folk singer-songwriter to take up rock music and subsequently achieved a major hit with 'Neue Männer braucht das Land' [This Country Needs New Men]. Ulla Meinecke was mentored by Udo Lindenberg who transformed her songs into versions of his own on her first three albums. Anne Haigis, to provide another example, turned from English-language jazz rock to *Deutschrock* with her eponymous album from 1984. Four more successful LPs followed until she returned to singing in English at the end of the 1980s.

The most notorious female German singer of the time was undoubtedly Nina Hagen. She largely owned her success to the excellent marketing by her manager Jim Rakete who secured regular TV appearances for her. Rakete also advised her to create a bad girl image in line with her punk-influenced music. For example, during a TV show in 1979, Hagen caused considerable outrage when she demonstrated various masturbation techniques for women. The fact that she originated from East Germany and had moved to West Germany in the wake of the infamous expatriation of her dissident stepfather Wolf Biermann in 1976, further contributed to the media interest in her. It soon faded in the early 1980s, however, as the quality and success of her album releases declined.

Finally, it is worth pointing out that when disco went mainstream in the mid-1970s, many international disco hits originated in Germany, although none were sung in German. Frank Farian scored more than twenty top ten hits in the UK with Boney M., while Giorgio Moroder and his Musicland Studios in Munich produced a total of eight top ten hits in the United States for Donna Summer. The first German to produce a world-wide disco hit, however, is the lesser known Michael Kunze with 'Fly, Robin, Fly', which secured Silver Convention the prestigious number one spot in the US charts in late 1975.

The synth-pop wave that hit Germany in the early 1980s after the success of British bands like Depeche Mode, OMD or Ultravox, led to two German bands that are notable not just for their success but also for the quality of their music. Both managed to produce immediate international top hits. Alphaville's 'Big in Japan', from their *Forever Young* album (1984), was a slick song with a melodious refrain that dealt with the reason why German bands chose to sing in English – to become a big success in other countries. Even though the Japanese market ironically only showed little interest in the band from Münster, the video directed by Dieter Meier from Yello propelled them to the number one spot in Sweden, Switzerland and the Billboard dance charts in the US.

Propaganda made their mark in 1980s pop music with 'Dr. Mabuse', a moody single named after the mysterious title character from three Fritz Lang films. This hit was soon followed by the extremely catchy song 'Duel'. The band originated from Düsseldorf, where it had been founded by Ralf Dörper, the keyboard player for the industrial pioneers Die Krupps. Propaganda's debut album *A Secret Wish* was released on Trevor Horn's ZTT label after Propaganda was signed by Paul Morley, who later married their lead singer Claudia Brücken. Their quick rise to international fame was, however, followed by a long string of problems including lengthy legal battles, internal disagreements, and repeated reshuffles of band membership. Whereas initially, it appeared that the band would have a major career, like that of their label mates Frankie Goes To Hollywood and Art of Noise, this sadly never happened.

The Rise and Demise of *Neue Deutsche Welle* – German Pop Music in the 1980s

The massive upheaval caused by the British punk explosion at the end of the 1970s also left its mark on the German music scene, albeit in a very different way, given the specific social and cultural context against which musicians in Germany rebelled. As Cyrus Shahan explains in his chapter, the short-lived German punk movement, which had its epicentre in the Ratinger Hof bar in Düsseldorf, was contemporary with the left-wing terrorism orchestrated by the Red Army Faction (RAF) and operated in the context of a well-to-do society still very much haunted by the repressed legacy of German fascism. The political thrust of German punk was to undermine the success of the prosperous, confident, forward-looking society that had emerged from the German Economic Miracle.

While, for example, the Sex Pistols appropriated the Union Jack for their iconography and invective against the British royalty and class stratification, the German punk band Male once burned the national flag during a performance of the national anthem, a visual and sonic embrace and destruction of the worst in German history that could never have the same significance in Britain.[17] Thus, British punk's battle cry 'no future' could not have the same effect in a rebuilding West Germany. The same applied to provocative displays of the swastika. When the Sex Pistols, The Clash, or Siouxsie Sioux used the swastika, they did so to invert the rhetoric of British might and to repudiate Britain's post-war sense of moral superiority and social-democratic progress.[18] In contrast, although unthinkable without its British variant, German punk's scattered use of the swastika was a nihilistic embrace of a past national culture so as to indict its ominous and undeniable echoes in punk's present.

However, just as in the UK (and the US), the sudden rise and quick demise of punk resulted in a new wave of German music. The original moniker of the *Neue Deutsche Welle* [German New Wave] or NDW for short, was soon appropriated and exploited by the record industry. The story of the NDW, as outlined by Christian Jäger, is an exemplary tale of how subcultural dissidence is cannibalized by the commercial mainstream and turned into a commodity.

As Jens Reisloh affirms in his extensive study of the history and development of German pop music, the NDW marked a new phase for pop music both in terms of musical (as well as lyrical) innovation and a massive boom in the production of German-language songs. 'About fifty musical styles abound in 1981 in German music. In 1979, there were already more than one thousand bands [...] which can be attributed to the NDW.'[19] A hallmark of the initial phase of the German New Wave, or NDW I as Jäger puts it, is the literary quality of the lyrics, which was due to the fact that NDW I's musicians were usually educated and had connections to local art schools.

This arty influence gave birth to the DADA-pop of bands such as Der Plan and Palais Schaumburg, a style destined to be subsumed – as were other wayward bands such as Freiwillige Selbstkontrolle (FSK), Deutsch-Amerikanische Freundschaft (DAF) and Einstürzende Neubauten – under the deliberately misspelled moniker of *Geniale Dilletanten*. German pop music of the early 1980s fused the intellectual with the bohemian and made for remarkable sonic times in which the meta-pop music and subversive artistic strategies – such as (feigned) affirmation as a form of criticism – were not only unique in Germany but also internationally.

---

17 Cf. Koch, *Angriff aufs Schlaraffenland*, p. 120.
18 For more on British punk and the swastika, see Karen Fournier's forthcoming essay 'Nazi Signifiers and the Narrative of Class Warfare in British Punk', in *Beyond No Future: Cultures of German Punk*, ed. by Mirko Hall, Seth Howes and Cyrus Shahan (New York: Bloomsbury, 2016).
19 Jens Reisloh, *Deutschsprachige Popmusik: Zwischen Morgenrot und Hundekot. Von den Anfängen um 1970 bis ins 21. Jahrhundert* (Münster: Telos, 2011), p. 142.

The music industry soon took advantage of this new development in German music and flooded the market with every new German band they could get a hold of. The commercial inversion of subversive affirmation pushed NDW I into its sell-out phase. Ironically, NDW II launched the very stars who also had an impact outside Germany: Nena in particular enjoyed phenomenal popularity in the English-speaking world in 1983 with the original German version of '99 Luftballons', while the Austrian singer Falco had already caused ripples on the European and Scandinavian charts the previous year with 'Der Kommissar' [The Inspector].

Three German Bands – Kraftwerk, Einstürzende Neubauten, Rammstein

Setting aside such brief moments of individual international success, three German bands deserve closer examination in this volume. The most important and influential among them is Kraftwerk. A *Gesamtkunstwerk* (total work of art), and not just a musical project, Kraftwerk are still touring extensively across the world. Between 1974 and 1981, their pioneering albums laid the foundation of electronic pop music by discarding guitars, drums, and other key elements of Anglo-American rock 'n' roll. Their groundbreaking machine music represented, in a very literal sense, the sound of the future. With startlingly prophetic accuracy, their songs predicted both the advancements and the cost of a world dominated by digital technology. Since Kraftwerk now regularly plays retrospectives of their musical œuvre at major art institutions around the world (such as the MoMA in New York, the Tate Modern in London and the Sydney Opera House), there has been a remarkable academic interest in the band and their music over the last few years, ranging from conferences to books. For this reason, an entire chapter has been devoted to them.

In this chapter, Schütte explores the key theme of ambivalence, which runs throughout Kraftwerk's œuvre and challenges simplistic perceptions of the band as ardent technophiles. As he shows, Kraftwerk's attempt to forge a new identity for their generation was inevitably a double-edged sword. If they were to create a better future, they had to address the abominable Nazi past and incorporate the lessons learned. This led to the unique, retro-futurist aesthetic that shaped their work and distinguished them from their contemporaries. Kraftwerk's aim was to revive cultural traditions truncated by the Nazis (such as the Bauhaus movement and Expressionism) and to (re-)introduce German modernism to the late twentieth century.

While Kraftwerk's robot imagery deliberately played on clichés such as German efficiency and engineering achievements, both Einstürzende Neubauten [Collapsing New Buildings] and Rammstein adhered to widely-held stereotypes about Teutonic brutalism. Formed in 1980 in West Berlin, Einstürzende Neubauten found an original approach to industrial music by largely discarding standard pop-musical instruments and repurposing tools (such as power drills and pneumatic hammers) or building musical equipment out of scrap materials. Such radical approaches to music-making were not entirely new, however. They can be traced back to the Krautrock band Faust and even further to Futurists such as Russolo and Marinetti.

As Alexander Carpenter outlines in his chapter, it is tempting but problematic to claim a continuum in German industrial music from Kraftwerk to Rammstein via Einstürzende Neubauten. Nevertheless, the industrial soundscape on Kraftwerk's *Trans Europa Express*, particularly the clanging in 'Metall auf Metall' [Metal on Metal], clearly inspired the radical music in the early releases of Einstürzende Neubauten.

Although conceptually and structurally similar to Throbbing Gristle, Einstürzende Neubauten and their confrontational (anti-)music had no equivalent until Test Dept emerged in the UK. During a career that spanned across three decades, Einstürzende Neubauten underwent several stylistic transformations and, although it would have been inconceivable in the 1980s, they now even serve as official representatives of German culture at the behest of government organizations such as the Goethe-Institut.

Like Tokio Hotel, a marketing package parading as a teen rock band that also hails from East Germany, Rammstein had a phenomenal career outside Germany during the first decade of this century. The band created the genre *Neue Deutsche Härte* [New German Hardness] with their crossover style of metal, industrial and electronica backed up by carnevalesque stage shows. Their ambiguous play with fascist imagery is clearly modelled on the Slovenian band Laibach, but they lack the latter's bravery and sophistication.

Nevertheless, as Carpenter shows, Rammstein's strategic package of music, style, artwork and stage show is based on a highly successful formula of calculated provocation that merits critical attention. For now, Rammstein remains the prime embodiment of German pop music across the globe and warrants Carpenter's close look at the Teutonic version of Germanness they convey to mass audiences who often do not speak the language of their songs.

Soundtrack of the New Germany – Rap and Techno in Germany

Kraftwerk's ground-breaking efforts to create music using machines rather than traditional instruments was especially well-received amongst black communities in the US in the early 1980s. Sampling and looping beat patterns from two Kraftwerk records, DJ Afrika Bambaataa from the South Bronx, New York, created the genre-defining electro track 'Planet Rock' in 1982, which exerted a major influence over the development of hip-hop culture.[20] Rap music, being the most visible manifestation of hip-hop culture, turned into one of the most successful musical styles in the US and began to inspire German artists to contribute to the genre in the 1990s.

As Marissa Munderloh explicates in her chapter, the term 'German rap' is problematic since many artists operating in this field are not ethnic Germans and rap lyrics are delivered in both German and other languages. The often highly creative use of language(s) in rap is certainly worthy of academic attention, not least because in some cases the lyrics convey minority narratives and socio-political criticism that would otherwise remain unheard.

Similar to the development of hip-hop in the US, where rap crossed over from its roots as a cultural expression of black minorities to the white mainstream (with bands like the Beastie Boys), rap in Germany is largely produced by ethnic middle class Germans such as the mainstream bands Freundeskreis or Fettes Brot but also (self-styled) gangsta rappers like Haftbefehl [Arrest Warrant], Kollegah, Sido or Fler. The considerable variety of sub-styles within the genre makes it a highly interesting topic of study. Furthermore, some products of rap in German warrant the interest of linguists who study the new variants of spoken German known as *Kiezdeutsch* ['hood German], but they are also of interest to sociologists concerned with migrant cultures in urban hotspots such as Frankfurt or the Neukölln district of Berlin.

German rap is also a media phenomenon since public discourse on the question of migration and integration of immigrants often arises in connection with various cleverly devised scandals by gangsta rappers. Germany's most successful rapper, the German-Tunisian Bushido, is regularly sued for slander by politicians and investigated by the police for anti-Semitic, sexist or homophobic statements.

---

20 It needs to be added, however, that both the producer Arthur Baker and keyboard player John Robie also played a major role in the creation of the seminal track.

His close involvement with a Berlin-based organized crime gang run by Palestinians caused considerable furore in the press in 2013.

At the same time, some politicians seek proximity to rappers so as to win over minority audiences and gain 'street cred' with younger voters. Haftbefehl's 2014 album *Russisch Roulette* [Russian Roulette] was given a rapturous reception in several highbrow papers, proof of a remarkable middle-class desire to incorporate apparently untamed, authentic street music into their normally elitist cultural canon. In her chapter, Munderloh explores this fascinating continuum from immigrant ghetto to official cultural approval and shows that rap in Germany is the musical mirror of the country's increasingly multicultural make-up since re-unification.

The first Love Parade took place in the summer prior to the fall of the Berlin wall when the organizer, Dr Motte, marched through Berlin followed by about 150 techno music enthusiasts. Eight years later, in 1997, that number had swelled to more than a million people. What started as an underground phenomenon became a major commercial mainstream operation that in turn helped to launch the phenomenal success of a band like Scooter that peddles a tedious catalogue of techno-inspired pop songs to mass audiences.

As Alexei Monroe details in his chapter, the explosive growth of techno in Germany happened to coincide with the fall of the Berlin wall. During the 'techno interregnum', which lasted until approximately 1996, the Berlin techno scene flourished thanks to the availability of empty urban spaces and a general spirit of freedom in the wake of reunification. Or as Ulrich Gutmair puts it in the subtitle of his book on Berlin techno, the new music indeed became the soundtrack of this decisive turning point in the post-war history of Germany.[21]

Even though German techno started in Frankfurt, the capital soon became the main venue for electronic dance music. While a far cry from its anarchic beginnings, the Berlin club scene – which includes the famous Tresor, the notorious Berghain and many more – has developed into a major tourist magnet, attracting the so-called 'easyJet Generation' from across Europe and beyond. In addition, producers like Richie Hawtin, Karl O'Connor (a.k.a. Regis) and Ricardo Villalobos relocated to Berlin permanently from the late 1990s onwards and contributed to the development of a specific Berlin strand of minimal techno.

Despite Berlin's role as the techno capital of Germany, the music also prospered in cities across the country. Thus, in addition to Berlin and Frankfurt, Monroe also analyses the specific techno cultures that developed in Cologne around the Kompakt conglomerate and focuses on the Munich scene associated with the

---

21 See Ulrich Gutmair, *Die ersten Tage von Berlin: Der Sound der Wende* (Berlin: Ullstein, 2014).

Disko B label and DJ Hell. During techno's spread in Germany, various other re-markable dance music and electronic labels emerged, such as the Hamburg-based Dial Records (whose roster includes artists like Efdemin, Lawrence, Roman Flügel or Pantha Du Prince) and the more experimental Raster-Noton label located in Chemnitz (the former Karl-Marx-Stadt) run by the artist-producer Carsten Nikolai alias Alva Noto. One should also note the glitch productions of Markus Popp alias Oval and dub techno artists such as Jan Jelinek or Stefan Betke alias Pole.

This vital array of producers and labels is a testament to Germany's contri-bution to the history of electronic music. Karlheinz Stockhausen is the 'founding father' of electronic music, albeit in the academic context. He was the inspira-tion for various experiments with electronic music in the Krautrock era, such as the ambient soundscapes of Tangerine Dream or the proto-techno on the *E2–E4* album recorded in 1981 (though released in 1984) by former Ash Ra Tem-pel guitarist Manuel Göttsching.[22] Apart from these Berlin-based musicians, the remarkable history of electronic pop music in Germany started, of course, with Kraftwerk in Düsseldorf. This early musical axis between Berlin and Düsseldorf continues today, with a number of excellent bands operating on an interface be-tween electronica and post rock, such as Kreidler, Tarwater or To Roccoco Rot, who all prefer to sing in English.

Diskursrock – Pop Music Made for and by German Intellectuals

There is no pronounced tradition of writing songs with intellectual lyrics in Anglo-American pop music. Scritti Politti, for example, devoted an homage to the originator of deconstruction with their 1982 song 'Jacques Derrida', and re-printed a page from Lacan's *Ecrits* on the cover of their UK top ten hit 'The Word Girl' (1985). Stephin Merritt a.k.a. The Magnetic Fields sang about 'The Death of Ferdinand De Saussure' on his epic *69 Love Songs* collection from 1999 which, upon closer inspection, turns out to be a deconstructive meta-album about the format of love songs in which Merritt questions, amongst other things, the heteronormativity of this prime form of popular music from a queer perspective.

---

22 Conrad Schnitzler, an early member of Tangerine Dream and a founding member of Kluster, also needs to be mentioned in this context.

Nevertheless, lyrical engagement with intellectual figureheads, contemporary theory and philosophy remains restricted to individual, isolated examples in the English-speaking world and cannot be compared to the trend that began in Germany in the early 1990s with the so-called Hamburg School. Taking their cue from the Frankfurt School moniker of Critical Theory (as developed by Walter Benjamin, Theodor W. Adorno and others), a number of bands began to write intertextual, self-reflective songs that engaged with contemporary theoretical discourses, often in a highly self-ironic manner. This genuinely German phenomenon also came to be known as *Diskursrock*.

In their chapter, Christoph Jürgensen and Antonius Weixler look at the various phases of *Diskursrock*. They focus on the two main protagonists of its initial phase, Blumfeld and Tocotronic. Blumfeld, who took their name from a short-story by Kafka, can certainly lay claim to be the most intellectual exponents of the Hamburg School. Their œuvre comprises six studio albums, released between 1992 and 2007, not all of which attain the quality of their sophomore effort *L'Etat Et Moi* (1994).

Tocotronic is still very much an ongoing affair, and has released more than ten studio albums since their debut in 1993. Despite undergoing a major change in conceptual direction at the end of the 1990s, the band has released a body of work that ranks amongst the very best in contemporary German pop music. While the second generation of *Diskursrock* bands (such as Tomte, Kettcar and Virginia Jetzt!) did not attain the excellence of their predecessors, according to Jürgensen/Weixler, the current third generation, which includes acts such as Trümmer and Die Nerven, makes for rewarding listening. The most remarkable band of their peers, however, is Ja, Panik from Austria. Along a varied range of musical styles, the often multilingual, highly intertextual lyrics written by Andreas Spechtl manage to marry the poetic with the political in a way that is unique in current German-language pop music.

An extensive interview with Diedrich Diederichsen, Germany's leading pop music theorist, concludes this volume. Following a long career in music journalism and cultural criticism, he has held visiting professorships at various universities and, since 2006, a chair at Vienna's Academy of Fine Arts. In his conversation with Heinrich Deisl, Diederichsen elaborates on his definition and interpretation of pop music in his landmark work, *Über Pop-Musik* (2014). Furthermore, he explores historical perspectives on German-language pop theory, as well as the social contexts and technological infrastructure of pop music. The interview closes with a discussion of the relationship between pop music and the sociopolitical developments in Germany from the 1970s to the present.

Diederichsen's pioneering *Über Pop-Musik*, which has more than 450 pages, puts the academic study of pop music in Germany on a solid scholarly footing.

Indeed, the underlying critical approach of this volume shares Diederichsen's premise that pop music is a complex web of interrelated functions which comes to life in the interplay between those who make the music and those who listen to it. Although Diederichsen's discussion is complex and challenging at times, *Über Pop-Musik* is a long overdue German-language theoretical work that finally puts the academic investigation of German pop music on an equal footing with pioneering work already undertaken on English-language pop music by Anglophone scholars and critics.

At the end of his book, Diederichsen sets out an ambitious agenda for future research: 'In academia, Pop Music Studies will have to set itself off from Musicology, just as Film Studies had to set itself off from Theatre Studies (and Theatre Studies, in turn, from Literary Studies): a secession with certain qualifications.'[23] By providing an extensive overview of this emerging field of academic study, the aim of this volume is to encourage further research by Anglophone scholars in the wider area of German Studies, sociology, cultural studies and beyond.

---

23 Diedrich Diederichsen, *Über Pop-Musik* (Cologne: KiWi, 2014), p. 457.

Julio Mendívil

Schlager and Musical Conservatism in the Post-War Era

Popular music in academic circles has time and again been associated with youth culture, generational struggle and resistance and rebellion. However, not all popular music genres are anti-hegemonic. The upbeat genre of the German *Schlager* is a good example of ideological and musical conservatism. Despite the difficulties in defining *Schlager*, here the genre will be regarded as a concrete discourse that reproduces a cultural image of Germanness by way of 'musicking', or, in other words, the act of taking part 'in a musical performance, whether by performing, by listening, by rehearsing or practicing, by providing material for performance [...] or by dancing'.[1] In that sense, *Schlager* constitutes a field rather than a form of music. Therefore, this chapter will focus on the time period between 1945 and 1975 – an era which is commonly regarded as the golden age of German *Schlager* music, since many of the *Schlager* evergreens were recorded during that period. However, it will also make reference to the 1980s and 1990s when necessary.

In order to understand the conservative character of *Schlager* music, one must first delve into its history, specifically into the post-war transformation of the term and the sounds associated with it. Accordingly, this chapter will begin with a short historical account of the term before and after the war before focusing on *Schlager* music's opposition to Anglophone popular music genres, such as rock 'n' roll, beat and rock music during the 1960s and 1970s. While discussing this distinction, it will examine how *Schlager* became a conservative field of music in Germany, allocated to an imaginary space closely related to romantic ideals associated with music as an expression of beauty. Finally, it will attempt to explain why, in the early 1970s, numerous foreign performers became successful in Germany, in spite of the fact that the musical environment surrounding *Schlager* explicitly rejected external cultural influences. Fundamentally, the aim of this chapter is to demonstrate how *Schlager* constructed an arena within which conservative streams of expression were able to rebel against the modern, liberal tendencies prevalent in the international popular music landscape by defending traditional values such as family and homeland.

---

1 Christopher Small, *The Meaning of Performing and Listening* (Middletown: Wesleyan University Press, 1998), 9.

DOI 10.1515/9783110425727-002

Born to be Well-Behaved – *Schlager* Before 1945

The term *Schlager* first appeared in the Viennese press during the late nineteenth century and was then used to denote catchy melodies.[2] *Schlager* could be found across the spectrum of popular song, including dance hall music and genres such as waltz, polka, gallops, couplets, operetta songs and arias, polonaises, etc. – basically any form of music that could be turned into a success.[3] In this sense, the word *Schlager* was not used to describe the musical qualities but rather the commercial success of different and divergent songs.

Popularity, however, did not always mean acceptance. Music specialists complained that musical taste was no longer being determined by connoisseurs but rather by inexpert listeners.[4] Consequently, Schlager became a derogatory term denoting an inferior musical product, which was often used by journalists as a synonym for sensationalism and simplicity in music.[5] Shortly thereafter, the word *Schlager* began to refer to a kind of song that easily captivated audiences.

No longer conceived as a part of an operetta, revue or musical theatre, *Schlager* gained its independence and began to be composed with success in mind. This desire for popularity and success started to determine some of the musical parameters of *Schlager* songs. Dance forms, simple melodic lines and elemental harmonic structures caught on and became the basis of the so-called 'light music' style of easy listening.

A perfect example of an early *Schlager* is the song 'Schenk' mir doch ein kleines bißchen Liebe' [Give Me a Little Bit of Love], from the operetta *Frau Luna* [Lady Luna] (1899) by Berlin composer Paul Lincke and lyricist Heinrich Bolten-Baeckers. The song's massive success led songwriters to use the same formula in other songs in the hopes of replicating the economic achievements of their predecessors.[6] Since then, the word *Schlager* has come to mean an effective and schematic composition that guarantees success – a replicated formula rather than an original work of art. Consequently, *Schlager* music was looked down

---

2 See Markus Bandur, 'Schlager', in *Handwörterbuch der musikalischen Terminologie*, ed. by Hans Heinrich Eggebrecht. Sonderband 1 (Stuttgart: Franz Steiner, 1995), pp. 384–395 (p. 384).
3 Peter Czerny and Heinz Hoffmann, *Der Schlager: Ein Panorama der leichten Musik*, vol. 1 (Berlin: VEB Musikverlag, 1968), pp. 12–14.
4 Peter Wicke, *Von Mozart zu Madonna: Eine Kulturgeschichte der Popmusik* (Frankfurt: Suhrkamp, 2001), p. 26.
5 Bandur, 'Schlager', p. 386.
6 Wicke, *Von Mozart zu Madonna*, p. 80; Czerny and Hoffmann, *Der Schlager*, p. 166.

upon by music specialists as a parasitic, 'deficient musical product'[7] or as a 'musical commodity for mass audiences fabricated by the numbers'.[8]

At the beginning of the twentieth century, African American dance music reached the European market, unsettling the moral landscape in Germany due to its physicality. During that time, *Schlager* had been disqualified as a commodity. However, during the Weimar Republic, the discussion on *Schlager* gained a chauvinistic and moralistic character, and several opponents of *Schlager* also criticized foreign influences such as the one-step, shimmy, foxtrot, jazz and tango. Towards the end of the Weimar Republic, the nationalist discourse demanded a return to good German traditions: 'We Germans want to celebrate the return of this beautiful, old, quintessentially German dance: the waltz. It is the most important contribution the German people have made to dance around the world.'[9]

This led to the first stage in the Germanization of German popular music and foreign influences were frowned upon as perversions.[10] The following comment from 1940, which first appeared in the nationalist magazine *Musik-Woche* [Music Week] and are here taken from Wulf, offers a paradigmatic example of such a discursive formulation in the history of *Schlager* music:

> The decline of the operetta [...] fostered the tendency towards indecency, so much so that even people with an artistic consciousness became desensitized and began to pervert operetta masterpieces with arrangements that only catered to the tastes of uncultivated people in order to make money. Jews have a particularly detrimental influence here. Many popular

---

7 Bandur, 'Schlager', p. 390.

8 Monika Sperr, *Das Große Schlager-Buch: Deutscher Schlager 1800–Heute.* (Munich: Rogner & Bernhard, 1978), p. 100.

9 Quoted in Christian Schär, *Der Schlager und seine Tänze im Deutschland der 20er Jahre: Sozialgeschichtliche Aspekte zum Wandel in der Musik- und Tanzkultur während der Weimarer Republik* (Zürich: Chronos Verlag, 1991), p. 100.

10 The consequences of this cultural policy were detrimental. Due to the Nazi regime's musical 'cleansing', the *Schlager* scene experienced an exodus. Leading composers like Jean Gilbert, Victor Hollaender, Franz Lehár, Emmerich Kálmán or Ralph Benatzky were forced to emigrate, while Fritz Löhner and Fritz Grünbaum died in concentration camps. A new generation of composers such as Michael Jary and Franz Grothe adjusted to the new cultural policy and actually benefitted from it, since there was significantly less musical competition. Also, the repertoire diminished, as masterpieces by Jewish composers like Offenbach and Kálmán were forbidden. See Peter Wicke, 'Das Ende: Populäre Musik im faschistischen Deutschland', in *Ich will aber gerade vom Leben singen…: Über populäre Musik vom ausgehenden 18. Jahrhundert bis zum Ende der Weimarer Republik*, ed. by Sabine Schutte (Reinbek: Rowohlt, 1987), pp. 418–429 (p. 420).

musicians, directors of ensembles, managers who organize popular music events and, above all, most composers were Jews.[11]

Before the rise of National Socialism, there was no differentiation between German and English lyrics in *Schlager*. However, during the Germanization of German popular music, a distinction between Anglo and German forms of *Schlager* began to take shape. In its opposition to the 'exotic', rhythmic and sensual '*Negermusik*' ['negro' music], the Nazi music industry fostered what Peter Wicke has described as 'sentimentality and pathos',[12] that is to say highly sentimental, melodic songs without stressed rhythmic patterns. *Schlager* stars such as Zarah Leander and Marika Rökk recorded music meant to entertain and also encourage people to obey the tenets of the National Socialist Party – a situation that remained unchanged until the final years of the war. During the Allied bombing campaigns against Germany, the production and release of new music ground to a halt, and the *Schlager* industry had to wait until the defeat of the Nazis in order to resume production.

'A Little Bit of Peace' – *Schlager* in the Post-War Era

The German music industry experienced such a profound crisis after the allied victory that it drew upon unpublished songs from the final years of the war.[13] Nostalgia, distance and *Heimat*[14] were some of the major topics at this time,

---

11 *Musik im Dritten Reich: Eine Dokumentation*, ed. by Joseph Wulf (Gütersloh: Sigbert Mohn, 1963), p. 263.

12 Wicke, 'Das Ende', p. 425.

13 The first hit in the post-war era was 'Capri Fischer' by Rudi Schuricke. The song was produced in 1943, yet the record was not immediately released due to the new political situation. In the meantime, Benito Mussolini had been overthrown and killed and Italy had switched sides and declared war on Germany, see André Port le roi, *Schlager lügen nicht: Deutscher Schlager und Politik in ihrer Zeit* (Essen: Klartext, 1998), p. 36. The song was finally released after the capitulation of Germany and quickly garnered success.

14 Although *Heimat* can sometimes be translated as homeland, this particular German concept is strongly related to the desire for familiarity and a peaceful life. Boa and Palfreyman affirm that *Heimat* is 'a physical place, or social space, or bounded medium of some kind which provides a sense of security and belonging [...] As a surrounding medium, Heimat protects the self by stimulating identification whether with family, locality, nation, folk or race, native dialect tongue [...] Heimat is an intrinsically conservative value connoting originary or primary factors

just as they had been in the *Schlager* of the Nazi era. But with the advent of the German Economic Miracle, the tone of popular music became more enthusiastic and optimistic. One of the more noteworthy songs of the time was 'Die Eingeborenen von Trizonesien' [The Natives of Trizonesia] (1948) by Karl Berbuer, which alluded to the occupying forces (France, Great Britain and USA), but in a humorous way, and celebrated capitalistic consumerism and the Americanization of German society.

Straightaway, the song became an unofficial anthem of the thriving new Germany, owing to its political and symbolic implications. At that point, *Schlager* oscillated between sentimental songs by Rudi Schuricke, Freddy Quinn and Peter Alexander, and humorous songs by Catarina Valente, Vico Torriani and other non-German musicians who introduced 'exotic' rhythms such as Brazilian samba and Latin American rumba, but always moderated for the German audience. Still the ideal *Schlager* star in the early post-war years was well-behaved, dressed in a three-piece suit and sang about heterosexual love.[15] This trend was broken as soon as the occupying forces imported rock 'n' roll. The German musician Udo Lindenberg recalls that:

> There were many Schlager songs around, the sky was full of mandolins and everything was quite sentimental until suddenly, like a grenade, rock 'n' roll hit the scene somehow causing an earthquake that activated a healthy disturbance throughout the country, kind of like a riot [...] And all of a sudden young people had their own music, and came into conflict with adults who suddenly felt completely taken aback and flabbergasted.[16]

Until the arrival of rock 'n' roll, dance music was made by adults for an adult audience. However, with the advent of rock 'n' roll, the music industry began to pay attention to a younger audience which saw waltz, polka, fox, rumba and polonaise as antiquated forms of music for an older generation.[17] Rock 'n' roll also turned English into the *lingua franca* of popular music all around the world. The American music industry had generated a considerable amount of wealth in the previous years, but – first with Bill Haley and the Comets, and later with Elvis Presley – it now conquered the entire world, spawning imitators in Bangkok, Buenos Aires, Paris, Berlin and Accra. In the US, confrontation

---

in identity', Elizabeth Boa and Pamela Palfreyman, *Heimat, A German Dream: Regional Loyalties and National Identity in German Culture 1890–1990* (Oxford: OUP, 2000), p. 23.

15 Thommi Herrwerth, *Katzeklo & Caprifischer: Die deutschen Hits aus 50 Jahren* (Berlin: Rütten & Loening, 1998), p. 13.

16 Udo Lindenberg, *Rock'n'roll und Rebellion: Ein panisches Panorama* (Munich: Heyne, 1984), p. 16.

17 Sperr, *Das große Schlager-Buch*, p. 232.

around rock 'n' roll was both musical as well as moral. The sensuality and corporeality with which the music was associated was seen as threatening to the fundamental values of white American society. Consequently, African American music (blues, rhythm & blues etc.), and its by-products rock 'n' roll and boogie, were vehemently opposed in conservative circles.

In Europe, criticism of rock 'n' roll was also based on puritan ideological positions, closely related to the traditional disembodiment of music in the Christian tradition. Performers such as Rudi Schuricke, René Carol, Freddy Quinn and Peter Alexander had inundated the *Schlager* scene with melodic, romantic and consequently self-affirmative songs, reinforcing the dichotomy between African American – and to a lesser extent Latin American music – (as physical) and German music (as intellectual). Another criticism levelled against African American music was based on an elitist, bourgeois positioning against a perceived commodification and Americanization of German culture.[18]

Americanization was a concrete threat, as one composer criticized: 'When rock 'n' roll came to Germany a few years ago, all our *Schlager* composers were derailed. Suddenly they were no longer up to date.'[19] The more *Schlager* music was put under pressure by rock 'n' roll, the more it acquired a national character which further narrowed the meaning of the word *Schlager*. Now a distinction was made between American and German songs, and the expression 'German *Schlager*' was primarily restricted to certain popular songs in the German language, whereas the English word 'hit' was used in reference to the earlier meaning of '*Schlager*' in German.[20]

Despite this, there were performers such as Peter Krause and Connie Froboess who – unlike Peter Alexander and Freddy Quinn – played rock 'n' roll music, albeit without the rebellion and resistance of American rock 'n' roll icons. German rock 'n' roll was 'compliant rock 'n' roll, rock ballads and sentimental stuff'.[21] The sexual allusions in the English were replaced with harmless German

---

18 Peter Wicke, *Vom Umgang mit Musik* (Berlin: Volk und Wissen, 1993), p. 75.

19 Siegfried Schmidt-Joos, *Geschäfte mit Schlagern* (Bremen: Schünemann, 1960), p. 32. The anti-American attitude was more idealistic than real. Several *Schlager* were translations of American songs produced for the German market. For example 'Heimweh', the former king of *Schlager* Freddy Quinn's first hit, was a German adaptation of the American evergreen 'Memories Are Made of This' by Dean Martin. See Hans-Christian Worbs, *Der Schlager: Bestandsaufnahme, Analyse, Dokumentation* (Bremen: Schünemann, 1960), pp. 46–47.

20 Peter Wicke, 'Schlager', in *Musik in Geschichte und Gegenwart*, vol. 8, ed. by Ludwig Finscher (Kassel: Bärenreiter, 1998), pp. 1063–1070 (p. 1064).

21 Port le roi, *Schlager lügen nicht*, p. 66.

lyrics about flowers and idyllic landscapes – the very topics Freddy Quinn and Peter Alexander also sang about.

In the 1960s, British Invasion bands such as The Beatles and The Rolling Stones completed the revolution Bill Haley and Elvis Presley had begun a decade earlier, further isolating German *Schlager*. English lyrics became the expression of an international youth culture bent on rebellion, while *Schlager* songs turned into the manifestation of a self-affirmative nationalistic culture. There was a clear polarization of target audiences: youth versus adults or beat fans versus *Schlager* listeners.[22] Radio DJ Hans Verres recalls in an interview that every Thursday there was a media battle between *Schlager* and beat music fans on his programme *Schlagerbörse* [The Schlager Stock Exchange]. Verres' idea was to create a chart of the highest nationally and internationally ranked songs and for listeners to call in and name their favourite songs. But instead of giving points to the music they did like, listeners instead began to deride the kind of music they did not – Freddy Quinn versus The Beatles, Rudi Schuricke versus Bob Dylan and so on.

The discussions often took on a nationalistic character because the issue was not only music, but also the image of young people in Germany: 'We received a lot of letters against songs in foreign languages, arguing "We are German", and on the other hand many got angry and said: "Why this German garbage?"'[23] This polarization also took place inside the music itself. Electric guitars, drums and shouts of 'yeah-yeah-yeah' were characteristic of loud beat music and youth rebellion, while violins, orchestration and bel canto intonation were audible symbols of *Schlager*. 'English stands for beat, for renewal and above all for an abandonment of clichés about love in Schlager', sums up one *Schlager* researcher.[24] Beat songs in German possessed less symbolic capital than songs in English:

> There were beat groups such as The Rattles and The Lords and others. But twenty years after the end of the war, it was obviously not possible to express their new lifestyle and feelings in the language in which brown-shirted hordes had shamelessly spread panic with their incendiary shouts. For this reason, there was an unwritten law for such groups: If one wanted to be taken seriously, they had to avoid the German language like the plague and sing in English.[25]

---

22 Herrwerth, *Katzeklo & Caprifischer*, p. 51.
23 Elmar Kraushaar, *Rote Lippen: Die ganze Welt des deutschen Schlagers* (Reinbek: Rowohlt, 1983), p. 102.
24 Dieter Baacke, *Beat: Die sprachlose Opposition* (Munich: Juventa, 1970), p. 161.
25 Herrwerth, *Katzeklo & Caprifischer*, p. 53.

The beat attack initiated the 'ageing process of *Schlager*', a period within which the German music industry waged a battle of the 'sweet' against the beat. Not only did adults listen to *Schlager*, but also the German *Schlager* community unmistakably distanced itself from the international Anglophone youth counterculture, and thereby more or less consciously sided with a kind of music not associated with rebellion and protest, but rather with conformism and decency.

The consolidation of young people as a target group for the international music industry, the canonization of beat music through its identification with liberal social forces, such as the feminist movement or minorities groups, and the demonization of the German language all put pressure on the social values of *Schlager*, transforming it into a conservative genre of popular music. Previously, criticism of *Schlager* had come from politicians and academics, but since then, *Schlager* music became a disqualified genre even within the field of popular music.

For young people in Germany in the 1960s, to declare interest in or love for sappy *Schlager* songs meant to accept to be well-behaved and, thus, antiquated. Accordingly, cool young people rejected *Schlager*, even those songs that aimed to be hip and modern rather than conservative and self-affirmative. In a certain sense, the cultural devaluation of *Schlager* influenced the academic reception of the genre and explains why even the majority of popular music scholars tend to assert so vehemently that *Schlager* are only 'Omamusik' [music for grannies],[26] although a minimum of empiricism would demonstrate that *Schlager* audiences are diverse and also include young people (even including Peruvian ethnomusicologists in Europe, like the author of this article.)[27]

Hitparade and the 'Son-in-law-ization' of *Schlager*

During the 1970s, *Schlager* discourse experienced an enormous centralization. TV entertainer Dieter Thomas Heck became the director of the television channel ZDF's program *Die Hitparade*, which gave him direct influence over the produc-

---

[26] See Gerhard Schulze, *Die Erlebnisgesellschaft: Kultursoziologie der Gegenwart* (Frankfurt: Campus, 1993), p. 300; Herrwerth, *Katzeklo & Caprifischer*, pp. 158–159.

[27] During my fieldwork in the early 2000s, I confirmed that the age of *Schlager* audiences could vary greatly. Although most fans are in their fifties or sixties, there are a lot of young people who consume *Schlager*, see Julio Mendívil, *Ein musikalisches Stück Heimat: Ethnographische Beobachtungen zum deutschen Schlager* (Bielefeld: Transcript, 2008).

tion of *Schlager*. The initial concept of the show was that during every episode, the audience could select its favourite song from the week's top-ten list.[28] However, the relationship between audience and producers rapidly reversed. At the beginning, the main condition for inclusion in the program was the popular recognition of the songs in question as *Schlager*. Later on, however, it was the very inclusion of songs that defined them as *Schlager*. Hence, *Hitparade* grew into a powerful authority that could unilaterally decide if a song belonged to the genre of *Schlager* or not:

> Hitparade became a monthly, televised ritual for those who wanted Schlager no longer to be consumed as a supplement to comedy-movies or shows, but as an independent form of music. There, new stars were born, old hands were pitted against new competitors and trends took shape, became fashionable and subsided. In spite of all that, Hitparade lasted for a long time with this format and defined in uncertain terms what 'Schlager' was, thus shaping the parameters of the genre.[29]

In doing so, *Hitparade* rewrote the concept of '*Schlager*', since, from that point on, neither the music nor its commodification were decisive factors in the classification of a song as *Schlager*, but rather merely its compatibility, or the lack thereof, with the show's format.[30]

The centralization of *Schlager* went hand in hand with what could be called its 'son-in-law-ization'. German *Schlager* aged musically, politically and morally with *Hitparade*. While longhaired young people sang 'Revolution' by The Beatles and protested against the Vietnam War to the tune of rock songs, Heck, in his program, presented decorous sunny boys in three-piece suits and ties who ostensibly captivated mums and grannies with toothpaste-commercial smiles and romantic lyrics. Elvis Presley, Paul McCartney and Mick Jagger were musicians, but they were also objects of desire. However, *Schlager* performers such as Chris Robert, Tony Holiday and above all, the epitome of the obedient son-in-law, Jürgen Marcus, were conceived to be the compassionate, charming and biddable

---

28 Burkhard Busse, *Der deutsche Schlager: Eine Untersuchung zur Produktion, Distribution und Rezeption von Trivialliteratur* (Wiesbaden: Athenaion, 1976), p. 39.

29 Matthias Bardong, Hermann Demmler and Christian Pfarr, *Das Lexikon des deutschen Schlagers* (Mainz: Schott, 1993), p. 37.

30 For a description of Dieter Thomas Heck's method for making stars see Jürgen Häusermann, *Und dabei liebe ich euch beide: Unterhaltung durch Schlager und Fernsehserien* (Wiesbaden: Breitkopf & Härtel, 1978); Herrwerth, *Katzeklo & Caprifischer*, pp. 73–99. For a truly revealing description of a recording session for *Hitparade* see Kraushaar, *Rote Lippen*, pp. 192–203.

young men every mum wanted her daughter to marry.[31] In this sense, the son-in-law-ization was a further step towards an overall desexualization of *Schlager*.

In the 1970s, Heck imposed his aesthetic and moral conceptions as the parameters of what did or did not constitute German *Schlager*. But his imagination was far from progressive. He fostered Gypsy romanticism, silly love songs and everything that young people abhorred. Admittedly, *Hitparade* accepted all kinds of performers, that is, apart from its repertoire of representative, traditional singers, there were also artists that tried to construct an alternative image of themselves, such as the 'German Joan Baez' Juliane Werding, the alleged working-class hero Gunter Gabriel, or the social democrat Katja Ebstein who sang about social problems and new gender roles in Germany.

Hitparade domesticated not only performers but also instruments such as the electric guitar, bass, keyboards and drums. At the beginning of the 1970s, The Flippers began to play minimalistic romantic songs with these instruments, which until then had been associated with rock music. At the time, producers attempted to gain new target audiences and recorded songs with traditional musical elements such as Heino's 'Die schwarze Barbara' [Black Barbara] and 'Es war einmal ein Jäger' [Once Upon a Time a Hunter] by Katja Ebstein, or soft rock songs such as 'Über sieben Brücken musst Du gehen' [Seven Bridges You Have to Cross] by Peter Maffay. Also worth mentioning in this context is the disco song 'Er gehört zu mir' [He Belongs to Me] by Marianne Rosenberg – probably the only *Schlager* singer with a Roma background.[32] The search for new consumer groups shows that the centralization of the de facto discourse had diminished the audience. However, the son-in-law-ization also allowed *Schlager* producers to test various strategies to deal with the problem, flirting with both rock elements and folkloristic tendencies.

The 1970s are considered the Golden Era of *Schlager*, and many songs from that time are now considered classics of the genre. 'Ein bißchen Frieden' [A Little Bit of Peace] – composed by Ralph Siegel[33] and performed by the then young singer Nicole in 1982 – may well represent the end of that era. The song is one of the most famous German *Schlager* evergreens, since its structure corresponds exactly to the minimalistic parameters of *Schlager*, but above all since, with it, Nicole won first place in the Eurovision Song Contest in 1982. Its title has led par-

---

31 Kraushaar, *Rote Lippen*, p. 131.

32 Her father Otto was an Auschwitz survivor and a long-time political activist for Sinti and Roma issues.

33 Ralph Siegel is one of the most important post-war producers and composers of *Schlager* in Germany. His father was the renowned musical publisher and composer Ralph Maria Siegel. For his biography see Bardong, Demmler and Pfarr, *Das Lexikon des deutschen Schlagers*, p. 291.

allels to be drawn between the song and the political tensions of the Cold War in Europe, in spite of the fact that *Schlager* songs normally do not have political themes. It has been argued that the song won the ESC not because of its musical qualities, but due to the 'very typical German mixture of emotionality with a hysterical apocalyptic mood'.[34] It is indeed true that the musical structure of 'Ein bißchen Frieden' is very simple, but the orchestral arrangement was as convincing as Nicole's performance of it.

The conservatism of *Schlager* was a determining factor in its negative reception within academia. The *Schlager* was a social and not a musical phenomenon for musicologists. For sociologists, it was an obvious case of cultural affirmation and was therefore considered to be of less cultural value than other kinds of music associated with resistance or protest. Furthermore, concepts such as progress, liberty, protest and revolution had no place inside *Schlager* discourse, whereas conservative concepts like homeland, family and romantic, heterosexual love were fundamental for the reproduction of a hegemonic, white and self-affirmative German image.[35] In the humanities and social sciences, *Schlager* became an example of conservatism, a scapegoat to which researchers could refer in order to condemn the domestication and commodification of recorded music, and in so doing, to increase their own cultural capital.[36]

Greek Wine and Fiesta Mexicana: The Representation of the Other in *Schlager*

German *Schlager* developed as a musical form in opposition to American and British genres such as rock 'n' roll, Mersey beat and the rock of the 1970s. As such, *Schlager* could be thought of as reluctant to assimilate foreign influences. Still, during the first half of the 1970s, many songs that referred to exotic topics in remote countries and to foreign nationals such as Greeks, Mexicans or Italians – often incorporating musical elements from these countries – flourished in the field of German *Schlager*. Throughout this period, there were also many performers with non-German backgrounds, such as Costa Cordalis, Roberto Blanco, Bata Illic, Howard Carpendale and Vicky Leandros, who achieved success singing *Schlager* songs. Although, at first glance, it seems contradictory that a national

---

34 Port le roi, *Schlager lügen nicht*, p. 206.
35 Herrwerth, *Katzeklo & Caprifischer*, p. 87.
36 Mendívil, *Ein musikalisches Stück Heimat*, pp. 147–148.

form like Schlager would incorporate otherness, in actuality this was a strategy to reinforce German musical conservatism.

Scholars have commonly criticized that *Schlager* songs always offer false descriptions of remote places in a typical romantic style.[37] Such criticism is based on the assumption that *Schlager* composers and lyricists distort the realities they describe. For example, Wolfgang Dietrich has analysed how Latin America is represented in several *Schlager* songs, concluding that lyricists use the region as a blank page in order to allow German listeners to fill it with clichés about domination and exploitation in that region. According to Dietrich, songs such as 'Popocateppetl Twist', 'Ananas aus Caracas' [Pineapple from Caracas] and 'Habanero' convey nothing about real life in Latin America, nothing about exploited *campesinos* and factory workers, and nothing about cruel dictators. Also, he maintains that such songs only reinforce the image consumers have of Latin America as a mixture of banana republics and primitive settings.[38] Evidently, there is a false general assumption at work here in the argument that the social function of popular music is to truthfully illustrate political or religious realities around the world to its audience.

The representation of the Other effectively changes its meaning if one abandons the idea that signifiers have natural relationships to the signified and rather assumes that the description of the Other is a strategy for the construction of the self. This can be demonstrated by analyzing the lyrics and music of two evergreens that deal with foreign objects from exotic places. The first example is 'Griechischer Wein' [Greek Wine], recorded by the Austrian singer Udo Jürgens in 1974. He was considered to be a liberal performer inside the conservative world of *Schlager*, an artist who put great emphasis on the quality of his lyrics and who tried to comment on current social developments in his songs. In this sense it was not a surprise that Jürgens chose the social situation of migrant workers in the 1970s as the topic for a *Schlager* song. 'Griechischer Wein' was a

---

37 See René Malamud, *Zur Psychologie des deutschen Schlagers: Eine Untersuchung anhand seiner Texte* (Winterthur: Keller, 1964), p. 62; Werner Mezger, *Schlager: Versuch einer Gesamtdarstellung unter besonderer Berücksichtigung des Musikmarktes der Bundesrepublik Deutschland* (Tübingen: Tübinger Vereinigung für Volkskunde, 1975), p. 181; Mark Terkessidis, 'Die Eingeborenen von Schizonesien: Der Schlager als deutscheste aller Popkulturen', in *Mainstream der Minderheiten: Pop in der Kontrollgesellschaft*, ed. by Tom Holert and Mark Terkessidis (Berlin: Edition ID-Archiv, 1996), pp. 115–138 (p. 131); Eckhart Höfig, *Heimat in der Popmusik: Identität oder Kulisse in der deutschsprachigen Popmusikszene vor der Jahrtausendwende* (Gelsenkirchen: Triga Verlag, 2000), p. 138.
38 Wolfgang Dietrich, *Samba, Samba: Eine politikwissenschaftliche Untersuchung zur fernen Erotik Lateinamerikas in den Schlagern des 20. Jahrhunderts* (Strasshof: Vier-Viertel-Verlag, 2002), p. 221–227.

huge success, often celebrated as one of the best *Schlager* songs that tackle real social problems.

Jürgens fans are less critical of his songs than are *Schlager* scholars, most of whom criticize Jürgens and lyricist Michael Kunze for distorting reality:

> At first sight, the content of Udo Jürgens' hit seems to place it in the category of protest songs rather than Schlager. It describes the situation of Greek migrant workers in the Federal Republic of German, who find their situation depressing. The song's listeners, however, are not confronted with any truth which might be uncomfortable to them. The Schlager contains only generally touching statements and descriptions of living conditions, for which listeners can by no means made responsible.[39]

However, the song should instead be interpreted in accordance with what could be called an 'aesthetic of difference'. The lyrics describe a lonely German man walking through the streets and hearing foreign music coming from a bar. He enters the bar and sees a group of black-haired men drinking and listening to music from their homeland, Greece. When one of them notices the German 'intruder', he invites him to join the group for a glass of wine. Notably, the roles are inverted in the lyrics: it is the German who is out of place in the bar and confronted with a strange situation in his native country.

The topic of their conversation is ostensibly the homelessness of the migrant workers, but the impossibility of communication between Greeks and Germans is also implied. Thus, the song suggests that spatial approximation of people from different countries is not enough to overcome cultural distance: 'Ich werde hier immer ein Fremder sein' [I will always remain a stranger here], the Greek laments, and the German reports: 'Sie sagten sich immer wieder: Irgendwann geht es zurück.' [They continually told themselves: One day we will go back home].

Although Greeks and Germans share the same space, they do not share the same cultural norms and memories. The link between these two worlds is not a shared moment while drinking wine, but rather their patriotic love of the homeland. As Höfig has pointed out, the images of the Greek motherland in 'Griechischer Wein' are the same as those praised in German *Schlager* songs: a picturesque landscape with green hills, the beautiful sea, a blue sky and so on.[40] In this sense, 'Greece' stands for the idea of 'homeland', and thus could also be interpreted as a metaphor for Germany.

---

39 Höfig, *Heimat in der Popmusik*, p. 142.
40 Ibid.

The musical poetics can be seen as signs of difference as well. The initial bouzouki melody suggests that the first-person narrator abandons the realm of German culture without leaving Germany. This is also suggested by the minor mode played on the bouzouki during the stanzas of the song. But at the height of the song, the refrain changes to F major, thus following the typical harmonic structure of *Schlager:* tonic, dominant and subdominant. Accordingly, the song recaptures its German character, and reduces and suppresses the foreign topic.

Such a musical strategy can be called an 'aesthetic of difference' because the topic of the song is an encounter between two different cultural identities in which, in spite of a short-lived alliance, each side remains foreign to the other. It should be borne in mind that these boundaries are self-affirmative as long as they reproduce cultural clichés and mechanisms of exclusion. It therefore must be argued that the character of the German subject in 'Griechischer Wein' is constructed through the recognition of inexorable otherness. The momentary alliance between these strangers takes places in the context of the German concept of *Heimat.*

Another pertinent example is the evergreen 'Fiesta Mexicana', also composed by Ralph Siegel. The song was recorded in 1972 by Rex Gildo, who gained popularity in the 1970s with hits such as 'Marina' and 'Speedy Gonzales'. Dietrich interprets the lyrics as follows:

> The identity of the singer, the guest of honour at a large farewell party in Mexico, is unclear. It is unlikely that a tourist could organize such a big party, although some verses bring to mind the lyrics of holiday songs. He is not Mexican since nothing indicates that the singer has his roots there [...]. He is someone who comes, goes and comes back to be happy and fall in love. [...] One can assume that these diffuse descriptions are calculated, because the central topic of the song is not Mexico, which is reduced to tequila, sombreros and guitars, but the beer pavilion from whose stage the singer can call to the audience: 'We are celebrating a Mexican fiesta'. [...] It is pointless to search for meaning in this song.[41]

This song, however, should be understood differently. The singer is clearly a German living in a Mexican village who must leave it temporarily for unspecified reasons. Therefore, the first-person narrator organizes a farewell party, which all the people in the village attend. The mere fact that the German is the host reveals how profoundly he is integrated into the village. The party takes place in the *plaza*, not at the *hacienda* or house of the stranger. And the *plaza* is also the place where the German kissed Carmencita: 'Und ich küsse Carmencita / Denn ich weiß, die Stunde des Abschieds ist da.' [And I kiss Carmencita because / since I know that it is time to say goodbye]. Accordingly, the *plaza* is

---

41 Dietrich, *Samba, Samba*, p. 188.

also a place of love and happiness. The suggestion is that this Mexican *plaza* is also a projection of German *Heimat* and is thus transformed into an object of nostalgia and desire.

The song is not about a real but rather an imagined Mexico with tequila, sombreros and *señoritas* – a Mexico that only exists in the fantasy of the German listener. Thus, the song replaces categories like 'German' or 'Mexican' with the German notion of *Heimat*. It is pointless to attempt to place the song in the context of Mexican history or relations between Germany and Mexico, as Dietrich did, since the main topic is not the life of Carmencita, Juanita, Pepe, or of any of the other people celebrating the fiesta in the *plaza*, but rather the life of the German in the Mexican village.

Therefore, *Schlager* songs about Italians, Greeks, cowboys, South-American Indians or happy Mexicans playing guitar do not have the function of opening a cultural window for German audiences or enabling sophisticated insights into foreign countries. Such songs have a different function. They should be seen as pacifist versions of the expansionist thrust of German nationalism in that they incorporate foreign territories into the German *Heimat*.

The inclusion of foreign performers represents the second aspect of this cultural expansionist policy. According to Heck, speaking with a foreign accent on stage was highly beneficial to the performer's success.[42] The Greek singer Costa Cordalis, Cuban entertainer Roberto Blanco, Chris Howland from Britain, and American singers Gus Backus, Connie Francis and Bill Ramsey, among others, enjoyed popularity as foreigners singing in German for audiences in the Federal Republic. In fact, as Helms has ironically noted, at that time those with names such as Norbert Berger, Jutta Gusenburger or Rosamarie Böhm stood no chance of success in the *Schlager* industry and had to take on artistic names like Cindy & Bert or Mary Roos.

It seems contradictory for a musical category that rejected African American and British genres to prefer stars with Anglicized names. However, in light of the cultural strategies German *Schlager* producers used to achieve worldwide success, it is clear that the presence of foreign performers during the 1970s was not an expression of liberal cosmopolitanism but rather another form of conservatism. The clash between the dominance of English in popular music and *Schlager* listeners' longing for the familiar led *Schlager* producers to attempt to

---

42 Quoted in Siegfried Helms, 'Schlager Stars', in *Schlager in Deutschland: Beiträge zur Analyse der Popularmusik und des Musikmarktes*, ed. by Siegfried Helms (Wiesbaden: Breitkopf & Härtel, 1972), pp. 159–176 (p. 163).

'domesticate' foreign languages and, in general, reduce cultural otherness by promoting singers with foreign accents and foreign-sounding names.

Conclusion

Schlager evolved from a commercial concept to a musical genre. During this process, the success of a song came to depend on its containing certain musical elements. Accordingly, *Schlager* transformed into a musical form that relied on certain types of songs and followed tried-and-tested formulas in order to sell records. In the post-war era, *Schlager* first came to be associated with the adjective 'German' to distinguish between German songs and American or British hits. In this sense, German *Schlager* became a conservative field, standing in stark contrast to the Anglo-American music industry that was commonly associated with liberal political stances and sexualized notions of the body.

During the 1970s, *Schlager* music experienced a process of what can be called 'senescence' as well as one of 'son-in-law-ization', which made it even less appealing to young people whose musical tastes were geared towards the new musical forms from abroad. Whereas rock 'n' roll, beat and rock subverted areas of social life such as sexuality and morality, *Schlager* music was produced and consumed for an easy-listening experience. The desire for the beautiful and the simple in music, it can be argued, is a political one, and *Schlager* can therefore be considered an act of rebellion against the successful advance of Anglophone music. It was a conservative rebellion against the liberalization of the German popular music scene.[43] The conservative genre of *Schlager* protested against the liberal character of democracy in the post-war era, contrasting physical music (rhythm) with mental music (melody).

The term 'conservatism' refers here to the defence of a hierarchical, religious and anti-modern world view – the attitude of those who advocate old-world values and reject what Anthony Giddens has described as 'the reflexivity of radical modernity', i.e. the fact that, in modernity, social practices are constantly examined and reformed in light of ever-changing information about those very practices, which constitutively alters their character.[44] In order to conserve this imagined land of beauty in music, the *Schlager* community converted exotic places

---

43 Mendívil, *Ein musikalisches Stück Heimat*, p. 348.
44 See Anthony Giddens, *The Consequences of Modernity* (Stanford: Stanford University Press, 1990).

into German territories and domesticated Otherness by accepting foreign singers and English stage names.

However, this only worked until the German New Wave surfaced in the 1980s, which posed a new problem for *Schlager*. Until then, *Schlager* were the only German music using the national adjective as a marker. When the German New Wave also claimed the adjective and native language for itself, *Schlager* were forced to develop new forms of musical conservatism in order to be more German than the German New Wave. While rock music distanced itself more and more from *Schlager*, becoming an important field in the German musical landscape, the fusion between *Schlager* and folk turned out to be dominant during the 1980s.

New *Schlager* ensembles such as Original Naabtal Duo or the Austrian soft rock ensemble Schürzenjäger assaulted the German charts by accompanying *Schlager* songs with accordions and singing in regional German dialects. The considerable success of 'Patrona Bavariae' [Virgin Mary of Bavaria] provoked an avalanche of similar songs that generated a new trend in *Schlager* – German folkloristic *Schlager* – and further radicalized its 'senescence', making it more melodic, more conservative and, as it were, more German. During the 1990s, singers such as Guildo Horn and Dieter Thomas Kuhn tried to modernize *Schlager* with rock versions of evergreens such as 'Aber bitte mit Sahne' [With Whipped Cream, Please] or 'Siebzehn Jahr, blondes Haar' [Seventeen and Blonde] in the hopes of winning over young people.

However, conservative *Schlager* audiences did not really accept these modernized renditions, overlooking the ironic aspect and perceiving Guildo Horn as a rocker who had surrendered to *Schlager*. Indeed, the German *Schlager* community colonized Horn's ironic renditions and, in doing so, turned him into an 'ordinary' *Schlager* singer. After his ephemeral success, Horn fell out of favour with *Schlager* audiences and attempted a comeback years later by singing old Nordic folkloristic songs. As in many comparable attempts, Horn's *Schlager* reform was short-lived, and Schlager ensembles like De Randfichten achieved popularity during the 1990s by singing folkloric melodies supported by techno beats.

In spite of the dogged resistance of *Schlager* to change, in the first years of the 21st century certain new *Schlager* performers, including Andreas Gabalier or Helene Fischer, have revolutionized the *Schlager* landscape, re-orientating it towards other (diverse) musical genres such as rock, pop and musicals. Fischer, for example, has changed the image of the Schlager singer progressively but radically. Her stage show, in which she sings, dances and even performs stunts, displays not only her great ability as a performer but also, more unusually for *Schlager*, great sensuality. Furthermore, she performs many different personalities on the stage: the timid, innocent and ladylike woman, the party-queen, the *femme fatale*, the techno-dancer, the pop star, and so on. Her musical aesthetic is strongly oriented towards pop and displays innovative choices. Her songs are strongly orchestrated and are often supported by electronic beats. In addition, her lyrics are more conservative and contain many of the *Schlager* clichés regarding heteronormative love, which is also not incompatible with her orientation towards (mainstream) pop. Today, German *Schlager* remains a strongly conservative and self-affirmative musical genre, whose vocalists sing about morality, beauty and idyllic landscapes in an increasingly insecure and hostile world.

David Robb

The Protest Song of the Late 1960s and Early 1970s – Franz Josef Degenhardt and Ton Steine Scherben

As well as being a time of great innovation in German popular music, the late 1960s and early 1970s in West Germany saw a high degree of politicized song-writing in the genres of *Liedermacher* [song-makers] and rock. This chapter looks at two distinct examples: firstly, Franz Josef Degenhardt, one of the most prominent singers of the folk, political song and chanson scene that affili-ated itself with the Extra-Parliamentary Opposition (APO) from the mid-1960s onwards, and secondly the agitrock band Ton Steine Scherben in the anarchist milieu of West Berlin in the early 1970s.

While aesthetically very different, both were countercultural forms within their respective political movements which used music as a galvanising force for the expression of oppositional identity and political demands of the time. Each in their own way, they contributed to the re-emergence of the *Protestlied* [protest song] as a prime medium of cultural expression for the political de-mands of the student movement.

Insofar as the *Liedermacher* and Ton Steine Scherben made music an out-spoken mouthpiece of social critique and political agitation, their protest songs markedly differed from the avant-garde bands such as Tangerine Dream, Amon Düül or Can, who came to the fore in the early 1970s. These groups, de-spite their revolutionizing of established popular music models, generally es-chewed direct political messages. All of these artistic innovations, however, rep-resented distinctive German musical responses to the political and cultural situation of the time.

The musical developments of the mid-to-late 1960s occurred against a back-drop of American and British musical and cultural influence combined with the political theory of the European New Left. Anglo-American culture had filled the void created by the isolationist cultural policies of the Nazis. Young German mu-sicians initially imitated the musical blueprints of English-language rock and pop music which they perceived as a protest against the conservative *Schlager* music their parents listened to.

The initial musical impetus for the German *Liedermacher* came from the new wave of folk and protest songs represented by American singers such as Bob Dylan and Joan Baez. Folk anthems like 'We shall overcome' were sung at the anti-nuclear Easter Marches in Germany from 1960 onwards. The democratically

DOI 10.1515/9783110425727-003

orientated US folksong revival with its affiliation to the Civil Rights movement was a point of identification for young German political singers, eager to distance themselves from the legacy of the Third Reich.

But the misuse of folk songs by the Nazis had rendered Germany's own folk song culture virtually unsingable. In response to the question from international visitors: 'Where are your own songs?' Franz Josef Degenhardt in 1966 sang:

> Tot sind unsre Lieder, unsre alten Lieder
> Lehrer haben sie zerbissen
> Kurzbehoste sie verklampft
> Braune Horden totgeschrien
> Stiefel in den Dreck gestampft
>
> [Our songs are dead, our old songs
> Teachers sang them to death
> The boys in short trousers strummed them to death
> The brown hordes screamed them to death
> Jackboots stamped them in the dirt]

The reaction to this perceived lack of German song was two-fold: on the one hand, the search began for a lost tradition of German oppositional folk songs. The bass baritone singer Peter Rohland, who had emerged from a democratic wing of the *Bündisch* German Youth Movement which had been banned in the Third Reich,[1] was the first to revive the tradition of socially critical German folk songs such as those of the 1848 revolution.[2] Other performers such as Degenhardt strove to create a contemporary satirical German chanson akin to that of the French. This heralded the emergence of the *Liedermacher*, a term allegedly coined by the East German protest singer Wolf Biermann in reference to Bertolt Brecht's literal term 'Stückeschreiber' [playwright]. Such endeavours of the *Liedermacher* to create something distinctively German mirrored Krautrock's search for a new musical identity untainted by the Nazi past.[3]

---

1 See Eckard Holler, 'The Burg Waldeck Festivals, 1964–1969', in *Protest Song in East and West Germany*, ed. by David Robb (Rochester, NY: Camden House, 2007), pp. 97–132 (pp. 98–103 and pp. 115–116).

2 David Robb and Eckhard John, 'Lieder der 1848er Revolution', in *Populäre und traditionelle Lieder. Historisch-kritisches Liederlexikon* (www.liederlexikon.de/ueber_liederlexikon_de/projekte/ahrc-dfg_projekt).

3 If Krautrock had partly represented, as argued in the chapter by Littlejohn, a turning away from US musical culture by the increasingly politicized youth as a result of the Vietnam War, the development of the *Liedermacher* to create a new German type of song was not necessarily in opposition to Anglo-American cultural models. The American folk revival as promoted by

The *Liedermacher*, who included Franz Josef Degenhardt, Dieter Süverkrüpp, Walter Mossmann and Hannes Wader, first came to prominence playing at the annual festivals in the grounds of the castle ruins of Burg Waldeck in Hunsrück between 1964 and 1969. They came to be closely affiliated with the Extra-Parliamentary Opposition which emerged alongside the student movement of the late 1960s and many were later active within the New Social Movements of the 1970s. The rock band Ton Steine Scherben, on the other hand, inhabited the radical anarchist and squatter scene of West Berlin of the early 1970s and had loose connections to the terrorist groups Rote Armee Fraktion (Red Army Faction) and the Bewegung 2. Juni (June 2 Movement). Both examples are distinct in their creative combination of German political music traditions with international popular musical trends of the time. A further aspect of commonality lies in how both the *Liedermacher* and Ton Steine Scherben had to address the perennial tension between art and politics whilst operating within their respective movements.

Degenhardt – From Nuanced Critique to Militant Opposition

The years from the early 1960s leading up to the highpoint of the oppositional student movement of 1968 represented a utopian period in German popular music culture, in which a young generation attempted to shake off the shackles of a Nazi cultural legacy and forge a new creative path as an alternative to the petty bourgeois conformism of society under Konrad Adenauer, who had dominated German culture as Chancellor between 1949 and 1963. Young folk singers, such as Peter Rohland or Hein & Oss Kröher, rediscovered suppressed traditions of oppositional German folk songs. At the same time political songwriters, such as Degenhardt, Süverkrüp, Mossmann and Hanns Dieter Hüsch, produced a degree of satirical innovation in song that had not been seen since the literary cabaret of the Weimar Republic forty years earlier.

Degenhardt's songs reflected the new cultural non-conformism emerging among the intellectual youth, who rejected the complacency of a German mainstream society celebrating its post-war Economic Miracle. Degenhardt, a doctor of law, initially came to the public eye at the first Burg Waldeck festival in 1964. His compositions, singing style and guitar accompaniment were noticeably influenced by the French chansonnier Georges Brassens. In his early songs, social

---

John and Alan Lomax with its emphasis on the democratic voices of the people, as in the songs of Woody Guthrie and Pete Seeger, was constantly seen as an exemplary model.

conformity and the image of uniform wealth propagated by the media are countered by the skeptical view of the social outsider. In his ballad 'Rumpelstilzchen' [Rumpelstiltskin] from 1963 Degenhardt plays the anarchic outsider who has come to create disorder: 'Es ist gut, daß niemand weiß / daß ich Rumpelstilzchen heiß' [It is good that nobody knows / that my name is Rumpelstiltskin].[4]

It was significant, however, that the gesture of non-conformity was not transmitted via an overt political message, but via the upside-down imagery that constitutes the narrative of 'Rumpelstiltskin's' fairy-tale world. As the 1960s progressed, Degenhardt's lyrics became more politically specific. In 'Spiel nicht mit den Schmuddelkindern' [Don't Play With the Scruffy Kids] from 1965, a middle-class boy's development is examined against the background of an underprivileged fringe existence. Here Degenhardt's insights into the class-character of Adenauer society contradict the view that a prosperous West Germany had successfully dissolved class boundaries thanks to the introduction of the so-called Social Market Economy, a tamed version of capitalism in which an extensive social security system is supposed to help eliminate the harmful effects of a free market system. The constant opposition of 'uptown' and the proletarian quarter implies the necessity of being in the right class and playing by its rules. The refrain, which urges for a cessation of contact with the scruffy kids, provides an ironical counterpoint:[5]

> Spiel nicht mit den Schmuddelkindern
> Sing nicht ihre Lieder
> Geh doch in die Oberstadt,
> Mach's wie deine Brüder'
>
> [Don't play with the scruffy kids
> Don't sing their songs
> Go uptown
> Just like your brothers][6]

Through the mid- to late-1960s Degenhardt began targeting his songs toward the increasingly politicized students and intellectuals in the Extra-Parliamentary Opposition which had formed in response to the Grand Coalition of the Christian

---

4 Franz Josef Degenhardt, *Spiel nicht mit den Schmuddelkindern: Balladen, Chansons, Grotesken, Lieder* (Reinbek: Rowohlt, 1969), pp. 15–17. Excerpts of this section on Degenhardt have appeared in David Robb, 'Narrative Role-Play as Communication Strategy in German Protest Song', in Robb (ed.) *Protest Song in East and West Germany*, pp. 67–96 (pp. 74–80).
5 Heinrich Vormweg, 'Degenhardt dichtend', in *Franz-Josef Degenhardt: Politische Lieder 1964– 1972*, ed. by Heinz Ludwig Arnold (Munich: Edition Text und Kritik, 1972), pp. 28–43 (p. 35).
6 Degenhardt, *Spiel nicht mit den Schmuddelkindern*, p. 45.

Democrats (CDU) and Social Democrats (SPD).[7] In 'Adieu Kameraden' [Farewell Friends] from 1965, he symbolically renounced his friends who did not share his developing political awareness. 'Väterchen Franz' [Little Papa Franz] from 1966 saw him breaking with his role as the drunken chronicler and renouncing the pure entertainment value of his cabaret-like art. The text 'Wenn der Senator erzählt' [When the Senator Tells His Story] (1967) subtly addresses the fact that former Nazis were still occupying positions of financial and political power.

Performed in the style of *Sprechgesang* in which the singer alternates between spoken and sung parts, it is an example of a typical Degenhardt *Rollengedicht* [dramatic monologue]. This functions by means of the singer donning a character mask and – via an ironic self-exposure – revealing that character's hypocrisy or self-interest.[8] In the text, the accumulation of the senator's wealth in the steel industry is traced from the German Empire through to the interwar period of the Weimar Republic, the Third Reich, and up to the present. After the war, he turns the land into a holiday park with the blessing of an old Nazi colleague who is now in government. The disingenuousness of the senator's narrative reflected by the sarcastic refrain 'Ja, ja, ja, ja, ja – Wenn der Senator erzählt' [Yeah, yeah, yeah, yeah, yeah – When the senator tells his story][9] is underlined by the false innocence of the peaceful string quartet music.[10]

A similar technique of *Sprechgesang* and ironic role-play is employed in 'Vatis Argumente' [Daddy's Points of View] from 1967, a father's tirade against the student leader Rudi Dutschke. Due to Degenhardt's distancing technique, nothing the father says may be taken seriously:

Lieber Rudi Dutschke [...]
wissen Sie was das hieß
studieren damals
keine Bücher, kein Brot, kein Bier
[...] aber gewaschen haben wir uns.
Und wenn's keine Seife gab
mit Sand,
jawohl mit Sand

---

7 See also Alexander von Bormann, 'Franz-Josef Degenhardt', in *Kritisches Lexikon zur deutschsprachigen Gegenwartsliteratur*, ed. by Heinz Ludwig Arnold (Munich: Edition Text & Kritik, 1978), pp. 5–6.
8 Ibid.
9 Degenhardt, 'Wenn der Senator erzählt', in *Spiel nicht*, pp. 91–93.
10 Hans-Klaus Jungheinrich, 'Protest-Noten', in *Franz-Josef Degenhard*, ed. by Arnold, pp. 45–54 (p. 50).

[Dear Rudi Dutschke [...],
do you know what that meant
to study in those days?
No books, no bread, no beer
[...] but we washed ourselves.
And when there was no soap
with sand,
yes with sand][11]

The satirical distancing betrays that throughout his life the father has been no more than a conformer, far from the rebel in the Hitler Youth he claims to have been:

Als ich so alt war wie sie
ich habe mir auch nichts gefallen lassen.
Hatte immer Krach mit dem Fähnleinführer [...]
Aber bei aller Aufsässigkeit,
wenn Not am Mann war,
da hieß es doch
ÄRMEL AUFKREMPELN ZUPACKEN AUFBAUEN

[When I was your age
I didn't put up with anything either.
I was always getting into trouble with our patrol leader [...]
But despite all the rebellion,
in times of emergency,
it was
ROLE UP YOUR SLEEVES GET TO IT DO SOMETHING][12]

The satire reflects the bitter feud between the students and their parents, whom they accused of silent complicity in the crimes of the Third Reich. The undercurrent of rebellion is further cemented by the rock music accompaniment in the style of The Doors.

By 1968, a clear radicalization was taking place within the German *Liedermacher* scene. This brought about the resurfacing of the historical tension between music and politics, posing the question of the extent to which music can ever be subservient to political goals. The fifth Burg Waldeck festival took place in May 1968 amidst an escalation of protests after the Vietnam conference in February in Berlin, the assassination attempt on Dutschke, and the controversial passing of the Emergency Laws which restricted constitutional rights in the

---

11 Degenhardt, 'Vatis Argumente', in *Spiel nicht*, p. 99.
12 Ibid., p. 101.

case of public unrest. The political atmosphere at Waldeck was heightened by the presence of members of the Socialist German Student League (SDS) who had little interest in music and saw the festival as a vehicle for furthering their political agenda.

In an atmosphere resembling an inquisition the satirical cabaret performer Hanns Dieter Hüsch was asked to account for his views and ultimately forced to call off his concert. A militant group came up with the slogan 'Stellt die Gitarren in die Ecke und diskutiert' [Put the guitars in the corner and discuss], calling for Degenhardt to turn his concert into a teach-in, a demand to which he complied after performing a few numbers.[13] Such developments rested uneasily with many festival goers. The tensions, which continued at the International Essen Song Festival in September that year and again at Burg Waldeck in 1969, were indicative of a growing incompatibility between the goals of artists and those of an increasingly splintering left-wing movement.

Throughout 1968, Degenhardt's songs became more militant and direct in their demands for change. He went on the offensive, embracing Marxist ideology and advocating a People's Front between the Social Democratic Party (SPD) and the newly formed German Communist Party (DKP) to overthrow the capitalist system. From now on, with echoes of Hanns Eisler's theory for the political song from the early 1930s,[14] he saw his songs as no longer for the aesthetic gratification of an educated audience, but for explicit agitation in the class struggle. Consequently, the music became harder-edged, his texts less ironic and more dogmatic. The radical sentiment of a new final verse which was premiered at the Essen Festival was representative of the feeling of the time among activists. In 'Manchmal sagen die Kumpanen' [Sometimes the Chums Say] (1968) he sings:

Vom Protest zum Widerstand, doch dabei bleiben wir nicht stehn,
denn wir müssen bald vom Widerstand zum Angriff übergehn.
Ja, genau das ist jetzt richtig, alles andre nicht so wichtig.
Alles andere ist Krampf – im Klassenkampf

[From protest to resistance, but it won't stay as that,
because we must soon go over from resistance to attack.
Yes, precisely this is important now, everything else is not so important.
Everything else is cramp in the class struggle]

---

13 See Holler, 'The Burg Waldeck Festivals', p. 120.

14 Hanns Eisler was an Austrian communist composer who wrote a theory on the role of music in songs for the political class struggle. He composed numerous *Kampflieder* (battle songs) with Brecht in the 1930s as well as music for the latter's plays. See Robb, 'Mühsam, Brecht, Eisler, pp. 54–57.

The lack of melody was indicative of how the balance between music and politics had tipped in the direction of the latter. This undoubtedly contributed to the impression held by many *Liedermacher* critics that the musical form was merely being used as a vehicle for political theorizing.[15]

The presence of new avant-garde groups such as Tangerine Dream and Amon Düül at the Essen Festival alongside the *Liedermacher* has been celebrated as a unique utopian coming together of starkly contrasting genres. This, nonetheless, also caused tensions at the time. Degenhardt, for example, distanced himself from the hippie supporters of Amon Düül, a Munich-based commune that performed as a radical art group in the alternative scene. For him, hippie existence was decadent; it meant escape from the world, not engaging in it and trying to change it.[16] His attitude was typical of the revolutionary didacticism of many of the 1968 political activists who were suspicious of the mysticism and anti-rationalism of the hippie, psychedelic bands.

1968 was the climax of the student and the *Liedermacher* movement, but it was also the end of a utopian period in which political and artistic aims had been in apparent unison. The realities of political in-fighting on the Left and sectarianism between different subcultural groups began to set in. The final Burg Waldeck festival of 1969 was marked by arguments between various left-wing groups including the newly founded German Communist Party (DKP) and various new Marxist-Leninist and Maoist K-Gruppen [cadre parties], each accusing the other of being counter-revolutionary.[17] The student movement ran out of steam by late 1969, their revolutionary idealism having lacked a concrete goal. However, the legacy of Franz Josef Degenhardt and his fellow *Liedermacher* was substantial in their reinvigoration of the tradition of socially critical German song

It even gained access to the pop mainstream, as exemplified by Degenhardt's 'Befragung eines Kriegsdienstverweigerers' [Interrogation of a Conscientious Objector] which reached the number one position in the WDR chart in 1972. At the same time, *Liedermacher* created the practice of writing popular song lyrics in German, influencing the likes of Udo Lindenberg, Konstantin Wecker, BAP and Herbert Grönemeyer, amongst many others. Politically, while these singers of 1968 did not achieve their utopian aims, it became clear that the reform movement had shaken the pillars of the German conservative establishment. The Willy

---

15 See, for example, Florian Tobias Kreier, *Die Band Ton Steine Scherben: Subpolitiker einer Gegenkultur?* (Hamburg: Diplomica, 2012), p. 11.

16 See Detlev Mahnert and Harry Stürmer, *Zappa, Zoff und Zwischentöne: Die Internationalen Essener Songtage 1968* (Essen: Klartext, 2008), p. 97.

17 Holler, 'Die Burg Waldeck Festivals', pp. 125–126.

Brandt-led governments of the 1970s successfully contained this protest by funding clubs, festivals and the New Social Movements, in which these musicians continued to perform and enjoy a prominence.[18]

Ton Steine Scherben – Anarchy and Agitrock in West Berlin

It was in a completely different niche within the oppositional political spectrum that the agitrock band Ton Steine Scherben existed. They have seldom been examined in relation to the *Liedermacher* before, largely because of this different location. Moreover, the two constituted separate musical genres at a time when electric and acoustic music were quite distinct taste group categories. According to the group's first drummer, Wolfgang Seidel, the altogether more anarchic and proletarian Ton Steine Scherben found the *Liedermacher* 'zu normal' [too normal] with their connections to the romantic German song tradition and their roots in cabaret.[19]

Still, both these musical approaches belong together in terms of the *Protestlied* as a musical vehicle for the expression of dissent in times of political change. After all, both had a nationwide impact as oppositional musical forms and both encountered similar issues in reconciling artistic with ideological ambitions within political movements. Unlike the *Liedermacher*, who for the most part constituted a network of folk and political song performers in a closely linked scene of clubs and festivals throughout the 1970s, Ton Steine Scherben were more of a unique phenomenon.[20]

Their story is set within the post 1968 countercultural scene of the Kreuzberg district in West Berlin. Since 1961, sandwiched between the Berlin Wall and middle class areas, this frontier district with its high Turkish immigrant population and cheap, run-down tenements had become a haven for those seeking an alternative existence: junkies, artists, militant students, young men escaping military service. It correspondingly became a focal point for underground culture.

---

18 See Eckard Holler, 'The Folk and *Liedermacher* Scene in the Federal Republic in the 1970s and 1980s', in Robb, *Protest Song*, pp. 133–167 (p. 136).
19 Wolfgang Seidel, 'Berlin und die Linke in den 1960ern: Die Entstehung der Ton Steine Scherben', in *Scherben. Musik, Politik und Wirkung der Ton Steine Scherben*, ed. by Wolfgang Seidel (Mainz: Ventil Verlag, 2005), pp. 25–50 (p. 42).
20 At the same time, they were not the only German-language political rock group. Others included Floh de Cologne, Checkpoint Charlie and Lokomotive Kreuzberg.

In the aftermath of the student movement and the dissolving of the APO-linked Kommune 1, the scene of communes and squats which characterized Kreuzberg had become more autonomous and militant. Emerging political groups such as the Blues, radical bohemian anarchists who had links to the terrorist groups RAF and Bewegung 2. Juni, existed alongside a number of the new anarchist K-Gruppen. As elsewhere in West Germany at that time, the latter saw their task as mobilising the political consciousness of the working class youth in their local environments.[21] This was mirrored in the approach of Ton Steine Scherben, who evolved in late 1969 and early 1970 out of the radical street theatre Hoffmann's Comic Teater and the apprentices' agitprop group Rote Steine [Red Stones].

The group name literally means 'Clay Stones Shards'. There are several stories in circulation regarding the origin of the band's name. According to Seidel, the group's singer Rio Reiser had come across this exact word combination while reading Heinrich Schliemann's account of excavating the ruins of Troy. In this respect the words had connotations of destruction as well as of piecing together and rebuilding.[22] As Sichtermann, Johler and Stahl remember, the name was also aptly reminiscent of the trade union Bau Steine Erden or the *volkseigene Betriebe* (VEB) [People's Own Industries] of the GDR.[23] At the same time there was an ambiguity in the words whereby musical associations to 'sound' ('Ton') and the Rolling Stones ('Steine') could be exploited.

The original group members were Ralph Möbius a.k.a. Rio Reiser (vocals, guitar), R. P. S. Lanrue (guitar), Kai Sichtermann (bass guitar) and Wolfgang Seidel (drums). Their early years were marked by a series of well publicized scandals such as inciting a riot at a major rock festival and their manager and saxophonist Nikel Pallat taking an axe to a table on a late night TV political discussion in December 1971. Forerunners of the punk ethos seven years later, they pioneered an independent system of record production and distribution under their own David Volksmund label.[24] By the end of the 1970s, the group had shifted 300,000 albums despite no advertizing and being shunned by radio sta-

---

21 Timothy S. Brown, 'Music as a Weapon? Ton Steine Scherben and the Politics of Rock in Cold War Berlin', *German Studies Review* 32/1 (2009), 1–22 (p. 7).

22 Seidel, 'Scherben...' in *Scherben: Musik, Politik und Wirkung*, pp. 69–114 (p. 77).

23 See Kai Sichtermann, Jens Johler and Christian Stahl, *Keine Macht für niemand: Die Geschichte der Ton Steine Scherben* (Berlin: Schwarzkopf & Schwarzkopf, 2003), p. 14.

24 See Sichtermann et al, *Keine Macht*, pp. 75–77. 'David' was a reference to the underdog David who challenged the giant Goliath. 'Volksmund' means 'people's voice'.

tions.[25] In particular their first three albums, *Warum geht es mir so dreckig?* [Why Do I Feel So Awful?] (1971), *Keine Macht für Niemand* [No Power for No-One] (1972) and *Wenn die Nacht am tiefsten...* [When the Night is at Its Darkest...] (1975), function as historical documents of the Kreuzberg anarchist underground scene in the volatile period of the early 1970s.

What is distinct about Ton Steine Scherben's work is the clear unifying narrative of the songs: on their seminal album *Keine Macht für Niemand*, which forms the focus of this study, lead singer Rio Reiser is the squatter anarchist. Each song tells a different story of life in their community: street battles with police; occupying houses; dodging fares on the Berlin public transport system; the communal squat as a haven from the boredom of apprenticeships; the quest for freedom from the constraints of the post-war Economic Miracle; the longing for utopian alternatives to capitalist reality.

The narrative is enhanced by the real-life dialect and mannerisms of Reiser in his vocal delivery, reflecting an attitude which verges on delinquency. Here we see an element of ambiguity in the role-play of Reiser stemming from the masked figures of Hoffmann's Comic Teater: on the one hand, he is a performer enacting various roles ranging from violent anarchist and teenage delinquent, to political philosopher or sensitive lover. At the same time, he is playing his authentic self: the stories, such as the occupation of a former hospital in 1971, are based on radical actions in which the group directly participated. The listener is caught up in this musical enactment of the hopes, aspirations and conflicts of the young Kreuzberg anarchists, apprentices and workers.

The musical soundtrack aids this portrayal: the Woodstock-style blues rock reminiscent of Joe Cocker or Jimi Hendrix, a style which at that time was laden with the symbolism of rebellion, is uniquely combined with the countercultural tradition of Berlin agitprop. This approach can be heard in the chanting and political sloganeering, which lend an air of proto-punk to the proceedings, and in the stage backdrops with political slogans such as Georg Büchner's infamous demand 'Peace to the shacks, war on the palaces'.[26] This proletarian theatrical influence, which would be highly unusual in a British or American rock context, stems very much from a post-Russian Revolution European tradition.

In the radical milieu of late 1960s West Berlin it was a feature of the alternative scene, where art was perceived as a tool or 'weapon'[27] in the class struggle

---

25 Brown, 'Music as a Weapon?', p. 10. See also Albrecht Koch, *Angriff aufs Schlaraffenland – 20 Jahre deutschsprachige Popmusik* (Frankfurt: Ullstein, 1987), p. 53.

26 For example, see Sichtermann et al, *Keine Macht für niemand*, p. 64.

27 See manifesto 'Musik ist eine Waffe' published in *Agit 883*, 24 December 1970. Quoted in Brown, 'Music as a Weapon', p. 16.

and the active participation of the audience (in a Brechtian breaking down of 'the fourth wall') was a precondition. Ton Steine Scherben consciously referenced this political artistic heritage in their rock version of Brecht and Eisler's 'Einheitsfrontlied [Song of the United Front] at the end of their first single 'Macht kaputt, was euch kaputt macht' [Destroy Everything That Destroys You] in 1971. A further element reminiscent of Brecht's Epic Theatre was the inclusion in their performances of spoken political texts and parables between songs.

This proletarian agitprop heritage should simultaneously in no way diminish Ton Steine Scherben's credentials as an authentic blues rock band and Reiser as one of the great German rock vocalists. There is also an air of experimentalism: distorted guitars – a hallmark of early 1970s progressive rock – are used to augment the soundscape of chaos. Sound effects such as sirens and gunshots (as in 'Menschenjäger' [Head Hunters]) denote street battles between urban guerrillas and police.

A dystopian darkness emanates from the sound, not atypical of West Berlin rock groups of the 1970s and 1980s. This is juxtaposed, however, with the utopianism of lyrics such as 'Schritt für Schritt ins Paradies' [Step By Step Into Paradise] or the joyful exuberance and Berlin humour of the life-affirming 'Mensch Meier' [Joe Bloggs] or 'Rauch Haus Lied' [Rauch House Song]. It was the latter aspect of fun which, as we will see, was to be rejected by the ideologues in the anarchist scene who wanted to use the group for their own political gains.

Ton Steine Scherben are acknowledged to be one of the first ever German rock bands to sing in German. Their motivation to do so overlapped with that of the *Liedermacher* in their need to be understood by an audience.[28] Here there was a strong didactic element, again stemming from the agitprop culture of the Weimar Republic. Indeed, one of the tenets of the proletarian song theory of Hanns Eisler was that lyrics and message had to be clear.[29] The element of political instruction is evident in the songs, which often share acquired knowledge about class exploitation with their targeted audience.

In 'Die letzte Schlacht gewinnen wir' [We'll Win the Final Battle] from *Keine Macht für niemand* [No Power For No-One] (1972) – again proto-punk in style with its staccato yet melodic guitar riff – Reiser shouts: 'Wir brauchen keinen starken Mann, denn wir sind selber stark genug / Wir wissen selber, was zu tun ist, unser Kopf ist groß genug' [We don't need a strong man, because we are strong enough / We know ourselves what we have to do, our heads are big

---

28 Siedel, 'Berlin und die Linke', p. 28.
29 See Hanns Eisler, 'Unsere Kampfmusik', in *Musik und Politik: Schriften 1924–1948* (Leipzig: VEB Deutscher Verlag für Musik, 1973), pp. 169–170. See also Robb, 'Mühsam, Brecht, Eisler', pp. 54–57.

enough]. A good example of an agitprop text set to popular music, the song is practically an anarchist manifesto with its list of demands:

> Wir brauchen keine Hausbesitzer,
> denn die Häuser gehören uns
> Wir brauchen keine Fabrikbesitzer,
> die Fabriken gehören uns
> Aus dem Weg, Kapitalisten,
> die letzte Schlacht gewinnen wir
> Schmeißt die Knarre weg, Polizisten,
> die rote Front und die schwarze Front
> sind hier

> [We don't need house owners
> because the houses belong to us
> We don't need factory owners,
> because the factories belong to us [...]
> Throw your guns away, police,
> the Red Front and the Black Front
> are here][30]

In 'Schritt für Schritt ins Paradis' the image of waking (a traditional symbol in revolutionary song for enlightenment) is juxtaposed with sleeping; knowledge with fear:

> Ich hab lang gewartet und nachgedacht,
> hatte viele Träume und jetzt bin ich wach
> Wenn wir suchen, finden wir das neue Land
> Uns trennt nichts vom Paradies außer unserer Angst

> [I've waited long and thought about it,
> had many dreams and now I'm awake
> If we search, we'll find the new land
> All that separates us from paradise is our fear]

Interestingly, the opening verse of this song echoes Degenhardt's theme of 'Für wen ich singe'. But unlike the latter's exclusivity, mostly listing the social groupings he is not singing for, Ton Steine Scherben's call in 'Schritt für Schritt ins Paradis' is inclusive, reaching out to all who may yet need to be convinced of the cause:

> Du hörst mich singen, aber du kennst mich nicht
> Du weißt nicht, für wen ich singe, aber ich sing für dich

---

30 The Red Front is a reference to communists, the Black Front to the anarchists.

Wer wird die neue Welt bauen, wenn nicht du und ich?
Und wenn du mich jetzt verstehen willst, dann verstehst du mich

[You hear me singing, but you don't know me
You don't know who I'm singing for, but I'm singing for you
Who will build the new world, if not you and I?
And if you want to understand me then you will understand me]

The illustration of unequal power relationships in society, encouraging the need for 'self-liberation through action'[31] is another striking characteristic of Ton Steine Scherben. Here the texts demonstrate in song similar conflicts to those which Hoffmann's Comic Teater and Rote Steine acted out in their agitprop scenes. In the songs, the demand for freedom is frequently juxtaposed with the social restrictions that prevent this. Freedom is embodied by the political struggle on the streets, the communal life of the squats and the wilful violation of rules and regulations. The latter are represented by the work-place, the family home, institutions and figures of authority such as politicians, factory bosses and parents.

'Wir müssen hier raus' [We Have to Get Out of Here] describes the prison-like existence of daily work and the stifling life at home with parents. The father, who drinks in the pub to forget, represents the cynical viewpoint that the world will not change, while the youth maintains that his generation can break out of these shackles. Like the dialogue of Degenhardt's 'Vatis Argumente', the song express- es the generational conflict between father and son. But this is no intellectual satire, rather an anguished cry of desperation mixed with utopian anticipation:

Wir müssen hier raus!
Das ist die Hölle!
Wir leben im Zuchthaus!
Wir sind geboren, um frei zu sein,
wir sind sechzig Millionen,
wir sind nicht allein.
Und wir werden es schaffen,
wir werden es schaffen

[We have to get out of here!
This is pure hell!
We live in a prison!
We are born to be free,
we are sixty million people.
We aren't alone.

---

31 See Brown, 'Music as a Weapon', p. 1.

And we'll do it,
we'll do it]

With its lyrical concentration on a unifying theme and theatrical elements, the *Keine Macht für Niemand* album bears resemblances at times to the concept album, popular in the late 1960s and early 1970s, such as The Who's *Tommy* or *Quadrophenia*. There are even parallels with the elements of fantasy which creep into the stories, which appear at times to be the wishful thinking of a would-be urban terrorist. The song 'Feierabend' [Closing Time], for example, celebrates the laying down of tools at the end of the working day as a possibility to let off steam: 'Es ist Zahltag und die Arbeit ist vorbei' [It's payday and the work is over]. But in an ironic twist, playing on the ambiguity of the word 'Lohn', which means 'just deserts' as well as 'wage', it will also be 'payback' time for the boss when the narrator goes to his home and drives off in his Mercedes.

The song 'Mensch Meier'[32] depicts another real life situation, this time about dodging tram fares, but again embellished with theatrical fantasy. On his way to work the singer refuses to buy a ticket, saying he is saving up to keep pace with tax increases. The Berlin Transport Authority (BVG) should rather claw its debts back from the factory bosses 'die uns beklauen' [who steal from us]. When the conductor threatens to call the police, the workers on the bus show solidarity with the singer, threatening to throw the conductor off instead. The group chant the chorus in Berlin dialect in the style of a football crowd:

Nee, nee, nee, eher brennt die BVG!
Ich bin hier oben noch ganz dicht,
der Spaß ist zu teuer, von mir kriegste nüscht!

[No, no, no, we'd sooner burn down the BVG!
There's nothing missing between my ears,
this lark is too dear, you'll get nothing from me!]

The 'Rauch Haus Song', one of the group's most famous tracks, relates to an historical event in which Ton Steine Scherben were among the main protagonists. On 8 December 1971 in the Old Mensa of the Technical University (TU) in West Berlin, the group had performed a teach-in in memory of Georg von Rauch, a member of the anarchist group Bewegung 2. Juni, who had been killed by police in a shoot-out four days earlier. After the concert, the group, together with members of the audience, occupied the former nurse's home of the disused Bethanien

---

32 This is a pun on the expression of surprise 'Mensch Meier' [jeepers creepers].

hospital in Kreuzberg's Mariannen Square and re-named it the Georg-von-Rauch-Haus in honour of the dead comrade of aristocratic descent.[33]

Strategically placed towards the end of the album, the song consolidates the sense of youthful fun in putting one over on authority. The reappearance of the character 'Mensch Meier', furthermore, adds to the conceptual unity of the album. The song recreates the euphoria of the squatters who ultimately win their stand-off with the police. It is set to a bright, life-affirming, sing-along pop-rock melody featuring a recurring riff played by piano and bass. The festive atmosphere of the piece prevails despite the references to tear gas and truncheons – it is a celebration of the everyday life of the Kreuzberg anarchist:

> Der Mariannenplatz war blau,
> soviel Bullen waren da,
> und Mensch Meier mußte heulen,
> das war wohl das Tränengas
> Und er fragt irgendeinen:
> 'Sag mal, ist hier heut 'n Fest?'
> 'Sowas ähnliches', sacht einer
> 'das Bethanien wird besetzt'

> [The Mariannen Square was all blue[34]
> so many cops were there,
> the man Meier was crying
> from all the tear gas
> And he asked someone:
> 'Hey, is there a festival on today?'
> 'Something like that', said someone'
> 'The Bethanien [hospital] is being occupied']

In the chorus the squatters respond to the police attempts to clear the square, chanting:

> Doch die Leute im besetzen Haus
> riefen: 'Ihr kriegt uns hier nicht raus!
> Das ist unser Haus,
> schmeißt doch endlich Schmidt und Press und Mosch[35]
> aus Kreuzberg raus'

---

33 See Sichtermann et al, *Keine Macht*, pp. 90–94. Also Rio Reiser, *König von Deutschland: Erinnerungen an Ton Steine Scherben und mehr* (Berlin: Möbius Rekords, 2001), p. 239.
34 Berlin policemen wore blue uniforms at that time.
35 The named persons here were builders and speculators associated with the planned new centre of Kreuzberg. This was part of an urban renewal project in West Berlin geared towards

[But the people in the occupied house
shouted: 'You won't get us out of here!
This is our house,
kick rather Schmidt and Press and Mosch
out of Kreuzberg']

It is arguably this sense of fun in Ton Steine Scherben's songs which led to conflicts with the anarchist political leaders in their local West Berlin milieu. It is well documented how the group felt increasingly alienated from the seriousness – the theory, dogmas and calculation – of the left-wing militants who wanted to use the group for their own purposes. This interference even went as far as censorship: according to Reiser the 'Rauch Haus Song' was rejected by the political committee governing the squat itself as having 'nichts mit der Realität zu tun' [nothing to do with reality]. It even forbade the group to play the song at the teach-in at the Audimax of the TU in March 1972, for which occasion the song was originally written.

The group had also encountered scepticism with their song 'Keine Macht für Niemand'. It had been commissioned by Reiser's friend Anne Reiche, a member of the militant anarchist group Blues. The RAF, however, allegedly dismissed the song, which originally had the working title 'Hymne für den bewaffneten Kampf' [Anthem for Armed Struggle], as 'Blödsinn, irrelevant und für den antiimperialistischen Kampf unbrauchbar' [stupid, irrelevant and unusable in the anti-imperialist struggle].[36] Another example of diverging goals was the teach-in at the TU in April 1974 when the group performed in front of colourful backdrops of trees and flowers and sprinkled glitter over the audience. The anarchist leaders were allegedly horrified, unable to see how such an accessory of the currently fashionable glam rock could have a role in the class struggle.[37]

One can postulate that in the narrative role-play of a song and the theatrical element of a show – where performance is not reality, but in Brechtian terms can be used to demonstrate aspects of reality – there was already great potential for misunderstandings with ideologues, who only sought an unambiguous message.[38] The freedom which Ton Steine Scherben desired for their artistic and professional development was ultimately inhibited. The group gradually became

---

the demolition of old buildings which was heavily contested by the alternative youth in Kreuzberg. See also Brown, 'Music as a Weapon', p. 10.

36 Sichtermann et al, *Keine Macht*, pp. 112–113.

37 Ibid, pp. 161–163.

38 Such ambiguous role-play is, according to Simon Frith, also an aspect of rock singers in the creation of their narratives. See Frith, *Performing Rites: Evaluating Popular Music* (Oxford and New York: Oxford University Press, 1998), p. 171.

weary of their position as 'Hochkapelle' [favoured band] of the leftist scene[39], having their lyrics and performances constantly scrutinized and being expected to play political benefit concerts for nothing whenever asked. Such pressures were to contribute to the group's decision in 1975 to leave Berlin for the countryside in Fresenhagen in North Germany, thus ending the first and historically most significant phase in the life of the group.

Conclusion

Taking case studies of Franz Josef Degenhardt and Ton Steine Scherben, this chapter has demonstrated the direct role that politics was able to play across the spectrum of the resurgence of the protest song in the late 1960s and the early 1970s in West Germany. In the aftermath of the APO and the student movement, it was a highpoint of grassroots political activism where music was promoted for the mobilization of political consciousness. While this relationship inspired the artistic creativity of Degenhardt's satirical role-play songs and Ton Steine Scherben's hybrid agitrock, it also led to an impasse when music suffered under the demands of political ideology and dogmas.

Political song remained a highly relevant and visible category in West Germany and the GDR[40] throughout the 1970s and 1980s with artists such as Degenhardt (†2011), Mossmann (†2015), Süverkrüp, Wader, Bettina Wegner, Konstantin Wecker, Wolf Biermann etc., but the genre has waned in importance particularly since the fall of communism and the end of the ideological debate of the Cold War. The lack of a unifying political movement to which musicians can affiliate has undoubtedly been a contributory factor to this.

The *Liedermacher* brand has continued, however, as a significant niche within the singer/songwriter, folk and world music festival environments, with artists such as Hans-Eckardt Wenzel, Heinz Ratz, Dota Kehr and many others. The annual Festival Musik und Politik [Festival of Music and Politics] has functioned as a meeting point for *Liedermacher* every spring since 2001 in Berlin.

Ton Steine Scherben finally broke up in 1985, after which Rio Reiser embarked on a solo career achieving his most notable success in 1986 with the single 'König von Deutschland' [King of Germany]. Since Reiser's premature death in 1996, the political and musical legacy of Ton Steine Scherben has been enthu-

---

39 Sichtermann et al, *Keine Macht*, p. 162.
40 *Liedermacher* also had a high presence in the GDR but form a separate story. See Robb, 'Political Song in the GDR: The Cat-and-Mouse Game with Censorship and Institutions', in *Protest Song in East and West Germany*, pp. 227–254.

siastically promoted in books, films and tribute concerts, a testament to the degree of nostalgia felt towards a bygone era when musical protest played an active role in street and urban politics.

John Littlejohn

Krautrock – The Development of a Movement

Since Krautrock began in 1960s West Germany, its impact has permeated innovative music all around the world. One hears the purest and most striking impact of Krautrock in the works of post-punk and new wave bands like The Fall, Public Image Ltd., and Talking Heads,[1] and even today, one can still hear recent music which conspicuously bears the influence of Krautrock. The Berlin-based Camera, for instance, can sound hauntingly like Neu! did in its prime. If, however, the reverberations of Can, Neu! and other Krautrock artists have generally become less pronounced, it is because their works have so thoroughly integrated themselves into both mainstream and experimental music. Yet Krautrock survives as more than a mere precursor to later music. True, Krautrock often serves as a sonic template for younger musicians and arms them with novel ways of creating their art, but a great deal of the music stands the test of time. *Neu!*, *Musik von Harmonia* [Music by Harmonia] and Can's *Monster Movie* still captivate listeners decades after their first release. In the words of Simon Reynolds, 'Krautrock is simply fabulous music'.[2]

The word 'Krautrock', however, presents some problems. The term – almost undoubtedly of English origin – was reportedly coined by DJ John Peel,[3] yet that remains uncertain to this day. As David Stubbs notes, this word 'retains the condescension of the British music press, who found the very fact that these groups were German inherently amusing'.[4] Furthermore, one cannot overlook the anti-German slur contained in the word, a lasting sign of its English origin. Perhaps unsurprisingly, several musicians indeed preferred the name 'kosmische Musik'

1 Jim DeRogatis, *Kaleidoscope Eyes: Psychedelic Rock from the '60s to the '90s* (Secaucus, NJ: Carol, 1996), p. 126; John T. Littlejohn, 'Introduction', *Popular Music and Society*, 32/5 (2009), 577–578 (p. 578).
2 Simon Reynolds, 'Kosmik Dance: Krautrock and its Legacy', in *Modulations: A History of Electronic Music: Throbbing Words on Sound*, ed. by Peter Shapiro (New York: Caipirinha, 2000), pp. 24–37 (p. 34).
3 Ulrich Adelt, 'Machines with a Heart: German Identity in the Music of Can and Kraftwerk', *Popular Music and Society*, 35/3 (2012), 359–374 (p. 361).
4 David Stubbs, 'Introduction', *Krautrock: Cosmic Rock and its Legacy*, ed. by Nikolaos Kotsopoulos (London: Black Dog, 2009), pp. 4–18 (p. 4).

DOI 10.1515/9783110425727-004

[cosmic music] in the early 1970s, but many of the artists have accepted the 'Krautrock' label over time.[5]

Even after overcoming the verbal baggage of the term, many enthusiasts argue about the definition of Krautrock. What exactly is Krautrock? What groups and music do we include with or exclude from this term? Which subcategories distinguish themselves? Many musicians did not consider themselves part of a movement, which intensifies the problem of defining it. Michael Rother, for instance, states:

> Even though I respected Kraftwerk and Can, I wanted my music to be different from what they did. [...] Any box or label that is attached to our music tries to neglect the fact that we weren't a 'family' of German musicians, we had no common goals or identity.[6]

When one considers the great variety in music uncontroversially regarded as Krautrock masterpieces – Can's *Ege Bamyasi*, Klaus Schulze's *Irrlicht* [Ghost Light] and Cluster's *Zuckerzeit* [Sugar Time], for instance, sound nothing alike – an attempt at a working definition of Krautrock appears unavoidable.

Scholars and critics vary on the level of inclusiveness the term Krautrock may have. Ulrich Adelt calls it:

> an all-encompassing name for the music of various German performers from roughly 1968 to 1974, ranging from the electronic music of Klaus Schulze and the jazz rock of Kraan to the political songs of Floh de Cologne, the folk rock of Witthäuser & Westrupp and music that is even harder to classify but had a long-lasting impact, like that of Faust, Cluster, or Popol Vuh.[7]

Ulrich D. Einbrodt's definition proves more restrictive:

> Krautrock is the music, which has not much or nothing to do with usual rock & roll. For instance, the successful German band The Scorpions played a kind of international hard rock in the seventies, so the term cannot be applied for their music. Therefore, the term does not cover the total range of German popular music from the seventies, it indeed indicates a very special style, often meditative, spherical, or somehow crazy.[8]

---

5 DeRogatis, *Kaleidoscope Eyes*, p. 125.

6 Mark Pilkington, 'Harmonia', in Kotsopoulos, pp. 100–103 (p. 103).

7 Adelt, 'Machines', pp. 360–361.

8 Ulrich D. Einbrodt, 'Space, Mysticism, Romantic Music, Sequencing, and the Widening of Form in German Krautrock during the 70s', in *Giessener Elektronische Bibliothek* (http://geb.uni-giessen.de/geb/volltexte/2001/592/pdf/p010004.pdf), p. 1.

Einbrodt also claims that this music has its roots in the California psychedelic rock of the Grateful Dead and similar groups,[9] which downplays the influence of British psychedelic rock bands such as Pink Floyd, as well as the tremendous importance of the Velvet Underground or Karlheinz Stockhausen. Melanie Schiller provides convincing insights into the music, while noting the difficulty of defining the term:

> Even though it might be problematic to try to summarize the essential features of the genre, it can be said that, [...] in musical terms the Krautrock bands experimented with sounds, instrumentation, musical structures, and compositions. Their songs could be 10, 20 minutes long, and many musicians would explore the margins of music, sound, and literal noise.[10]

Geographically, Krautrock began as and remained a solely West German phenomenon. Krautrock was decentralized, with key bands coming from all over the country,[11] from Munich in the south to Hamburg in the north. The music therefore developed as a nationwide sensation rather than a local one. However, Krautrock did not expand into East Germany due to its cultural isolation and the official ban on popular culture from the West enforced by the regime in the GDR.

The key element of Krautrock is experimentation. Whether the artists were taking consciousness-expanding drugs, taping hours of jams and editing the material down, or crafting compositions under the influence of Stockhausen and Fluxus artists (or any combination of the three), they strove for something new and different. The artists belonging to this movement tried to expand their sounds in many different ways. Some artists attempted to play instruments they had not mastered well, some used instruments not usually associated with rock music, and some played standard rock instruments but in non-standard relationships to one another. Still other musicians 'played' non-instruments (such as drills or pinball machines)[12] or invented their own. As Schiller mentions above, Krautrock groups often tested musical boundaries and explored different manners of composition,[13] which often led to tracks which explode the typical rock-song format and length.

Furthermore, as this author has noted in an earlier article, a very high percentage of Krautrock consists of instrumental music, much more so than was

---

9 Ibid.

10 Melanie Schiller, 'Fun Fun Fun on the Autobahn': Kraftwerk Challenging Germanness', *Popular Music and Society*, 37/5 (2014), 618–637 (p. 634).

11 Adelt, 'Machines', p. 363.

12 Julian Cope, *Krautrocksampler*, 2nd edn (Great Britain: Head Heritage, 1996), pp. 25–26.

13 Schiller, 'Fun Fun Fun', p. 634.

typical of other popular music of the era.[14] Krautrock music often eschews lyrics, and, in many songs which do have a text, those lyrics make no logical sense. True, Krautrock has some great and original vocalists and some fine texts, yet the focus more typically remains on the ensemble of the band. Just as Krautrock musicians attempted to use their instruments in different ways, some Krautrock vocalists used their voices like musical instruments, providing percussive or textual effects to the music in addition to – or instead of – conveying a meaning through words.

Due to its experimental nature, the formal aspects of Krautrock accordingly prove difficult to pin down. At times, the artists expand the music to its limits and tracks become quite lengthy, but at other times, they construct tight, short songs. Some tracks exhibit a droning or harmonic uniformity similar to the best of James Brown's œuvre, yet some tracks maintain a state of flux, always changing and rarely repeating. The enormously influential 'Motorik' drumbeat became widely identified with Krautrock – Brian Eno stated that 'There were three great beats in the '70s: Fela Kuti's Afrobeat, James Brown's Funk and Klaus Dinger's Neu! beat'[15] – while many Krautrock classics do without drums altogether. Much of the music is instrumental, yet many tracks feature prominent vocals. The vocalists themselves may sing lyrics, or simply use their voice as another instrument. In songs with lyrics, the text may be extensive or consist of a mere handful of words. Singers may sing in their native German, in English, or any number of other languages.[16] Few if any lyrical themes prove consistent throughout the Krautrock canon.

Therefore, the following working definition is proposed: Krautrock is a rock-based experimental music which emerged in late 1960s West Germany. Many bands formed between 1968 and 1971, and the music saw its full flowering in the early 1970s. By mid-decade, however, the genre declined as the primary bands broke up or set off in vastly different musical directions. Few masterpieces appeared after 1975.

While the author recognizes the incompleteness and fallibility of this definition, it should prove to help readers zero in on the wide variety of music commonly referred to as Krautrock without sending them astray. Even though the Stones-influenced Ton Steine Scherben, East Germany's Puhdys and singer-song-

---

14 John T. Littlejohn, 'Kraftwerk: Language, Lucre, and Loss of Identity', *Popular Music and Society*, 32/5 (2009), 635–653 (pp. 636–637).

15 Ben Sisario, 'Klaus Dinger, 61, Drummer of Influential German Beat', *New York Times*, 4 April 2008, p. 6.

16 'Kanaan', the opening track of Amon Düül's first album *Phallus Dei* contains a version of the Lord's Prayer in Greek. The album's title is, of course, Latin.

writer Udo Lindenberg and his Panik-Orchester each produced excellent pop-rock music in the early 1970s, few would consider them Krautrock bands. The above characterization of the Krautrock bands and their music will hopefully prevent confusion for new listeners.

If one accepts that the one musical aspect key to all Krautrock music is experimentation, one must look at the reason behind that experimentation. The musical touchstones commonly referred to as influences – Stockhausen, the Velvet Underground, American psychedelic rock – all explored musical boundaries, and that may be a reason these bands look back to them for inspiration. Clearly, the social conditions of the late 1960s and early 1970s affected the West German musicians just as forcefully as they did those in New York and San Francisco. The major cultural shift which kindled the youth movement and resulted in a generation gap throughout large parts of the Western world at that time did not bypass West Germany, however, an additional aspect was at play there.

During the 1960s and 1970s, 'a generation of young people was searching for an identity amid the cold war tensions, the lingering consciousness of Nazism and World War II and the same experimentations with alternative lifestyles, sex and psychedelic drugs that was happening in the West'.[17] Those who came of age during this time had been born in the years following World War II, the time of the Economic Miracle which saw West Germany rise from the rubble of war to become one of the world's great economic powers. During this time of rebuilding and growth, the adult generation swept aside the events of the past, and National Socialism and the Holocaust were forbidden topics. As Schiller notes, 'The post-war period is often described in terms of a lost identity',[18] in which Germans tacitly rejected many aspects of their Germanness and their German cultural history because of the events of the 1930s and 1940s. By the late 1960s, the younger generation began to confront their parents about the events of the War and the roles they played in it, leading Germany to attempt a *Vergangenheitsbewältigung*, a coming to terms with the past. Only then could they create a new German identity.

Yet the older generation was not the only social adversary they had to overcome. Many youths also shunned the culture of Britain and, in particular, of America – two of the former Allied Powers which had divided Germany after the War and still maintained a prominent military presence in West Germany. Nascent Krautrock bands – as a part of this younger generation – therefore distanced themselves from rock music, perceiving it as a continuation of cultural

---

17 DeRogatis, *Kaleidoscope Eyes*, pp. 124–125.
18 Schiller, 'Fun Fun Fun', p. 619.

imperialism. Rock 'n' roll music had its roots in America, but quickly became an international phenomenon, as had British beat music. In the 1950s and 1960s, West Germany had its own cadre of rockers, imitating American and British sounds and songs, but only infrequently adding anything to the originals except enthusiasm. In an attempt to free themselves from the negative colonial and parental forces, Krautrock musicians, many of whom had played in rock cover bands in the early 1960s, tried to create a new music, a music imprinted with neither Anglo-American rock music nor the popular German music of the day. Inasmuch as these groups were attempting to escape both the popular culture in Germany – which was controlled by the older generation – and the international youth culture – which was dominated by the US and the UK – this generation of musicians had little choice but to find their own art through experimentation.

This period is 'characterized by attempts to reconstruct a lost German cultural and national identity in delimitation from its international counterparts and in negotiation with its own past'.[19] Therefore, the fact that several of the most prominent Krautrock bands included members from other countries and/or worked with musicians from outside Germany is a curious circumstance to which scholars and critics have paid little attention. Faust's line-up included Frenchman Jean-Hérve Péron, and the band also released the album *Outside the Dream Syndicate* with American Tony Conrad. Englishman Dave Anderson played bass on Amon Düül II's first two albums before joining Hawkwind. American Malcolm Mooney gave Can their name, and was the group's first vocalist, succeeded by Damo Suzuki, a native of Japan. Ash Ra Tempel recorded *Seven Up* with Timothy Leary, while Cluster recorded an album with Brian Eno.

One can, however, see that the presence of a foreign member in the band could change the perspectives of all involved. Péron would later state 'We're German, we're not afraid of it, we're not ashamed of it'.[20] Contrast that statement with Kraftwerk founding member Ralf Hütter's comment during the band's first flush of major success in 1975:

> We are the first group to record in our own language, use our electronic background, and create a Central European identity for ourselves. So you see another group like Tangerine Dream, although they are German they have an English name, so they create onstage an Anglo-American identity, which we completely deny. We want the whole world to know our background. We cannot deny we are from Germany.[21]

---

19 Ibid.
20 DeRogatis, *Kaleidoscope Eyes*, p. 129.
21 Lester Bangs, *Psychotic Reactions and Carburetor Dung* (New York: Knopf, 1987), p. 158.

True, these two quotes stem from interviews almost two decades apart, yet one notices clearly how the French Péron positively seizes Germanness, something Hütter cannot quite manage. Kraftwerk had an exclusively German line-up, they did indeed take a German name, and this interview came about as a result of the success of their hit record 'Autobahn' which simulated a trip on the German motorway. Yet, despite the wholly German line-up of his band, and although he is clearly attempting to do so, Hütter was unable to take on the mantle of German identity. He and several other Krautrockers refused to claim an Anglo-American identity which was not theirs, but, although he could not deny the Germanness for which he was then known, he did not identify himself as German and rather claimed to be fashioning a Central European identity. A 2005 interview reveals the thoughts of an older Hütter:

> 'Being born in Germany', Hütter shrugs, is simply a 'biological fact'. But he stresses that growing up in Düsseldorf, a cosmopolitan city close to the border with the Netherlands and Belgium, made him far more European than German. 'Berlin is farther away than Paris. You might even say we are from the British sector'.[22]

Hütter's continued conflicted opinion on his own Germanness three decades after the first interview is telling. He still refuses to fully accept a German identity, and, in the intervening years, has even moved towards the Anglo-American identity he had previously denied. The issue of German identity, which was so important to the development of Krautrock, as indeed it was to the youth of West German in the 1960s and 1970s in general, is a fascinating one, especially in light of such major socio-political events as the end of the Cold War and the reunification of Germany in 1990.

As noted earlier, Krautrock did not emerge from one particular region of West Germany. This does not, however, mean that these artists always worked in isolation. Rother's statement above that '[a]ny box or label that is attached to our music tries to neglect the fact that we weren't a "family" of German musicians, we had no common goals or identity',[23] tells an important part, but only one part, of the story. While the idea that all Krautrock bands shared a single prevalent artistic or political agenda is an obvious oversimplification, it would be equally misleading to argue that these bands had no common ground and that they did not influence each other.

---

22 Stephen Dalton, 'That was then, This is now', *The Times (London)*, 3 June 2005 (http://www.thetimes.co.uk/tto/arts/music/article2416696.ece). Hütter's home region of North Rhine-Westphalia was part of the British occupied territory after World War II.
23 Pilkington, 'Harmonia', p. 103.

In addition to the influence Krautrock artists had on each other, fluctuations in band line-ups played a large part in the development of Krautrock. As in rock music around the world, band membership could be fluid, and some artists followed their muse from one project to the next. When musicians left one group – or groups simply broke up – experiences gained on one project were naturally transferred to the next. Some artists used similar compositional and recording techniques in different bands, while others attempted to break free of an earlier band's methods and seek new paths. Continual shifts in band membership for many Krautrock bands therefore help explain the great variety of Krautrock and the number of distinctive strains within this genre.

The following section should therefore act not only as a brief introduction to some of the best-known Krautrock artists, but also outline the development of the music by following various nexus of artists when applicable. Unfortunately, this section can neither cover these artists in the depth they deserve nor mention all the artists which merit inclusion.

Amon Düül

Amon Düül I and Amon Düül II routinely appear early in histories of Krautrock music, not only because their names begin with the first letter of the alphabet, but also because these two groups were among the earliest and best-known Krautrock bands. Both of them stem from the same Munich commune, starting out together in 1967 as one large communal band before the more proficient musicians and composers split off to form Amon Düül II the following year.

Amon Düül I stayed together until 1971, releasing four albums during that period, although three of these albums supposedly date from a single 1968 jam session.[24] The fourth album, 1970's *Paradieswärts Düül* [Towards Paradise Düül] proves much more satisfying. Largely casting off the band's typically percussion-heavy sound, this album has the pastoral feel and musical vibe of a communal get together, and yet the loose, borderline lazy sound stops short of being shambolic. The peace-and-love lyrics are definitely of their time, but they remain charming throughout and fit with the music. *Paradieswärts Düül* is not a great Krautrock record. However, it is a snapshot of its time and holds up as a fine early album from this movement.

Unlike Amon Düül I, much of Amon Düül II's early work transcends the era whence it came. From the very first recordings, one can hear why the best mu-

---

24 David Stubbs, 'Amon Düül', in Kotsopoulos, pp. 54–55 (p. 54).

sicians broke away from the original group. 'Phallus Dei', the side-long title track of the band's 1969 first album, was atmospheric, sometimes scary and already miles ahead of anything on *Paradieswärts Düül*, which would not be released until the following year. Amon Düül II simply had a different vocabulary at their disposal. Another classic appeared the following year, the double LP *Yeti*. Not only did *Yeti* contain even stronger playing and more complex writing than its predecessor, it also bore on its sleeve one of the most iconic images in all of Krautrock: a picture of drummer Wolfgang Krischke holding a scythe, posed like the Grim Reaper.[25] Thereupon followed another double album, the experimental *Tanz der Lemminge* [Dance of the Lemmings] (1971) with its broad palette of styles and textures. The year 1972 saw the release of both the fine and somewhat underrated *Carnival in Babylon* and the muscular *Wolf City*, but after these two albums, the band's musical output grew increasingly uneven. The band broke up in 1981, but would later re-form for performances and occasional recordings.

Tangerine Dream

While, as Stubbs notes, the original Amon Düül has been called 'Krautrock's most hated band',[26] Tangerine Dream may well be Krautrock's most derided band. The group, long centred around founder Edgar Froese, has made music which ranges from the rapturous to the frankly tedious. In the words of Jim DeRogatis: 'Tangerine Dream progressed from imitating Pink Floyd to delivering snooze-inducing synthesized instrumentals'.[27] In addition, the band's massive output (well over 100 recordings overall) and remakes of earlier triumphs such as *Phaedra 2005* or *Tangram 2008* may not have ingratiated it with critics.

Tangerine Dream's best known and most innovative music comes from its first decade. The band started out as a recording unit with the 1970 album *Electronic Meditation*, featuring Klaus Schulze and Conrad Schnitzler alongside Froese. Like the overwhelming majority of Tangerine Dream's work, *Electronic Meditation* is an instrumental album – the only vocal here being the spoken section, recorded backwards, at the beginning of 'Resurrection'. Cacophonous and beautiful, the album's five tracks interweave instruments masterfully, starting with the sounds of Schnitzler's strings before moving to the organ or Froese's guitar,

---

25 Julian Cope also used this image for the cover of his *Krautrocksampler*.
26 Stubbs, 'Amon', p. 54.
27 DeRogatis, *Kaleidoscope Eyes*, p. 127.

while Schulze enters and exits the fray, seemingly at whim. While one doubts this trio of restless and prolific artists could have stayed together for an extended period, one wishes this version of Tangerine Dream could have existed longer than a mere few months before Schulze and Schnitzler departed. Froese soon found a fine foil in Christoph Franke, however, and with additional keyboardist Peter Baumann soon in tow, the group developed its sound across a series of releases in the first half of the 1970s. *Alpha Centauri* (1971), the double-album *Zeit* [Time] (1972), and *Atem* [Breath] (1973) are largely of a piece, with the band creating novel textures from its atmospheric and increasingly synthesizer-focused music. 1974's *Phaedra*, which ranks alongside *Electronic Meditation* as the best of their work, represents a consolidation of the band's earlier works and its commercial breakthrough: *Phaedra* and the following year's *Rubycon* both reached the Top 20 of the UK album charts. Unfortunately, the band would thereafter never quite have the same commercial success, nor attain the same artistic level or relevance, although they would chalk up five consecutive Grammy nominations for Best New Age Album in the 1990s.

While it would be foolhardy to label a band with such an extensive catalogue unindustrious, a sense of complacency soon crept into Tangerine Dream's work, as indicated by the four live albums released between 1975 and 1982. During the 1980s and 1990s, they worked steadily on music for movies, the best known of which is probably *Risky Business*. More recently, the band recorded the soundtrack for *Grand Theft Auto V*, one of the best-selling video games of all time.

While Edgar Froese remained with Tangerine Dream for the rest of his life, the other two musicians who created the LP *Electronic Meditation* soon set out for new musical horizons. Conrad Schnitzler would amass a prodigious catalogue in the following decades.[28] Yet music fans might well remember the band he helped found, Kluster (later Cluster), more than they remember Schnitzler himself. Two Kluster studio albums, *Klopfzeichen* [Tap Code] and *Zwei-Osterei* [Two-Easter Egg], and the live album *Eruption*, had limited releases in 1970 and 1971, after which time Schnitzler left the band.[29] While these records are not essential, they are well worth hearing for those who enjoy *Electronic Meditation* or The Cosmic Jokers.

---

28 Schnitzler released the track 'Krautrock' on his solo album *Rot* [Red] in 1973, the same year Faust more famously released a track by that name as the opener of *Faust IV*.

29 Henning Dedekind, *Krautrock: Underground, LSD und Kosmische Kuriere* (Höfen: Hannibal, 2008), p. 254.

Hans-Joachim Roedelius & Dieter Moebius, Klaus Schulze & Manuel Göttsching

The two remaining members, Hans-Joachim Roedelius and Dieter Moebius, re-named the group Cluster after Schnitzler's departure. Their first record, *Cluster* (1971), is more cohesive than Kluster's work, although it covers much of the same ground as that earlier incarnation. In *Cluster II* (1972), however, the group experiments with tighter, more structured material and evinces the elec-tronic, repetitive sound for which Cluster would soon become known. 1974's *Zuckerzeit* and 1976's *Sowiesoso* [Anywayway] sound both tighter and more ex-pansive than earlier works, with the latter often sounding similar to Kraftwerk's music of the era, i.e. it was years ahead of nearly everyone else. The band con-tinued to record, including a collaboration with Brian Eno that led to 1977's *Cluster and Eno*[30] (which features some fine bass work by Can bassist Holger Czu-kay), until it split up in the early 1980s. Roedelius and Moebius re-formed the band and sporadically worked together under the Cluster banner between 1990 and 2010. Roedelius would form Qluster in 2010, and has recorded several albums under that name since 2011. As for Conrad Schnitzler, he went on to re-vive the Kluster name in the twenty-first century without Roedelius or Moebius.

Like Schnitzler, his colleague from Tangerine Dream, Klaus Schulze would also go on to co-found a second great Krautrock band – Ash Ra Tempel, with gui-tarist Manuel Göttsching – before quickly leaving it to set out on a solo career. Their first album, *Ash Ra Tempel* (1971), contains two side-long instrumental tracks, and Göttsching's sonic invention helped establish it among the best gui-tar records of the era. Schulze quit before the band recorded its sophomore ef-fort, *Schwingungen* [Vibrations], which provides exhilarating, though at times frustrating listening. The band's idea to collaborate with Timothy Leary on *Seven Up* (1972) may have been good, but the album was not. Luckily, the band released one last classic, *Join Inn* (1973), a project for which Schulze very briefly rejoined the band. Göttsching later retired the group and began releasing solo work under the name Ashra, although he resurrected the name Ash Ra Tem-pel for collaborations with Schulze which resulted in the *Friendship* and *Gin Rosé at the Royal Festival Hall* releases in 2000. Under his own name, Göttsching re-leased the classic *E2–E4* in 1984. *E2–E4* 'prefigures developments in electronica in the 1990s and beyond as effectively, perhaps even more fully than Kraftwerk's

---

30 A second collaboration, 1978's *After the Heat*, is attributed to Eno Moebius Roedelius.

Computer World.[31] The album remains a tour de force of repetition rarely equalled and almost never surpassed in its vitality.

By the time of Ash Ra Tempel's *Join Inn*, Klaus Schulze had already begun his solo career. His first solo album, *Irrlicht* (1972), shares a similar aesthetic to Tangerine Dream's work from that time and is considered by many a classic. The following year's double album, *Cyborg*, takes *Irrlicht* as a starting point, ramps up the rhythmic intensity and thereby becomes an altogether more immediate work than its predecessor – and no less engaging upon repeated listening. His string of recordings from the middle of the decade – *Timewind* (1975), *Moondawn* (1976) and *Mirage* (1977) – retain their influence on ambient electronic music decades after their original release and arguably represent the high point of his creativity. As of the time of writing, Schulze remains active, releasing music on a more regular basis than artists one-third his age.

Early Kraftwerk

If Schulze's influence on later music is vast – and it is – Kraftwerk's influence is incalculable. However, Kraftwerk's early work fails to impress. One can discern little musical growth between the 1969 album *Tone Float* recorded by Ralf Hütter and Florian Schneider's early group Organisation and the first two albums by the renamed Kraftwerk. These first works show a band searching for its identity. Schneider's flute features prominently on *Kraftwerk* (1970), as do acoustic drums, but Kraftwerk would soon stop using both instruments. Although the band had not yet found its signature sound, one can already distinguish the seeds of its later success in the album opener 'Ruckzuck' [In No Time]: clear echoes of this track can be heard in the band's breakthrough 'Autobahn' four years later. *Kraftwerk 2* (1971) lacks much of the rock influence that was prevalent on its predecessor, which makes this second album an altogether more placid affair, although it contains oases of willful turbulence. One notable addition to the Kraftwerk sound was the rhythm machine on 'Klingklang', the track which would later provide the band with the name of its Düsseldorf studio.

Kraftwerk's third album, *Ralf und Florian* [Ralf and Florian] (1973), proves altogether more inspired and livelier than its previous work. The band expands its sound here in several ways, not least via increased use of electronic percussion and the band's first, very tentative attempts at a lyric: the vocodered repetition of

---

31 David Stubbs, *Future Days: Krautrock and the Building of Modern Germany* (London: Faber & Faber, 2015), p. 404.

the title 'Ananas Symphonie' [Pineapple Symphony]. *Autobahn* (1974) presents yet another step forward, though not the leap forward some might assert. In fact, most of the music on the B-side of the album could have appeared on earlier Kraftwerk albums. The 22-minute title track, on the other hand, occupies the entire A-side and conveys a cohesiveness only hinted at before. An edited version of 'Autobahn' with a running time of less than four minutes became a surprise hit internationally, which prompted Kraftwerk to fundamentally change its sound and even its visual aesthetics.

Michael Rother and Klaus Dinger

Rother and Dinger both briefly played in Kraftwerk before splitting off and forming Neu! In the words of Julian Cope, 'If Neu! had split right after the opening track on their first LP they would still have changed rock 'n' roll'.[32] This track, 'Hallogallo' from *Neu!* (1972), features the simple, driving motorik beat for which Dinger became known. With the tones Rother wrings from his guitar on top of that beat, the band builds an exciting, atmospheric track which not only stands as its best work, but also ranks among the very best rock music of the 1970s. Like their first album, *Neu! 2* proves thought-provoking and exceedingly listenable, especially the album opener 'Für Immer (Forever)' – a 'Hallogallo' rewrite almost as good as the original. After *Neu! 2*, the band split but reunited briefly to record *Neu! 75*, an LP split into two distinct halves.

The A-side of the vinyl features typically dreamy Neu! music, while the B-side augments the band with more musicians and rocks considerably harder. Critics have called 'Hero' proto-punk,[33] while 'After Eight' sounds wonderfully like a poor quality Rolling Stones live bootleg. Neu! split up again after *Neu! 75*, though they reunited a decade later for some ill-fated and ultimately abandoned recordings which were released much later as *Neu! 4* (later revised as *Neu! 86*).

During the band's brief split between *Neu! 2* and *Neu! 75*, Michael Rother joined with the duo in Cluster to found Harmonia, a Krautrock supergroup which earns the appellation 'super'. Their first album, *Musik von Harmonia* (1974), sounds less influenced by Rother's Neu! material than his new bandmates' work. Only 'Dino' with its propulsive beat immediately brings Rother's other band to mind. 'Watussi', with its languid polymetre, and the regal 'Sonnen-

---

32 Cope, *Krautrocksampler*, p. 125.
33 Ibid., p. 127; Leon Muraglia, 'Neu!', in Kotsopoulos, pp. 116–121 (p. 120).

schein' [Sunshine] are highlights, while the markedly un-catchy 'Ohrwurm' [Ear-worm] confirms that the group had a sense of humour. On Harmonia's next album, *De Luxe* (1975), Rother has a much greater presence. One can more clearly hear the DNA of Neu! in *De Luxe* than in *Musik von Harmonia*. Standout tracks include 'De Luxe (Immer wieder)', 'Walky-Talky' and 'Monza (Rauf und runter)' [Monza (Up and Down)], the last of these being both a companion piece to the title track and a close cousin of Neu!'s 'Hero'. After producing two excellent albums, Harmonia broke up in 1976. Not long afterwards, however, the band reunited to record with Eno in September of that same year,[34] though the music would not appear until 1997. In 2007 Harmonia reunited for a series of performances in Europe, the United States and Australia that would last until 2009.[35]

After Neu! split in 1975, Rother's partner Klaus Dinger continued where the band left off with their last record. The second side of *Neu! 75* features Hans Lampe and Dinger's brother Thomas in addition to the band's core duo. Lampe and the Dinger brothers formed La Düsseldorf and released their eponymous first LP in 1976. If the tracks 'Düsseldorf' and 'La Düsseldorf' arguably lack Michael Rother's atmospheric guitar, his ex-partner's manic energy more than makes up for the deficit. This album features 'Silver Cloud', a single that placed high in the charts in 1976 and is probably the band's best-known song. The follow-up album, *Viva* (1978), is poppier, darker and more shambolic. One can hear the influence of punk in this album, particularly in the vocals, which should come as a surprise to no one, considering that their first album – like 'Hero' from *Neu! 75* – frequently sounds like early punk shortly before that music hit big.[36] After *Viva*, La Düsseldorf released only one more album, *Individuellos* [Individualless] (1981), before breaking up.

Faust

Faust does not have the myriad musical and personal connections of the preceding artists, but the band's inclusion in the Krautrock pantheon remains uncontested. Taking a name that would necessarily recall Goethe's drama as well as a fist (the word's meaning in German), the band 'was determined to tear down rock 'n' roll and romp in the debris'.[37] The band's eponymous first album, re-

---

34 Pilkington, 'Harmonia', p. 103.

35 Ibid., p. 103.

36 David Stubbs, 'La Düsseldorf', in Kotsopoulos, pp. 108–111 (p. 109); DeRogatis, *Kaleidoscope Eyes*, p. 140.

37 DeRogatis, *Kaleidoscope Eyes*, pp. 128.

leased in 1971, gives an indication of that determination. Fragments of the Beatles' 'All You Need Is Love' and the Rolling Stones' '(I Can't Get No) Satisfaction' appear alongside brass, chanting, alternatingly warm and shrill guitar distortions, and moments strongly reminiscent of Stockhausen's 'Gesang der Jünglinge' [Song of the Youths]. The contrast forced by the inclusion of the Beatles' music does the album a disservice, and *Faust* comes across as an extended – and less successful – 'Revolution 9', particularly on the album's more disjointed A-side.

Faust So Far (1972) shows the band largely abandoning the collage-like form of their first album for more traditional structures, using these structures to subvert song form, the recording process and perhaps music in general. The opener, 'It's A Rainy Day Sunshine Girl', contains many elements common to pop-rock songs of the time, almost every one of which denies listeners the pleasure of getting lost in the music and so alienates them in the Brechtian sense. Similarly, the abrupt and jarring shift in instrumentation, mood and tempo of 'No Harm' tears the audience out of the calming first section, breaks the spell of the music and forces listeners to think about the recording instead of simply enjoying the music.

Faust would only release two more LPs in the 1970s. *The Faust Tapes* (1973) sounds as little like *So Far* as that album did to their first one. Most of its 26 tracks run less than two minutes. Many do not reach the one-minute mark. *The Faust Tapes* serves as a masterful synthesis of the band's first two albums. The group fleshes out some longer pieces as in *So Far*, while the way the snippets frame these pieces constructs a stronger collage than *Faust*. *Faust IV* (1973), which famously opens with the instrumental entitled 'Krautrock', once again presents an entirely different listening experience than the LPs which preceded it. The album represents a mix of the sublime ('Krautrock' and 'Jennifer') and the silly ('The Sad Skinhead' and 'Giggy Smile'), with the silly songs being the better. Faust broke up after this fourth album, but members of the band revived the Faust name two decades later. In different configurations they have both performed live and released new material beginning with 1994's *Rien*.

Can

Can ranks as the best known of the great Krautrock groups, surpassing even Faust and Neu! Also, Can is arguably the Krautrock group whose late 1960s and early 1970s music has been the most influential. Furthermore, this band follows a general timeline and evolution typical of Krautrock artists. For these reasons, among others, Can will receive a more in-depth analysis than the other artists mentioned in this chapter.

The core band consists of the four instrumentalists Holger Czukay, Michael Karoli, Jaki Liebezeit and Irmin Schmidt. Keyboardist Schmidt, born in 1937, was the oldest of the four. He had been trained as a classical instrumentalist and composer, taught piano and singing and achieved some success as a conductor before co-founding Can.[38] Bassist Czukay was born in 1938 and, like Schmidt, had studied composition with Stockhausen. Born in 1948, Karoli was by far the youngest of the four, and had been a student under Czukay.[39] His relative youth was perhaps the reason he initially found himself much more interested in popular music than the others. He played guitar in Can, although, like the others, he often switched to other instruments. Liebezeit, 'one of the architects of modern rhythm',[40] was born in 1938. He was a free-jazz drummer who had become tired of free jazz and was ready to make a change at the time Can was formed.[41]

These four musicians hardly seemed the type to form a legendary rock band. Indeed, they did not particularly set out to become a rock band, which is a large part of the reason Can developed as it did. Another, equally large part of this equation is that they did not mind when they realized that they were a rock band. However, Can did not want to make typical Anglo-American rock music. Liebezeit states: 'We tried to stay out of the rock business and find our own direction: something that was not so strongly tied to English and American music.'[42] Stockhausen proved to be a key reference point for the fledgling band. The Velvet Underground was another. According to Czukay, 'They were the first group we had ever heard who were playing something with a completely new relation to their instruments, very unconventional in their way of playing, a magic way'.[43] One can distinctly, if infrequently, hear echoes of the Velvet Underground's music in Can's œuvre, but it was the earlier band's novel play and creation of an individual sound which most influenced Can, just as Can would go on to influence later artists.

The band which later became known as Can first began working together in 1968. Within months, American Malcolm Mooney would join the band as singer,

---

38 Pascal Bussy, *The Can Book* (Harrow: SAF, 1989), pp. 52–54.

39 Andy Gill, 'We Can Be Heroes', *Mojo*, 41 (1997), 54–80 (p. 70).

40 Stubbs, *Future Days*, p. 111.

41 Hildegard Schmidt and Wolf Kampmann, *Can Book Box* (Münster: Medium Music, 1998), p. 58.

42 Ibid., pp. 317–318.

43 Bussy, *Can Book*, p. 70.

and the band's sound changed immediately. According to Schmidt, 'Jaki and Malcolm were a unit from the first moment. A rhythmic cell with unbelievable strength. From that moment on, the possibilities gelled and we were suddenly a rock band'.[44] Mooney and Liebezeit came up with the band's name, originally The Can. The cover of their first album, *Monster Movie*, still bears the definite article the band would later drop.

Monster Movie (1969) stands as a landmark recording, and arguably the best album of the band's career. Three of the four tracks are undeniably great pieces of music and two are genuine classics. Only the nursery rhyme play of 'Mary, Mary So Contrary' disappoints by being both slightly less excellent than the material surrounding it, and also more clearly a product of its time. The album's opening track 'Father Cannot Yell' finds the band at full power. Schmidt's organ opening immediately seizes the audience's attention, Karoli pulls many different voicings out of his guitar, and Czukay's playing runs the gamut from complex to naïve. Mooney accents and repeats phrases and sounds, and all this happens on top of Liebezeit's unrelenting momentum.

The powerful 'Yoo Doo Right' takes up the entire B-side of the original album. Mooney famously based the lyrics on a letter he had received from his girlfriend. Though both 'Father Cannot Yell' and 'Yoo Doo Right' sound like Can and like no other group, they are two vastly dissimilar works. 'Yoo Doo Right' clocks in at almost three times the other track's length, starts out at half its speed, undergoes many shifts in style and appears altogether sparser. The band's process of improvising music and editing the best parts together hits its stride with 'Yoo Doo Right'. The song came about as the band 'sat around for twelve hours and played the same groove. At the end, there were three takes available, out of which [the group] then edited a final version. The end was actually the beginning of a new version'.[45]

Liebezeit has termed Can's way of creating music 'instant composition'. The group would record their improvisations and listen to them in order to form their music through editing, very much in the way Miles Davis created his early jazz fusion works such as *In A Silent Way* and *Bitches Brew* at around that same time. In regard to their production process, Irmin Schmidt states: 'Sometimes we played for two days in the studio, recording almost everything. Then we listened and when everybody liked it we worked on it. Sometimes we cut in the tape, sometimes we played it again.'[46] Holger Czukay, who tended to most of

---

44 Schmidt and Kampmann, *Can Box Book*, p. 61.
45 Ibid., p. 148.
46 Bussy, *Can Book*, p. 156.

these editing duties, would later say: 'It used to be a composer would imagine the music; it would only be realized and performed later. What we do is we make the music first and then compose it.'[47]

Of course, studio costs require an immense amount of money under ordinary circumstances and most bands could not afford the luxury of endless days experimenting in the studio. Luckily, like Faust and Kraftwerk, Can had their own studio. A friend of the group's let them use part of a castle, Schloß Nörvenich, as a recording facility. This full-time access to a recording studio with minimal outlay allowed Can to develop their music and find new ways to create.

Like Tangerine Dream, Popol Vuh and other Krautrock bands, Can produced a large amount of soundtrack work. Especially in the early days, the group recorded the soundtrack or individual pieces for several feature films, television movies, and even the theme tune of the German TV culture programme *Aspekte*. In 1970, Can released *Soundtracks*, a compilation of seven tracks from five movies. The LP has not attained the classic status of *Monster Movie*, nor does it deserve it. Nevertheless, *Soundtracks* remains engaging throughout and inclusion of the long version of 'Mother Sky' makes the album essential.[48] The relatively unheralded 'Soul Desert' has a strong, steady groove, and is likewise available only on *Soundtracks*.

The recordings collected on *Soundtracks* stem from a time when the group experienced its first great change: vocalist Malcolm Mooney left the group and returned home to America. The majority of *Soundtracks* therefore features Can's new vocalist Kenji 'Damo' Suzuki, although Mooney sings on two of the album's seven tracks. Many factors differentiate these two vocalists. Suzuki hailed from Japan and was barely 20 when he joined the group – ten years younger than his predecessor. The difference between Mooney's and Suzuki's vocals also establishes itself immediately. Whereas the former possesses a deeper and gruffer voice, the latter often emits a whisper which searches for the perfect spots to manifest itself. Even when screaming, Suzuki does not convey the same power Mooney does in the band's early recording. Furthermore, the other members of Can repeatedly talk about the musical connection Mooney had with drummer Liebezeit.[49] Their new singer formed a bond not with the drummer, but with guitarist Karoli. According to Schmidt: 'When Damo joined, something

---

47 Reynolds, 'Kosmik Dance', p. 37.

48 The compilations *Cannibalism 1* and *Anthology* both contain a much shorter edit of 'Mother Sky'.

49 Schmidt and Kampmann, *Can Box Book*, pp. 61, 214, 296.

happened between him and Michael that was similar to what had happened between Malcolm and Jaki. It just took off.'[50]

Despite this major personnel change, *Tago Mago* (1971) finds the band, arguably, better than ever.[51] The new line-up sounds much more coherent than on *Soundtracks*, despite *Tago Mago* being a double album originally planned as a single LP. Opening track 'Paperhouse' sounds the most like Can's earlier material, while the spare sound of the following track, 'Mushroom', highlights each member's ability and provides a prime example of the band's wonderful interaction. Can would never get much funkier than they do on 'Oh Yeah'[52] and the side-long 'Halleluhwah'. Julian Cope declares that 'The whole instrumental side of 'Hallelujah' [sic] is so confident that it's like the Meters playing avantgarde music'.[53] Indeed, the first album of the set features some of Jaki Liebezeit's best drumming, which is equivalent to saying some of the best rock drumming overall. Album 2 sounds more like the work of some of the more 'cosmic' Krautrock groups – Cope mentions a similarity of the track 'Aumgn' to the work of Organisation, Amon Düül I and Kluster.[54]

After *Tago Mago*, Can converted an old cinema in the small town of Weilerswist, some fifteen miles from Cologne, into their new recording facility which they dubbed the Inner Space studio. They recorded the majority of their next album in this studio. Like *Tago Mago*, *Ege Bamyasi* (1972) contains seven tracks, though it manages to fit them all on a single vinyl disc. Three songs are well under four minutes and therefore shorter than anything on either *Monster Movie* or *Tago Mago* – and these shorter songs are the highlights of the album. 'Spoon' had appeared as a single before the release of *Ege Bamyasi* and was the band's sole top-ten hit in Germany. It also serves as an excellent album closer. Like 'Spoon', the band released 'Vitamin C' as a single and both of these relatively short tracks rank among the band's best work and add a variety to the album which allows the longer tracks such as 'Pinch' and 'Soup' to shine.

Future Days (1973) is such an icon that David Stubbs named his 2014 Krautrock book after it. This LP acts as a perfect end to what many see as Can's great period. In terms of album structure, Can comes full circle. Breaking away from

---

50 Ibid., p. 70.
51 The uneven but often excellent 33 1/3 book series released a volume on *Tago Mago* in 2014. This author cannot recommend the volume for those seeking an in-depth analysis of the album or its production.
52 'Oh Yeah' would serve as a template for the Fall's homage to Can, 'I Am Damo Suzuki'.
53 Cope, *Krautrocksampler*, p. 106.
54 Ibid.

Ege Bamyasi, which contained many briefer tracks combined with a single longer piece on each side, *Future Days* follows the four-song path of *Monster Movie*. Like *Monster Movie*, the A-side consists of two extended songs with a shorter one at the end, while the B-side features only one epic track. Although *Future Days* returns structurally to the first album, it also finishes a journey from that album's aggression and unease to the most peaceful and perhaps even relaxing music the band ever created. Rob Young notes that, on this album and its successor, 'Can had found a never to be repeated levity combined with agility that made their music impeccably weightless'.[55] And though the members of Can could not know that a great change lay before them, the album felt like a turning point. Both the album title and opening track refer to the future, yet the music distinctly recalls the band's past, particularly on Side 2's 'Bel Air', with its echoes of the previous album's 'Sing Swan Song' and *Tago Mago*'s 'Oh Yeah'.

After *Future Days*, Damo Suzuki left Can. Even more so than Malcolm Mooney's departure, the loss of Suzuki would affect the group for the rest of its career. Suzuki had been with the group twice as long as Mooney had and during that time, the group had crystallized significantly. With Suzuki, Can had recorded three full albums (not counting the material collected on *Soundtracks*), earned their first hit record with 'Spoon' and built a recording studio together. In a musical collective like Can, where each individual plays an equal part, chemistry can easily become unbalanced when a member joins or leaves. Schmidt notes: 'There was certainly an interruption when Damo left. One-fifth of the group was suddenly gone. Afterwards, we did "Soon Over Babaluma". Without him. That was naturally something different'.[56] Although they tried out other vocalists, the remaining members of the band, mainly Michael Karoli, took over vocals after Suzuki's departure. Yet it is unlikely that anyone within or outside the band could have taken Suzuki's place, not merely because of the individuality of his voice. After years of collaboration in which they learned how to play rock music together and found a voice for the band, any of its members would have been irreplaceable.

The fall did not, however, occur immediately. *Soon Over Babaluma* (1974) sees Can in good, if not great, form, though some classify it as Can's last great album.[57] It also represents Can's move in earnest into what later would be called World Music. The change to the band's sound on this album should come as no

55 Schmidt and Kampmann, *Can Box Book*, pp. 355–356.
56 Ibid., pp. 102, 105.
57 Stubbs, *Future Days*, p. 145; Schmidt and Kampmann, *Can Box Book*, p. 357.

surprise, as tracks off earlier albums, such as 'Spoon', display the band's interests in non-Western music. Nonetheless, problems presented themselves even during the recording of *Soon Over Babaluma*. Czukay worried that the band had deviated too far from its core practice of instant composition and he called the production 'indistinct'.[58] Karoli stated: 'The whole thing became much more formal and conventional.'[59] Inasmuch as Can changed both their sound and way of creating music during the recording of *Soon Over Babaluma*, one may consider *Future Days* their last Krautrock album. Can then began their development into a more conventional pop/rock band, albeit one with clear world music leanings.

Most listeners and critics agree that Can's material after *Soon Over Babaluma* paled alongside their earlier work, though they continued to regularly release new material until their break-up in 1979. 1975's *Landed* was followed by *Flow Motion* (1976), which contained the track 'I Want More', the band's only hit single in the UK. On *Saw Delight* (1977), two former members of Traffic join the band. Rebop Kwaku Baah plays percussion, while Rosko Gee takes over bass from Czukay who busies himself with non-instrumental sound. Czukay, who quit the band in 1977 does not appear in *Out Of Reach* (1978), though he does get a credit as editor on the following year's *Can* (also known as *Inner Space*). Some years after the band dissolved, the *Monster Movie*-era Can reunited to record *Rite Time* (1989), which by no means ranks with the group's classic early work, but neither does it desecrate the legend of the band, as some reunion projects do.

The Krautrock Aftermath

Besides being the most famous and arguably the best Krautrock group, Can had many ideas and followed a similar career path to other artists in this genre. The group formed in 1968, within the four-year period from 1968 – 1971 in which many of the most prominent Krautrock bands came into being. Can also wanted to create a music that had little to do with Anglo-American rock. Creating a powerful rock music while breaking free of the sounds of Memphis, Chicago, Liverpool, and London, required experimentation, which is a key tenet of Krautrock. And like other groups, Can built a studio to facilitate that experimentation. By 1975, bands associated with this wave of experimental German music had either split up – for instance Neu! and Faust – or dramatically changed their sound and

---

58 Uwe Schütte, *Basis-Diskothek Rock und Pop* (Stuttgart: Reclam, 2004), p. 40; Schmidt and Kampmann, *Can Box Book*, p. 168.
59 Schmidt and Kampmann, *Can Box Book*, p. 244.

method of producing music – such as Kraftwerk and Can. Can also reunited several years after splitting up, as did Faust, Neu!, Amon Düül II and several other groups. One final aspect of Can typical of Krautrock artists is so obvious that it may be overlooked: Can was a band. Very few solo artists fell into this music and even Klaus Schulze, the most prominent exception to this rule, had played in multiple Krautrock bands before embarking upon a solo career.

Can maintained a relatively consistent level of renown after its prime, but some Krautrock bands found a larger audience only after their break-ups. Neu!, for instance, achieved only modest success during its early 1970s existence. Yet Grönland Records' release of Neu!'s albums in CD format in 2001 not only brought these works to a new generation of listeners, but also cemented the band's reputation as one of the great bands of the 1970s. Similarly, Harmonia could not find an audience during its brief existence. The records sold poorly and the band failed to draw a large live following.[60] An audience for Neu! and Harmonia did, however, slowly amass.

More than 30 years after the break-up of the band, Michael Rother joined forces with drummers such as Hans Lampe (from Neu! offshoot La Düsseldorf) or Steve Shelley (from the US band Sonic Youth) to play well-received concerts, featuring songs from Harmonia and Neu! While Klaus Dinger, who died in 2008, lived to experience the enthusiastic reception of the Neu! reissues, Dieter Moebius passed away in July 2015 and did not see either that autumn's release of an elaborate vinyl box set containing Harmonia's *Complete Works* or the nine-album box set containing the remastered oeuvre of Cluster that came out in spring 2016. The renaissance of Harmonia, Cluster and Neu!, as well as the enduring success of Can, demonstrate that the legacy of Krautrock remains very much alive.

The ideas inherent in Krautrock, and the music from bands connected with Krautrock, remain common currency for popular music decades after the music was recorded. However, Krautrock does not only merit consideration as inspiration for later artists. Like British beat music in the early to mid 1960s – one of the only periods to enjoy more influence than this German music a few years later – Krautrock is one of the great flowerings in Western popular music in the second half of the twentieth century. Much of this music is now just as fascinating, thought-provoking and utterly magnificent as when first released.

---

60 Stubbs, *Future Days*, p. 343.

Uwe Schütte

Kraftwerk – *Industrielle Volksmusik* between Retro-Futurism and Ambivalence

The most important watershed moment in the history of popular music in post-war Germany came in November 1974 when Kraftwerk released its groundbreaking album *Autobahn*. Although the album largely met with disinterest in Germany at the time, its title track is today considered to be the most iconic song in German popular music. While the B-side featured atmospheric instrumentals in a vein similar to the band's three previous, more experimental, albums – which were the result of the creative direction of Ralf Hütter and Florian Schneider – the entire A-side of *Autobahn* was taken up by the stunning title track, which ran to nearly 23 minutes. An edited three-minute version of the track entered the US Billboard charts and also became a top 20 hit in the UK in 1975.

Scholars argue that, in a complex way, 'Autobahn' 'reflects upon the state of German cultural, artistic, and musical identity'[1] and 'explicitly addressed aspects of German identity loaded with references to the Nazi era and beyond'.[2] After all, the German *Autobahn* symbolized individual mobility and freedom on a motorway system with no (official) speed limit. The *Autobahn* is further connected with car manufacturing, which formed the backbone of the post-war economy, as well as the quality of German engineering as captured by the marketing slogan 'Vorsprung durch Technik' [advancement through technology].

On its original cover, *Autobahn* featured a painting by Emil Schult which is full of references to Germany's past. As Bussy describes, it 'juxtaposes images of the countryside, mountains, an exaggerated sun, green grass, blue sky and floating clouds against the most potent symbol of the industrial era – the car on the motorway'.[3] As well as projecting this idealistic harmony between nature and technological civilization, the two cars in the painting are also loaded with symbolic meaning: while the black Mercedes, a make of car used by political leaders such as Adolf Hitler and West Germany's first chancellor Konrad Adenauer, is shown driving towards the viewer, a VW Beetle, like the one Ralf Hütter

1 Melanie Schiller, '"Fun, Fun Fun on the Autobahn": Kraftwerk Challenging Germanness', *Popular Music and Society*, 37/5 (2014), 618–637 (p. 623).

2 Sean Albiez and Kyrre Tromm Lindvig, '*Autobahn* and Heimatklänge. Soundtracking the FRG', in *Kraftwerk: Music Non-Stop*, ed. by Sean Albiez and David Pattie (New York: Continuum, 2011), pp. 15–43 (p. 19).

3 Pascal Bussy, *Kraftwerk: Man, Machine and Music* (London: SAF, 2001), p. 54–55.

DOI 10.1515/9783110425727-005

owned at the time, can be seen driving towards the sunrise on the horizon, symbolizing the hopes of a younger generation for a brighter future beyond the troubled Nazi past.

The song, or rather the musical composition, differed greatly from the previous work of Kraftwerk and their Krautrock contemporaries. It emulated a car journey on the *Autobahn* and set out to mimic the boredom and monotony of driving through its repetitive rhythm and the recurrent refrain 'Wir fahr'n, fahr'n, fahr'n auf der Autobahn' [We drive, drive, drive on the motorway]. This emulation was also enhanced by synthesized tooting horns, the simulated Doppler shift of passing cars and the *mise-en-abyme* of 'Autobahn' being played on a car radio.

In addition to the cover art, Schult was also responsible for writing the track's minimalist, rhyming lyrics, which relate directly to his cover image and further enhance the immersive, multi-medial setting of the journey:

> Vor uns liegt ein weites Tal
> Die Sonne scheint mit Glitzerstrahl
> Die Fahrbahn ist ein graues Band
> Weiße Streifen, grüner Rand

> [Ahead of us a valley wide
> The sun shines with sparkling light
> The lane is a grey concrete strip
> White stripes, green ditch]

Hütter repeatedly described Kraftwerk's music as *industrielle Volksmusik*,[4] a deliberate expression that resonates deeply in German culture. The phrase's literal translation as 'industrial folk music' does not do justice to the ambiguities in the German language. The use of '*industrielle*' here is not a stylistic reference to the noisy (anti-)music developed by Throbbing Gristle. Instead, it refers to the highly-industrialized Rhein-Ruhr region in which Hütter and Schneider both grew up. In other words, it refers to a modern civilization based on technology, manufacturing and the use of machines. This further implies an association with the modernist notion that noise can be beautiful and hence typifies a contemporary musical aesthetic.

Likewise, what Hütter calls '*Volksmusik*' is not the 'folk music' British or American audiences might expect. On the contrary, the term refers to Kraftwerk's

---

4 See the interview 'Maschinen sind einfach lockerer', *Der Spiegel*, 50 (2009), p. 138 or the interview with Chris Bohn in *New Musical Express*, 13 June 1981 (http://www.rocksbackpages.com/Library/Article/kraftwerk-a-computer-date-with-a-showroom-dummy).

modern take on regional musical traditions in Germany and therefore suggests an originality which distinguishes Kraftwerk's techno pop from the dominant Anglo-American cultural influences which pervaded post-war Germany. Furthermore, the term refers to the democratic nature of popular music, namely in the sense that it is music made both *for* and *by* the people. Overall, then, the label *industrielle Volksmusik* captures the band's aim to challenge the dominance of Anglo-American rock music, whilst constructing a new, legitimate national identity in the wake of the atrocities committed by the Nazis.

Throughout the track, 'Autobahn' encapsulates Kraftwerk's notion of *industrielle Volksmusik* by setting out to reflect every-day life in modern West Germany or, more precisely, the Rhein-Ruhr area with its extensive *Autobahn* network. The music incorporates mechanical noise and was largely, although not entirely, produced using electronic music technology in favour of traditional instrumentation. The song and its German lyrics are deceptively simple, appealing even to children, yet they also constitute the central piece of a complex *Gesamtkunstwerk* [total work of art] because of their connections with the music and cover art. The track updates avant-garde ideas and techniques (e.g. Russolo's futurism) to create a contemporary, specifically German aesthetic that had a major impact on the development of popular music across the globe.

Radio-Aktivität (1975)

The ambiguous title of Kraftwerk's next album caused confusion. *Radio-Aktivität* [*Radio-Activity*] was largely deemed to be a paean to nuclear energy, which was a subject of considerable political protest at the time by the emerging ecological movement. In later remixes, Kraftwerk dispelled all doubts about their position on nuclear energy by changing the lyrics of the title track to '*stop* radioactivity'. Yet, at the time of release, Kraftwerk agreed to have promotional shots taken which showed the band members wearing white lab coats in a Dutch nuclear power plant. This move further contributed to the common view that *Radio-Aktivität* is about the theme of nuclear energy, though it was in fact inspired by the band's visit to the USA during their extended tour in 1975 to promote *Autobahn*. Whilst travelling in the USA, Hütter and Schneider were impressed by the large network of radio stations, and also discovered that *Billboard* magazine featured the most played singles under the heading 'Radio Activity'. 'Suddenly', wrote band member Wolfgang Flür, 'there was a theme in the air, the activity of radio stations, and the title of 'Radioactivity Is In The Air For You And Me' was born. All we needed was the music to go with it. [...] The ambiguity of the theme didn't come until later'.[5]

Radio-Aktivität was Kraftwerk's first fully-realized concept album, a 37-minute-long musical radio play with 12 tracks which segue seamlessly into each other. Particularly on CD, the album provides a succinct, continuous listening experience, connecting upbeat techno pop songs such as 'Radio-Aktivität' or 'Antenne' with moody experimental pieces of electronic music which act as intermissions.

The ambiguity mirrored in the album's title reflects the core concept of *Radio-Aktivität*. Like *Autobahn* before, Emil Schult provided striking artwork which shows the front and back sides of an outdated radio receiver on the front and back covers of the album, respectively. Not only did this suggest a tension between obsolete technology and the avant-garde music heard on the record, but clearly referenced the Nazi past through the image's strong resemblance to a DKE 38 model *Volksempfänger*, which was used to receive Nazi propaganda in German homes.

Radio-Aktivität was the first album release to feature bilingual lyrics in German and English. The song text would first be sung in English, followed by the German original, which mostly, though not neatly, mirrored the English translations. Littlejohn sees this addition of English lyrics as a tactical move which not only unduly lengthened the duration of the tracks, but also created an 'important break with the earlier albums, a break indicative of the band's attempt at commercialization'.[6]

Bussy considers the title track to be 'a humorous denunciation of the nuclear industry',[7] though Kraftwerk is careful to present this ironic aspect subtly:

Radioactivity
Is in the air for you and me
Radioactivity
Discovered by Madame Curie
Radioactivity
Tune in to the melody
Radio Aktivität
Für dich und mich in All entsteht [originates in space for you and me]
Radio Aktivität
Strahlt Wellen zum Empfangsgerät [sends waves to the receiver]

5 Wolfgang Flür, *Kraftwerk: I Was A Robot* (London: Sanctuary, 2000), p. 77.
6 John Littlejohn, 'Kraftwerk: Language, Lucre, and Loss of Identity', *Popular Music and Society*, 32/5, 635–653 (p. 644).
7 Bussy, *Kraftwerk*, p. 72.

Radio Aktivität
Wenn's um unsere Zukunft geht [if our future is at stake]

These lyrics are neutral in tone, not least because there is no explicit mention of nuclear power plants. As Buckley noted, the reference to Marie Curie is inaccurate, or at least imprecise.[8] Only the last line in German appears to relate to nuclear energy, though its meaning, again, is neither strongly affirmative, nor critical. Indeed, John Foxx has pointed out that 'the song is actually as neutral a Warhol statement, as all their songs tend to be'.[9] Given that Hütter and Schneider admired Warhol as a model artist, their highly ambiguous writing could well have been derived from him.

'The album delights in wordplay and allusion', observed Buckley.[10] Notable, for instance, is the play on the popular English expression 'home sweet home', which turns into 'Ohm Sweet Ohm', i. e. alluding to the unit of electrical resistance named after the German physicist Georg Simon Ohm. Elsewhere in the album, other lyrics are used to associate the ambivalent title with related aspects, often in minimalist ways. 'Radio Sterne' ['Radio Stars'], for example, deals with the radio frequencies emitted by planets, quasars and pulsars. Meanwhile, the lyrics of 'Antenne' ['Antenna'] anticipate the very state of mutual connectedness and constant interchange of information made possible today by the internet:

I'm the transmitter
I give information
You're the antenna
Catching vibration

'Die Stimme der Energie' ['The Voice of Energy'] is the bleakest track on *Radio-Aktivität* – it is essentially an experimental spoken word piece in which a vocoded voice speaks the following warning:

Hier spricht die Stimme der Energie
Ich bin ein riesiger, elektrischer Generator
Ich liefere Ihnen Licht und Kraft
Und ermögliche es Ihnen, Sprache, Musik und Bild
Durch den Äther auszusenden und zu empfangen

---

8 Radioactivity was actually discovered by Henri Becquerel; Curie discovered the two elements polonium and radium and later coined the term 'radioactivity'.
9 Quoted in David Buckley, *Kraftwerk: Publikation* (London: Omnibus, 2011), p. 78.
10 Buckley, *Kraftwerk*, p. 78.

Ich bin Ihr Diener und Ihr Herr zugleich
Deshalb hütet mich gut
Mich, den Genius der Energie

[This is the Voice of Energy
I am a giant electrical generator
I supply you with light and power
And I enable you to receive speech
Music and images through the ether
I am your servant and lord at the same time
Therefore guard me well
Me, the Genius of Energy]

Yet again, the crux of this piece is its ambivalent outlook. It discusses the potential for technology to be used for either beneficial or destructive ends. In the light of the album title, this can be attributed, on the one hand, to the generation of electrical energy and the devastation caused by nuclear bombs, and on the other hand, to the spreading of totalitarian political propaganda and the broadcast of music via the radio.

Although Kraftwerk never acknowledged it, the track bears a very close resemblance to a speech synthesis experiment undertaken by the physicist Werner Meyer-Eppler in 1949. In fact, the German text is a direct, slightly enlarged translation from Meyer-Eppler's original. In this sense, it could be described as Kraftwerk's only 'cover version'. Continuing their previous use of a vocoder in *Autobahn*, *Radio-Aktivität* contains a number of songs with vocoded voices that consolidated the band's position as 'pioneers in the use of phonetic experiments in pop music'.[11]

With 'Die Stimme der Energie', Hütter and Schneider also paid their homage to the early innovators of electronic music with which they had become acquainted through the night-time broadcasts of the Cologne-based Westdeutscher Rundfunk (WDR). The WDR's Studio für elektronische Musik, founded in 1951, served as a platform for a number of avant-garde composers, most notably Karlheinz Stockhausen who realized *Elektronische Studien* (1953–54) and *Gesang der Jünglinge* (1955–56) using the studio's equipment. It is quite possible that WDR broadcasts brought the two core members of Kraftwerk into contact with Meyer-Eppler's experiments.[12] Indeed, in 1981, Hütter indicated that he and Schneider

---

11 Carsten Brocker, 'Kraftwerk: Technology and Composition', in *Kraftwerk*, ed. by Albiez and Pattie, pp. 97–117 (p. 106).

12 For details see Elena Ungeheuer, *Wie die elektronische Musik 'erfunden' wurde: Quellenstudien zu Werner Meyer-Epplers Entwurf zwischen 1949 und 1953* (Mainz: Schott, 1992), pp. 110–112.

were regular listeners of the WDR: 'They played a lot of late-night programmes with strange sound and noise. So [*Radio-Aktivität*] was like our dedication to the age of radio, and radiation at the same time, breaking the taboo of including everyday political themes into the music.'[13]

Stubbs describes *Radio-Aktivität* as 'a milestone in electronic music, one that marks a precise and signal midpoint between Stockhausen and Depeche Mode'.[14] In addition, the album marked an important stage in the development of the band as they pursued full artistic control over their output. Not only was *Radio-Aktivität* the first album conceived entirely with electronic instruments, but its production was handled entirely by Hütter and Schneider for the first time, the band having previously relied upon Conny Plank's services. The record was also the first to feature the classic Kraftwerk line-up by adding Wolfgang Flür and Karl Bartos and, having signed with EMI, it was the first release on their vanity label *Kling Klang Schallplatten* [Ding Dong Records]. This onomatopoeic name was also given to their new artistic head quarters in Düsseldorf, the Kling Klang Studio, which was located until 2008 in an anonymous building on 16, Mintropstrasse, near the main Düsseldorf railway station.

Trans Europa Express (1977)

With *Trans Europa Express*, Kraftwerk 'moved from experimental sounds to formal structures and melodies'.[15] This album about train travel through Europe revisited the theme of transportation in *Autobahn*, but expanded it from a German national icon to an idea of European integration as expressed in a transnational railway system. The Trans Europ Express (TEE) network was in operation from the late 1950s until the early 1990s. At its height, it connected 130 cities across western Europe with regular services every two hours. As such, the system represented a modern, if expensive, lifestyle as the trains only offered first-class fares.

The railway was a strong symbol of modernization due to its role as a driving force of industrialization. Historically, railway technology can be seen, along with the car, as another key German technology: The first railway line was opened in 1835 to connect the Bavarian cities of Fürth and Nuremberg. In

---

13 Quoted from Brocker, 'Kraftwerk', p. 106.
14 David Stubbs, *Future Days: Krautrock and the Building of Modern German* (London: Faber & Faber, 2014), p. 181.
15 Brocker, 'Kraftwerk', p. 107.

1885, Germany's railway network was the largest in Europe, running to a total length of about 40,000 kilometres (clearly exceeding its next contender, Great Britain, which totalled around 30,000 kilometres).

As with the *Autobahn* network, however, the railway is an ambivalent symbol in the context of German history, given the Nazi's use of the railway system to transport deportees to death camps in the East.[16] The *Reichsbahn's* key role in the murder of many hundreds of thousands is remembered today by several memorials erected at trains stations throughout Germany. Furthermore, it is this past which drove the Federal Republic to proactively develop greater political integration with Europe and create a shared European cultural identity. The latter impulse clearly underpins Kraftwerk's artistic efforts. Given that France and Germany were the early driving forces of European integration under Adenauer and France's first post-war president, de Gaulle, it is fitting that the lyrics of the title song sketch a journey on the TEE from Paris via Vienna to Düsseldorf, a route often travelled by members of Kraftwerk (though, obviously, without the detour via Vienna).[17]

The album's artwork offers a prime example of Kraftwerk's guiding retro-futurist aesthetic in practice. This concept aims to fuse utopian notions with nostalgic images to create an aesthetic tension that confronts the present with unredeemed past promises of a better future. In Kraftwerk's case, as Grönholm explains, their 'futuristic nostalgia is a special way of creating historical narratives and images; it excludes sentimentality and rejects the idea of a Golden Age, but instead reimagines the past as a continuum of progressive development'.[18]

Following what seems to be a conventional design approach, the cover features a photo of the four band members. The album was released at the apex of the punk explosion, yet the image conveyed was totally at odds with the spirit of the times. The band portrait was taken by the American celebrity photographer(s) Maurice Seymour,[19] and shows the band members dressed conservatively in suit

---

16 In this context, see also Steve Reich's composition *Different Trains* (1988).

17 Coincidentally, Kraftwerk took their inspiration for *Trans Europa Express* from an avant-garde piece of *musique concrète* that originated in France: Pierre Schaeffer's *Etude aux Chemins de Fer*. Worth mentioning is also Conrad Schnitzler's 20-minute piece *Zug* [Train] which was issued on a private tape in 1974.

18 Pertti Grönholm, 'When Tomorrow Began Yesterday: Kraftwerk's nostalgia for the Past Futures', *Popular Music and Society*, 38/3 (2015), pp. 372–388 (p. 372).

19 This name actually refers to a team of two brothers: Maurice (1900–1993) and Seymour (1902–1995) Zeldman who were Russian Jews and both legally changed their names to Maurice Seymour.

and ties in the style of a group portrait typical of the 1930s or 1940s. Only a Rhinestone brooch in the form of a musical note worn by Schneider hints at the irony involved in staging the musicians in this way.

There is even a second portrait that aims to underline this conservative, conformist impression of the band. In it, Kraftwerk could pass as a conventional string quartet, but hardly as innovators of futuristic electronic music. It shows the band sitting at a table under a large oak tree against the backdrop of a lush, Alpine landscape. Its colour was retouched by Schult to increase the air of nostalgia. According to Stubbs: 'It's ironic, it's ridiculous, but at another level it is reclaiming for Germany and its popular music a sense of poise and unapologetic confidence.'[20]

Such out-of-date and traditionalist imagery stands in marked contrast to the decidedly futuristic music on *Trans Europa Express*, which was released at the very moment when 'no future' provided the call to arms for England's punk movement. Moreover, whilst British punk was denouncing royalty and the British establishment, Kraftwerk was singing the praises of a 'Europe endless' in the opening track of the album.[21] Against the gritty urban realism of punk, *Trans Europa Express* paints a rather romantic and often melancholic picture of the continent, grounded in the natural beauty of its landscape (although also taking care not to fall prey to clichés):

Flüsse, Berge, Wälder
Europa endlos
Wirklichkeit und Postkarten-Bilder
Europa endlos
Eleganz und Dekadenz
Europa endlos

[Rivers, mountains, forests
Europe endless
Reality and postcard views
Europe endless
Elegance and decadence
Europe endless]

The theme of German romanticism is taken up by the instrumental track 'Franz Schubert', named after the noted nineteenth-century Austrian composer. Haglund argues that much of Kraftwerk's music can be aligned with Schubert's ro-

---

20 Stubbs, *Future Days*, p. 190.
21 A reprise, entitled 'Endlos, Endlos', also closes the album, rounding up the theme of European unity.

mantic song cycles, as they are both 'based on the romantic notion of "Der Wanderer". [...] Not only are there structural similarities in the use of repeats and layering. All through, the music is about physical and mental movement. The state of longing and melancholy that arises is based on similar melodic figures.'[22]

With 'Schaufensterpuppen' ['Showroom Dummies'] and 'Spiegelsaal' ['Hall of Mirrors'], *Trans Europa Express* features two songs whose lyrics follow an unusually expansive, narrative structure, focusing in both cases on the theme of identity loss and objectification. 'Schaufensterpuppen' and 'Spiegelsaal' prefigured the key conceptual theme – the man-machine – which Kraftwerk explored on the follow-up album in two important ways. Firstly, the songs responded to the accusation that the band performed like mannequins on stage. Secondly, they critically examined the (psychological) pitfalls of stardom. 'Besides providing abundant material to the theme of identity loss [...], 'The Hall of Mirrors' is also a fine example of the riches which lie hidden in [Kraftwerk's] under-researched lyrics', according to Littlejohn.[23]

'Spiegelsaal' can be read on various levels,[24] not least from a cultural anthropological perspective as a rite of passage according to the three-stage model proposed by Arnold van Gennep (i. e. separation, liminality, incorporation).[25] In a more obvious sense, the lyrics can be seen as a warning about what happens to pop stars (such as David Bowie, who is evidently referred to in the chorus): fame condemns them to 'live their lives in the looking glass' of public scrutiny, which forces them to 'change themselves' and live a public persona. With hindsight, it is clear that Hütter and Schneider took heed of the transformative, problematic aspects of fame, as exemplified by Bowie, by retreating into privacy, essentially refusing to discuss their work and shielding their private lives.

---

22 Magnus Haglund, 'Franz & Robert: The Romantic Machine', in *Influenser, referenser och plagiat: Om Kraftwerk estetik*, ed. by Andréas Hagström (Göteborg: Röhsska Museet, 2015), pp. 153 – 159 (p. 153 – 154). An early edition of Kraftwerk, comprising Ralf Hütter and Klaus Dinger (later of Neu!), used Beethoven's late string quartet *Opus 132 in A minor* as the starting point for a lengthy improvisation during a concert in 1970, see ibid., p. 158.

23 Littlejohn, 'Kraftwerk', p. 640.

24 The title also alludes to the hall of mirrors at Versailles where the German Empire was founded in 1871. Subsequently, it was chosen as the venue for Germany to sign the treaty of Versailles in 1919 which poisoned the political relations with France and contributed to the rise of the Nazis during the Weimar period. The problem of a fractured personal identity could hence also be applied to German national identity in the twentieth century.

25 See Arnold van Gennep, *The Rites of Passage* (London: Routledge 2010 [1960]).

The album's title track, which is often regarded as one of Kraftwerk's master-pieces, proved to be of crucial importance for the development of electronic music. It is actually a suite of three tracks which merge smoothly into one another. The techno pop track 'Trans Europa Express' is followed by the instrumental 'Metall auf Metall' ['Metal on Metal'], which features ferocious metal percussion, and is concluded with the short outro 'Abzug' (essentially the sound of a train departing).[26] The 13-minute 'Trans Europa Express' suite is based on relentless repetition, propelling the listener onward, emulating the velocity of train travel by marrying it with the constant forward flow of beat-driven music. Extending the approach heard in 'Autobahn', this musical simulation of train travel exemplifies Kraftwerk's artistic aim to translate the industrial sounds of pulsating noise and metal clanging into a modern machine-based music.

With the 'Trans Europa Express' suite, Kraftwerk had 'found a disciplined and streamlined way of incorporating the sounds of everyday industry and transport into structures that were essentially pop songs'.[27] Harking back to the attempts of Dadaists and futurists of the 1920s and 1930s to incorporate industrial modernity into art, Kraftwerk's techno pop paved the way for the future of electronic dance music. This particularly applied to *Metall auf Metall*, 'the pounding, percussive anvil work of Flür and Bartos' which, according to Stubbs, is 'one of a handful of the most influential tracks in the entire canon of popular music'.[28]

The retro-futuristic, highly danceable combination of pop music with avant-garde soundscapes resonated particularly with black communities in the US: 'I don't think they even knew how big they were among the black masses in '77 when they came out with *Trans Europa Express*. When that came out I thought, that was one of the weirdest records I ever heard in my life.'[29] Indeed, as Rietveld rightly stresses, 'Kraftwerk's electroacoustic soundscapes responded to a (post-)industrial social experience that affected societies beyond the Ruhrgebiet, Germany and western Europe.'[30]

---

26 'Abzug' was dropped as a title and merged with 'Metall auf Metall' for the 2009 remasters.
27 Bussy, *Kraftwerk*, p. 90.
28 Stubbs, *Future Days*, p. 189. Simon Reynolds described it as 'a funky iron foundry that sounded like a Luigi Russolo Art of Noises megamix for a futurist discotheque'. (See ibid.)
29 Afrika Bambaataa, in David Toop, *Rap Attack: African Jive to New York Hip Hop* (New York: South End Press, 1984), p. 130.
30 Rietveld, in Albiez and Pattie, p. 222.

Die Mensch-Maschine (1978)

Die Mensch-Maschine is Kraftwerk's key conceptual work. 'Strictly speaking, rather than the LP being a concept, the group themselves was now a concept, and the LP was merely a vehicle to further it.'[31] In stark contrast to the retro style of photography in *Trans Europa Express*, Kraftwerk now appeared on their latest album cover as a uniform group of pale mannequins in red shirts and black ties. The futurist styling of the album is also coupled with the bold graphic art of Karl Klefisch, whose design and typography visibly reference the work of the Soviet avant-garde artist El Lissitzky, which strongly influenced suprematism, constructivism and the German Bauhaus movement.

Mensch-Maschine is central to Kraftwerk's *Gesamtkunstwerk* in that it constructed their corporate identity, although its music also proved vital to their career. After all, the album contains their only UK number one hit single 'Das Modell' ['The Model']. As Stubbs points out, 'on certain tracks, including 'Spacelab' and 'Metropolis', they were playing catch-up with the innovations by [Giorgio] Moroder and [Robbie] Wedel',[32] who had enjoyed great success with the disco hit 'I Feel Love' in 1977.

Tellingly perhaps, 'Das Modell' hardly ranks amongst Kraftwerk's best work musically. The song, written in a typical pop style and featuring the only female protagonist in their oeuvre, was a nod to Düsseldorf's status as Germany's leading fashion capital at the time.[33] However, the themes of its lyrics – commerce, sex, drinking and dancing at a chic nightclub – are rather at odds with the highly posthuman, futuristic orientation of the album. It may have been for this reason that the song's chart success only came three years after the release of *Mensch-Maschine*.[34]

The romantic 'Neonlicht' ['Neon Lights'], much loved and often covered because of its lilting melody, is likewise a song about Düsseldorf, paying tribute to the many colourful neon signs that advertise shops, hotels and bars in the city. Indeed, many examples of neon advertisements, though mostly for sex shops and seedy bars, can be found to this day in the area where the Kling Klang studio

---

31 Bussy, *Kraftwerk*, p. 99.

32 Stubbs, *Future Days*, p. 192.

33 On Kraftwerk and the fashion industry see Philip Warkander, 'The Mechanical Body: Kraftwerk and Contemporary Fashion', in Hagström, pp. 183–190.

34 The song originally served as the B-side to the UK 'Computer Love' single released in July 1981; when it turned out that 'The Model' proved more popular than the A-side, the song was re-issued in December 1981, with the song now as the A-side, upon which it reached the number one position in February 1982.

was originally located. 'Metropolis' pays homage to the masterpiece of German Expressionist cinema by Fritz Lang. His film *Metropolis*, one of the first science-fiction movies, featured a robot and exerted a major influence on Kraftwerk. Indeed, posters promoting their 1975 USA tour already showed an artist's impression of the futuristic city of Metropolis as envisaged in Lang's film and announced Kraftwerk (in German) as 'Die Mensch-Maschine' to their American audience.

Accordingly, the band appropriated the image of the robot to act as the avatar for their concept of the man-machine. To promote the album, robot mannequins were built of each member in the band and, to this day, these likenesses of the band members appear on stage to accompany their theme tune, 'Die Roboter' ['The Robots']. The robot mannequins embody a fitting metaphor for the work ethos of the band. In one of his various attempts to construct an artistic identity distinct from the band's rock contemporaries, Hütter claimed, 'We are not scientists nor musicians. We are workers.'[35] Indeed, Kraftwerk's highly conceptual electronic music project 'represented a conscious, deliberately constructed aesthetic offence to traditional rock values [...] where a sense of unbuttoned maleness, of hair and heart and emotive authenticity was paramount'.[36]

As Hütter has repeatedly stressed, he sees the band as the human vehicle for their man-machine concept. Accordingly, a robotic voice has for years announced the band as 'die Mensch-Maschine Kraftwerk' before the beginning of their concert performances. On the subject of man and machine and music, Hütter explained in 1978: 'The machines are part of us and we are part of the machines [...] They play with us and we play with them. We are brothers. They are not our slaves. We work together, helping each other to create.'[37]

Later on, Hütter talks about the band's 'symbiotic relationship with machines',[38] again stressing both the mutual benefit and temporary nature of the unity between man and machine, be it in the studio or on stage. In light of this, the man-machine concept can be described as the artistic *dispositif* (Foucault) that emerges when Kraftwerk operate their machines to produce electronic music. Crucially, the humans behind the consoles on stage embody a convergence that clearly differs from a mindless, heteronomous robot.[39]

---

35 Quoted in Bussy, *Kraftwerk*, p. 69.
36 Stubbs, *Future Days*, p. 194.
37 Interview with Ralf Hütter in *Future*, 5 (1978), p. 24.
38 Ibid.
39 See the feminist analysis by Kajsa G. Eriksson, 'Kraftwerk's Soft, Smooth, Erotic Bodies and Feministic Resistance', in Hagström, pp.171–181.

From a performance point of view, the occasional mistakes that the band make during concerts underline the fact that humans, not machines, are making the music. Similarly, close examination of the robot and man-machine concepts reveals a characteristic degree of ambivalence. Though Kraftwerk's overall faith in the positive capabilities of technology remains unbroken, they do not communicate this naïvely. In this respect, Kraftwerk connects their artistic project to the cultural-historical tradition of the man-machine. From Julien Offray de La Mettrie's treatise *L'homme machine* [*Man a Machine*] (1747) and the first mechanical automatons in the eighteenth century, to the depiction of uncanny characters in nineteenth-century literature (such as Olimpia in E.T.A. Hoffmann's *Der Sandmann* [*The Sandman*] from 1817 or Mary Shelley's *Frankenstein* from 1818), to the female robot Futura in Lang's *Metropolis*, man-machines are hybrid-beings that inspire in us ambivalent feelings of fear and hope with regard to technology.

Kraftwerk's characteristic play with ambiguity can be detected in the paramilitaristic look the band has on the *Mensch-Maschine* cover. At first glance, it evokes unwelcome associations for many Germans, not least because the colour scheme matches the colours of the Nazi flag. In this light, the quartet of robots could be seen as a reminder of the 'willing executioners', upon which German fascism relied to obediently follow orders without asking questions. Thus, in yet another retro-futuristic turning of the tables, the band managed to fuse a reference to the German past with our technologically-governed future.

It is also no coincidence that the lyrics of 'Mensch-Maschine' are typically minimal, refusing to define the exact nature and characteristics of Kraftwerk's artistic paradigm. The vagueness and ambiguity are increased by the fact that the lyrics subtly differ in German and English. The German original describes the man-machine as 'halb Wesen und halb Ding' [half a being and half a thing]. In the English version, though, this duality becomes 'semi-human being', which reduces the dichotomy expressed in German. Hence, the dialectical nature of the man-machine remains open to discussion. It is unclear whether they combine man and machine into something fundamentally new via a transcendent ontology or whether they are envisioning a cyborgian hybrid.

This theoretical question is complicated by the shift that occurs when the posthuman man-machine is also described as 'halb Wesen und halb Überding' [half a being and half a super-thing], which is rendered in the English version as 'super-human being'. While the German original implies technological improvement and development of the man-machine, the conflated English version opts for a term that is strikingly close to the Nietzschean *Übermensch* and yet also indirectly evokes its opposite, i.e. the fascist notion of the 'subhuman'.

Kraftwerk's techno-optimism can, in any case, be situated within current discourses in the field of post- and trans-humanism which challenge traditional dichotomies such as the man-machine duality. 'The predominant concept of the "human being" is questioned by thinking through the human being's engagement and interaction with technology'[40] – this definition of post-humanist trends in contemporary philosophy could equally be used to describe Kraftwerk's artistic concept.

In this light, the gratuitous note on the back sleeve of the album reading 'Produced in W. Germany' offers an important indication that *Mensch-Maschine*, too, is an album which acknowledges Germany's Nazi past and fuses it with the prospect of trans-humanity. This, then, is yet another figuration of the retro-futurist principle of Kraftwerk's central aesthetics.

Computerwelt (1981)

With *Computerwelt*, the band attained their musical peak and completed a seven-year series of ground-breaking albums. The album, released in May 1981, 'was arguably Kraftwerk's most cohesive and conceptual piece of work yet'.[41] Three years in the making, its release went on sale shortly before the first personal computers (PCs) came on the market. IBM launched the rather expensive 5150 in August 1981, Commodore launched the more affordable Commodore 64 – the first true home computer – in August 1982, and Apple launched the first Macintosh computer in January 1984 – all within two and a half years of the release of *Computerwelt*.

On their prophetic album, Kraftwerk 'do not predict a robotised, sci-fi future. However, they do predict, with complete accuracy, that our modern-day lives will be revolutionised'[42] by computer technology:

> Automat und Telespiel
> Leiten heut' die Zukunft ein
> Computer für den Kleinbetrieb
> Computer für das Eigenheim
>
> [Machines and video games
> Introduce us to the future
> Computer for the small business
> Computer for the home]

---

40 Robert Ranisch and Stefan Sorgner, '*Introducing Post-and Transhumanism*', in *Post- and Transhumanism. An Introduction*, ed. by Robert Ranisch and Stefan Sorgner (Frankfurt: Lang, 2014), p. 8.
41 Bussy, *Kraftwerk*, p. 106.
42 Buckley, *Kraftwerk*, p. 165.

Ironically, the studio production of the album was analogue and did not involve any computer technology, underlining the visionary power of the album. *Computerwelt* is less retro than any other Kraftwerk album – and consequently their most futuristic work.

Schneider's interest in gadgets and the ubiquity of microchip technology throughout everyday life at the time is reflected in the playful 'Taschenrechner' ['Pocket Calculator'], which proved so successful in Japan that a Japanese version 'Dentaku' was issued. 'Computerliebe' ['Computer Love'] with its seductive melody was yet another track of visionary quality given the manifold opportunities the internet now provides via social networking and matchmaking sites, whether for romantic or erotic ends:

> Ich bin allein, mal wieder ganz allein
> Starr auf den Fernsehschirm (2 x)
> Hab heut Nacht nichts zu tun (2 x)
> Ich brauch ein Rendez-vous (2 x)
>
> [Another lonely night
> Stare at the TV screen
> I don't know what to do
> I need a rendezvous]

However, this song captures a degree of sadness and alienation by envisaging a scenario of personal isolation in a future saturated with technology and lacking in purpose and emotional connection. The pronounced ambivalence at the heart of this vision of the advent of our present day computer world can hardly be overlooked. And in a way, this prediction was correct considering that increased digital communication has been seen to foster the dissolution of established traditional social interactions and communities.

As Bussy points out, 'lost on many was that the album was as much a warning about the dangers of a "computer world" as it was a celebration of the microtechnology that had brought computerization into people's everyday lives'.[43] From today's perspective, in the context of revelations surrounding British and US government surveillance operations, the dystopian mood of *Computerwelt* turns out to be chillingly prescient. After all, Kraftwerk not only correctly predicted the triumph of computer technology, they also envisaged the near-totalitarian control it would take over our lives and its immense potential to exert power over society.

---

43 Bussy, *Kraftwerk*, p. 114.

Arguably, such wariness towards instruments of social control can be attributed to the German experience of both the totalitarian regime under Hitler and the dictatorial system of the GDR. The disciplinarian reach of the Nazi apparatus and the East German secret police (*Stasi*) were strong enough already, but, as Kraftwerk perhaps sensed, the introduction of a computerized means of surveillance would give authorities even stronger powers to police the population.

In the late 1970s, the Bundeskriminalamt [Federal Crime Agency] introduced the new technique of *Rasterfahndung* [dragnet investigation] in order to identify the location of wanted terrorists in the Baader-Meinhof group. The public hysteria about terrorism at the time clearly abetted this innovative way of computer-aided database analysis.[44] Its success was rather limited but raised considerable unease amongst many due to the dystopian prospect of government agencies collecting and analysing the data of innocent citizens on a large scale. Accordingly, alongside other crime agencies and financial institutions, the Bundeskriminalamt is referenced by its acronym BKA on 'Computerwelt':

> Interpol und Deutsche Bank
> FBI und Scotland Yard
> Finanzamt und das BKA
> Haben unsre Daten da
>
> [Interpol and Deutsche Bank,
> FBI and Scotland Yard
> Inland Revenue and BKA
> Have our data available][45]

Uncharacteristically, in promotional interviews for the album, Hütter explicitly spelled out Kraftwerk's political stance on the matter:

> By making transparent certain structures and bringing them to the forefront – that is a technique of provocation. First you have to acknowledge where you stand and what is happening before you can change it. I think we make things transparent, and with this transparency reactionary structures must fall.[46]

---

44 Flür reports that the apartment of Schneider had once been raided erroneously by antiterrorist police prior to his joining the band and that he himself was once falsely identified as a known terrorist and questioned by the police (see Flür, *Kraftwerk*, pp. 78–80).

45 The last two lines are missing in the English version of the text. The extent to which West Germans felt uneasy about state control over their personal data was vividly evidenced in 1987 by the massive protest against the national census.

46 Interview with Neil Rowland, *Melody Maker*, 4 July 1981.

Monroe emphasizes the dystopian quality of the apparently innocuous 'Nummern' ['Numbers'], with its obsessively repeated numeric sequences: 'In our present context, the track brings to mind the massively disruptive automated trades and high speed money transfers that accelerate and proliferate as austerity degrades the offline life conditions of entire continents.'[47] By replacing words with numbers (or strictly speaking: numerals), Kraftwerk arguably anticipated (at least in part) that a merciless flow of numeric data would increasingly replace traditional communication and cultural exchange based on words and literacy. With *Computerwelt*, Kraftwerk not only displayed a remarkable degree of foresight in predicting a world based on computer technology, but, crucially, they backed this up with an uncompromising and serene musical vision of the emerging sound of the future: '"Nummern" was a [...] successful attempt to define a new sonic aesthetic, directly inspired by the then small flow of numerical data.'[48]

Compared to previous records, the now truly futuristic sound of *Computerwelt* was markedly brighter, cleaner and more clinical. In line with their self-styled image as music workers, audio engineers and sound researchers, Hütter explained to an interviewer: 'We aim to create a total sound, not to make music in the traditional sense with complex harmony. A minimalistic approach is more important for us. We spend a month on the sound and five minutes on the chord changes.'[49]

This painstaking work produced truly ground-breaking music, the repercussions and resonances of which would also be heard across the Atlantic. The centrepiece of the album in this respect was 'Nummern'. It 'is a striking work, not only in the general context of Kraftwerk's output, but also because it seems so different and more experimental than the other tracks'[50] on *Computerwelt*. 'Nummern' represents a radical exercise in reduction, making it a minimalistic, almost brutal piece of music. The relentless drum pattern, written by Bartos, made this pivotal track more typical of techno than pop. The beat pattern from 'Nummern' and the melody from 'Trans Europa Express' formed the sampled backbone of 'Planet Rock' by Afrika Bambaataa and Soulsonic Force in 1982. From the black ghettos of New York (albeit with the help of white producer Arthur Baker), this song spawned the electro genre and was striking evidence of the

---

47 Alexei Monroe, paper given at Electri_City Conference, Düsseldorf, 29 October 2015.

48 Monroe, Düsseldorf, 29 October 2015.

49 Quoted in Buckley, *Kraftwerk*, p. 169.

50 Joseph Toltz, '"Dragged into the Dance": The role of Kraftwerk in the Development of Electro-Funk', in *Kraftwerk*, ed. by Albiez and Pattie, pp. 181–193 (p. 185).

keen reception the machine music from Düsseldorf received amongst black communities in the USA.[51]

Kraftwerk's music clearly provided a crucial contribution to the development of electronic dance music styles such as house and techno. Particularly in Afro-futurist works, Kraftwerk's retro-futurist aesthetic offered unexpected synergies with artists like the Detroit production duo Drexciya or the Underground Resistance collective, with the latter paying emphatic homage to the music from Düsseldorf later on with the track 'Afrogermanic' from 1998.

Techno Pop / Electric Cafe (1986) & The Mix (1991)

Over the course of the decade following *Computerwelt*, Kraftwerk only released two albums as their musical lead over their competitors waned. This decline in productivity can be attributed to various factors. Bartos and Flür had left out of frustration with Schneider and Hütter's preoccupation with cycling rather than making new music. Years were devoted to the painstaking digitalization of the back catalogue from *Autobahn* onwards, a time-consuming work mostly undertaken by their studio technician Fritz Hilpert. Whilst cycling, Hütter also suffered serious head injuries which further delayed the release of the follow-up to *Computerwelt*.

Eventually released in November 1986, *Electric Cafe* was the first album since *Autobahn* not to feature a coherent theme or overarching concept and also the first album to be recorded digitally. Its working title, *Techno Pop*, was changed to *Electric Cafe* (but restored again to *Techno Pop* upon its re-release in 2009). 'Sex Objekt' ['Sex Object'] represents a rare thematic excursion into typical pop music subjects, while 'Der Telefonanruf' ['The Telephone Call'] became the only song released sung by Karl Bartos. On 'Electric Cafe', the erstwhile title song, Buckley commented that 'its unmemorable melody is disappointingly derivative of "Trans Europa Express"'.[52] Although *Techno Pop* is indeed Kraftwerk's least adventurous studio album, it is still inventive and the addition in 2009 of the remix 'House Call', a sort of technofied version of 'Telefonanruf', further increased its quality.

Its centrepiece, however, is the suite of three tracks which open the album. The minimalistic 'Boing Boom Tschak' consists of three onomatopoetic words

---

51 For an in-depth discussion see Toltz, 'Dragged into the Dance.'
52 Buckley, *Kraftwerk*, p. 213.

borrowed from comic strips (with 'peng', 'zong' and 'tsss' being occasionally thrown into the mix). It leads seamlessly into 'Techno Pop' whose multi-lingual lyrics deliver, as it were, a proud summary of Kraftwerk's landmark achievements in electronic music:

> Musique non stop, techno pop
> Elektroklänge überall
> Dezibel in Ultraschall
> Es wird immer weitergeh'n
> Musik als Träger von Ideen
> Techno pop
> La musica ideas portara
> Y siempre continuara
> Sonido electronic
> Decibel sintetico
> Synthetic electronic sounds
> Industrial rhythms all around

> [Music non stop, techno pop
> Electronic sounds all around
> Decibel in ultrasonics
> It will always go on from here
> Music, the carrier of ideas
> Techno pop
> Music is the carrier of ideas
> And will always carry on
> Electronic sounds
> Artificial decibel
> Synthetic electronic sounds
> Industrial rhythms all around]

'Techno Pop' then segues into 'Musique non stop', which varies the rhythm of the preceding track, endlessly repeating the lines 'musique non stop' and 'techno pop'. As Stubbs dryly summarizes: 'Kraftwerk's work was done. The electrification of pop music was complete.'[53]

With *The Mix* in 1991, Kraftwerk aimed to update highlights from their back catalogue for the rave generation. This compilation of the band's popular favourites showcased the sonic improvements and new possibilities which resulted from their incorporation of digital studio technology. According to Bussy, 'it is important to make the distinction that *The Mix* was not merely an exercise in re-

---

53 Stubbs, *Future Days*, p. 196.

mixing, hence the title wasn't "The Remix", but the tracks were digitally reconstructed using sampled elements of the originals.'[54]

The songs were not just reworked with 'a bright if thin new digital sound',[55] but, importantly, both new musical material and new vocals were added. Such experimentation showed that Hütter and Schneider regarded Kraftwerk's music to be very much a work in progress and pre-empted the constant live reworking of their music during the band's many concerts since 2009. The most notable change, however, was that 'Radio-Aktivität' now featured as 'Radioactivity' and was preceded by a list of places associated with nuclear disasters, adding the word 'stop' to remove the ambivalence of the original track.

Tour de France Soundtracks (2003)

The first musical evidence of the cycling obsession which gripped Hütter and Schneider during the early 1980s was the *Tour de France* single released in June 1983. It was not included on *Techno Pop* but reappeared in various versions and (re)mixes between 1984 and 1999. A completely new recording, though, was made for Kraftwerk's surprise return in 2003 with the release of *Tour de France Soundtracks*, their first new studio album in 17 years. Indeed, the only release between *Techno Pop* and *Tour de France Soundtracks* was the 1999 *Expo2000* EP written for the 2000 World Fair in Hanover. Similarly, *Tour de France Soundtracks* was meant to celebrate the centenary of the famous cycling race, but the release date missed the actual anniversary.

Whilst the album continues the theme of travel heard in *Autobahn* and *Trans Europa Express*, the focus on the bicycle seems odd at first glance due to its low technological complexity in comparison to cars and trains. However, apart from the biographical connection, according to Hütter, the bike can also act as an instrument:

> The bicycle is already a musical instrument on its own. The noise of the bicycle chain and pedal and gear mechanism, for example, the breathing of the cyclist, we have incorporated all this in the Kraftwerk sound, injecting the natural sounds into the computers in the studio.[56]

---

54 Bussy, *Kraftwerk*, p. 155.
55 Buckley, *Kraftwerk*, p. 233.
56 Quoted in Bussy, *Kraftwerk*, p. 125.

The incorporation of sounds produced by technological objects in a song, such as rhythmic clanking of train wheels on steel tracks, enables Kraftwerk to redefine everyday noise as music, but also manages to create a sense of velocity and pushing forward. Significantly, *Tour de France Soundtracks* also adds sounds of the human body. Hütter explains: 'We took the results of medical tests I had had over a couple of years, heartbeat recordings, pulse frequencies, lung volumes, and used those on the album. [...] It's percussive and dynamic.'[57]

Not only does the title track incorporate the sounds of a cyclist gasping for oxygen, but the beginning of 'Elektro Kardiogramm' also includes the sound of deep breathing alongside a bass beat which mimics the beating of a human heart. The track's minimalistic lyrics – 'Elektrokardiogramm / Minimum-maximum / Beats per minute' – suggest a connection between the tempo of electronic dance music and the beat of a human heart (which creates small electrical impulses that can be made audible with a machine). Connected with this somatic theme is 'Vitamin', one of Kraftwerk's best songs musically. Lyrically, it just runs down a list of food supplements thought to increase health and physical performance. Like other tracks on the album, this song can serve as a paradigm for achieving maximum aesthetic gain via minimum artistic means. Tellingly, this formula was later adopted as the title of the *Minimum-Maximum* live album that appeared in 2005.

To complement the songs featuring English and German lyrics, the album also includes a group of songs sung entirely in French. These tracks deal with the overall culture, techniques and other aspects of professional cycling such as 'Aéro Dynamik', 'La forme' or 'Titanium' (the corrosion-resistant material commonly used in the manufacturing of bicycle components). The album is also framed by tracks derived from the original 'Tour de France' single. Following the short opener 'Prologue', there is the central trio 'Tour de France Étape 1–3', which segues into the instrumental 'Chrono'. This collection, which lasts close to 20 minutes, is dominated by a soundworld echoing developments in house, ambient and trance music.

In the closing track, 'Tour de France', the unity of man and mechanics reflected in cycling represents yet another figuration of the man-machine concept. Or, as Hütter explains: 'Cycling is the man-machine. It's about always continuing straight ahead, forwards, no stopping.'[58] Though often unfairly underrated by critics, *Tour de France Soundtracks* accomplishes a conceptual coherence that links it with the great concept albums from the latter part of the 1970s. Interest-

---

57 Quoted in Buckley, *Kraftwerk*, p. 249.
58 Quoted in Buckley, *Kraftwerk*, p. 251.

ingly, it also turned out to be Kraftwerk's first and only number one record on the German album charts.

Der Katalog (2009)

The release of Kraftwerk's long-delayed retrospective *Der Katalog* [*The Catalogue*] box-set in October 2009[59] represented a major milestone in the history of the band for a number of reasons. Firstly, the digital remasters presented their music in much better sound quality with greater clarity and definition (though some aspects of the remastering work were also severely criticized).[60] Secondly, by compiling the eight albums from *Autobahn* to *Tour de France*, this also officially delineated the band's canon (marginalizing their first three albums).

Thirdly, the cover designs and overall visual character were overhauled and updated. This also included changes to titles (such as the renaming of *Electric Cafe* and the dropping of the word 'Soundtracks' from *Tour de France*). Overall, the visual presence of the musicians was reduced, allowing for even more minimalistic designs. The front design of the box set shows a highly stylized portrayal of four band members in a pixelated design evocative of 8-bit graphics. Similar anachronistic design is also used on the Kraftwerk website. Although constantly updated and furnished with simple flash-based games, its deliberate retro look and feel is a far cry from comparable band websites.

In most cases, the cover designs of the key albums contained in *Der Katalog* were fully overhauled: for *Autobahn*, the painting by Schult has been replaced with a blue German road sign and *Radio-Aktivität* now features a bright yellow cover with the trefoil symbol in bright red. While *Trans Europa Express* now displays the logo of the Trans Europ Express on a stylized white train against a black background, the photo of the four band members on *Mensch-Maschine* has been removed and only its constructivist typography remains against a plain red background. The colour scheme of the band's artwork was thereby reduced to a small palette of black and white alongside the primary colours red, yellow and blue. This greatly enhances the visual coherence of Kraftwerk's catalogue, giving it a thoroughly modern design. This in part sacrificed their earlier retro-futurist slant, but their later designs, from *Computerwelt* to *Tour de France*, have been been left untouched.

---

59 The box-set was originally scheduled for release in 2004 under the title *12345678*, marking the thirtieth anniversary of *Autobahn*.

60 This particularly regards the albums *Computerwelt* and *Techno Pop*, see 'Kraftwerk: a remastered retrospective', *5:4* (http://5against4.com/2009/11/08/kraftwerk-a-remastered-retrospective).

Last but not least, *Der Katalog* also marked the final phase in Kraftwerk's development since Schneider had left the band in 2008, a move which left Hütter as the only remaining original member. In a symbolic break with the band's past, Hütter also moved the Kling Klang studio from its original location to its new premises in a business park outside Düsseldorf. No details were given regarding Schneider's decision to leave the band, although it was well-known that he was very uncomfortable with touring. In any case, it is noticeable that in the years which followed, Hütter revamped the stage show by introducing full 3D visuals to each song and took the band on extensive international tours. For eight evenings in April 2012, the band took up a high profile residency at the Museum of Modern Art in New York. This was the first of a number of *Katalog* retrospectives to be held at renowned art institutions such as the Tate Modern in London, the Sydney Opera House, the Kunstsammlung NRW in Düsseldorf, the Burgtheater in Vienna and the Neue Nationalgalerie in Berlin.

As far back as 1975, Schneider explained to *Rolling Stone:* 'Kraftwerk is not a band. It is a concept. We call it "die Mensch Maschine". [...] Kraftwerk is a vehicle for our ideas.'[61] Some forty years later, now under the sole guidance of Hütter, the Kraftwerk *Gesamtkunstwerk* based on the man-machine concept has been recognized as a major achievement of contemporary culture by the world of art. Accordingly, their updated 3D graphics were exhibited in a purely visual format in art galleries in both Munich and Berlin. Kraftwerk are hence undergoing a process of museumization that is exceptional for any music group, let alone one from Germany.

However, Kraftwerk's drive towards official acknowledgement and recognition as a cultural milestone should not be equated with artistic inertia. Whilst the very high standards of quality which Hütter (and Schneider) imposed on themselves had indeed resulted in little new original material being released since the classic period from 1974 to 1981, the 'definitive versions', as it were, which appear in *Der Katalog* did not mark an endpoint. Instead, they provided a stronger foundation for further development. Their oeuvre represents an 'open work' of art and the lack of new musical material was compensated for by varied efforts in visual design.

Playing extensive tours is a key aspect of Kraftwerk as a work in progress. The use of advanced technologies such as 3D projections and multichannel surround sound systems has made them an immersive concert experience unique in pop music. Moreover, live performances also enable the band to constantly present its music in different arrangements and new live mixes. This combination of

---

61 Quoted in Hagström, *Influenser, referenser och plagiat*, p. 115.

stage performance in futuristic costumes, live music in surround sound and 3D visuals marries art and technology, man and machine, to deliver both musical entertainment and intellectual pleasure.

Not only does Kraftwerk offer a sophisticated commentary on German cultural history through their retro-futuristic aesthetics, they also raise pressing questions about the future. In addition to provoking fans' curiosity about how Hütter will continue to unfold or advance the band's concept in the years to come, the band crucially invites us to reflect on how our societies will face a future that promises to be even more threatening than Kraftwerk's ambivalent projection of it. Future generations of post-human beings may well look back to their techno-optimist visions with benign nostalgia for the future envisaged when Kraftwerk began their remarkable career, a future that was, sadly, never realized.

Cyrus Shahan
Fehlfarben and German Punk: The Making of 'No Future'

'Geschichte wird gemacht' [History is being made], declared the singer of Fehl-farben, Peter Hein, in the 1980 song 'Ein Jahr (Es geht voran)' [One year (it's mov-ing forwards)].[1] What at first blush might read as another phrase in the tradition of self-aggrandizing rock lyrics asserting relevance or path-breaking production, Fehlfarben's entry into the practice of declaring historical significance is, rather, a crucial cipher for understanding the aesthetic and socio-political currents that constituted West German punk. The lyrical appraisal of history making for better times ahead illustrates a fundamental contradiction that underwrote German punk: both fly in the face of punk's anarchic mantra 'no future' and its desire to commit to the dustbin any value of time's forward march.

'No future', the infamous line from the Sex Pistols' song 'God Save The Queen', was the band's seminal response to the absolute lack of any hope for youth caught in the wake of Britain's crumbling post-war economy, and its res-onance highlights how the Sex Pistols' socio-aesthetic response to their present was not specific to the band. Rather, 'no future' channelled and gave voice to what Jon Savage has called the 'appalling frustration' of working-class kids of the 1970s.[2] Instead of a cure for boredom, punk songs and style sought to accel-erate Britain's downfall through 'cut-up form' and to accelerate 'no future' – in-cluding punk's own – through chaos.[3] And although the apocalyptic fantasies and fleeting materiality easily legible in punk textualities (songs, sartorial style and fanzines) clearly disavow temporal duration and aesthetically distance punks from hippies, it seems Fehlfarben's song about forgetting the perils of the present threatens to cleave punk to the utopic future fantasied by its archene-mies. When understood through the logic of punk as a subculture, however, Fehlfarben's lyrics make public how the mantra 'no future' put into action an aesthetic imaginary resolutely invested in rejecting the future promised by its present.

---

1 All references to 'German punk' throughout this essay are shorthand for West German punk.
2 Jon Savage, *England's Dreaming: Anarchy, Sex Pistols, Punk Rock and Beyond* (New York: St. Martin's Griffen, 2002), p. 114.
3 For more on UK punk's sartorial disruption, see Dick Hebdige, *Subculture: The Meaning of Style* (London: Methune, 1979).

DOI 10.1515/9783110425727-006

'No future' is a dystopic mantra because of its desire to sustain unsustainable contradictions and, as detailed below, it signals punk's unyielding investment in its past, present and future. This chapter unveils how the West German iteration of 'no future' was about performing – not resolving – the recurrent crises of politics, identity, history and violence that defined the Federal Republic in the late 1970s and early 1980s. While its subsumption into the mainstream indicates how punk's performances failed to stave off the affirmative culture of postwar Germany, its a-programmatic, decentralized and antagonistic factions illustrate punk's unique contribution not just to music history but also to socio-political history.

For just as Fehlfarben's making of history cannot be taken at face value, neither can the blatant failure of German punk dystopia once it had – circa 1983 – come to be represented by bands such as Die Ärzte and Nena, by bands trafficking in punk aesthetic performances and angst (social demise), but which were too choreographed and inauthentic in their postures. Punk's demise must be read as more than rock stars selling out and instead as a mirror and medium of social change, because the will to failure was sacrosanct: it was the realization of punk's unwavering strategy of ironic nihilism. To that end, this chapter frames punk ephemera as worthless but nevertheless producing powerful effects, it parses the traces of failure in punk's aesthetic products and translates the echoes of punks screaming in German to shed light on the unique critical purchase this spectral subcultural moment brings to broader understandings of the intersections of social transformation and sound subcultures.

Fehlfarben is a particularly effective axis to frame factions of West German punk because so many music journalists, scholars and punks bristle – to say the least – at the appellation 'punk' for the band. If we divorce performers and lyrics from the sound, then it is easy to locate Fehlfarben's two-tone, upbeat rhythms squarely within *Neue Deutsche Welle* [German New Wave] or NDW. That harsh contextual bracketing, though, would obscure the conditions of possibility for Fehlfarben to reconnoitre British ska for Düsseldorf, Germany, and the logic of Fehlfarben's sounds within the sonic genealogy of its band members' roles in the undisputedly-punk bands Charley's Girls, Mittagspause [Lunch Break] and S.Y.P.H.[4] Most problematically, periodization contributes to the treatment of punk as a genre rather than a socio-political subculture.[5] Obviously, musical

---

4 Of course, my appellation 'British ska' itself elides the colonialist present that made it possible for middle class white Britons to make such music.

5 Punk music, as Mittagspause member Gabi Delgado frames it, was one way to avoid fruitlessly choosing a side in the battle in and over culture witnessed in the early 1960s and 1970s. Instead, punk music consisted of 'songs, [...] various tracks, that one could turn on and off' as an escape

genres differ and periodization aids the understanding and organization of music history, but this chapter eschews such a framing to rather parse punk as structure of feeling – the way its aesthetics confronted 'objective' social reality – as witnessed in the lived moment of punk subcultures.[6]

I therefore argue that punk's contradictions made it possible for the subculture to advocate a politics of 'no future'. Its politics denied the possibility of future human prosperity because the affirmative and authoritarian present of the Federal Republic was in punks' eyes merely the Fascist past in new clothes. German punk was neither a mere imitation of its Anglo forefathers nor a facile opposition to its domestic predecessors such as Krautrock or the chimeric bogeyman hippie music.

To illustrate that, this chapter examines violence, fantasies and social construction to illustrate the twin pillars of punk's cunning inner-logic: no future and failure. The former is the most fundamental means by which to delineate UK and German punk, because for early punk bands such as Male and Mittagspause, the mantra 'no future' represented not a rejection of the legacies of British class stratification (as it did for UK punk), but a rejection of the legacies of German fascism. Against the continuation of what they saw as an endless chain of failed interventions into the present, German punk's no future was no antidote to the utopian fantasies of hippie culture, but a unique and disingenuous position signalling punk's will to failure.

Punk's position in the well-known historical teleology of the current Berlin Republic is crucial because punk envisioned itself a bulwark to that very narrative. If the canonical waypoints leading to reunification can be marked as the 'zero hour' of German historical consciousness after 1945, the rejections of this silence by post-war generations (*Halbstarke*[7] and hippies), student revolutions

---

from dead-end binaries of social intervention. See Jürgen Teipel, *Verschwende deine Jugend: Ein Doku-Roman über den deutschen Punk und New Wave* (Frankfurt: Suhrkamp, 2001) p. 292.

6 While it can ease discussions – and for record labels, marketing – to cast genres as concrete entities in toto, natural differences of opinion amongst fans and journalists/academics and the documented description of bands' members ensure that any confidence in the definitions of a genre is suspect. As such, this essay paints contradictions in punk's present as fundamental to the numerous iterations of post-punk and the transformation of the forward-looking logic of 'no future'. While his definitions verge close to clear delineations of genres, Simon Reynolds offers a similar argument against ossified conceptions of genre. See *Rip It Up and Start Again: Postpunk 1978 – 1984* (New York: Penguin, 2006).

7 The *Halbstarken* – typically rendered in English as hooligans – denotes the groups of working-class kids in the mid-1950s who emerged in the wake of World War II and modeled their stylization from American 'rebel' films such as *The Wild One*, *Rebel Without a Cause*, *Blackboard Jungle*, and *Rock Around the Clock*. True to the image of 'outsiders' such as James Dean and Marlon

circa 1968 and the violent insurrection of domestic terrorism, then this chapter shows how German punk's own fantasies of social action sought to block for-ward-marching time and a resurgent, militarized and powerful German state. Rather than merely another waypoint in that canonical trajectory of post-war German history, punk's moment therein vehemently resisted neat periodization precisely because it stole from previous failures and it sought to end the hegem-ony of a better tomorrow as witnessed by the ironic lyrics in Fehlfarben's song.

Through sounds and bands sometimes in sync and sometimes out of sync with the stereotype of punk as a genre, I consider the lived moments of bands by articulating their lyrics, aesthetics and performances within the politics of their present rather than merely as a reaction to the sounds of their past. To un-veil one anecdotal marker of punk's spatial and temporal wryness that does just that, witness Peter Hein's assertion about the lifespan of German punk. For the singer of the punk bands Mittagspause, Male and Fehlfarben, punk was 'summer 1977 to summer 1978, in one city, on one street, in one bar'.[8] Certainly, Düssel-dorf's Ratinger Hof, the bar Hein has in mind, was fundamental for a particular faction of West German punk.

It is equally certain that punks such such as Blixa Bargeld in the metropolis of Berlin and Rocko Schamoni in the hamlet of Lütjenburg would beg to differ with Hein's geographical and temporal limits. But the following is not to be some kind of tête-à-tête betwen record store employees on the 'real' timeframe for, or representatives of, a musical genre witnessed in Nick Hornby's novel *High Fidelity* (1995). For the rise of post-punk circa 1979, the constitution and re-constitution of countless punk bands into the 1980s, the wealth of punk fanzines produced after 1978 or the band S.Y.P.H.'s 1980 recording of 'Zurück zum Beton [Back to Concrete] – a quintessential song of German punk – all testify to the ab-surdity of Hein's claim. But that absurdity is simultaneously its absolute punk quality of acting and feeling: the ironic rejection of its accepted present in an at-tempt to stave off duration, co-option and facile understanding. That is what makes punk such a rich query. Through internal fracturing and ironic nihilism, punk sought in its own time to complicate general understandings of Germany's present and past, its affective apprehensions and its threads of violence.

Brando, *Halbstarke* wore Levis jeans, T-shirts, greased hair, and performed auto repair. For a thorough reading of the *Halbstarken*, see Uta Poiger, *Jazz, Rock, and Rebels: Cold War Politics and American Culture in a Divided Germany* (Berkeley: University of California Press, 2000).
8 Peter Hein, 'Alles ganz Einfach', in *Zurück zum Beton: Die Anfänge von Punk und New Wave in Deutschland 1977–'82: Kunsthalle Düsseldorf, 7. Juli–15. September 2002*, ed. by Ulrike Groos and Peter Gorschlüter (Cologne: König, 2002), pp. 131–134 (p.131).

To understand the aesthetic strategy punk used to engage its present by inverting practices of violence and the rhetoric of social progress, one must consider Germany's historical avant-gardes and their use of shock. German punk again distinguishes itself from its UK and US predecessors, precisely through its explicit engagement with theories and traditions of historical avant-gardes, aesthetic moments that operated at the intersection of socio-political unrest and violence, albeit in conjuncture with a hot war – World War I – rather than a cold one. The presentness of violence notwithstanding, Dada and Futurism in Germany reckoned with the theretofore unseen horrors of modern warfare, an instance of industrialization that, for practitioners of the avant-garde, unveiled any promise of the Enlightenment and its rhetoric of progress as a lie.

After 1977, once theory (university students circa 1968) and violence (domestic left-wing terrorism) failed to bring forth any believable national reckoning with a National Socialist past and present, punks from Düsseldorf, Munich, Hamburg and West Berlin fused their rejection of the present and the future it assured to the practices of historical avant-gardes by channelling dada and cultural theorists such as Walter Benjamin. In 1980, Gabi Delgado, a member of the bands Mittagspause and Deutsch-Amerikanische Freundschaft (DAF, a play on the Deutsche Arbeitsfront[9]), linked punk's aesthetic quest for anarchy to Dada, specifically to 'that revolutionary element: We are going to do something really different and blow up society with it. Or at least shock it.'[10]

Three years later, Blixa Bargeld of Einstürzende Neubauten quoted Benjamin when framing punk's anarchistic tendencies. 'When someone tells us that we are destructive', Bargeld asserted, 'then that is something positive for me: "The destructive character [...] does not know what it wants, but rather only, that everything that is, it does not want."'[11] Beyond testifying to punk's indebtedness to aesthetic practices of avant-gardes, Delgado and Bargeld's aesthetic genealogies demonstrate the willed self-destructive and fractal nature of any geographic, temporal or sonic iteration of punk.[12]

---

9 The Deutsche Arbeitsfront was the Nazi association for workers and employers. DAF also toys with the East German state organization Gesellschaft für Deustch-Sowjetsiche Freundschaft (Society for German-Soviet Friendship), which fostered, or rather enforced, friendship between the GDR and the USSR.

10 Teipel, *Verschwende deine Jugend*, pp. 78–79.

11 Bargeld, *Stimme frisst Feuer* (Berlin: Merve, 1988), p. 106.

12 Although it differs significantly from my argument on German punk because it focuses on band managers and not members, Greil Marcus' *Lipstick Traces* links British punk to avant-gardes, specifically through the person Malcom McLaren. As manager of the Sex Pistols, McLaren made flyers for the Sex Pistols that mimed Situationist International flyers (of which McLaren was a member). Marcus uses this evidence to correlate punk style with Guy Debord's 'dé-

As the next section illustrates through a sampling of punk album covers and lyrics, the disquiet incited by punk performances reveals the uncanny normalization of violence in the post-war period. The framing of punk through the avant-garde signals how the making of 'no future' was inseparable from – and illogical without – an absolute engagement with the future punk feared.

The Aesthetics of Violence

The making of 'no future', just like the making of the present Berlin Republic, cannot be separated from the history of post-war violence in West Germany. This chapter is not the space to detail that narrative, but two moments are absolutely necessary for deciphering punk's aesthetic insurrection: the intersection of state violence and non-violence in the student protests in the 1960s, and the intersection of state violence and non-state violence in the 1970s, the age of German domestic terrorism. As is well documented in primary materials, critical readings and cinematic re-imaginings, the 1960s in the Federal Republic, as in countries around the globe, saw violent clashes between university students and various markers of (US) capitalist imperialism, from the Federal Republic's support for the Shah of Iran to Siemens and IG Farben's restitutions to the sham of denazification.[13]

In Germany these conflicts happened under the spectre of a recently remilitarized Germany that remained a US and British proxy in those nations' attempts to halt the forward march of the Soviet Union.[14] To many students, the Federal Republic chose remilitarization over adequate social reckoning with the National Socialist past, political silence over the persecution of war criminals and corporate subsidies over socio-economic equality. On the micro level, the first post-war generation found the silence vis-à-vis the past in their homes paradigmatic for the rebuilding nation. Despite (or perhaps because of) its utopic fantasies, the

---

tournement', the theft of aesthetic artefacts from their contexts and their diversion into contexts of one's own devise. See Greil Marcus, *Lipstick Traces: A Secret History of the Twentieth Century* (Cambridge, MA: Harvard University Press, 1989).

13 Jermey Varon provides an excellent comparative reading of West Germany's Red Army Faction and the USA's Weather Underground. See *Bringing the War Home: The Weather Underground, the Red Army Faction, and Revolutionary Violence in the 1960s and 1970s* (Berkeley: University of California Press, 2004).

14 Clearly, France's occupation of West Germany is omitted here. However, the French zone was perhaps more dominated by American culture than French. It is a historical fact that, by 1951, 750,000 American troops were stationed in the German state of Rhineland-Palatinate, which was originally part of the French occupation zone.

academic epicentre of the student movement foreclosed the possibility, for some, of effecting real change. Though the intent was to put theory into action, the students' use of Critical Theory[15] and the Marxist-Leninist theories of Mao Zedong ultimately alienated swaths of the population, including future terrorists who saw students stuck in a quagmire of debate.

The members of what would come to be interchangeably called the Baader-Meinhof Gang and the Red Army Faction (RAF) tired of what they saw as ineffective discussion and marching and instead chose a language they felt the Federal Republic would understand: that of the gun. If student protests only resulted in police violence and, infamously, in the death of innocent bystanders,[16] if German politicians were comfortable aiding the United States' bombing campaign in Vietnam, Laos and Cambodia, if former National Socialists continued to retain positions of social and economic power,[17] then bombs had to supplant theory as the vector of social change for youth in Germany. In addition, punk was born in West Germany concurrently with the highly suspect simultaneous suicides of jailed terrorists Gudrun Ensslin, Jan-Carl Raspe and Andreas Baader in 1977.[18]

Punk was not immune to the threads of violence that produced it, but it was unconcerned about radically distancing itself from the dialectic of state or citizens' violence. Instead, it chose a position that took advantage of all available positions, the music, images and texts punks produced narrate a subculture aiming to radically disrupt the rhetoric of progress, social change and national stability. Prior to the sounds under investigation in this chapter, the shifting and often contradictory radio broadcasts heard on the airwaves of an occupied nation narrate temporal, geographical, political and (inter)national tensions and crosspollinations.

As previous chapters on the *Schlager* and Krautrock in this collection have shown, the music soundscapes of West Germany are inextricable from the logic of American, British and French occupation, a quiet kind of violence

---

15 By 'Critical Theory' I refer exclusively to the work coming out of the Institute for Social Research (aka the Frankfurt School) at the University of Frankfurt. Theodor Adorno was the erstwhile theoretical lighthouse for many students, a role that Herbert Marcuse would come to inherit.

16 Here I refer to the infamous murder of protest bystander Benno Ohnesorg by policeman Karl-Heinz Kurras on 2 June 1967. Ohnesorg's murder would catalyse German domestic terrorists to action and give the group Bewegung 2. Juni (Movement 2 July) its name.

17 See, for example, the persons Chancellor Kurt Georg Kiesinger, Siegfried Buback, Hanns-Martin Schleyer or industries such as BASF, Siemens, Bayer, Krupp, etc.

18 For one account of the deaths of Ensslin, Raspe and Baader, see Stefan Aust, *The Baader-Meinhof Group: The Inside Story of a Phenomenon* (London: Bodley Head, 1987).

done to German culture in the name of post-war rebuilding. Just as those sounds were, punk in Germany is inseparable from the contradictory rhythms and lyrics of the British rock that John Peel broadcast in northern Germany and the American country music that dominated in southern Germany. By contrast, however, punk never envisioned itself as a solution to the tensions the Allies' nationbuilding created among working class youth (as was the case with the *Halbstarke*)[19] or as a corrective to the affirmative image of the *Schlager* (as was the case with Krautrock). In the wake of the mainstreaming of the *Halbstarke* style or the commercial successes of Krautrock and the concomitant distancing of performer and fan, punk insinuated itself into the late 1970s' cultural landscape as an escape from the endless cycles of protest, resistance and affirmation.

What that subculture saw as an absolute deadening of progress is crystallized in the 1979 song 'Testbild' [Test Screen] by the band Mittagspause. Through screeches, feedback and lyrics that narrate only the circadian broadcast of a test screen, the song pulls back the curtain on incendiary presses and media in their present and nowhere mentions the saturation of violence and rhetoric of national security. Three years later, the band made abundantly clear their awareness of simplified signs and signifiers as paradigmatic for the continuing media and public hysteria that buttressed the mainstream inability to grasp the socio-historical logic of German domestic terrorism. With an album cover featuring their *détournement* of the RAF-star – the Mittagspause logo is a machine gun in front of a coffee canister with a circle around it – the band makes clear that, (years) after the ostensible defeat of the Red Army Faction at the hands of the Federal Republic and its Emergency Laws curtailing public freedoms, West Germany was still preoccupied with the legacies of internal violence. Mittagspause was not alone in thinking this.

The album *Viel Feind, viel Ehr* [Lots of Enemies, Lots of Honour] by S.Y.P.H. sonically and visually broadcasts the belatedness, intersections and misuses of state-sponsored violence and violence 'from below'. The album's cover consisted of what seems to be innocuous enough pictures: a baby carriage and a young man wearing sunglasses carrying a camera. But S.Y.P.H.'s album was just as provocative as Mittagspause's playful version of the RAF-star because the photo of the baby carriage was from the kidnapping of leading industrialist and erstwhile

---

19 As Uta Poiger argues, flying in the face of the Federal Republic's attempts to normalize its post-war society, 'West German authorities, if they imagined a society devoid of class hierarchies, certainly did not want to see it symbolized by' the working class, because a contented labour-force was the foundation for the 'Economic Miracle' of the 1950s. Poiger, *Jazz, Rock, and Rebels*, p. 82.

SS member Hanns-Martin Schleyer by the RAF in 1977 and the young man was second-generation RAF-terrorist Christian Klar.

Both images were widely recognizable to German citizens because the band lifted the photos from the mainstream weekly *Stern*. With their 1979 song 'klammheimlich' [clandestine] on *Viel Feind, viel Ehr*, S.Y.P.H. completes the picture of organized chaos that punk sent forth into the afterglow of the German Autumn.[20] This song consists of three parts – newscasts of terrorist actions sampled from the evening news broadcasts, sequencer distortion and the lyrical coordinates 'stammheim / eigenheim / heldentum / eigentum' [stammheim / home / heroism / possession]– and traffics in the very kind of media broadcasts heard in 'Testbild'.

The wordplay in the German-language original, including its disavowal of standard German rules for the capitalization of nouns, is significant and absent in translation. The lyrics – 'stammheim / eigenheim / heldentum / eigentum' – are rhetorically parallel and rhyme, which increases the slipperiness between Stammheim, the maximum security prison outside Stuttgart built specifically to house Baader-Meinhof terrorists and 'Eigenheim', one's own property. Furthermore, the idea of ownership in 'Eigentum' traffics syntactically with the front of 'Eigenheim' and end of 'Heldentum', but also philosophically with the Marxist critique of consumerism, imaginary ownership of consumer goods and value in the prefix 'eigen' (own). These two songs make audible how in punk's hands, the incendiary becomes the banal, the news becomes the droning background noise of nothingness, the bystander becomes the suspect and the state becomes the maniac.

Through the absolute lack of sensationalism in either song, punk music turns what political theorist Hannah Arendt in 1963 called the 'banality of evil' in her report on the trial of the Nazi bureaucrat Adolf Eichmann into an indictment of the state: the Federal Republic had perfected the banality of violence.[21] These album covers and lyrics make clear how punk saw its present differently, not as a landscape of a state seeking to organize itself and re-enter the global society or as various factions of (student then terrorist) youth pushing

---

20 'German Autumn' is the term given to the culmination of the Baader-Meinhof group terrorist activities in late 1977. Since the early 1970s, the West German state found itself at odds with domestic terrorism in the form of the Red Army Faction, its subsequent iterations and numerous other splinter groups. For more on German punk and German domestic terrorism, see Cyrus Shahan, 'The Sounds of Terror: Punk, Post-Punk and the RAF After 1977', *Popular Music and Society* 34/3 (2011), 369–386.

21 As such, there is a tacit indictment of the proto-fascist tendencies of which Baader-Meinhof was accused in punk's operational logic.

against their father's generations, but rather as the complete failure of their contemporaries to offer any kind of viable solution for the past and future in the
present.

The sounds of violence and the national news reports on that violence are
audible in punk music and fanzines also took up a position on the border between actual violence and mundane production. These publications were independent, low-budget magazines not to be confused with music journalism or
mere information for fans by fans. Fanzines – as with underground cassette ex-
changes that transferred music north and south[22] – signal a punk investment in
literary production that, like punk's chaotic sounds and images, made journalism militant, aggressive and anarchistic. By turning literature into the unforesee-
able and unsustainable through the aesthetics of collage and detritus, and by
using underground networks of recording, publishing and distribution, fanzines
were part of punk rock's political intervention.

Although punks did not confuse their fleeting publications with a solution to
the dead end trap of violence and counter-violence, the flotsam and jetsam pil-
fered for the fanzines, the juxtaposition of images and the assembly itself formed
a triptych that made visual the violence punks channelled. Whereas hippies' fantasies of utopic peace and terrorists' deployment of counter-violence against violence are easily understood as inverted strategies, punk's aesthetic violence in
fanzines turned inward while broadcasting the quagmire engendered by the violence binary.[23]

No longer seeking to fill gun barrels with daisies or car trunks with explo-
sives, punk fanzines turned to razor blades and safety pins to channel and con-
join the violence of the previous two decades. The turn to weapons whose potential for real violence is laughable in the face of the militaristic options chosen by
the state or terrorists is, as was Hein's bracketing of punk to one year in Düsseldorf, an ironic gesture intent on unveiling itself as disingenuous and dilettantic:
it promised only failure. Just as punk's sartorial style made the quotidian abject
its object of choice (safety pins, garbage bags, tattered clothes and all kinds of
vile things smeared in one's hair), fanzines pair images and reconstituted headlines from mainstream weeklies to unveil their understood truth of the late 1970s

---

22 For more on cassette exchange in the Federal Republic, see Frank Apunkt Schneider, *Als die
Welt noch unterging: Von Punk zu NDW* (Mainz: Ventil, 2006).
23 It is in no way intimated here that punk's fanzines were the first instance of literary-aesthetic
violence, only that its synchronicity with the subculture as a whole differentiates punk fanzines
from, for example, the flyers made by the various avant-gardists, or even, to keep it in a German
context, from pre-punk Rolf Dieter Brinkmann's collages. See for example Brinkmann's *Schnitte*
(Reinbek: Rowohlt, 1988) or *Westwärts 1 & 2* (Reinbek: Rowohlt, 1975).

and early 1980s.[24] Because the binary of violence had normalized modes of resistance, and because it blunted people's feelings and actions in response to violence, punk declared that the only alternative left – as various fanzines illustrate – was the absurd, and thus they juxtaposed Adolf Hitler with Blondie, Siouxsie Sioux with the fascist rhetoric 'Germany awake', or the RAF, Clark Kent and Vietcong with SS-officers.

Ralf Dörper, the author of S.Y.P.H.'s lyrical montage in 'klammheimlich', conjured for the cover of his fanzine *Die Düsseldorfer Leere* [The Düsseldorf Void] the latter schizophrenic list of 'personal friends'.[25] However, just as his four choice words in 'klammheimlich' use keywords from nightly news headlines to blow up the sanctimonious comfort they were meant to instil in the general public through their 'clear' binaries, his fanzine cover of a 'void' makes visual the incendiary and antagonizing monikers adopted by punks.

Gudrun Gut, Harry Rag or Robert Görl's[26] band DAF, and song titles such as Mittagspause's 'Herrenreiter' (the word equates to 'gentleman rider' in English and refers to Hitler's vice chancellor Franz von Papen) were punks' absurd and aggressive riposte to the violence structuring the Federal Republic.[27] Together, album covers, song texts, punk's names and Dörper's fanzine catalogue the obliquely subversive nomenclature that punk misused in its attempt to unmake their present.

(Middle Class) Fantasy

Another band, bearing the English name Middle Class Fantasies, embodied an aspect of punk and many subcultures across the globe: A large quotient of punks were indeed middle class youths who were predominantly male and white. Such a demographic fact led – and leads – easily to the critique that those who protest (students, terrorists or punks) are precisely those who can afford to do so. This privilege was used to indict students in the late 1960s, whose institutional base and lack of connection to the working class undermined their

---

24 For the seminal reading of punk semiotics, see Dick Hebdige, *Subculture: The Meaning of Style* (London: Methuen, 1979).

25 For images of fanzines, see Ulrike Groos and Peter Gorschlüter, *Zurück zum Beton: Die Anfänge von Punk und New Wave in Deutschland 1977 – 82: Kunsthalle Düsseldorf, 7. Juli–15. September 2002* (Cologne: König, 2002).

26 The first and third names could be translated as 'Be Good Gudrun' and 'Robert the Girl' (or perhaps, a toyed-with version of 'brat' [Görl]).

27 See Mittagspause, *Mittagspause* (1979) and Middle Class Fantasies, *Tradition* (1981).

anti-institutional aims, and also Baader-Meinhof, whose founding members were a failed artist, a pastor's daughter and an established journalist. Their real or presumed individual privilege notwithstanding, middle class youths with fantasies of resistance – even through rituals[28] – are indeed a force for social change, because the middle class is usually the locus of hegemonic consent.

In another doubled punk gesture of ironic nihilism and self-indictment, Middle Class Fantasies celebrated their own culpability in the unequal Economic Miracle of post-war rebuilding, the election of the socio-politically regressive Grand Coalition and consumption of the hysterical content of mainstream media such as the magazine *Stern* and the tabloid paper *Bild*, in order to then set their sights on post-war West German prosperity. For Middle Class Fantasies, reconstruction, economic success and remilitarization cannot be seen as anything other than a debauched party at the site of mass human extinction.

As Melanie Eis and Fabian Eckert argue, the song 'Party in der Gaskammer' [Party in the Gas Chamber] hyperbolizes the titular sadomasochistic narrative in order to insist 'on the guilt of the sadistic onlooker [and charge] the band and every listener as a potential perpetrator'.[29] Such self-indictment certainly targeted an older generation, but also indicted their own aesthetic strategies and questioned punk's staging of affect, violence and masculinity. DAF, as will be explained in more detail later, perfected the latter performance in conjunction with a scathing and unflinching critique of the inadequate reckoning with the Nazi past.

Like their British predecessors, West German punks used sartorial style to critique the gender norms parents foisted upon their children. Although it drew inspiration from masculine greasers who cried (James Dean and Marlon Brando), hippies who 'freed' the body and sex it also drew from Andreas Baader who enacted physical and sexual male violence, thus punk in the Federal Republic did not escape the heteronormative and male-centric vortex of rock 'n' roll. Although the presence of a few female-fronted, all-female bands and

---

28 Here I reference the canonical work on subcultures – *Resistance through Rituals* – that came out of the Centre for Contemporary Cultural Studies at the University of Birmingham, England. Subsequent publications from the CCCS, such as Dick Hebdige's *Subculture: The Meaning of Style* or its feminist corrective, Angela McRobbie's 'Settling Accounts with Subculture: A Feminist Critique', are indispensible for an analysis and understanding of the intricacies of subcultures and their work. See McRobbie's *Feminism and youth culture: from 'Jackie' to 'Just seventeen'* (Basingstoke: Macmillan, 1991).

29 See Melanie Eis and Fabian Eckert, '"1979 Deutschland": Holocaust, West German Memory Culture, and Punk's Intervention into the Everyday', in *Beyond No Future: Cultures of German Punk*, ed. by Mirko M. Hall, Seth Howes and Cyrus M. Shahan (New York and London: Bloomsbury, 2016), forthcoming.

women such as Carmen Knoebel (owner of Düsseldorf's Ratinger Hof) testify to momentary escapes from the historical male rock experience, the subculture, as existing material evidence testifies, remained overwhelmingly male.[30]

One important break within this trend of maleness is the band DAF, whose channelling of sadomasochism and National Socialism through homosexuality in their lyrics, album covers and performances were explosive amongst their fellow punks and within the very structures of power punk used to sow disquiet. Members Robert Görl and Gabi Delgado purposely pushed the kind of gender-bending initiated by McLaren and Vivian Westwood to a political extreme unavailable in the UK. In the Federal Republic, after all, the trafficking in pleasure and pain or in discipline and punishment was inextricable from the historical paring thereof in the aesthetics and practices of Weimar Germany and the Nazi SS. With songs titled 'Greif nach den Sternen' [Reach for the Stars], 'Der Mussolini' [The Mussolini] and 'Absolute Körperkontrolle' [Absolute Body Control], DAF was not using clever double entendre. Far from Dörper's slippery punk verse in 'klammheimlich', DAF forced their audiences to confront historical and contemporaneous fantasies about fascism via the fusion of sound and bodies.

Rather than declaring deceased or living fascists as their enemies, DAF's performance tried to out-fascist National Socialism and the Federal Republic with their embrace of the infamous lines from the well-known Hitler Youth anthem promising 'heute da hört uns Deutschland / Und morgen die ganze Welt'[31] [today, Germany listens to us / And tomorrow the whole world] in addition to the clean, hard, male bodies it prized.[32] No doubt because on consecutive albums they told young Germans 'euch gehört / die ganze Erde' [the whole world / belongs to you], implored them to 'tanz den Adolf Hitler / und jetzt den Mussolini' [dance the Adolf Hitler / and now the Mussolini] or because their leather pants on the cover for *Gold und Liebe* [Gold and Love] fuse Nazi

---

30 As a corrective to the male subculture narrative, see for example Lauraine Leblanc's *Pretty in Punk: Girls' Gender Resistance in a Boys' Subculture* (New Brunswick, NJ and London: Rutgers University Press, 1999). For a corrective on the whiteness of subcultures, see *White Riot: Punk Rock and the Politics of Race*, ed. by Stephen Duncombe and Maxwell Tremblay (London: Verso, 2011).

31 The lines belong to the chorus of 'Es zittern die morschen Knochen' [The rotten bones are trembling] by Hans Bauman.

32 See Klaus Theweleit, *Male Fantasies* (Minneapolis: University of Minnesota Press, 1987) or Alexander and Margarete Mitscherlich's ground-breaking study of German reckoning with the atrocities of the Nazi past in *Inability to Mourn: Principles of Collective Behavior* (New York: Grove Press, 1975).

jodhpurs with fetish clothing, their contemporary Peter Glaser remembers, 'all social pedagogues hit the roof because of DAF'.[33]

DAF fused punk, the desire to shock and bondage clothing with electronic instruments and dance in sounds that were seemingly incongruous with stereotypical punk songs. As such, it sought to make its antagonistic performances and aggressive sounds a 'trigger' able to blow up and shock the Federal Republic out of what Delgado described at the time as a neurotic, psychosexual bunker in the liner notes of *Gold und Liebe*. Through the brilliance of the 'DAF-machine', punk's dystopic fantasies drew unchained on the anti-humanist élan of a mechanized war machine and of middle class aspirations for a better Germany in its attempt to make 'no future', for a moment, reality.[34]

Bands such as Mania D and Malaria! (constituted by former members of Mania D) were anti-humanist in ways that seem anti-punk and produced aggressive, pulsing sounds that conjoined analogue and digital instruments that complicated classical definitions of punk as a genre. Whereas the name Middle Class Fantasies indicts the band as part of the hegemonic malaise then plaguing the Federal Republic, the name Mania D diagnoses the affect plaguing West Germany in the late 1970s and early 1980s to then use it as the impetus of their aesthetic intervention.

Stuck in the wake of failed subcultures and caught in the iron grip of the re-built nation-state, Mania D embraced the performance of psychological sickness as a punk mode of acting through feeling. Mania D's self-stylization is another practice drawn from the tradition of avant-gardists, such as Marinetti and his madhouse murderers of the moon's light, and fuses the vibrant colours of punk with heavy blacks and asymmetric hair, putting their aesthetic in a liminal space, one that clearly channels the kind of dramatic aesthetics of Robert Wiene's seminal expressionist movie *Das Kabinett des Dr. Caligari* [*The Cabinet of Dr. Caligari*], colour theories practiced by groups such as Bauhaus or De Stijl and the pop art drama of artists such as Martin Kippenberger.

Unsurprisingly, the complexity of their music reflects their deviation from mainstream and subcultural modes of acting and feeling.[35] The 1980 song 'Herzschlag' [Heartbeat], dominated by noise and distortion, slips into a happening music style with a wailing, sometimes droning saxophone and a blend of English and French lyrics. Certainly a gesture to the transnational seeds of jazz, punk, post-punk and the occupied landscape of the Federal Republic,

---

33 Teipel, *Verschwende deine Jugend*, pp. 304–307.
34 Ibid., p. 304.
35 In part due to their work in other bands such as Liaisons Dangereuses, Einstürzende Neubauten and Die Krupps.

'Herzschlag' really sets its sights on the slipperiness of punk as a subculture. As if a retort to the infamous titular misunderstanding of *Der Spiegel*'s 1978 issue 'Punk: Kultur aus den Slums: brutal und häßlich' [Punk: Culture from the Slums: Brutal and Ugly], singer Bettina Köster both mocks the mainstream weekly's quaint shock and demarks Mania D's disinterest in codifying punk.

In English rather than the native tongue typical of German punk, she screams 'You're punk rock? What the fuck is that? I don't know'.[36] The image of sickness and contagion that the band name calls forth is infolded into the categorization of the subculture itself, wielded against the stuffy parents, politicians and kids who need clear definitions to understand the world around them. Mania D unflinchingly indicts any static punk subcultural resistance as affirmative, a heartbeat that is ever-present and fundamental for the smooth functioning of the process it seeks to undermine. Between sickness and health, between keystone and periphery, Mania D and 'Herzschlag' are emblematic of the transnational qualities of punk and the Federal Republic.

The aesthetic problems Mania D causes fit into the avant-garde schooled faction of German punk, often subsumed under the umbrella group 'Geniale Dilletanten' [sic]. Insofar as this chapter pushes against strong cordoning off of genres, it is concurrently suggested that the 'Ingenious Dilletants' group was not the sole domain of art school punks,[37] but inherently punk as such – as a mode of thinking and feeling that, when put into action, resisted through rituals the persistent, authoritarian imperatives of affirmative culture and its mainstreaming of subcultural initiatives.[38] Members of Mania D trafficked with avant-garde artist Martin Kippenberger, members of Lou Reed's band and Jean-Michel Basquiat, so it is not surprising that they détourned beatnik happenings, harnessed Krautrock unevenness à la Can and the punk distortion of S.Y.P.H. Precisely the use of all available material – a mania of the band's own – cast Mania D as resistive to genre (punk, post-punk and no wave), an intention unmistakable in 'Herzschlag', a song that opposes the definition of a subculture and is a female rebuttal of the male arrogance of defining and delimiting punk rock. Malaria! continued the genre-bending fusion of jazz, sequencer, proto-EBM and dark wave punk sounds.

---

36 See the Mania D, *Track 4* (1980). *Spiegel*'s title represents a misunderstanding because punk was anything but 'culture from the slums'. It was overwhelmingly middle-class kids donning clothes who sought to refute their privilege.

37 Though some 'Ingenuous Dilletants' groups intentionally used aesthetic practices pioneered by Dada and Futurism, this was not the case for DAF and other bands under that umbrella.

38 See *Mainstream der Minderheiten: Pop in der Kontrollgesellschaft*, ed. by Mark Terkessidis and Tom Holert (Berlin: Edition ID-Archiv, 1996).

Above all, Malaria! advocates nonconformity and is relentless in advocating the need for subcultures to harness the flexibility that makes them – temporarily, of course – an effective agent of social resistance. As witnessed in 'Herzschlag', the 1982 song 'Your turn to run' is another instance of the band seeking to fracture the subculture itself. No doubt sensing contemporaneous commercial interests in German punk music, Malaria! confronts the spectre of selling out to the music industry, claiming 'I can't pay your price'.[39] While this moment of not selling out is, for the band, one of success, this song also signals a shift in punk practices since it points out that it is the mainstream's 'turn to run'. 'Your turn to run' is a transformation of acting and feeling that indeed could be chosen as another of punk's endings. Leaving it up to the listener to decide what price is too much – be it entry into a punk, new wave or male-dominated scene, or be it a prosperous German present – is Malaria!'s only chance to derail the suffocating normalization and levelling of its present.

Conclusion: Collapse, Americanism and New Cities

The 'Federal Republic of Germany' moniker that emerged after 1949 was meant to signal a unified nation and buttress the future-oriented ideology of teleological progress, reconciliation and prosperity. Punk's soundscapes belie that myth and concurrently testify to the flexible, aggressive and a-programmatic practices of punk well into the 1980s. The performances and sounds coming from Munich, Hamburg and Berlin by the bands Freiwillige Selbstkontrolle (FSK),[40] Palais Schaumburg and Einstürzende Neubauten are so radically different from one another that one would be hard pressed to associate them with the same subculture.

However, if punk, as this chapter has endeavoured to demonstrate, is understood as an aesthetic moment in the tradition of European avant-gardes that informs a mode of acting and feeling, as a subculture invested in taking up all

---

39 See the Malaria! 12' *New York Passage* (Das Büro, Büro 001, 1982).

40 Freiwillige Selbstkontrolle [Voluntary Self-Censorship], the name for Germany's equivalent to North America's parental advisory system for cinematic releases, was ironically appropriated by the band. As they famously defined it in their fanzine *Mode & Verzweiflung* [Fashion & Despair], 'Heute Disco, morgen Umsturz, übermorgen Landpartie. Dies nennen wir Freiwillige Selbstkontrolle' [today disco, tomorrow revolution, the day after tomorrow an outing to the country. This is what we call voluntary self-censorship]. See Thomas Meinecke, *Mode & Verzweiflung* (Frankfurt: Suhrkamp, 1998), p. 36.

available positions and as sounds that are purposively discordant with one another, then mere sonic differences cannot be the foundation for suggesting an absolute schism between stereotypical punk sounds and those that, like Mania D's, push back against a preconceived notion of what punk rock is. Freiwillige Selbstkontrolle was an important band of the 1980s and continues to make music and tour today. They were and are post-punk, but 'post' must not be confused with anti. It is, rather, something *of* and *within* punk.

Aggressively affirmative, alternatingly wry, overt and obscure, FSK's lyrics incensed subculture and mainstream alike. These lyrics, which were conjoined to sounds that range from wistful to cacophonic to cliché, told FSK's audiences that 'it doesn't get any better than right here, right now', demanded that their listeners make 'Ein Kind für Helmut' [A Child, for [Chancellor] Helmut [Kohl]][41] or reduced German domestic terrorism to 'In Mogadishu' and 'Gudrun E' (i.e., Baader-Meinhof terrorist Gudrun Ensslin). Their lyrical content thereby unmistakably continues the socio-political complaints of the 1960s and 1970s, but that continuation is punk to its core. FSK's content is ironic nihilism par excellence.

The salience of FSK's faux-praise for economic equality and the chancellor's crypto-fascist rhetoric of producing more German babies, and of their sly critique of the continued misunderstanding of the RAF, was confirmed in 1980 at FSK's second concert when a massive fight broke out between the punks in the audience over the apparently affirmative content of the band's songs.[42] That fight splendidly narrates punk's internal fractures, but also the effectiveness of FSK's ironic strategy of affirmation as resistance, a strategy clearly sympathetic with Fehlfarben's lyrical irony in 'Ein Jahr'. In a fascist register starkly distinct from their contemporary, the band DAF, FSK's buttoned-up style took up a position of resistance between Kraftwerk's subversively nerdy fashion and DAF's 'fist fuck'[43] aesthetic.

The least spectacularly punk band in this chapter, FSK, saliently distils punk's 'no future' and dystopic fantasies in ways not witnessed in other bands. If the strategically mercurial FSK stood for anything, then it was unflinchingly dedicated to remaking itself so as to continue to effectively criticize the Federal Republic's inability to reconcile with its National Socialist past, its welcoming of US capitalist hegemony and the cultural violence done by the American troops stationed throughout the country.

---

41 In the songs 'Moderne Welt' [Modern World] on *Herz aus Stein* [Heart of Stone] (1980) and 'Ein Kind für Helmut' [A Child for Helmut] on *Stürmer* (1982), respectively.
42 Thomas Meinecke, liner notes, *Verschwende deine Jugend*.
43 See Gabi Delgado, quoted in Teipel, *Verschwende deine Jugend*, p. 306.

It is, as such, quintessentially punk in its devotion to aesthetic anarchy and in its investment in halting the progress then haunting the Federal Republic. The unique fusion of English and transliterations of American phrases into German such as 'to fall in love' and the incendiary paralleling of American GI's and Nazi Storm Troopers[44] unmasked the myth of Germanness sown by the Federal Republic in response to national crises in the 1980s.[45] However, this chapter seeks to position FSK, alongside bands such as Einstürzende Neubauten and Palais Schaumburg, as a group that foregrounded the influence of the United States in the Federal Republic, the effacing of the scars of Germany's past through break-neck reconstruction and the paradoxes of the present.

Einstürzende Neubauten took punk's investment in detritus further than perhaps any other band. Stealing construction debris to make instruments and recording songs in the dark underneath highway overpasses, Einstürzende Neubauten's riposte to the prosperity of a rebuilt Germany broadcast the mechanical dystopia in Germany's present as a cacophony of nightmarish sounds. Similarly, Palais Schaumburg's 'Wir bauen eine neue Stadt' [We're Building a New City] broadcast out of Hamburg the sheer absurdity of the paving-over of the past that post-war construction engendered. Reconstruction and reparations, just as the discord between German reality (song text) and dreams of reconstruction (music), become in these songs something to dance to and laugh about.

Despite the extremely short shrift given to the previous two bands (and to others in this chapter), the triptych FSK-Einstürzende Neubauten-Palais Schaumburg maps for the ears (and with FSK's fanzine, the eyes) three distinct reactions in the 1980s to the fraught project of rebuilding a nation. The questions of identity, materiality and historical tension that the three bands call forth are so important because they – presciently – pushed strongly against the teleology of joyous unification. The damage which FSK asserted American troops were doing to German socio-political and daily life would become an undeniable reality once the troops, weapons and music began to return home. The mechanical dystopia that Einstürzende Neubauten turned into music indeed began again and caused

---

44 In the song 'I wish I could "Sprechen Sie Deutsch?"' the music fades to leave only the (drum-machine-created) sound of boots marching in step, an otic referent that in a German context cannot but recall Nazi jackboots and the spectre of *Lebensraum*, now as a warning of the project of American GIs stationed in the Federal Republic and of the contemporary remilitarization of the FRG. See also 'Liebe tut weh' [Love Hurts], *Stürmer* (ZickZack ZZ80, 1982).

45 Freiwillige Selbstkontrolle produced *Mode & Verzweiflung* well into the 1980s and – this is a testament to the transnational influence of German (post-)punk – recorded more songs for/with British producer John Peel's BBC radio show than any non-British band.

more pain for those in the way of progress after 1989, under the guise of rebuilding the East. Throughout the 1970s and 1980s, the kinds of distortions audible in Palais Schaumburg's quasi-atonal bleeps, twerps and saxophone cries became visible once, in punk's estimation, the Federal Republic chose political and economic expediency over the process of thoughtful, equal and just social progress.

The fall of the Berlin wall signalled the total failure of punk rock's desire to halt the forward march of time and to prevent a unified Germany from arising like a phoenix. However, punk had already witnessed its own monumental failure prior to that time. As early as 1983, the same year in which Bargeld cited Benjamin to describe punk's destructive character and a year after the 'fun punk' band Die Ärzte formed in Bargeld's debris and metal-ridden city, Nena recorded the German version of '99 Luftballons' ['99 Red Balloons']. Financial success certainly distances them from their punk moniker, but the real violence done to punk by having Nena or Die Ärzte represent it is that both bands – lyrically and performatively – destroy any critical distance between the object and its referent, a savage *unmaking* of punk's anarchic aesthetics.

Nena's hit and the poppy appeal of Die Ärzte testify to punk's failure to stave off co-option, as witnessed by New York City's Metropolitan Museum of Art's gala exhibition 'Punk: Chaos to Couture' or by Virgin Money's (the banking arm of Virgin Records) use of Sex Pistols' imagery on their credit cards. Although the English or German language versions of '99 Luftballons' are ubiquitous on jukeboxes in the Anglophone world, understanding punk as a mode of feeling and acting instead of a genre, and instead of spikey hair, highlights how contemporary representations of the subculture have reduced punk – literally – to a façade of what it once was.

While attention to Nena debases German punk's astute engagement with the intricacies of national violence past and present, and the Metropolitan Museum's exhibition signals a facile reduction of subcultures to fashion, the way Nena and the Met focus on easy consumption elides the national and sub-national instances of punk, but even worse, it vacates the sociocultural intervention into its present that remains audible today. 'No future' was, after all, directed against the promise of a fairy tale present and of economic prosperity at the price of forgetting the past.

Christian Jäger
Ripples on a Bath of Steel – The Two Stages of *Neue Deutsche Welle* (NDW)

In *Dialectic of Enlightenment*, Theodor W. Adorno and Max Horkheimer declare that 'Fun ist ein Stahlbad'[1] [Fun is a bath of steel]. They accuse fun – for them explicitly the products of the American cultural industry – of being a means to distract people from the true nature of contemporary society: exploitation for the good of capitalist companies. Opposed to high art's general capacity to provide tools for increasing perceptiveness, fun is bound to popular culture, which cannot provide insight into the machinations of the culture industries.

German music from the late 1970s onwards, which shall be discussed in this chapter on *Neue Deutsche Welle* [German New Wave, NDW], contradicts Adorno's condemnation of popular art. After punk's initial destruction of the conventional patterns of pop music created a vacuum waiting to be filled with all kinds of experiments, some German bands cleverly introduced techniques of modern art into popular culture. Although this remarkable phenomenon led to the astonishing success of pop music with German lyrics in the early 1980s, it mistook the ripples on the bath of steel for fun.

Some More or Less Productive Misunderstandings

During the 1970s, only a few bands were singing in German. Their songs addressed a mainly middle-aged audience for *Schlager* and *Liedermacher* music. Musicians who aimed at a younger audience and wanted to appear up to date sang in English. Some exceptions, though, are worth naming: Ton Steine Scherben and their highly politicized protest songs; Kraftwerk, the Düsseldorf pioneers of electronic music with minimalist lyrics; and Udo Lindenberg, the first rock singer to demonstrate that German lyrics could be witty and to the point (rather than just plain embarrassing).

The late 1970s were marked by the invasion of punk music, which was, in contrast to former musical invasions, also an appropriation. Punk led to the es-

---

[1] Theodor W. Adorno and Max Horkheimer: *Dialektik der Aufklärung* (Frankfurt: Suhrkamp, 1988), p. 149.

DOI 10.1515/9783110425727-007

tablishment of a new underground that opposed petty bourgeois popular music, as well as the remainders of hippie counterculture such as art-rock, progressive rock and folk music. Some of the main exponents of the new movement later called *Neue Deutsche Welle*[2] were musicians who had become unsatisfied with the kind of music they themselves were playing. Punk had opened up many new musical opportunities, in part through the availability of new sound technologies, and punk bands such as Kiev Stingl, Joachim Witt, the Nina Hagen-Band and Geier Sturzflug changed melodic rock songs into plainly structured pop songs, converted the lyrics from poetry to prose and used a less artsy, more colloquial tone.

The lack of experience in writing lyrics in German often led to grave misunderstandings, illustrated most clearly by Geier Sturzflug's 'Wir steigern das Bruttosozialprodukt' featuring the chorus: 'Wir steigern das Bruttosozialprodukt, ja, ja, ja, jetzt wird wieder in die Hände gespuckt' [We're going to increase the gross national product, yes, yes, yes, now we're going to roll up our sleeves again]. Although the subsequent lines provide enough indication of the song's ironic meaning, the audience listened only to the refrain and, in combination with the upbeat rhythm, mistook the song as an affirmative comment on the conservative politics of the Kohl government that had come into power in 1982.[3] However, just as Geier Sturzflug had ironically implied, Kohl's neoliberal agenda quickly put an end to the progressive policies under the social democratic chancellors of the 1970s, Willy Brandt and Helmut Schmidt.

The band Fehlfarben made a mistake similar to Geier Sturzflug's in their most successful song, 'Ein Jahr (Es geht voran)' [One year (we're moving on)]. Fehlfarben's membership originated from the first German punk bands, in particular Mittagspause, and they were closely connected to the Düsseldorf underground scene (e.g. S.Y.P.H., DAF and Der Plan). The refrain of their 1981 song, 'Keine Atempause, Geschichte wird gemacht – es geht voran' [No respite, history is being made – we're moving on], also misled many listeners to assume the band agreed with the political turn of events in the capital Bonn. However, the three remaining lines of lyrics narrate a clear refutation of the refrain:

---

2 The term was coined by the ZickZack label owner and music journalist Alfred Hilsberg in an article entitled 'Neue Deutsche Welle – Aus grauer Städte Mauern' [German New Wave – From Grey Cities' Walls] in *Sounds* of October 1979.
3 Klaus Pokatzky, 'Der Witz mit dem Hit: Geier Sturzflugs Dilemma zwischen Gesinnung und Hit', *Die Zeit*, 2 December 1983.

Spacelabs fallen auf Inseln, Vergessen macht sich breit, es geht voran!
Berge explodieren, Schuld hat der Präsident, es geht voran!
Graue B-Film-Helden regieren bald die Welt, es geht voran!

[Skylabs crash on islands, forgetfulness spreads, we're moving on!
Mountains explode, it is the president's fault, we're moving on!
Aged B-movie heroes will rule the world soon, we're moving on!][4]

The first line refers to the Skylab spacecraft that crashed down in Western Australia in 1979 due to NASA miscalculations and the second to the 1980 eruption of the volcano Mount St. Helens near Portland, Oregon, that released an energy blast equivalent to 1,600 times the size of the nuclear bomb dropped on Hiroshima. Although Jimmy Carter was the Democratic president of the USA at the time, the next American presidential election was won by the Republican Ronald Reagan who had starred in various low budget movies prior to entering politics. In combination with these historical events, the notion of progress, conjured up at the end of each line, is clearly intended as an ironic comment on the catastrophes mentioned.

However, the single's sales figure of around 200,000 units unmistakably indicate that many people were only too willing to praise the dawning of a new political era which they erroneously assumed to be welcomed in these two songs. In the early 1980s, there was strong desire to get rid off the depressive atmosphere of the late 1970s which had become encapsulated in the expression 'German angst': Germans had been afraid of *Waldsterben* [deforestation] due to acidic rain, environmental pollution from nuclear power stations and the industrial infrastructure. Apart from such ecological concerns, the continuing threat of left-wing terrorism in the aftermath of the 'German autumn'[5] of 1977 coincided with the country's increasingly becoming the prime battlefield for Cold War tensions.

This unease increased considerably when, as part of the nuclear arms race, the Soviet Union deployed medium-range missiles in East Germany in the late 1970s and NATO responded by deploying the same technology in West Germany in the early 1980s. Combined with other social and political issues, this strategy of 'mutually assured destruction' caused fear to prevail in the public conscious-

---

4 Musik und Text: Thomas Schwebel, Michael Kemner, Peter Hein, Frank Fenstermacher, Uwe Bauer, George Nicolaidis Lygon. © verlegt bei Fehlfarben Musikverlag GbR und SMV Schacht Musikverlage GmbH & Co KG. Mit freundlicher Genehmigung von Fehlfarben. All rights reserved. For a detailed interpretation of Fehlfarben's lyrics see Christian Jäger, 'Wörterflucht oder Die kategoriale Not der Literaturwissenschaft angesichts der Literatur der achtziger Jahre', *Internationales Jahrbuch für Germanistik* 1 (1995), 85–100.
5 See Stefan Aust, *The Baader-Meinhof Complex* (London: Bodley Head, 2008).

ness in West Germany. Against this backdrop, emerging bands with new sound and lyrics that differed strikingly from those of their predecessors tended to be mistakenly recognized as harbingers of hope and optimism.

The 1980 song 'Eisbär' [Polar Bear] by the Swiss band Grauzone [Grey Zone], highlights the breadth of German-spawned angst. From the perspective of a person longing to be a polar bear, the narrator sings of his hope to survive living in the cold and clear climate of the Arctic and rid himself of desperate emotions and worries. Protesting against an apparently over-complex world, the song fits in the general oeuvre of Grauzone's lyrics with lines such as 'Wir sind alle prostituiert' [We are all being prostituted] and 'Die Traurigen werden geschlachtet – die Welt wird lustig / Die Dummen werden geschlachtet – die Welt wird weise' [The sad are slaughtered – the world will become funny / The dumb are slaughtered – the world will become wise].[6]

Significantly, Grauzone disbanded shortly after their first album because of the success they experienced. They had never striven for commercial success but had rather been interested in a marriage between art and pop music. Thus, thereafter, Grauzone's members followed their individual non-commercial interests – a retreat similar to that of Fehlfarben's singer Peter Hein, who did not want to join the music business professionally and opted to keep his job at a company that sold and maintained photocopiers. 'Eisbär' is thus a testament to Grauzone's correct appraisal of their unwanted musical future and to their failure to escape the formidable forces of commercial interests. It can be found on virtually every compilation of *Neue Deutsche Welle* songs today, while their other material has since garnered a cult following and was re-released in 2010 as the 2-CD box set *Grauzone 1980–1982*.

Contributions From the Previous Generation

Kiev Stingl, who released a rather conventional rock album in 1975 entitled *Teuflisch* [Devilish], was one of the first musicians to capture and define the sound of NDW with *Hart wie Mozart* [Hard as Mozart], released in 1979. The album was produced by the famous singer/songwriter Achim Reichel, a former member of the 1960s beat band The Rattles who were regarded as the German Beatles. Holger Hiller (later singer for Palais Schaumburg) was on guitar and Walter Thielsch, who replaced Hiller in Palais Schaumburg in 1982, played drums. Stingl

---

6 These are quotes from the songs 'Marmelade und Himbeereis' [Jam and Raspberry Ice-Cream] and 'Schlachtet!' [Slaughter!] from Grauzone's eponymous 1981 LP.

also published poetry[7] and his verses – written or sung – usually mixed English and German, only occasionally sticking to just one language. His lyrics operate with few but precisely chosen words, a quality that echoes in the use of very short lines. In 'Süß und rein' [Sweet and Pure] from *Hart wie Mozart* the lyrics run thusly:

> Sie hängt sich in mich rein, ja; ich tu' mich in sie rein, ja
> Sie sagt sie ist noch klein. Sie sagt sie ist noch rein.
> Sie sagt sie ist nicht mein. Ich sag nicht ich bin dein.
> Es klopft sie sagt herein. Es klopft ich sag herein.
> Sie sagt sie ist noch klein, sie sagt sie ist noch rein.
> Sie sagt sie ist nicht mein, ich sag nicht ich bin dein.
> Sie sagt ich bin gemein. Ich bin, ich bin allein
> So süß und rein. Ich will nicht anders sein.
> Ich will nur in sie rein. So süß und rein.

> [She hooks herself into me, yeah; I put myself in her, yeah
> She says she is still small. She says she is still pure.
> She says she is not mine. I don't say I am yours.
> There's a knock, she says come in. There's a knock, I say come in.
> She says she is still small, she says she is still pure.
> She says she is not mine, I don't say I am yours.
> She says that I am mean. I am, I am alone
> So sweet and pure. I don't want to be different.
> I only want to get into her. So sweet and pure.]

The song has very simple words and syntax, employs a considerable degree of repetition, given that some lines are repeated five to ten times, and uses a rhyme that in German is very common (*rein – mein, dein – klein* etc.). Although the lyrics are rather lewd, the music is pleasantly arranged with an up-tempo beat: a repetitive rhythm guitar accompanied by the drums, a simple keyboard melody and the bass which accompanies Stingl's deep, barely modulated voice. During the bridge, a violin joins in, and a female singer performs in anti-phony with Stingl for the repetitions of the line 'so süß und rein'.

As witnessed with Fehlfarben, reduced language with an equally reduced message created a minor hit and established a small fan base for Stingl. The follow-up albums *Ich wünsch' den Deutschen alles Gute* [I Wish All the Best to the Germans] from 1981 and *Grausam das Gold, jublend die Pest* [Cruel the Gold, Jubilant the Plague] from 1989 did not achieve the success of *Hart wie Mozart* in terms of music or lyrical skill. Stingl stopped making music after 1989 and has

---

7 See *Flacker in der Pfote* (Kaufbeuren: Pohl'n'Mayer, 1979); *Die besoffene Schlägerei* (Berlin: Nixdorf, 1984); *Kainer Maria Cowboy* (Berlin: Edition Galrev, 1993).

prevented re-releases, so his music has become difficult to get a hold of. This is highly regrettable in terms of music history, since *Hart wie Mozart* is a key precursor to NDW.

Another musician active during the 1970s is Joachim Witt. He played in several bands before joining Duesenberg, which released three albums during the second half of the 1970s with at least one minor success among them. At the beginning of the 1980s, Witt decided that he would embark on a solo career and produced *Silberblick* [Sly Squint], which was released in 1981. In 1982 the second single 'Der goldene Reiter' [The Golden Horseman] became a major success:

> An der Umgehungsstraße, kurz vor den Mauern unserer Stadt
> Steht eine Nervenklinik, wie sie noch keiner gesehen hat
> Sie hat das Fassungsvermögen sämtlicher Einkaufszentren der Stadt
> Geh'n dir die Nerven durch wirst du noch verrückter gemacht
> Hey hey hey, ich war der goldene Reiter
> Hey hey hey, ich bin ein Kind dieser Stadt
> Hey hey hey, ich war so hoch auf der Leiter
> Doch dann fiel ich ab, ja dann fiel ich ab
>
> [At the by-pass, just outside the walls of our town
> There is a mental institution like nobody has ever seen
> Its mental capacity equals that of all the malls in our town
> If you lose your head, they will drive you even more crazy
> Hey, hey, hey, I was the golden rider
> Hey, hey, hey, I am a son of this town
> Hey hey, hey, I was so high up on the ladder
> But then I fell down, yes then I fell down]

Witt's lyrics reflect the progressive disintegration of someone's state of mind, a process completed in the last verse, where there are only a few words without conjunctions or verbs and eventually only the meaningless syllables 'lalalalo, lalalalalo ...'. The references to the rider and the city walls are significant for the cultural critique offered by *Silberblick*. Those allusions to a golden Germany predating the age of industrialization are contrasted to the song's references to features of our modern, everyday life, such as the by-pass road and the diminished mental capacity of consumers of commercial goods.

Witt's critical position on psychiatric clinics establishes a link to the antipsychiatric movement of the 1970 led by psychiatrists such as R. D. Laing in Britain and Franco Basaglia in Italy. They argued that the social purpose of clinics was to discipline those patients who otherwise could live more or less independently of the medical system. Clearly, in stark contrast to common topics dealt with in the lyrics of popular music, Witt uses unconventional characters and abnormal perspectives; his lyrics seem inspired by the kind of outlaw country music played by David Allen Coe or Townes van Zandt.

Joachim Witt used a classic band format for 'Der goldene Reiter', with keyboard, drums, guitar and bass. As was the case with Stingl, female backing vocalists join the singer for the refrain. The percussion is very reduced, the guitar only delivers rhythm with quite accentuated chords and the keyboard underscores the vocals by repeating the melody. Witt did not produce an altogether new sound, but combined parts of German rock music in the vein of Udo Lindenberg with quintessentially modern means.

Satire, Irony and the German Tradition

At the beginning of the NDW era, there was a considerable gap between the aesthetic and political intentions of the bands and the willingness or ability of the audience to understand those intentions. Deutsch-Amerikanische Freundschaft [German-American Friendship], which is best known by their acronym DAF, are yet another example for how easily artistic intentions were misunderstood by the larger public. With the 1981 release of their third album *Alles ist gut* [Everything's Fine], they simultaneously conquered the dance floors and ignited a heated debate about whether they were fascist with their single 'Der Mussolini'.

However, the DAF duo, singer Gabi Delgado and drummer Robert Görl, made clear that their song was about the oversimplifications peddled by political leaders and social movements that only fostered ideological rigidity among the public. Far from being affirmatively fascist, DAF's song is an attempt to exorcize that historical burden through re-signification (comparable to the artistic strategy of the Slovenian band Laibach, which uses totalitarian imagery).

The music of Palais Schaumburg – mockingly named after the (former) residence of the Federal President in Bonn – is drawn from completely different musical traditions than DAF's electronic beats. Palais Schaumburg's rhythm section was largely based on funk patterns and enriched with experimental industrial noise by F. M. Einheit, who also played percussion for Abwärts and Einstürzende Neubauten. The experimental noise driving Palais Schaumburg's sound was matched by singer Holger Hiller's Dada-influenced lyrics.[8]

---

8 Hiller left the band after their debut album to pursue a solo career that earned him much critical acclaim (but little financial reward). See Holger Hiller, *Ein Bündel Fäulnis in der Grube* (1984), *Oben im Eck* (1986), *As is* (1991) and *Demixed* (1993).

Palais Schaumburg were in fact one of the few art school bands that had sprung up in Germany, a background that explains their attempts at adapting aesthetic-cultural traditions from the Weimar Republic. One of their rather famous songs was a cover of 'Wir bauen eine neue Stadt' [We Are Building a New Town] by Paul Hindemith, originally composed as a light opera for children. They also covered 'Die Nacht ist nicht allein zum Schlafen da' [Night Is Not Only for Sleeping] from the soundtrack to the 1938 movie *Tanz auf dem Vulkan* [Dance on the Volcano],[9] a song that was controversial since its star Gustaf Gründgens had made his career in the Third Reich under the personal protection of Hermann Göring. During live performances, Palais Schaumburg played 'Jawohl, meine Herren' [Yes of course, Gentlemen], a duet between the famous UFA actors Hans Albers and Heinz Rühmann from the 1937 comedy *Der Mann, der Sherlock Holmes war* [*The Man Who Was Sherlock Holmes*].

However, the band did not limit themselves to cover versions of past German artistic productions. On their sophomore album, *Lupa*, produced by Coati Mundi, a member of Kid Creole and the Coconuts, they blended references to past German traditions with Latin American influences. Because of its German lyrics, the album, which met the international standards of early 1980s pop productions, sounded like a piece of 1950s avant-garde pop. Alongside other examples of bands emerging during the NDW era,[10] Palais Schaumburg's aesthetic concept resulted in a kind of music that can be associated with the concept of hauntology in contemporary pop music, i.e., to today's ears, it sounds like memories of a better past that never actually occurred.[11]

In a development which given the availability and increasing affordability of new sound production equipment might at first appear paradoxical, a number of the more interesting and innovative NDW bands turned to forgotten or overlooked German musical history for inspiration. To mention three examples: Extrabreit landed a hit with 'Flieger, grüß mir die Sonne' [Pilot, Give My Regards to The Sun], a song originally sung by Hans Albers in *F.P.1 antwortet nicht* [F.P.1 does not respond], an ambitious and successful science fiction movie from 1932. The Tanzdiele covered both the German folk song 'Lass doch der Jugend ihren Lauf' [Let Youth Take Its Course] and 'Musik, Musik, Musik', a title

---

9 The film, set in 1820s Paris and portraying the amorous competition between an actor and King Charles X., was directed by Hans Steinhoff who had strong Nazi affiliations.

10 See for example Ede & die Zimmermänner (later shortened to Die Zimmermänner), founded by Detlef Diederichsen and Timo Blunck (who was also a member of Palais Schaumburg) in the late 1970s.

11 See Mark Fisher, *Capitalist Realism: Is there no Alternative?* (London: Zero Books, 2009) and the releases on the London-based Ghost Box label.

which originally featured in a 1939 feel-good movie and then gained worldwide success as the theme tune of the Muppets TV show. KFC[12], clearly a punk band, covered 'Flamme Empor!' [Flame Arise!] which dated back to 1814 and was later used by the SS and other Nazi organizations for propaganda purposes.

However, such references to older songs, including those from the Third Reich, should on no account be taken as an expression of affection for conservative ideas, let alone as a dubious nostalgia for the culture of the Nazi period. Rather, for these bands, reanimating the past represented a strategy of calculated provocation directed against the last strongholds of hippie culture. The aim was to distinguish themselves from that subculture which they deemed outdated and shallow in its critical approach to contemporary politics.

Thomas Meinecke, frontman of the Munich-based band FSK, coined the slogan 'subversive affirmation' to characterize this tactic. For Meinecke and FSK, subversive affirmation meant appropriating even the most destructive and imprudent political or cultural features and demonstrating a degree of admiration for the people who represent them. Their intent was for such subversive action to give the audience insight into the true nature of the points critiqued. An example is the Fehlfarben lyrics quoted above: The song's claim that things are moving forward *seems* to affirm a notion of progress. However, understood through FSK's logic of subversive affirmation, the song actually highlights the failures and blunders at the core of the hollow claim of progress.

This strategy, however, proved unsuccessful and the public at large failed to understand the purpose of subversive affirmation. Meinecke was certainly aware of Fehlfarben's attempts in that area when he mourned the concept's many failures in his 1986 essay 'Das waren die 80er' [Those Were the 1980s].[13] His own band, however, has been continuing, with strikingly distinct sounds, the practice of subversive affirmation up to today.

Outstanding examples of how German cultural tradition also affected the way German New Wave music was performed can be found on the albums by Ideal (*Bi Nuu*, 1982) and Fehlfarben (*Glut und Asche* [Embers and Ash], 1983), where use of acoustic instruments increased and the dual influences of ska and punk replaced that of Weimar cabaret and revue culture. However, although songs like 'Magnificent Obsession', 'Die Kunst des Zitats' [The Art of Quotation], 'Tränen am Hafen' [Tears at the Harbour] or 'Die zweite Sonne' [The Second Sun] can be considered contributions to a new German chanson, these experiments

---

12 The KFC playfully offered two ways to decipher the acronym: Katholischer Fanfaren Chor [Catholic Fanfare Choir] or Kriminalitätsförderungsclub [Crime Promotion Club].
13 See Thomas Meinecke, *Mode & Verzweiflung* (Frankfurt: Suhrkamp, 1998), p. 117.

were commercially unsuccessful and the bands disbanded afterwards, effectively ending musical-cultural development in this direction.

In terms of financial success, bands that combined the latest technological opportunities with simple lyrics and rhythmical patterns were much more fortunate. Such bands fused nursery-rhyme lyrics and a modernized version of *Schlager* to create a kind of German synth-pop. Remarkably enough, as the result of a prank, a parody of that musical style turned into one of the first best-selling singles of the NDW genre. Andreas Dorau's 'Fred vom Jupiter' [Fred from Jupiter] emerged from a school project in which sixteen-year old Dorau wrote a song with the assistance of his teacher. As has been stated, Dorau's song drew on the NDW tradition, but an influence that has not been considered previously in connection with Dorau is the concept of de-evolution as formulated and popularized by the American band Devo. De-evolution implied the idea of having arrived at a turning point in history where progress was no longer possible and only regression and continuous decline could ensue. Devo, whose members had witnessed the Kent State shootings, considered American society convincing proof of their theory.[14]

Devo mimicked this postulation of cultural decline musically by playing very simple songs accompanied by highly absurd video clips, such as can be heard and seen in 'Jocko Homo' or 'Whip it'. Against this American background, 'Fred vom Jupiter' was meant to be a caricature of a pop song, but since the general public in Germany seemed immune to such subversive forms of irony, it was received as mere fun pop. Dorau, as such, delivered a blueprint for many further successful NDW songs. An entire sequence of novelty hits that quickly stormed the charts were then created, among which DÖF, short for Deutsch-Österreichisches Feingefühl [German-Austrian Sensibility], who used the absurd storyline of an alien visiting Earth in their one-hit wonder 'Codo' from 1983; a female singer with the moniker Fräulein Menke and her hits 'Tretboot in Seenot' [Pedalo in Distress] and 'Hohe Berge' [Mountains High]; or the Bavarian rock 'n' roll band Spider Murphy Gang with the lewd 'Skandal im Sperrbezirk' [Scandal In the Off-Limits Zone]. In the early 1980s, the music industry was flush with money and, after the first songs with German lyrics made the general charts, record companies entered into innumerable contracts with any band they thought might become a financial success in a not too distant future.

---

14 See for example Daniel Kreps, 'Mark Mothersbaugh Explains How Tragedy Inspired Devo', *The Rolling Stone* (US), 6 March 2015 (http://www.rollingstone.com/music/videos/mark-mothersbaugh-explains-how-tragedy-inspired-devo-in-animated-clip-20150306).

Those in Darkness Drop from Sight

Hundreds of bands emerged from German punk and wave and the associated DIY ideology. The implied message of the late 1970s and early 1980s – which originated from the subcultures of the time and was then promoted by a recording industry with riches in mind – was that everybody could team up and form a band, no experience required. However, by 1982/83, only a few of those hopefuls had actually met record industry expectations. There was no broad success, and German bands met three distinct fates: they became commercially successful, stopped making music or went underground. Some of the original punk and wave bands were among the first victims. Among the bands that had minor successes and proved influential in their time were Hans-A-Plast, Kosmonautentraum, Geisterfahrer, Wirtschaftswunder, Interzone and Neonbabies.

Hanover's Hans-A-Plast deserves particular attention. They released their own music on their self-founded No Fun label as well as the music of featured local bands like Bärchen und die Milchbubis, Mythen in Tüten and Rotzkotz. These bands spanned a broad spectrum in music and style, from early punk (Rotzkotz) to funky synth-pop (Der moderne Man). No Fun was thereby not only a local label providing a shared platform for most of Hanover's creative potential, it was also well-connected in the music scene. One of the label's founding members, Hollow Skai, was a journalist who helped distribute their records. In addition, radio broadcaster John Peel quite simply liked the No Fun label and played each single on his British Forces Broadcasting Service (BFBS) radio shows in Northern Germany and on the BBC's world service.

Accordingly, the small label reached a wide audience and its music received, relatively speaking, considerable airplay. All its bands allowed for ever more complex rhythmic patterns to dominate their increasingly electronic soundscapes, as exemplified by the one and only album by Bärchen und die Milchbubis and by *Ausradiert* [Rubbed Off], the last album of Hans-A-Plast, which no longer sound like punk but rather an elaborate post-punk. Although the Hanover scene was as determined by political lyrics as the Düsseldorf scene had been, the large presence of female singers ensured that Hanover-based lyrics addressed feminist topics (sexual desires and gender roles) in a rather aggressive tone. Unfortunately, the Hanover scene largely disintegrated after 1983.

The Berlin scene was mainly shaped by experimental bands like Einstürzende Neubauten, Mania D., DIN-A-Testbild, Sprung aus den Wolken, Geile Tiere and other genre-defying acts like Die tödliche Doris, Mekanik Destruektiw Komandoe [M.D.K.]. These groups formed a loose association referred to as the 'Geniale Dilletanten' [Ingenious Dilletantes (sic)]. The deliberately misspelled term was taken from the name of a 1981 music festival in Berlin and it describes a brief era of artistic upheaval in the subcultural German music scene that led to vociferous protest against the cultural mainstream.

Geniale Dilletanten can hardly be regarded as part of the NDW context, and might best be described as German avant-garde pop. Apart from these artful experiments, there were also some bands in Berlin that did contribute to the development of NDW. One of Ideal's founding members, Annette Humpe, originally played along with her sister Inga in Neonbabies, a band mainly influenced by two-tone ska with a very dominating saxophone sound. Like that of other ska bands, the Neonbabies' original sound ultimately moved toward pop.

One of the most underrated Berlin bands of the early 1980s is Der 1. Futurologische Congress (named after a novel by the Polish science fiction author Stanislav Lem). Usually shortened to 1. FC, the band was supposed to be an open project with three core members and various guest musicians, however, eventually, they had six members and played with up to seventeen musicians on stage. Their sound was rightly compared with that of the early Talking Heads – which was, after all, high praise in the German music scene. Their lyrics were mainly absurdist, as demonstrated by those of their single 'Rote Autos' [Red Cars] from their 1982 debut album *Schützt die Verliebten* [Protect Those in Love]:

> Die Orange ist so gesund
> Und rund und im Wald
> Ziemlich grün wirklich grün
> Alle Neger sind so Schwarz
> Ich bin weiß, viel zu weiß
> Rote Autos, schwarz und weiß
> Grüne Autos, schwarz und weiß
> Unsere Sonne ist so hell, viel zu grell
> Und der Himmel himmelblau wirklich blau
> Warum kann man in der Karibik keine Neger essen
> Rote Autos schwarz und weiß
> Grüne Autos schwarz und weiß
>
> [The orange is very healthy
> And round and in the forest
> Rather green really green
> All Negroes are so black
> I am white way too white
> Red cars black and white
> Green cars black and white
> Our sun is so bright, way too bright
> And the sky sky-blue, true blue
> Why can't you eat Negroes in the Caribbean

Red cars, black and white
Green cars, black and white]

Following their debut album, Der 1. Futurologische Congress released *Wer spricht* [Who is Talking] in 1983 before regrettably vanishing into the same abyss that swallowed hundreds of bands at the end of NDW.[15]

On the Way to Glory, or: Act Locally, Sell Globally

After Lokomotive Kreuzberg, a radical rock group from the 1970s, disbanded, some of its former members founded the Nina-Hagen-Band, which was named after their singer. Though Hagen ultimately became dissatisfied with the band and departed for a solo career, the remaining band members fulfilled their contractual obligations by recording *The Spliff Radio Show*, a kind of alternative musical about the rock business. Afterwards they stuck with the name Spliff and began recording their own material. *The Spliff Radio Show* was performed in English and though their second album, *85555* which was named after its catalogue number, had German lyrics, songs like 'Heut' Nacht' [Tonight], 'Carbonara' and 'Deja vu' went straight to top positions on the singles charts in 1982 and the album stayed on the hit charts for more than a year.

The sound of Spliff was, apart from a few ballads, rather funky and well produced. Although the band quickly released a follow-up album, *Herzlichen Glückwunsch* [Congratulations], in 1982 and then *Schwarz auf Weiss* [Black on White] in 1984, neither of them could match the great success of *85555*. After Spliff disbanded in 1985, keyboard player Reinhold Heil and guitarist Manfred Praeker became music producers. The best-known records produced by that team are Nena's first three albums. As fate – or the recording industry – would have it, these former members of a 1970s radical rock group were to cause the irrevocable downfall of NDW through their work with Nena.[16]

In stark contrast to her producers' musical past, there was nothing new about Nena's music. She played basic soft rock in the most conventional way,

---

15 To get an impression of the quantity as well as variety of German, Swiss and Austrian punk music bands, the best source is the website *Punk-Discography* (http://www.punk-disco.com/).
16 For a similar point of view see chapter 3 in Barbara Hornberger, *Geschichte wird gemacht: Die Neue Deutsche Welle. Eine Epoche deutscher Popmusik* (Würzburg: Königshausen und Neumann, 2011).

with lyrics that included all the clichés of the *Schlager* that seemed to have been forgotten at the dawn of NDW. The mediocrity of the music and the personal appearance of the singer – who opted for a clean, cute *Fräulein* image – helped her gain domestic and eventually even international recognition with her 1983 single '99 Luftballons'. The immense success of the song led to the release of an English-language version in early 1984. The original lyrics were only loosely translated and, supposedly because it would harm record sales, Nena never played the English version live, lest she be perceived as a protest singer.

The assumption that Nena's considerable success was due to her being part of the NDW remit has led to a major misunderstanding that prevails to the present day. One must make a salient distinction between genuine NDW artists and bands who merely imitated that sound and attitude for commercial purposes. To clarify the debate, the bands and musicians usually attributed to NDW must be placed into two distinct groups – which will here be described as NDW I and NDW II – even though both groups were similar in their use of German lyrics and the latest technological equipment. In my estimation, NDW I comprises those bands from the late 1970s to the early 1980s whose primary goal was to bring innovation, experimentation and renewal into the area of German music. NDW II, conversely, comprises bands of the same time period who played only slightly modernized forms of rock 'n' roll or *Schlager*. This terminological differentiation coincides with that of Diedrich Diedrichsen between Pop I (subcultural forms of dissidence) and Pop II (commercial forms of affirmation). This theoretical distinction between NDW I and NDW II thus allows for the analysis of the oeuvres of artists whose works fall into both categories, as is the case with Trio.

The East Frisian band Trio started out in 1981, although two of its members, Stefan Remmler and Kralle Krawinkel, had played together since the late 1960s. The new person in the mix was drummer Peter Behrens who, since Remmler had been obsessed since the early 1980s with reducing the sound structure of songs, limited his drum kit (for the most part) to hi-hat and snare drum. While Krawinkel played only a few chords on his guitar, Remmler, in turn, used a tiny Casiotone keyboard or a megaphone for his instruments to create a special, idiosyncratic sound. The first single released by Trio was 'Da da da' in 1982.

Trio's video, directed by Dieter Meier from Swiss synth-pop duo Yello, shows the members of the band drinking in a local bar. Annette Humpe, who sings in the chorus line, co-stars as a waitress. The video initially shows men playing the song with acoustic instruments while Remmler sings in black and white on a TV. After a while, the bar patrons sing along and dance and, finally, the band plays live in the pub. The video illustrates Trio's marketing strategy: they insisted on their status as a local band and refused to play concert halls or larger venues.

Accordingly, their management organized a tour where Trio played in record shops in the afternoon and in small bars in the evenings. To underline their rejection of pop star attitudes, the cover of their debut album, called simply *Trio*, featured an enlarged version of their address stamp with their home address and telephone number.

Although Trio's music, stage persona, image and lyrics can be regarded as minimalist, they told a short, simple and often funny story. 'Da da da' – with its plain yet playful reference to the Dada avant-garde movement – sold 30 million copies worldwide and the second single 'Anna (Lassmichrein Lassmichraus)' ['Anna (Letmein Letmeout)'] was also a global hit. While it is justifiable to classify the first Trio album, with its minimalism and distinctive radicalism, as NDW I, *Bye Bye*,[17] which was issued in 1983, belongs to NDW II and is close to nursery rhymes such as 'Tura-lura-lu' ['Tooraloolalooraloo'] and *Schlager* such as 'Herz ist Trumpf' ['Hearts are Trump']. After *Whats* [sic] *the password* (1985), Trio split up. Though its members all went on to make more music, only Stefan Remmler's *Schlager*-type songs would become hits.

The Trio phenomenon – a trajectory from local prominence to early international chart success to artistic decline – was repeated in the case of Falco, Austria's biggest-selling pop star. In 1981, this musician, who was born Johann Hölzel in Vienna, made a major contribution to NDW with the song 'Der Kommissar' [The Police Inspector]. At the time, he was a member of the Austrian anarchist rock group Drahdiwaberl under the stage name Falco. 'Der Kommissar' was actually written for a friend of his, Lukas Resetarits, an actor who played the role of a police inspector in the popular Austrian TV series *Kottan ermittelt* [Kottan Investigates]. Originally intended as a gesture of friendship, 'Der Kommissar' ultimately became an international hit. Even though Falco recorded an international version, the song had already become a huge success with its mixture of (an artificial) Viennese accent and English. A story set in the drug scene of Vienna, 'Der Kommissar' follows the narrator and a young woman consuming drugs as well as the police inspector observing them.

Musically inspired by Rick James' major funk hit 'Superfreak' and – as the song itself lays bare – by the nursery rhyme in the children's game *Plumpssack*, the quirky 'Der Kommissar' became the first German-language rap song and in all likelihood, the first commercially successful rap song by a white singer. Some of Falco's successive single releases proved successful both in the US and the German-speaking world. In particular, these included the 1985 songs

---

17 The English-language version of the album features a different cover design and was titled *Trio and Error*.

'Rock me Amadeus', an ironic attack on Austria's use of Mozart to attract tourists, and 'Jeannie', a song about rape that was banned by several radio stations.

In 1998, at the age of 40, Falco died in a drug- and alcohol-induced car crash in the Dominican Republic. Given that the drugs-related lyrics of 'Der Kommissar' propelled him to fame, the telling connection between his reckless lifestyle and the subject matter of his first hit struck a sad note.

Some Survived

Those who clung unabashedly to early 1980s ideals were few but nonetheless important, as evidenced by Foyer des Arts. A duo of singer and lyricist Max Goldt and multi-instrumentalist Gerd Pasemann, Foyer des Arts was augmented by a large number of guest musicians on stage and in the studio. Their first single 'Eine Königin mit Rädern unten dran' [A Queen With Wheels Attached to Her Lower Parts] was released in 1981, followed by the 1982 album *Von Bullerbü nach Babylon* [From Bullerbü to Babylon] and several quite successful singles. In the meantime, a member of Foyer des Arts, Max Goldt launched a career as an author of short prose, publishing several books and spoken word albums. On those, Goldt used his own voice to create the illusion of several people talking amongst each other, a technique also used on some Foyer des Arts albums. Accordingly, tracks by Foyer des Arts such as 'Familie und Gewaltanwendung' [Family and the Uses of Violence] from the 1986 album *Die Unfähigkeit zu frühstücken* [The Inability to Have Breakfast][18] can be regarded as a kind of audio drama.

Whereas that album mocked Germans reckoning with the Nazi past, other songs poked fun at musical genres, such as 'Sing' mir ein kleines Arbeiterkampflied' [Sing Me a Little Socialist Worker's Song] which mimed heavy metal, or 'Schleichwege zum Christentum' [Secret Paths to Christianity] which derided modern Christian pop songs. In the latter, the lyrics are full of irony, oppose traditional, conservative values, and express a dislike of bad manners. With the use of digital recording and production equipment, Foyer des Arts' experimental pop became more and more elegant as well as increasingly complex, although that cannot be solely attributed to technology, since on early recordings, such as 'Schimmliges Brot' [Mouldy Bread] or 'Bau mir ein Haus aus den Knochen von

---

18 The title is an evident allusion to *Die Unfähigkeit zu trauern: Grundlagen kollektiven Verhaltens* [*The Inability to Mourn: Principles of Collective Behaviour*] (1967), written by the psychoanalysts Alexander and Margarethe Mitscherlich. This important and influential work marked the beginning of an attempt by West Germans to come to terms with their recent history.

Cary Grant' [Build Me a House out of The Bones of Cary Grant], the band was simply absurd. The band released three more albums by 1995 and then disbanded.

Another experimental pop band that survived the demise of NDW I was Der Plan. They were an electronic band discernibly inspired by the US experimental outfit The Residents, the British industrial pioneers Throbbing Gristle and, to some degree, The Human League's first records. When Der Plan started out, the group consisted of four musicians, three of whom, Chrislo Haas, Frank Fenstermacher and Robert Görl, were also co-founders of DAF. Haas and Görl left after their first single was released and were replaced by another DAF-Member, Pyrolator (Kurt Dahlke). Moritz R. and Fenstermacher worked as musicians and fine artists, co-owned a gallery in Wuppertal and joined the independent Atatak label that Pyrolator founded in 1979.

Der Plan had some decidedly odd ideas about *Schlager* that recall Frank Zappa's similar deconstruction of 1960s mainstream pop on his album *200 Motels*. Their debut album, *Geri Reig*, as well as its follow-up, *Normalette Surprise*, were filled with sound bites and little melodies that mixed industrial music and minimalist pop. The lyrics addressed topics randing from everday life to debates in arts, whereby Der Plan sang of the quintessentially German question of genius (*Genie*) and, as expressed in Joachim Witt's songs, insanity and the productive qualities of schizophrenia. Another interest, which Der Plan shared with Kraftwerk, was their fascination with new media and gadgets, as evidenced in songs like 'Ich bin ein Komputer' [I am A Computer] and 'Robot-Bolero'.

Despite their noisy qualities, it is still fun to listen to tracks of Der Plan. Although some of their songs carry titles like 'Die Welt ist schlecht' [The World Is Bad], 'Erste Begegnung mit dem Tod' [First Encounter With Death] or 'Kleine Grabesstille' [Little Silence of the Grave], they do not create an atmosphere of fear or doom. Melodies that appear to be based on nursery rhymes and comparatively high production standards defined Der Plan's distinctive style, but, just as Ideal and Fehlfarben had done on their respective third albums, they also turned towards a more acoustic sound. With their 1984 single 'Gummitwist' [Double Dutch], Der Plan created a hit commonly misunderstood as belonging to the category of NDW II:

> Tanz den Gummitwist! Woher weht der Wind von morgen, wozu wird das Ding gebaut? Wonach schreit der Mensch von heute, wer hat mein Gehirn geklaut? Ich frage Leute auf der Straße, in der U-Bahn, im Büro, alle woll'n Computer haben, keiner weiß genau wieso. Gib mir Parallelschnittstellen, 64-Bit-Prozessor, Fortram, Logo, CPU und VisiCalc und RAM-Modul. Interslip und Floppy Chip, Pershing II und Apple Panic, sind die Russen unsre Feinde, ach, die Welt ist so verwirrend!
>
> Papi, schenk mir einen Computer! Hilfe für die ganze Familie! Liebling, nimm die Rüs-

tungsspirale! Tanz den Gummitwist! [Refrain] Kann ich morgen nicht mehr leben ohne Personalcomputer? Kann ich meine Blumen nicht mehr ohne den Computer gießen? Kann ich keine Suppe kochen ohne LCD-Display, und wenn ich meine Socken wasche, brauche ich ein Interface? Woll'n die Russen uns vernichten, oder sind die Amis schuld? Crazy Shoot Out, Space Invaders, Snack Attack und Roach Hotel. Von allen Dingen auf der Erde, die es gibt und geben darf, weiß ich eines völlig sicher, was war es gleich, grad wußt ich's noch? [Refrain] Ta ta ta ta tanz tanz tanz! Tanz den Gummi, tanz den Gummi! Co Co Co Co Com Com Com! Computer Computer!

Bin 'ne kleine Stubenfliege, nichts gelernt und weiß nicht viel, verstehe nichts von Mikro-Chips, Kernkraftbomben und so'n Zeugs. Fliege einfach um die Lampe, tausendmal, tagaus, tagein, weiß nichts über Gut und Böse, brauch ich mehr zum Glücklichsein! Reicht es nicht, so rumzuleben, so dahin, für einen Tag? Muß ich den nach Höherem streben, wozu will ich Müh und Plag? Ja, das mußt du, kleine Fliege! Ich bin der Hacker im System, ich schleich mich in die NATO ein, ich könnte auch ein Russe sein. [Refrain]

[Dance the Double Dutch! Where will the wind of tomorrow blow from? Why is the thing built? What does the man of today cry for, who stole my brain? I ask people on the street, in the subway, at work, all of them want a computer, nobody knows exactly why. Give me an auxiliary interface, 64-bit-processor, Fortram logo CPU and VisiCalc and RAM-module. Interslip and Floppy chip, Pershing II and Apple panic. Are the Russians our foes? Oh, the world is so confusing!

Daddy, buy me a computer! Help the whole family! Darling, take the arms race! Dance the Double Dutch! (Refrain) Can I live tomorrow without a PC? Will I be able to water my flowers without a computer? Can I cook a soup without an LCD-display, and when I wash my socks, do I need an interface? Do the Russians want to annihilate us or is it the Americans' fault? Crazy Shoot Out, Space Invaders, Snack Attack and Roach Hotel. About all things on earth, which exist and should exist, I am absolutely sure about one thing, what was it again, I was just thinking about it? (Refrain) Da da da da dance, dance, dance! Dance the Double, dance the Double ! Co Co Co Com Com Com! Computer Computer!

I am a little housefly, learnt nothing and hardly know anything, know nothing about micro-chips, nuclear bombs and that kinda stuff. I just fly around the lamp, a thousand times, day in day out, know nothing about good and evil, do I need more to be happy? Isn't it enough to live around, just so, just for one day? Do I have to aspire after something higher, why do I want labour and bother? Yes, little housefly, you have to! I am the hacker in the system, I creep into NATO, I could be a Russian too! (refrain)]

The lyrics of 'Gummitwist' mock contemporary concerns about the digitalitation of everyday life and technological advancements and present the new technology as a threat and as controlling people and their private lives. Just as had the Cold War arms race, the opportunity for unlimited data storage scared many Germans. In the face of this, Der Plan send out a reassuring message – 'don't worry, let's dance' – whereby the politics of dancing expressed an aversion to contemporary politics and aimed at a different type of political subject, one not driven by fear but by the hope that new technological opportunities might create new political possibilities.

In a certain way, such a stance could be regarded as the form postmodernism took in its transformation by popular culture. Der Plan went on to release records until its split in 1993. Its keyboard player, Pyrolator, carried on releasing a number of very interesting solo albums from 1979 to the present, and though beyond the scope of this chapter, those albums are dramatically diverse, ranging from a collage of found environmental sounds in *Inland* (1979) to the captivating, timeless minimal techno sounds of the bona-fide club music record *Neuland* [New Ground] (2011).

Conclusion

The considerable number of bands in this chapter illustrate the huge variety of musical approaches within the NDW.[19] Although only a few of them defined and constituted the soundscape of German new wave, it is crucial to understand how they and the NDW acted as a door-opener to the charts, and thereby to wider audiences, for the German-language music of (soft) *Deutschrock* artists such as Udo Lindenberg, Marius Müller-Westernhagen, BAP, Peter Maffay, Ina Deter, Ulla Meinecke, Klaus Lage and, the most successful amongst them, Herbert Grönemeyer. Even the successes of East German bands such as Karat, which include 'Der blaue Planet' [The Blue Planet] and Silly's 'Die wilde Mathilde' [Wild Mathilda], can be traced back to NDW. Despite those German-language successes, it must be stressed that, from the mid-1980s onwards, a number of German acts who sang in English became far more successful than their predecessors. These include the duo Modern Talking, whose Dieter Bohlen went on to become a major tabloid celebrity; the short-lived Alphaville with their major hit 'Big in Japan'; and the hugely successful hard rock band The Scorpions, whose excruciating 'Winds of Change' gained the status of the unofficial anthem for German reunification.

FSK (Freiwillige Selbstkontrolle) deserves another mention here, not least since they remain active today. Their highly intellectual form of meta-pop provides yet another paradigmatic argument for the view that the essential quality of the German new wave – NDW I – was based on an intelligent approach to creating an entirely new kind of German pop music, a quality that was also exhib-

---

19 Some scholars take a different view, accentuating more homogenous topics or motifs, see Katja Mellmann, 'Helden aus der Spielzeugkiste: Zu einem Motiv in den Texten der Neuen Deutschen Welle (NDW)', *Mitteilungen des Deutschen Germanistenverbandes: Songs*, 52 (2005), 254–274. By doing so, however, they usually confuse NDW I and NDW II, and also the differing musical backgrounds of the bands, hence failing to identify the specific nature of their songs.

ited by Palais Schaumburg, Fehlfarben, Foyer des Arts, Der Plan and others. FSK were instigators and part of this sonic-aesthetic movement from the very beginning, particularly through singer and lyricist Thomas Meinecke's theoretical reflections on NDW, the development of pop music and their intersections with social and cultural conditions. That intense theorization ensured that FSK never lost touch with (re)emerging trends or cultural shifts.

Independently of their aesthetic qualities, commercial interests and political intent, or lack thereof, NDW bands communicated sophisticated messages about West Germany's social conditions and political situations. This is a rare achievement in German popular culture after the Weimar Republic. After NDW's demise, its rather radical orientation towards contemporary society would be updated at intervals and its aesthetic practices would inform *Diskursrock*, which was itself followed by the contribution of German hip-hop's artistically advanced pop music to the project of political and social intervention.

There is a degree of tragedy involved in the popular perception that the NDW moniker applies only to commercially-oriented and artistically inferior bands whose songs dominate the great number of available *Neue Deutsche Welle* compilations. It is fitting evidence of the two iterations of NDW that NDW II compilations designed as soundtracks for 1980s parties are readily available for consumption, while key works of the sophisticated NDW I strand – which include the CD edition of Grauzone's debut album – are out of print. Thus, in this regard, Adorno's indictment of fun as a consumerist distraction from capitalist exploitation and political reality is entirely accurate. Nevertheless, that is a one-sided reading that does not square Adorno's claim with manifold attempts by German bands to raise awareness and unmask the social injustice upon which the culture industry is based. To put it more concisely: while NDW II was undoubtedly part of the culture industry, NDW I did create some ripples worthy of attention on Adorno's metaphorical bath of steel.

Alexander Carpenter

Einstürzende Neubauten to Rammstein: Mapping the Industrial Continuum in German Pop Music

'We are not Rammstein!', asserts Blixa Bargeld, singer of the seminal, avant-garde German band Einstürzende Neubauten. In making this proclamation, Bargeld is rejecting industrial metal band Rammstein's controversial image, provocative stage shows and martial music. He is also demarcating the gap – not merely chronological, but also aesthetic and philosophical – that separates Rammstein and Einstürzende Neubauten, even while tacitly acknowledging that the bands are linked, as both reside within the genre of industrial music. In this essay, critical scrutiny will be applied to the notion of 'industrial' music in German pop music culture and the evolution of the genre will be traced along a continuum, from Einstürzende Neubauten to Rammstein.

In the case of German industrial music, what is at stake are not merely questions of genre but also questions about the relatedness of genre to issues of national and cultural identity. The chapter begins with a general overview of the genre of industrial music, followed by a discussion on German national identity in music. It then moves on to the industrial music tradition in Germany, focusing narrowly on Einstürzende Neubauten and Rammstein, identifying some of the key differences and similarities between the bands. The chapter is concluded by locating both bands on the industrial continuum, demonstrating that Einstürzende Neubauten's modernist approach to industrial music – and by extension Germany's musical past – which privileges sonic excess, is ultimately superseded by a new kind of excess, in the form of Rammstein's postmodernist manipulation of musical and visual signifiers.

A Question of Genre: Industrial Music

'Industrial' is one of the trickier popular music genres to define: as music journalist Dave Thomson has argued, industrial music comprises 'one of the most readily identified, and most misunderstood forms in modern rock history'.[1] It has become commonplace for the term to be attributed to a kaleidoscopic

---

1 Dave Thomson, *Alternative Rock* (San Francisco: Miller Freeman, 2000), p. 69.

DOI 10.1515/9783110425727-008

array of performers, from European post-punk experimentalists to contemporary mainstream rock acts. The label 'industrial' is used promiscuously by the music industry and music journalists alike, such that Genesis Breyer P-Orridge, founding member of the seminal British industrial group Throbbing Gristle, could observe incredulously that it has simply 'become part of the vocabulary' of the music business and of journalists, 'and most of them have totally forgotten where it came from'.[2] Jennifer Shryane's scholarly study of German experimental music confirms the ambivalence and ambiguity of the generic designation 'industrial', noting that it is a problematic umbrella term that, in many respects, does not even apply to putatively original or pure, first wave industrial bands – notably Einstürzende Neubauten – and, as such, is ultimately only useful for the music industry 'to classify its commodities for promotion and sale'.[3]

The origins of industrial music can be traced back to the Italian futurists who sought to create modern music using the sounds of modernity. The futurist movement was launched by the Italian writer Filippo Tommaso Marinetti in 1909, whose 'Manifesto del Futurismo' ['Manifesto of Futurism'] laid out an iconoclastic aesthetic vision for the artwork of the future in which many of the key elements of industrial music are implicated: a celebration of machinery and technology, amateurism, a subversive approach to art and the glorification of violence. Early forays into futurist music are attributed to the painter Luigi Russolo, whose own 1913 manifesto, *L'arte dei rumori* [The Art of Noises] advocated the expansion of the contemporary musical palette to include a full range of noises from the urban soundscape. As a painter rather than a composer, Russolo was ideally positioned to approach the revisioning of modern music with complete freedom and he argued for music to adopt all noise as the raw material for composition. To this end, Russolo created what were arguably the first instruments of industrial music – *intonarumori* [noise machines] – to be used in conjunction with conventional instruments.

Indeed, futurism, as Marinetti himself described it, was concerned with 'the aesthetics of the machine' and made a case not only for the sheer, exhilarating vitality of machinery, but also for the innate interconnectedness of man and machine in the increasingly industrialized early twentieth century.[4] This aesthetic vision, coupled with an approach to performance that combined musical amateurism, theatre, sound machines and a fundamental desire to confront and dis-

---

2 Quoted in Thomson, *Alternative Rock*, p. 69.

3 Jennifer Shryane, *Blixa Bargeld and Einstürzende Neubauten: German Experimental Music – 'Evading Do-Re-Mi'* (Farnham: Ashgate, 2011), p. 56.

4 S. Alexander Reed, *Assimilate, A Critical History of Industrial Music* (Oxford: OUP, 2013), p. 22.

turb audiences, foreshadows the early ethos and efforts of European proto-industrial and industrial bands in the 1970s.[5]

While it is difficult to precisely reconstruct the genealogy of industrial music, Throbbing Gristle must be considered seminal: indeed, pop music scholar Simon Reynolds avers that Throbbing Gristle constructed industrial music 'from scratch...single-handedly creat[ing] one of the most enduring and densely populated fields of post-punk music'.[6] According to the band's pandrogynous singer Breyer P-Orridge, 'industrial' was a term that partly described the sound of the music and partly the process of its mass production and marketing. The band called its record label Industrial Records, reputedly after the American artist Monte Cazazza characterized Throbbing Gristle as making 'industrial music for industrial people'.[7] In 1975, the group began experimenting with a variety of traditional instruments and electronics in their East London studio called the Death Factory.[8] Throbbing Gristle's first album, *Second Annual Report* (1977), has been described by *Rolling Stone* as a 'disturbing' record of 'grinding, mechanical terror' that 'steamrolled a new path for underground noiseniks by eschewing most of the formal rules of rock music – drums, guitars, melody and, on Side B, pulse entirely – going directly for the primal appeal of distortion'.[9]

To characterize Throbbing Gristle as a band overlooks its background as an art collective. The group, having emerged out of the radical performance-art ensemble COUM Transmissions, is perhaps better understood as a kind of experimental music/performance art/sonic research hybrid: while Throbbing Gristle recorded 'songs' and released LPs like a conventional band, its output was highly mercurial, with the music typically coming into being through improvised performances that blended art and obscenity (the band's name itself is Yorkshire slang for an erect penis), *musique concrète* elements, noise and the grotesqueries of *Grand Guignol* and Dada theatre. Throbbing Gristle combined electronic beats with distorted noise that reflected the same urban sounds that inspired the futu-

---

5 Flora Dennis and Jonathan Powell, 'Futurism', in *Grove Music Online: Oxford Music Online* (http://www.oxfordmusiconline.com). The influence of the futurists is readily evident in the music of Einstürzende Neubauten: Marinetti is referenced in the song 'Let's do it Dada' and some of Russolo's noise instruments are depicted in the band's video for the song 'Blume'. See Reed, *Assimilate*, p. 23.

6 Simon Reynolds, *Rip it Up and Start Again: Post-Punk 1978 – 1984* (London: Faber and Faber 2005), p. 240.

7 Thomson, *Alternative Rock*, p. 69.

8 For a more detailed examination of the cultural context of Throbbing Gristle see Uwe Schütte, *GODSTAR. Der verquere Weg des Genesis P-Orridge* (Vienna: Der Konterfei, 2015).

9 'Throbbing Gristle: Second Annual Report', *Rolling Stone: Most Ground-Breaking Albums of All Time* (http://www.rollingstone.com/most-groundbreaking-albums-of-all-time).

rists, including motorized vehicles, power tools and factory sounds. The music strives for ugliness and seeks to overturn and dismantle normativity: industrial music declares, in P-Orridge's words, that 'beauty is the enemy'.[10]

Throbbing Gristle's members were patently unskilled on their instruments, did not cultivate a particular style, did not have a drummer (to avoid associations with rock music), built their own synthesizers and proto-sampling devices and focused on the power of sound as such rather than on traditional pop music parameters such as structure, melody and groove. As P-Orridge insisted, 'Let's have content, authenticity and energy. Let's refuse to look like or play like anything that's acceptable as a band and see what happens'.[11] This sentiment would be echoed by Einstürzende Neubauten's lead singer Bargeld, who recounted: 'I had an idea that music could be anything you wanted it to be... [Because we had no formal training,] it meant we had no rules to follow.'[12]

In this regard, first-wave industrial music and punk share some essential affinities: a do-it-yourself approach that celebrates amateur music making, an elemental rawness and energy and a kindred anti-authoritarian/anti-music ethos. However, they also differ in several key aspects, namely in that industrial music is fundamentally experimental and often improvisatory, whereas punk is musically conservative. Additionally, punk's pretence to anarchic proletarianism is largely absent from industrial music, which instead tends to proceed from coherent philosophical and artistic foundations.[13] While Throbbing Gristle may have been the first industrial band, there are other important sources – found in German popular music culture – for what would come to define the sound and spirit of industrial music in the early 1980s and beyond.

German Industrial Music

A precursor of German industrial music was the ground-breaking German electronic group Kraftwerk, whose members, like Throbbing Gristle, insisted they were not musicians but rather styled themselves as 'musical workers'[14] concerned with their artistic concept of *industrielle Volksmusik* [industrial peo-

---

10 Reed, *Assimilate*, p. 83.

11 Quoted in Reynolds, *Rip it Up and Start Again*, p. 228.

12 Quoted in Leigh Salter, 'Einstürzende Neubauten's Blixa Bargeld: "We are NOT Rammstein!"', *Faster Louder*, 7 January 2013.

13 See Shryane, *Blixa Bargeld and Einstürzende Neubauten*, pp. 58–59.

14 Pertti Grönholm, 'Kraftwerk – The Decline of the Pop Star', in *Kraftwerk: Music Non-Stop*, ed. by Sean Albiez and David Pattie (New York: Continuum, 2011), pp. 63–79 (p. 67).

ple's/folk music].[15] Kraftwerk's experimental music merged repetitive beats and pop song structure with synthesized mechanical sounds and, in so doing, shaped the future of both electronic pop and industrial music.

The first true 'industrial' band in Germany, however, was probably Einstürzende Neubauten. The group was formed in 1980 in Berlin and released its first album, *Kollaps* [Collapse], in 1981. From the outset, Einstürzende Neubauten was conceived as an anti-band, with an anti-pop music approach that was predicated upon using traditional instruments that were unconventionally tuned and played, along with a host of homemade and found 'instruments', comprised of tools and materials discovered amongst street detritus or stolen from construction sites and junk yards.[16] This collection of non-traditional instruments included an array of power tools, pieces of sheet metal and glass, metal fencing, pipes and steel drums which were employed to create noisy, evocative, percussive soundscapes, over the top of which Einstürzende Neubauten's singer Bargeld intoned and screamed apocalyptic lyrics of desolation and despair.

Einstürzende Neubauten emerged alongside Düsseldorf's DAF and Die Krupps, who melded synth-pop melodies with industrial percussion in the early 1980s. This ultimately led to a blurring of boundaries between pure industrial music and industrial-flavoured electronic music, inspiring a generation of young synthesizer bands in Europe and England. The real hybridization and commercialization of industrial music was arguably led by Hamburg's KMFDM, an electronic dance group that began to add layers of distorted guitars to its music in the mid-1980s, joining the Chicago-based label Wax Trax in the late 1980s alongside kindred industrial metal juggernaut Ministry.

KMFDM's noisy, guitar-driven electro-percussive music contributed to the rise of a new generation of hybridized North American industrial groups, including Skinny Puppy, Frontline Assembly and Nine Inch Nails, and eventually to the mainstreaming of the industrial genre. Contemporary industrial music and its subgenres are now firmly rooted in the mainstream, with groups like Marilyn Manson, Nine Inch Nails and Rammstein enjoying international fame. It is Rammstein – as the originator of *Neue Deutsche Härte* [New German Hardness] and as an industrial metal band – that seems to have inherited the generic label and the legacy of both its German and North American precursors.

The genealogy of industrial music is not easily sorted out: the genre and its offshoots constitute a rich, diverse field of music and musicians. Nonetheless, it

---

15 Ralf Hütter in conversation with Chris Bohn, *New Musical Express*, 13 June 1981.
16 This approach to sourcing the components of their instruments connects the band with their British successors Test Dept. See *Test Dept: Total State Machine*, ed. by Alexei Monroe (Bristol: PC Press, 2015).

is clear that German contributions to the industrial aesthetic – in response to the socio-political situation in German in the late 1970s – played a key role in the development and dissemination of the genre. As will be argued below, notwithstanding the putative origins of industrial music in Britain, it appears to be the case that there are organic links between industrial music and German culture and that 'industrial' music is, in important ways, 'German' music.

Music and German Identity

How do we approach this relationship between industrial music and German identity? Of course, the very notion of the inseparability of music and German identity is something of a truism. As some scholars maintain, the very words 'German' and 'music' may be said 'to merge so easily into a single concept that their connection is hardly ever questioned'.[17] While this notion is problematic – German national identity (as the 'people of music', for instance) is not so easily circumscribed and debates over the Germanness of certain musicians or types of music have raged unresolved for centuries – it is certainly the case, as Celia Applegate and Pamela Potter have argued, that music has made a 'fundamental contribution [...] to German imaginings of nationhood and collective identity', even if this contribution is facilitated largely through the discourses of critics, audiences and educators, and not necessarily through musicians and composers themselves.[18]

In terms of popular music, a number of scholars have pointed to fundamental tensions in post-war German popular music, between a desire to reflect tradition and the pressures of the music industry. Moreover, there is tension between the kind of hugely popular, homely songs used to construct a sense of 'Germanness' – *volkstümliche Musik* [folksy music] or *Schlager* – and what Simon Frith calls the 'historical reality and responsibility' that is proper to German identity.[19] Bands linked to what would become the industrial music tradition in Germany can be understood as confronting these tensions, as they sought to make commercially viable music while simultaneously endeavouring to rebuild or resurrect some idea of authentic Germanness – to make music that res-

---

17 Celia Applegate and Pamela Potter, 'Germans as the "People of Music": Genealogy of an Identity', in *Music and German National Identity*, ed. by Celia Applegate and Pamela Potter (Chicago: University of Chicago Press, 2002), pp. 1–35 (p. 1).
18 Ibid., p. 2.
19 Quoted in Edward Larkey, 'Postwar German Popular Music: Americanization, the Cold War, and the Post-Nazi *Heimat*', in Applegate and Potter, pp. 234–250 (p. 234).

onated both within and without the nation, that navigated the putative links between German musical culture, national identity and especially, the past.

Industrial Music as 'German Music'?

Just as Germans are legendarily the 'people of music', and just as music is essential to German national identity, so it is often asserted that industrial music is somehow an essentially German phenomenon. It is frequently correlated to German culture and, specifically, to the German language. Reed, for instance, has described 'German-ness' [sic] as a particular, formative feature of industrial music, noting that both musicians and fans of the genre assume an organic unity between the genre and the German language, culture and history. This understanding is predicated on the notion

> that Germany as a technological, political presence in history and that German as a spoken language together resonate uniquely with industrial music's penchant for technological and tragic themes and its rhythmic, timbral aggression. [...] The idea of nation runs through industrial identity, and in this regard Germany holds a privileged role.[20]

Certainly, in terms of the advent of German industrial music from the *Neue Deutsche Welle* [German New Wave], it seems that the wedding of the German language to the politicized post-punk music of the German new wave movement was a key aspect of its authenticity and that this musical renaissance was in many ways inseparable from issues related to national and cultural identity.

Tracing the roots of industrial music as a German cultural phenomenon goes at least back to Kraftwerk, who claim a direct link between the German language and the band's proto-industrial music, insisting that their use of German has to do with its affinities with a mechanistic aesthetic. As Kraftwerk co-founder Ralf Hütter avows, 'we create out of the German language [...] which is very mechanical. We use it as the basic structure of our music. Also the machines, from the industries of Germany.'[21] Kraftwerk's legendary breakthrough LP *Autobahn* from 1974 already demonstrates the group's engagement with what it calls 'industrial

---

20 Reed, *Assimilate*, pp. 89–90.
21 Quoted in Joseph Toltz, '"Dragged Into the Dance": The Role of Kraftwerk in the Development of Electro-Funk', in Albiez and Pattie, pp. 181–193 (p. 187).

movement [...]. The movement fascinates us [...] all the dynamism of industrial life, of modern life'. [22]

The connectedness of industrial music with a particularly German sensibility – and with Germany's musical past – was later proclaimed by members of Rammstein, who insist that the band makes music that is almost 'too German': it sits heavily on the beat, rather than stressing the offbeat (that is, it is not syncopated like music rooted in the African American tradition); it is 'angular and straight [...] heavy, bombastic, romantic'; and it reflects the inheritance of the German classical tradition – 'the classical music, the music of our ancestors' asserts Rammstein, '[...] is passed down in a certain way'.[23] Claire Berlinski has echoed these claims, asserting that 'Rammstein is the inheritor of the German tradition of musical genius. Their rhythmic craftsmanship – unerring and precise – is unmistakably German, as is their intuitive command of tension and release'.[24]

Critics like Berlinski are perhaps trying a little too hard to forge links between Rammstein and the German serious music tradition. She goes rather too far in likening Rammstein's 'bombast' to the music dramas of Richard Wagner, in crediting the influence of Carl Orff in Rammstein's orchestrations and in finding textures reminiscent of Franz Schubert's art songs in the band's vocal arrangements. However, Berlinski also identifies the German language as well-suited to Rammstein's industrial-metal aesthetic – with its 'sibilants, harsh fricatives, unique phonotactics and stress rules' – in terms of both its sound and its rhetoric.[25] While the question of musical Germanness certainly cannot be addressed in full here,[26] it is necessary to acknowledge the truism of industrial music as having innate Germanic qualities: it informs both the notion of an ongoing industrial music tradition in Germany and indeed how musical Teutonism is exported and consumed outside of Germany. Acknowledging this truism begins with Einstürzende Neubauten.

---

22 Pascal Bussy, *Kraftwerk: Man, Machine and Music* (London: SAF Publishing, 2005), pp. 91–92.

23 Quoted in Claire Belinksi, 'Rammstein's Rage', *Azure*, 5765 (2005), pp. 63–96 (p. 77).

24 Ibid., p. 68.

25 Ibid.

26 For a detailed exploration of this complex question see Friederike Wißmann, *Deutsche Musik* (Berlin: Berlin Verlag, 2015).

Einstürzende Neubauten

Like Throbbing Gristle, Einstürzende Neubauten is a band that, at least during its early years, was more a performance art collective and it insisted on a similarly antagonistic approach to music. This antagonism manifested itself in music that reflected an essentially nihilistic, avant-garde vision, a vision that emerged from a haze of noise, drug use and self-mutilation. Formed in West Berlin's rich artistic scene in the late 1970s, and fronted by the singer Blixa Bargeld (whose given name is Christian Emmerich), Einstürzende Neubauten's earliest performances and recordings – comprising 'noise-intensive, rhythmically ritual anti-pop' – were intended as a declaration of war on conventional music, and as 'an antidote for the frightened, paralyzed and media-sedated masses'.[27]

It is also true that Einstürzende Neubauten was part of an anti-establishment movement in Berlin that was determined to declare war not only on the music industry, but also on the city itself. Bargeld recounts West Berlin artists coming to blows with the physical infrastructure of Berlin, with art and politics co-mingling as people 'started to build barricades and they drummed for hours on the metal fences and barricades. [...] [Ours] was fundamentally the same music'.[28]

In the 1970s, West Berlin offered a fecund mixture of political idealism, robust social programs and blossoming youth subcultures that gave rise to a wealth of experimental art initiatives, all set in the midst of a tense dialectic of tradition and modernity, between old, decaying buildings and the modern new buildings – *Neubauten*. Berlin was and is the *sine qua non* of Einstürzende Neubauten: Bargeld and his band were inspired first by the enduring *bricolage* character of the cityscape and later by its on-going efforts to conceal its own past, through a process of layering, of applying make-up over scars, of making – in Bargeld's words – 'the old faces of history disappear'.[29]

Einstürzende Neubauten's approach to art, music and performance was driven by the ideas of the futurists, by French dramaturge Antonin Artaud's notions of the theatre of cruelty – rejecting traditional approaches to performance in favour of an elemental, energetic and irrational aesthetic, in order to provoke powerful emotional audience responses[30] – and by the philosopher Walter Benjamin. Bargeld credits Benjamin with providing an especially important part of the philosophical underpinning for Einstürzende Neubauten's industrial aesthetic,

---

27 'Einstürzende Neubauten.' *Neubauten.org* (https://neubauten.org/en/biography).
28 Quoted in Reed, *Assimilate*, p. 87.
29 Quoted in Shryane, *Blixa Bargeld and Einstürzende Neubauten*, p. 62.
30 See Albert Bremel, *Artaud's Theater of Cruelty* (London: Bloomsbury Press, 2014), pp. 5–7.

namely the notion of 'destruction'. In his essay 'Der destruktive Charakter' ['The Destructive Character'] from 1931, Benjamin argues for the critical socio-political necessity of destructive characters since they 'clear away' the past, making room for the new:

> The destructive character knows only one watchword: make room. And only one activity: clearing away [...]. The destructive character is young and cheerful. For destroying rejuvenates, because it clears away the traces of our own age; it cheers, because everything cleared away means to the destroyer a complete reduction, indeed a rooting out, out of his own condition.[31]

The destructive character rejects comfort, conformity, certainty and permanence, instead finding itself always facing a multiplicity of possibilities, of ways forward: the destructive character stands forever at a crossroads, surrounded by the rubble-of-the-now, which it creates as the very means to move forward.[32] In adopting Benjamin's destruction as an approach to making art, Bargeld and Einstürzende Neubauten come into alignment with a host of avant-garde strategies for sound organization and into direct confrontation with the past. Einstürzende Neubauten's music emerged from the isolated cityscape of West Berlin, haunted by both the deeper and the more recent past. It also emerged from a bifurcated, conformist contemporary popular music scene that was likewise mired in the past and which deferred uncritically and simultaneously to tradition and to the foreign influence of Anglo-American musical culture. In its confrontation with the past, the way forward for Einstürzende Neubauten as a German musical group was to make musical 'rubble' and present the sound of urban decay via gestures of sonic excess, 'found' instruments, noise and untraditional uses of the singing voice (screams and howls) that 'deny the accepted codes of musical or verbal communication [...] both are associated with the visceral and gestural [...] both are usually in excess, being dangerous and disruptive'.[33]

Einstürzende Neubauten's earliest albums, including *Kollaps* (1981) and *Zeichnungen des Patienten O.T.* [Drawings of Patient O.T.] (1983), offered an uncompromising, experimental industrial aesthetic: the title track from *Zeichnungen des Patienten O.T.*, for instance, consists of an unrelenting bass pulse and clattering sixteenth notes, metallic clanging and the sound of breaking glass, over which Bargeld screams and moans darkly opaque lyrics about heaven,

31 Walter Benjamin, 'The Destructive Character', in *Selected Writings. Vol 2, Part 2. 1931–1934*, ed. by Michael Jennings and others (Cambridge, MA: Harvard University Press, 1999), pp. 541–542 (p. 541).
32 Ibid., p. 542.
33 Shryane, *Blixa Bargeld and Einstürzende Neubauten*, p. 136.

hell and the edge of the world. Beginning in 1985, with the album *Halber Mensch* [Half Human], the band turned to less experimental, more structured (although no less radical) music and Bargeld sang rather than shouted the lyrics. Einstürzende Neubauten's music softened further still in the 1990s, when the band enjoyed increasing international acclaim and commercial success. In 1996, this culminated in the well-received single 'Stella Maris' [Star of the Sea], a gentle, minimalist ballad sung as a duet between Bargeld and actress Meret Becker.

The band celebrated its twentieth anniversary by releasing *Silence is Sexy* (2000). On this album, Einstürzende Neubauten's music, while still rooted in an ethos devoted to the creation of evocative soundscapes and still sometimes strikingly clangourous, had nonetheless evolved into restrained and moody ambient music, focusing on drones, subtle dynamic shading and long periods of silence. *Silence is Sexy* featured lyrics in both English and German that repeatedly referred critically to the drastically changing cityscape of Berlin during the 1990s. Particularly on the pulsating, melancholic central piece 'Die Befindlichkeit des Landes' [The Lay of the Land], allusions to Benjamin's angel of history are combined with visions of future decay and the destruction of the many proud *Neubauten* [new buildings] that signified the regained self-confidence of Germany's new seat of political and economic power: 'Die neuen Tempel haben schon Risse / künftige Ruinen / einst wächst Gras auch über diese Stadt' [The new temples are already showing cracks / future ruins / at one time the grass will grow again over this city].[34]

The band's listener-supported albums in the early twenty-first century, including *Perpetuum Mobile* (2004) and *Alles wieder offen* [Everything Open Again] (2007) – which were released directly to crowd-funding fans without the mediation of a record label – allowed Einstürzende Neubauten to return to more experimental and expansive music while retaining some of the pop trappings it had acquired over the preceding two decades.

The band returned to the studio in 2014 and released *Lament,* a long-form meditation on World War I that blends screaming and cabaret-like *Sprechstimme*, air compressor-derived sonorities, driving rhythms pounded out on plastic tubes and muted, moody melodies. *Guardian* music critic Alexis Petridis describes *Lament* as 'wilfully uneasy listening'. However, he also cogently observes that Einstürzende Neubauten has evolved into 'a marginally more user-friendly combo' than it was 30 years ago 'when every record [...] sounded like an industrial acci-

---

34 Lyrics by Blixa Bargeld. Used with permission.

dent happening at the same time as a catastrophic natural disaster and the finals of the All-German National Shouting Championship'.[35]

While Einstürzende Neubauten's more recent albums have certainly become more lyrical and song-like, eschewing sonic aggression for more evocative and atmospheric tone painting, the group's output in general remains largely non-commercial. Einstürzende Neubauten's music was and is experimental, designed primarily for live performance, with recordings providing merely contingent versions. If the group's sound has become markedly less cacophonous since the early 1980s, Einstürzende Neubauten nevertheless continues to insist upon the same unremittingly experimental compositional ethos that defined its earliest forays into 'industrial' music.

Rammstein

If Einstürzende Neubauten represents the beginning of the industrial music continuum in Germany, then Rammstein is at its opposite end. Rammstein was founded as a sextet in 1994 in Berlin, and its line-up of musicians has remained constant, consisting of singer Till Lindemann, guitarists Richard Z. Kruspe and Paul H. Landers, bassist Oliver 'Ollie' Riedel, drummer Christoph 'Doom' Schneider and keyboardist Christian 'Flake' Lorenz. Rammstein released its first album, *Herzeleid* [Heartbreak], in 1995, which stayed on the charts in Germany for almost two years. In 1998, the band completed a second album, *Sehnsucht* [Yearning]: it not only sold close to half a million copies in the immediate aftermath of its release, but also earned the band several prestigious national awards for its music and videos and reached number one on the German charts.[36] Between 2001 and 2009, Rammstein released four albums – *Mutter* [Mother] (2001), *Reise, Reise* [Journey, Journey] (2004), *Rosenrot* [Rose-Red] (2005) and *Liebe ist für alle da* [Love is There for Everyone] (2009) – all of which reached number one on music charts in Germany, Austria and a handful of other European countries.

Despite their lyrics being in German, all of Rammstein's albums, moreover, have reached the top 100 on the Billboard 200 chart in the United States, with

---

35 Alex Petridis, 'Einstürzende Neubauten: Lament review – The Weirdest First World War Commemoration of All', *The Guardian*, 4 December 2014 (https://www.theguardian.com/music/2014/dec/04/einsturzende-neubauten-lament-review-first-world-war).
36 Belinski, 'Rammstein's Rage', p. 63.

Liebe ist für alle da cracking the top 20 at number 13.[37] Rammstein has placed numerous singles on international song charts, has seen some of its songs on several mainstream movie soundtracks and in video games, regularly sells out arena tours and music festivals in Europe and has toured North America three times since 2001. While Einstürzende Neubauten was and still is an influential and well-known band, in terms of commercial success, it has been eclipsed many times over by Rammstein.

While Rammstein is often categorized in a number of different genres and subgenres – notably metal, extreme metal and industrial metal – the band is also credited with having founded the so-called *Neue Deutsche Härte*, a dog's breakfast of several distinct genres, including heavy metal, industrial music, electronic music and goth. In terms of musical style, *Neue Deutsche Härte* generally features strong German vocals over pounding, often martial rhythms and low-tuned, heavily-distorted guitars, with song textures typically being enlivened with an array of sampled sounds and synthesized choral and quasi-orchestral parts.

The 'hardness' of *Neue Deutsche Härte* stems from musical tropes borrowed from thrash metal and groove metal, namely tightly-orchestrated, minor-mode guitar riffs synchronized with steady, four-on-the-floor, unsyncopated drumming (often using a double-bass drum to emphasize the rhythm), with the guitars and bass playing below their normal ranges. Taken together with the drums, this creates a powerfully bottom-heavy effect. In Rammstein's case, this is enhanced by a male singer who combines guttural roars with bass-baritone crooning, further fleshing out the lower range and adding more depth and shading to the music's dark colour palette.

Additionally, the notion of hardness is emphasized through an array of arresting visual tropes. Rammstein's concert stage offers an assemblage of motifs and materials drawn from industrial and cyber-punk aesthetics (performing in a stylized power plant; wearing metallic exoskeletons and masks; stage design featuring metal scaffolding, cages, steel pipes and gratings).[38] In addition, the band's stage theatrics frequently involve flamethrowers and an assortment of violent pyrotechnics; and the band members wear futuristic outfits or bondage gear (leather outfits covered with buckles, rubber clothing, jackboots) or appear

---

37 'Rammstein', *Music Industry Data* (http://musicid.academicrightspress.com/search/result? artists[]=87252).

38 See David A. Robinson, 'Metamodernist Form, "Reader-Response" and the Politics of Rammstein: What Rammstein Means When You Don't Understand the Lyrics', in *Rammstein on Fire: New Perspectives on the Music and Performance*, ed. by John T. Littlejohn and Michael T. Putnam (Jefferson, NC: McFarland, 2013), pp. 30 – 52 (pp. 31 – 34 *passim*).

shirtless, with hyper-masculine, muscular torsos prominently on display. A hard image is further suggested through the band's frequent references to acts of social deviance and transgression, including murder, cannibalism, incest, graphic sexual acts and sexual violence, which appear in their song lyrics, album art and promotional material and are enacted symbolically on stage.

As Corinna Kahnke has observed, Rammstein is Germany's most successful musical export after Kraftwerk. The band's success, she argues, is predicated upon striking a careful balance of exotic 'otherness' – that is, as an authentically German rather than North American band – and generic, accessible musical and visual 'cues'.[39] Rammstein thus exports a particularly palatable and artfully packaged 'transnational' form of Germanness that melds music, provocative visual imagery and national identity into a *Gesamtkunstwerk* that manages to overcomes mere spectacle to 'convey sociocultural critique' to both German and international audiences.[40] Part of Rammstein's success, both in Germany and internationally, hinges upon a decidedly ambivalent and parodic deployment of musical and visual signifiers related to German national identity and the past. It is precisely this admixture of ambivalence and parody that has contributed to interpretations of Rammstein's music as neo-fascist. International audiences in particular are at risk of misinterpreting the band's semiotics, and indeed, many fans, critics and commentators – who do not understand the band's songs or its musical-visual semiotics – decode Rammstein as far right-wing, notwithstanding the band's protests to the contrary. The imputations of neo-fascism or neo-Nazism stem from several sources: singer Lindemann's trilled 'Rs' are often linked to Hitler's pugnacious oratorical style; the band has been accused of fostering a Nazi-like fetishization of the masculine, Aryan body; and Rammstein treats the rock concert as a kind of ritualized spectacle, reminiscent of the Nuremburg-style mass rallies orchestrated by Albert Speer, replete with provocative symbolism, including columns of light, fire, blood and steel.

To look for evidence of Rammstein as a neo-Nazi band in the mould of, say, Laibach (the Slovenian industrial-techno band that was a direct influence on Rammstein) is to miss the point. Whether or not Rammstein is actually engaging in parody in order to accomplish sociocultural criticism, it is certainly true, as Slavoj Žižek has asserted, that Rammstein is playing with – not 'flirting with', as some commentators would have it – neo-fascist musical and visual signifiers in such a way as to 'over-identify' with fascism/Nazism for the sake of pleasure,

---

39 Corinna Kahnke, 'Transnationale Teutonen: Rammstein Representing the Berlin Republic', *Journal of Popular Music Studies*, 25/2 (2013), 185–197 (p. 185).
40 Ibid., p. 186.

such that what the band does in its songs or on stage is disconnected from its original meaning and we, the audience, can enjoy the spectacle – or, the 'fascinating fascism', to invoke Susan Sontag.

Sontag's famous account of Leni Riefenstahl and fascist aesthetics seems, at first blush, to map neatly onto Rammstein. For Sontag, fascist aesthetics go beyond simply privileging 'sacred vitality' and 'primitivism' – which, in terms of music, we might locate in the band's hyper-masculine appearance, coarse lyrics, use of fire and brutally heavy martial rhythms – and rather emphasize a fundamental duality, a dialectic between master and slave, between control and submission:

> Fascist aesthetics...flow from (and justify) a preoccupation with situations of control, submissive behaviour, and extravagant effort; they exalt two seemingly opposite states, egomania and servitude. The relations of domination and enslavement take the form of a characteristic pageantry: the massing of groups of people; the turning of people into things [...] fascist dramaturgy centres on the orgiastic transactions between mighty forces and their puppets. Its choreography alternates between ceaseless motion and a congealed, static, 'virile' posing. Fascist art glorifies surrender; it exalts mindlessness: it glamorizes death.[41]

We can readily recognize some of the contradictory but essential aspects of fascist aesthetics in Rammstein's performance, namely the combination of domination and enslavement. In its most obvious form, it is acted out by Lindemann and keyboardist Lorenz in homoerotic vignettes during live concerts. In performances of the song 'Bück dich' [Bend Over], for instance, the skinny Lorenz assumes the submissive role: he is led around on a leash and then receives simulated anal sex from the massive and muscular Lindemann. In making sense of such displays – which seem to contradict the band's hyper-masculine 'hardness' – it is tempting to turn towards Sontag's master and puppet dualism. For other scholars, such as Patricia Simpson, however, this is simply an example of Rammstein's virtuosic manipulation of signifiers as part of an economy of exaggerated humour, which she links to Freud's account of comic mimesis.[42] Certainly, the culmination of this sequence of homoerotic sadomasochism – Lindemann ejaculates via a prosthetic penis that sprays the crowd like a fire hose for several minutes – seems to confirm this scene as a gesture of comic excess, rather than a fascistic orgy.

---

41 Susan Sontag, 'Fascinating Fascism', *New York Review of Books*, 6 February 1975 (http://www.nybooks.com/articles/1975/02/06/fascinating-fascism/).
42 Patricia Anne Simpson, 'Industrial Humor and Rammstein's Postmodern Politics', in Littlejohn and Putnam, pp. 9 – 29 (pp. 18 – 19).

Žižek argues that 'one should therefore resist the Sontagesque temptation to reject as ideologically suspect the music of Rammstein with its extensive use of "Nazi" images and motifs[43] – what they do is the exact opposite'. He states that they liberate these motifs from their ideological connection to Nazism, rendering them 'pre-ideological', not through irony, but rather 'by directly confronting us with [the] obscene materiality [of totalitarian ideology] and thereby suspending its efficacy'.[44] Ultimately, the notion of Rammstein as a band of the German far-right, or even as purveyors of totalitarian or Nazi music, is undermined not only by Žižek's arguments but also by the knowledge that Nazi or totalitarian music itself is nearly impossible to identify. Musicologist Pamela Potter has convincingly argued that the very concept of 'Nazi music' is itself 'amorphous' and anachronistic and that definitions of it are often negative ones, saying only what Nazi music is *not*.[45]

In a Freudian sense, Rammstein's 'martial' rhythms, knee-high leather jackboots, over-the-top masculinity and ubiquitous use of fire are not only over-identified but also 'over-determined', insofar as such signifiers stand for a multiplicity of meanings, not a one-to-one connection with fascism or Nazism. This, however, does not deter listeners, commentators and critics from asserting that Rammstein simply *sounds* like the music of totalitarianism. Indeed, a song like 'Rammlied' [Ramm Song] certainly seems to reinforce such a perception. 'Rammlied' consists of driving, on-the-beat industrial groove-metal, but it opens with a quasi-medieval, organum-like vocal dirge. In its opening invocation, Lindemann intones:

Wer wartet mit Besonnenheit,
der wird belohnt zur rechten Zeit.
Nun, das Warten hat ein Ende.
Leiht euer Ohr einer Legende:
Rammstein!

[Those who wait patiently,
will be rewarded at the right time.
Now, the waiting has ended.
Lend your ear to a legend:
Rammstein!] [46]

---

43 Including the use of clips from Leni Riefenstahl's film *Olympia* in the music video for the song 'Stripped'.
44 Slavoj Žižek, *Living in the End Times* (London: Verso, 2011), pp. 386–387.
45 See Pamela Potter, 'What is Nazi Music?', *Musical Quarterly*, 88/3 (2005), 428–455.
46 Written by Till Lindemann, Paul Landers, Richard Z. Kruspe, Christoph Doom Schneider, Doktor Christian Lorenz, Oliver Riedel. Used with permission. Author's translation.

In the song's bridge, Lindemann asserts, in mock-oratory style and with the band punctuating each phrase: 'Ein Weg / Ein Ziel / Ein Motiv / Rammstein!' [One path / One goal / One reason / Rammstein!].[47] Here, one might be tempted to make the leap Darryl Sterdan famously did in his laconic review of the album *Mutter*, decrying Rammstein's 'stomping goosestep rhythms and industrial Eurometal [...] typically Teutonic, totalitarian aggression and oppression [and] the slightly scary Nuremberg-rally chants': Rammstein, Sterdan concludes, makes 'music to invade Poland to'.[48]

In refuting such accusations of promoting totalitarianism or a right-wing viewpoint, Rammstein claims to reside on the left of the political spectrum. The band's well-known song 'Links 2, 3, 4' (from the album *Mutter*, 2001) directly confronts the imputation of neo-Nazism by invoking the chorus of Bertolt Brecht's and Hanns Eisler's workers' anthem 'Einheitsfrontlied' [United Front Song]. Lindemann sings:

> Sie wollen mein Herz am rechten Fleck
> Doch seh' ich dann nach unten weg
> Dann schlägt es links
> Links, zwo, drei, vier
>
> [They want my heart at home on the right
> But when I look down I see
> That it beats on the left
> Left, two, three, four] [49]

However, as Žižek would claim, even here where Rammstein claims to be overtly political, the band's message confounds interpretation and is ultimately non-ideological since its signifiers – *sinthomes*, or symptoms, in Žižek's terminology – continue to be over-determined. The music video for 'Links' is a kind of parody

---

47 'Rammlied' is strikingly reminiscent of the Laibach song 'Geburt einer Nation' [Birth of a Nation] from its 1987 album *Opus Dei*. A cover of Queen's 'One Vision', the opening verse of 'Geburt einer Nation', with its stark pauses between short, declamatory phrases, strongly evokes the bridge of 'Rammlied'. Such a connection between Laibach and Rammstein clarifies Daniel Lukes argument that Rammstein is dialectically linked to Laibach, the 'id' to Laibach's 'super-ego'. Rammstein, in this view, is the children's version of Laibach and enjoys much greater commercial success by aping some of the brutalism and symbology of Laibach but abandoning the latter's satire, social criticism and avant-garde approach. See Lukes, 'Rammstein are Laibach for Adolescents and Laibach are Rammstein for Grown-Ups', in Littlejohn and Putnam, pp. 53–78.
48 Darryl Sterdan, '*Mutter*', in *Canoe.com* – *Showbiz*, 13 April 2001 (http://jam.canoe.com/Music/Artists/R/Rammstein/AlbumReviews/2001/04/13/771725.html).
49 Written by Till Lindemann, Paul Landers, Richard Z. Kruspe, Christoph Doom Schneider, Doktor Christian Lorenz, Oliver Riedel. Used with permission. Author's translation.

of Riefenstahl's movie *Triumph des Willens* [*Triumph of the Will*] set in an ant colony, although the marching ants could certainly be rallying Brechtian workers as readily as Nazi phalanxes. In concert, when 'Links' is performed, audiences reproduce the ambiguous call-and-response effect heard on the recording. When Lindemann shouts 'Links!' the audience responds with what sounds very much like 'Heil!'. Again, however, as Žižek would insist, there is a 'gap' at the point where ideology would like to impose 'the illusion of seamless organic unity' or, in other words, precisely where ideology would fill in the gap between what is heard and what is not heard and its putative historical and political significance.[50] Instead, in that gap or space, we are left free to enjoy the aesthetic pleasures that these visual and musical motifs afford us.

Through its knowing play with an array of ambiguous signifiers – which is perhaps a form of deconstructive critique, insofar as it inverts and manipulates a number of tropes associated with German nationalism and cultural identity – Rammstein achieves the 'transnational' status that Kahnke observes: The band becomes an exportable, exotic 'Other' that connects with non-German fans not through a definable ideology, but by virtue of over-determined signifiers and ideological gaps that give international audiences access to '"knots" of libidinal investment'[51] interwoven with the music and spectacle, notwithstanding the German song titles and lyrics.

A German Industrial Music Continuum? – From Modernism to Postmodernism

It is difficult to draw a straight line between Einstürzende Neubauten and Rammstein and to understand both groups as representing German 'industrial' music. Lyrically, Einstürzende Neubauten's songs are more poetic, place stronger emphasis on existential angst and even verge upon the neo-psychedelic, whereas Rammstein's lyrics tend toward the harshness and grotesqueries of heavy metal, or simply to the obscene. Einstürzende Neubauten's pretentions to performance art and its associations with the avant-garde are conspicuously absent from Rammstein's approach to music-making and performance, as are the former's experimental ethos and mercurial combinations of traditional and non-traditional instruments – which, at one time, were a defining feature of industrial music. Above all else, the music of the two groups simply does not sound the

---

50 Zizek, *Living in the End Times*, p. 386.
51 Ibid.

same: sonically, Einstürzende Neubauten and Rammstein do not belong on the same evolutionary branch. So, how might we speak of an 'industrial continuum' in German industrial music and understand the relationship between these two bands?

Rammstein and Einstürzende Neubauten are connected in both substantial and superficial ways. Both sing unapologetically and nearly exclusively in German, and both are interested in the promotion of German language and culture, although Einstürzende Neubauten opposed the Anglo-American rock aesthetic whereas Rammstein has absorbed and exploits the North American heavy rock/metal sound. It could also be argued that both make music tied to a sense of place. For Einstürzende Neubauten, that place is Berlin, a mercurial and multi-layered city that stands for a dialectic of decay and creativity, whereas, for Rammstein, it is the former East Germany and a sense of *Ostalgie* – a nostalgic longing for the East German past, coupled with a mistrust of western European and American culture – that permeates the band's music.[52] Finally, both bands trade in 'excess'. In the case of Einstürzende Neubauten, it is a sonic excess that manifests itself through the use of non-traditional instruments and music as organized noise. In the case of Rammstein, the excess takes the form of a (sometimes-comical) overabundance of signifiers – a giant semen canon, face-mounted flamethrowers, exaggerated martial rhythms, pantomimed gay sex and allusions to Nazi-era spectacle.

It also is clear that Einstürzende Neubauten and Rammstein are linked in one more important way: both bands approach music-making and performance through engagement with the past, specifically with Germany's past, and this engagement also offers a way forward. Einstürzende Neubauten's music confronts the histories of the (once divided) city of Berlin, and has evolved via Benjamin's injunction that the past is a thing to be aware of – as 'historical man' is aware of the past, and this awareness leads to a mistrust of the 'course of things', of the certitudes of the future – but that all paths lead forward, via destruction. For Einstürzende Neubauten, it is a high-modernist, John Cage-inspired destruction of intent, of comprehensibility, of the very notion of 'music', through a focus on performance, process and the improvised organization of sounds. For Rammstein, the way forward is also via the past, likewise through Benjamin's 'rubble': in this case, the 'rubble' is a slippery, postmodern aggregate of musical and visual signs that co-mingle past and present, German and transnational identity, in a celebration of spectacle and excess. If we wish to think of an industrial contin-

---

52 See John T. Littlejohn and Michael T. Putnam, 'Rammstein and *Ostalgie:* Longing for Yesteryear', *Popular Music and Society* 33/1, (2010), 35–44.

uum, then, we might consider Rammstein to be a postmodern response to Einstürzende Neubauten's modernism, with the latter reveling in the rubble of the past and the former playfully manipulating it.

To end where we began: Einstürzende Neubauten is 'not Rammstein!', as Blixa Bargeld maintains, and Rammstein is certainly not Einstürzende Neubauten. Both are, however, emblematic of industrial music's essential characteristics: progress, technology, Reed's 'timbral aggression' and a desire to discomfit, if not shock audiences. They also both make the German language primary in their music and share an engagement – for better or worse – with German cultural history. Rammstein and Einstürzende Neubauten are sonically dissimilar, their music targets different audiences and Einstürzende Neubauten's music has over time evolved to the point where it bears but a distant resemblance to its origins, whereas Rammstein has been locked within a consistent, even inflexible aesthetic for nearly two decades. Nevertheless, no map of the industrial music continuum would be possible and no understanding of German popular music would be complete without a critical consideration of the contributions of both bands.

Alexei Monroe
Sender Deutschland – The Development and Reception of Techno in Germany

German techno history is marked by massive speed and scale. To fully document even its first five years would entail selecting from thousands of artists and labels. *When* and *where* such a history should start is also controversial. Mainstream techno historiography often presents the genre as having begun in Detroit circa 1988 (albeit with significant, though under-acknowledged German and European influences). German techno has contested beginnings, with what some consider its pre-history starting in Frankfurt in 1984 and its better-known advent beginning in late 1980s Berlin. While Frankfurt provided strong competition for many years, it was in the dramatic conditions of the aftermath of the fall of the Berlin wall that techno made its most dramatic breakthroughs, the effects of which would spill out across the country, with new scenes springing up overnight. By 1991, followers of the new dance music were enjoying 'Berlin and Germany's Summer of Love'[1] and institutions such as the Tresor nightclub and record label were founded.

Techno activity beyond Berlin also increased massively in the next years, with numerous producers, labels and new variants of techno emerging. Whilst even in its first years there were already significant differences within German techno, by the mid-1990s, sub-genres were proliferating and they were sometimes mutually antithetical and often bound up with regional identities. Vast stylistic chasms opened up and, even within the same cities, rival labels or clubs saw themselves not just as economic or stylistic rivals, but even as ideological opponents. Competing factions and fierce polemics were directed towards techno from within and without. Perceived offences included commercialism, promotion of a mindless/hedonistic lifestyle, de-politicization and even crypto-nationalism.

Techno gradually 'slipped from the utopian to the commercial as the movement was partially absorbed by the entertainment industry'.[2] Proponents of cryptic, counter-cultural, insurgent techno saw their revolution betrayed by commercialization, examples of which include the Berlin Love Parade and the emergence of superstar DJs and producers. During the imposition of the post-reunifi-

---

1 Théo Lessour, *Berlin Sampler: From Cabaret to Techno: 1904–2012, A Century* of Berlin Music (Berlin: Ollendorff, 2012), p. 311.
2 Lessour, *Berlin Sampler*, p. 318.

DOI 10.1515/9783110425727-009

cation order in the early 1990s, the new authorities sometimes took harsh measures against the underground sectors of techno, especially in Berlin, but other parts of the state embraced it. The Goethe-Institut used the international appeal of techno as a means to promote German culture *per se*, supporting talks, performances and even the *Chromapark* techno art exhibition. Despite fierce resistance from within and without, techno inexorably became used as a cultural symbol of the reunified country.

'German' became a marker of quality and innovation for techno listeners just as it had been for *Krautrock* listeners. Some of the German techno virtues appreciated by international listeners were intensifications of the harder and more coldly futuristic aspects of Kraftwerk's aesthetics on *Computerwelt* (1981), which is widely regarded as having been massively important for techno and electro in Germany and beyond.[3] Kraftwerk's increasingly digital, minimalist sound was a major influence on 1980s proto-techno in the US. Although their techno-Germanic archetypes were soon overshadowed by acid house and Detroit techno[4], they left huge traces on these forms.

Coldness, precision and hardness were frequently used terms of praise – the perceived (and increasingly popular) hardness of some strands of German techno was even used to market a series of British compilations documenting some of the more uncompromising examples. The compilation series *Hard Techno Classics From Deepest Germany* and *Hard Trance Classics From Deepest Germany* (both 1994 – 1997) exploited the already established connection in listeners' minds between Teutonic hardness and German-produced techno.

By the mid-1990s, the various strands of techno and related genres were being consumed, produced and exported in Germany on such a scale that techno was seen as an increasingly significant economic as well as cultural force.[5] An extensive German techno infrastructure emerged and facilitated techno's complex, ambivalent role as a transmitter [*Sender*] of (often conflicting) German techno aesthetics and a hyper-contemporary (if often sanitized or even naive) image of the new Germany. Although much of the new infrastructure was created *ex nihilo* from the underground (especially in Berlin), it was soon part of a huge scene, operating on a global, corporate scale.

---

3 David Cunningham, 'Kraftwerk and the Image of the Modern', in *Kraftwerk: Music Non-Stop*, ed. by Sean Albiez and David Pattie (London: Continuum), pp. 44 – 62 (p. 59).

4 For more on the origins of the term, see Sean Nye, 'Minimal Understandings: The Berlin Decade, The Minimal Continuum, and Debates on the Legacy of German Techno', in *Journal of Popular Music Studies*, 25/2, 154 – 184 (p. 154).

5 Unknown Author, '5 Jahre Groove', in *Localizer 1.0 The Techno-house book*, ed. by Die Gestalten Berlin, Chromapark e.V., Robert Klanten (Berlin: Gestalten, 1995), p. LOC 1.0 MAG 5.9 GR 0.

Throughout the 2000s, techno organizations grew into professional, quasi-corporate institutions. In the last decade, Berlin has become a magnet for international producers, drawn by its mythical techno history and the support network in what is now acknowledged as a techno metropolis.[6] Paradoxically, this very success has diluted the specifically German nature of the techno scenes in the 'Berlin Republic',[7] such that a distinctively 'German techno' is now harder to identify.

The history of techno has been marked by centrifugal and centripetal forces of aesthetic dehumanization and rehumanization, and structural decentralization and recentralization. Styles that were originally peripheral rapidly became central, some permanently and some transiently. When styles became too popular or accessible, there were sharp creative counter-responses. As soon as labels or artists perceived that an uncompromising, militantly underground position would only get them so far, they offered lighter, more consumable products. Even the softer variants of mainstream commercial techno would have been perceived as too 'extreme' a year or two previously and even at the peak of techno's mass popularity (larger in Germany than any other country) there were many for whom it remained unpalatable. In response to moves towards the mainstream, other labels and artists deliberately intensified the colder, more punitively dehumanizing aspects of the German techno aesthetic, which pushed the form further. Such stylistic conflicts intensified the momentum, forcing the vanguard to keep moving ahead so as to escape the relentless logic of *Konsumterror* [consumer/consumption terror] and the rapid assimilation of radical sounds.[8]

Techno emerged at the dawn of the Internet and some years passed before reliable online information on artists, styles and record labels emerged. The decentralized and recentralized development of German techno is best understood through labels – the key operational and creative agencies that drove it forward with such speed. Labels such as Tresor, Force Inc. or Kompakt played a more critical role in this phase of German post-war music history partly due to the often radically depersonalized mode of sonic production the labels released and shaped. This was true of all contexts in which early (pre-1993) techno emerged, but even more so in Germany because of the number of labels, which often transmitted austere, functional and faceless aesthetics. In common with early DJ culture,

---

6 Nye, 'Minimal Understandings', p. 154.
7 Ibid.
8 I first appropriated Ulrike Meinhof's concept to help explain the speed with which genres split during the 1990s. See Alexei Monroe, 'Thinking about Mutation: Genres in 1990s Electronica', in *Living Through Pop*, ed. by Andrew Blake (London: Routledge, 1999) pp. 146–158.

the facelessness of the techno aesthetic was central to the scene. Photos of the producers were rarely seen on the often generic covers and the actual personal identities of some of the legions of more obscure techno producers remain unknown to this day. In the absence of personalities, lyrics or anything but minimal and cryptic slogans, label aesthetics assumed far greater importance.[9]

Labels were not only bearers of the national, German techno identity, but of specific regional ways of engaging with techno. As in the Krautrock era, there was 'a strong sense of the identity of great cities',[10] which endured through the first 15 years of the techno era, when Berlin's dominance was actively and successfully challenged by distinctive, regionalized labels. In the larger cities, all the (often antithetical) techno tendencies were present to some extent, with the popular perception of a city's techno sound shifting according to which tendencies became dominant at which times.

Some of the tensions surrounding techno loosely corresponded to regional identities and differences within re-unifying Germany and techno was also marked by strong cultural, class and philosophical-aesthetic differences. The speed, beat patterns, textures and smoothness (or lack of it) of tracks and labels rapidly became entangled with questions of regional and national (or anti-national) identity. Over time though, Berlin became ever more central at the expense of the innovative and dynamic scenes in Cologne, Frankfurt and Chemnitz. This reflected both the triumph of the capital as an international techno brand, but also the normalization of reunified Germany and loss of the regional diversity that animated and massively contributed to the development of techno in Germany. Yet even today, 'Berlinification' isn't as complete as it might seem from within Berlin or outside Germany.

Frankfurt – The Overlooked Initiator

The term *Techno* was first used in Germany in 1982. Frankfurt-based Talla 2XLC (Andreas Tomalla) used it as a record shop genre label grouping more dance-oriented forms of synth-pop and (post-)industrial. In 1984, he founded the *Techno-club*, which became important for promoting the new styles, particularly the nas-

---

9 See the analysis of PCP label aesthetics by Soenke Moehl and Low Entropy, *PCP Legends in Their Life: The Unofficial PCP book* (self-published PDF, 2014, http://pcplegendsintheirlife.blog spot.be/).
10 See David Stubbs, *Future Days. Krautrock and the Building of Modern Germany* (London: Faber & Faber, 2014), p. 31.

cent Electronic Body Music (EBM) sound.[11] EBM shifted the dystopian themes and harshness of industrial music onto the dancefloor, emphasizing regimented electronics over raw noise. Over time, some of the darker themes in EBM faded away and the Frankfurt variant associated with the Zoth Ommog label became more minimal and hedonistic, but without fully sacrificing force and aggression.

One of the key (proto-)techno acts also emerged from Frankfurt. Moskwa TV featured Talla 2XLC, which began as a primarily instrumental project, but, with the addition of a vocalist, incorporated a poppier element with similarities to the hugely popular British group Depeche Mode. Their track 'Tekno Talk' was an early example of techno memes in a pop context and their instrumentals were a model for those wanting to produce a new mode of 'Futuristic Dance'.

In 1989, Jürgen Laarmann helped establish *Frontpage* magazine in Frankfurt. It was initially closely connected to the *Technoclub* and Talla's musical operations. Although, within five years, it was a mass-circulation rave magazine, in its first two years it retained a strong EBM orientation, while also covering the nascent techno scene. It featured the *Official German Technocharts*, which in 1991 showed an uneasy coexistence between acts such as Front 242 and Nitzer Ebb and early techno and house projects such as T99 and Tricky Disco. This combination would have been unthinkable in Britain and reflected the brief period when the two tendencies were presented on equal terms in the same media. Ultimately, this tension was unsustainable. In April 1992 the magazine formally split with *Technoclub*, signalling a victory for the 'technohouse'-oriented Berlin team over the EBM-aligned Frankfurt faction.

Stylistic and ideological tensions between the two cities still affect the perceived importance of Frankfurt in the history of techno. Some resented the gradual loss of Frankfurt's leading edge status as the centre of gravity shifted East. Frankfurt lacked the dystopian, underground allure of 1990s Berlin and wasn't the focus of international interest. It was a commercial West German city, far more regulated than the new capital. Yet this didn't preclude active cultures of resistance expressed through techno.

One of the most prolific Frankfurt producers came from an industrial/EBM background. Uwe Schmidt applied his interest in postmodern theory to his work as Lassigue Bendthaus, which blended alienated, electronically-processed vocals with colder, digital textures. Sonically, Lassigue Bendthaus was even more futuristic and advanced than much early techno. It was distributed in the industrial market, but the techniques Schmidt perfected on these releases

---

11 The term was first used by Kraftwerk's Ralf Hütter in 1978 to describe their work. It's also strongly associated with fellow Düsseldorf groups Die Krupps and DAF.

fed into his many techno and ambient projects. His best known alias was Atom Heart (now Atom™). Working with artists such as Pascal F.E.O.S. (Resistance D and Heiko M/S/O), he helped define the emergent Frankfurt trance techno sound with increasingly lengthy and abstract tracks. From 1992, Schmidt worked with Peter Kuhlmann's Frankfurt label FAX +49 – 69/450464.

FAX released both ambient and dance-oriented productions. Some of the definitive Atom Heart releases appeared on FAX – deep and often ominous soundscapes distant from mainstream techno and trance hedonism. In 1994, Schmidt established the FAX sub-label Rather Interesting, primarily releasing his own digital music experiments. These releases appeared monthly for over 5 years and less frequently since then. However, it would be a massive undertaking even to listen to, let alone own, the total output of these two influential Frankfurt labels. Schmidt moved to Chile in 1997, but continues to release music and remains a respected figure in German electronic music.

Another Frankfurt-based producer/DJ who played a key role in the development of German trance was Sven Väth. In 1991 he founded the Eye Q label, releasing his own material and that of local allies. The initial releases were unremarkable acid house/rave, but, with the release of Barbarella's *The Art Of Dance* album in 1992, the label's sound began to develop a more cosmic (and sometimes kitschy) sound, particularly in Väth's solo work. Eye Q was designed as a commercial label, but its cinematic Goa-influenced trance sound matured and expanded from 1993. Barbarella inaugurated the more underground sublabel Harthouse intended to release harder and more minimalistic sounds.

Frankfurt was also home to the Mayday organization, which organized increasingly corporate mega-raves, becoming associated with commercially-oriented artists such as Mark Spoon. Techno and rave culture were intensively industrialized in Frankfurt and began to attract an increasingly smart and materialistic crowd that would never previously have attended raves. Yet other local scenes and audiences were appalled by such trends. The mythical label and group Planet Core Productions (usually known as PCP) was founded in 1989 as an independent operation to release new forms of dance music rejected by established companies. In 1990 it released the first of a series of *Frankfurt Trax* compilations. As the series developed, the sounds became much darker and rawer, representing the emerging 'hardcore' strand of techno, situated somewhere between dancefloor populism and sonic dystopianism.

PCP grew to include at least 27 sub-labels, each pursuing increasingly specialist variants of the hardcore techno sound. Thematically, releases varied between a hooligan/gangster aesthetic associated with acts like Ace The Space, to the cold, dystopian sci-fi mythologies of Alien Christ, Mescalinum United or The Mover. Although the more populist PCP-affiliated artists played increasingly large-scale events, their sound and aesthetic remained taboo to many in techno, tainted by association with gabber and populism, although for some on the hardcore scene PCP was not extreme enough.[12] This isolation reinforced a dynamic of (self-) exclusion and a spirit of defiance. Leathernecks' 'At War' was a macho riposte to the commercially dominant Low Spirit agency and PCP often defiantly insisted on the Frankfurt component of their identity, which was so clearly at odds with much of the local scene. Ultimately, PCP represented an escapist mode of resistance, drawing its fanatical listeners into a netherworld of hyper-machismo or the bleak scenarios associated with the apocalyptic 'doomcore' sound it had helped establish.

Frankfurt's other centre of resistance to commercialized techno saw escapism as inherently suspect and aimed to bring listeners back to earth without sacrificing the pleasures of the dancefloor. Force Inc. was created in 1991 by Achim Szepanski, who, like Uwe Schmidt, had an interest in French post-structuralism. Early releases showed a clear influence from UK hardcore and rave, incorporating breakbeats and British style utopian rave chords. Over the next 15 years, more than 300 releases appeared, which ranged widely in style and quality but were loosely bound together by the overall Force Inc. strategy. In 1992, the first of what became a 15 volume compilation series appeared. At that stage, some of the music remained relatively basic and not particularly experimental, but the semi-academic theoretical text printed with the first *Rauschen*[13] CD instantly differentiated Force Inc. from other labels and the artwork of the second featured a German language quote from Gilles Deleuze's work on Foucault.

Force Inc. was ideologically rooted in the work of Gilles Deleuze and Félix Guattari. Szepanski attempted to release electronic music that would materialize the duo's concepts sonically and provide an ideological counterweight to the rapid political and economic 'territorialization' of techno and dance music. This theoretical-political background informed some of the stylistic choices the label made. For different but related reasons, Szepanski and Alec Empire were inherently suspicious of over-linear or simplistically hedonistic techno and its potential for de-politicization or even right-wing mobilization. The compilation *Destroy Deutschland* (1993) took an openly oppositional stance, with artists including Alec Empire and label regulars Mike Ink and Exit 100 (Thomas Heckmann). Empire's militantly-titled tracks made a point of using British-style break-

---

12 Moehl/Low Entropy, *PCP Legends in Their Life*, PDF (http://pcplegendsintheirlife.blogspot.be/).

13 *Rauschen* can mean 'roar, rustle, rush, or intoxication' and was a concept used to symbolize the liberating, excessive power of the new dance music.

beats, rave chords and reggae samples in an attempt to disrupt the allegedly Fascistic flow of linear Germanic techno.[14]

In April 1994, a sub-label, Mille Plateaux, appeared that was to play a vital role in the growth of post-techno electronic music in Germany and internationally. It was named after the title of Deleuze and Guattari's mammoth book, with Deleuze's blessing. Its releases were intended as demonstrations of the duo's opaque writing on electronic music and its liberatory potential. Space was given to new artists and Force Inc. regulars were encouraged to release more experimental work. Mille Plateaux (and its four further sub-labels) released some ground-breaking work and injected genuine theoretical-philosophical depth into the electronic music of the time. It helped popularize the work of Deleuze and Guattari and affected techno by providing contrasting models of sonic 'deterritorialization' and disruption that were then re-applied by some Mille Plateaux artists when they returned to the dancefloor. After releasing a vast body of work including some genre-defining (and genre-disrupting) classics such as 'Trope by Age' (Thomas Heckmann), 'Life's A Gas' by Love Inc. (Wolfgang Voigt) and a series of influential compilations including the *Modulation and Transformation* series, the Force Inc./Mille Plateaux operation was fatally damaged by the bankruptcy of the EFA distribution network in 2003. Yet the collective work of Szepanski's improbable but aesthetically significant group of Deleuzo-Guattarian labels left a definitive imprint on the electronic music of its time.

Berlin – The Fall and Rise of a New Form

While Frankfurt was already established as a centre of electronic dance music, still-divided Berlin was trying to catch up. In 1988, the West Berlin-based Swiss national Thomas Fehlmann set up a label and series ambivalently called *Teutonic Beats*, playfully presenting the work of the nascent dance scene and some of its future stars via 'an ironic form of "electronic nationalism"'.[15] In the same period, Berlin industrial music promoter Dimitri Hegemann used his Interfisch organization to launch the short-lived but legendary UFO Club. The year 1989 also saw the opening of the still influential Berlin record shop Hard Wax and the first *Love Parade*.

---

14 Empire's punk background marked his approach to dance music and his suspicion of (German) techno. He went on to form the group Atari Teenage Riot, fusing elements of punk, breakbeats and hardcore in an explicitly political approach that in 2002 led to its album *The Future of War* being restricted in Germany. See Lessour, *Berlin Sampler*, pp. 325–326.
15 Ibid., p. 298.

Yet, while there was already strong momentum around the nascent but relatively separate German techno scenes, the opening of the wall and the effective collapse of East German state authority in November 1989 accelerated it massively. It was in this techno interregnum[16] that the scene exploded. Rave, techno and related forms became the ready-made and natural soundtrack to the end of the Cold War and East Berlin was the playground in which it was celebrated most intensively. The vast, decaying spaces of the East were dramatic and ready-made backdrops to the scale and ambition of the new scene in which East and West German youth encountered each other far more positively than elsewhere in the country.[17]

It is striking how closely two of the major cultural and political events of German history are linked. It's now almost a truism to state that the fall of the wall in autumn 1989 massively accelerated the meteoric rise of techno and house culture in Berlin, but it is also hard to dispute. To fully understand this cultural response to the collapse of the East German regime, it's useful to explore the context from which it emerged.

The extent of sub- or counter-cultural activity in East Germany (and the wider Eastern Bloc) is still under-appreciated. When East German youth rushed to embrace (and massively strengthen) the emerging techno culture, they were not doing so from a position of complete ignorance. During the 1980s, some of them had already embraced breakdance and hip-hop (seen by the authorities as less ideologically suspect than punk). This form of dance music did not suffer the same degree of repression and, in the last years of the country's existence, officials tried half-heartedly and semi-competently to incorporate and neutralize it as a safety valve for youth.[18] When some of these youth heard early acid house played on Western radio, it led to a logical and inspiring progression in their musical tastes. Western dance records were smuggled into the country and the trusted official radio DJ Peter Niedziella was even able to play some on his programme *Die musikalische Luftfracht* [Musical Airfreight, an allusion to the Berlin airlift of 1948/49].[19]

---

16 This refers to the period between 1989 and roughly 1996, seen by some as a utopian interlude between the collapse of GDR control and the imposition of FRG authority (and West German property/commercial laws). See the photographic anthology *Berlin Wonderland. Wild Years Revisited 1990–1996*, ed. by Anke Fesel and Chris Keller (Berlin: Die Gestalten, 2014).

17 See Olivia Henkel and Karsten Wolff, *Berlin Underground. Techno und Hiphop: Zwischen Mythos und Ausverkauf* (Berlin: FAB, 1996), p. 64.

18 See Felix Denk and Sven von Thülen, *Der Klang der Familie* (Berlin: Suhrkamp, 2014), pp. 25–27.

19 Ibid., p. 28.

In West Berlin, Westbam, a commercial dance DJ and producer, was gaining influence and developing contacts in the East. In September 1989, as protests escalated and GDR state authority ebbed, the Low Spirit label staged a show in an official GDR venue that featured Westbam and fellow DJs. It was prophetically titled *Macht der Nacht* [Power of the Night] and was the first major Western-style event held in the GDR. Yet rather than uncritical gratitude, Westbam's hit-oriented set was met with disappointment by fans expecting more radical mixing in the style of his radio shows. While Westbam felt he had to exercize caution, some of his fans felt patronized or cheated, an experience that spurred them to make their own efforts.[20]

When the wall fell, some East Germans knew exactly what clubs and records to seek out in West Berlin. With the West Berlin techno/acid house scene centred on UFO still in its infancy, new blood was welcome, and the Easterners quickly became part of the scene as active protagonists rather than awe-struck consumers, shifting its centre of gravity definitively towards East Berlin, where all the key techno clubs would soon be established. Besides the enthusiasm of the East German protagonists, another factor was the anarchic physical condition of post-wall East Berlin. Many spaces had been abandoned when the regime collapsed but were still in operational condition. *Tekknozid* was started by ex-GDR citizens in the Haus der Jungen Talente, a venue originally belonging to the FDJ state youth organization.[21] The largest-scale appropriation was the techno club E-Werk, which ran from 1993 to 1997 in a 1920s transformer station in the Mitte district of Berlin. The power stations, factories and bunkers in which techno music was played also helped shape it. DJs and producers began to shape their sounds for performance in specific acoustic spaces since the architecture (such as the former vaults at the Tresor club) had a direct structural influence on the sounds and was also a romantic, doom-laden inspiration.

The most meteoric rise was that of Tresor, which emerged from its subterranean base to become one of the most significant techno clubs and labels in the world. In its early days, the space had a hellish aspect, with visiting Detroit DJ Blake Baxter recalling how his ears bled on his first visit. In addition to the sonic assault, the sheer number of dancers in the confined space led to problems

---

20 Ibid., pp. 66–67. From this point onwards, Westbam contributed mainly to the mass commodifiction of the form, although his friendship with writer Rainald Goetz resulted in an experimental book collaboration entitled *Mix, Cuts & Scratches* (1997) which tried to portray the new techno culture from the personal perspective of both the DJ/producer and writer turned rave participant.

21 Ibid., p. 100.

– condensation raining down on equipment and DJs bringing in oxygen tanks so as not to pass out while performing.

Tresor grew out of Dimitri Hegemann's Interfisch label, which in 1988 – 89 released three classic singles and an album by the English dark EBM group Clock DVA. Their music had a very advanced sound for its time and many early techno productions sound quite primitive in comparison. Their work attracted the interest of the American label Wax Trax, which licensed many European EBM and industrial groups. Wax Trax gave Hegemann a demo by Detroit industrial group Final Cut, then a duo of Anthony Srock and the soon-to-be-legendary Tresor artist Jeff Mills. When Mills left Final Cut to work with Mike Banks and form the militant techno group Underground Resistance, Hegemann selected their *Sonic Destroyer* EP to launch the Tresor label in September 1991.

After its first four releases, all by Detroit artists, Tresor began to release local techno. Tresor's fifth release by 3 Phase Featuring Dr. Motte was the canonical *Der Klang der Familie* (1992). It was a tense blend of sinister strings and dark acid textures, yet it worked as a unifying anthem, breaking out of Tresor's underground zone and attracting a much wider audience. In 1992, NovaMute released Tresor's first compilation under the same title, reinforcing it as a definitive Berlin techno slogan. Tresor swiftly established itself 'as German techno's avantgarde',[22] releasing some of the most significant German and international techno artists. The 1993 compilation *Berlin-Detroit A Techno Alliance* acknowledged the huge influence of Detroit techno, particularly that of Underground Resistance, on Berlin, and the reciprocal influence of German artists across the Atlantic. German contributions included DJ Hell and Maurizio's epic percussive remix of *Lyot* by Vainquer (René Löwe). Together with Maurizio (a duo of Mark Ernestus and Moritz von Oswald), Löwe created what became known as the Berlin dub techno sound, associated most strongly with their various aliases and the labels Basic Channel (1993 – 1995) and Chain Reaction (1995 – 2003).

Basic Channel's minimal artwork and cryptic or functional titles (such as *e2e4 Basic Reshape*, *Q1.1*) complemented a dub-influenced sonic aesthetic of stretching, scouring, faltering and splitting. At a time when much of techno was marked by ever greater velocity and force, their approach was often characterized by deceleration and reduction. Leaving increasingly blurred and skeletal traces of the techno structures, their work functioned as a poetic critique. Chain Reaction moved still further from the strict definition of techno, releasing the cinematic soundscapes of artists such as Robert Henke (Monolake) and Various Artists (Torsten Pröfrock), in addition to international collaborators.

---

22 Lessour, *Berlin Sampler*, p. 318.

The increasing internationalization of techno in Berlin was accompanied by the growing centrality of the capital in German life. Just as foreign artists and labels were attracted by Berlin's growing reputation, so were their German counterparts. From the end of the 1990s to the present, Berlin has been shaped by normalization, centralization and internationalization. Incomers were attracted by the uniquely abnormal conditions of the post-1989 city, but their arrival was a sign of and a contributor to normalization. The anarchic conditions and open possibilities of the techno interregnum were as much a historical legacy as a concrete reality, although even today many non-Berliners look on its unique conditions (relatively low rents, high number of available ex-industrial spaces) with envy.

Another sign of normalization was the move away from outright dancefloor-oriented tracks to what would become codified as a 'minimal' style by the mid-2000s. This was an often self-consciously tasteful style that at its best had a cool elegance and at its worst faded into entirely generic and undistinguished background music. The label Sender Records helped develop this tendency. Founded in 1999 by Benno Blome in Cologne, it followed many others to Berlin and is seen as a Berlin label, in part due to its stylized TV tower logo, which could be taken as a reference to East Berlin's iconic *Fernsehturm* [TV tower]. The 2009 trailer *10 Years Sender Records* plays with the transmitter motif to promote the German anniversary tour and presents its artists in a carefree mode, very far from the austere visual strategies normally associated with techno.

In 2005, at the height of the minimal boom, a new label appeared. The still-influential Ostgut Ton is a subsidiary of the Berghain club, which in the last decade has become the physical space most associated with Berlin techno. The historic former power station in which it is located rapidly became a cult attraction, attracting huge queues undeterred by an exclusive door policy. The fifth anniversary compilation *Fünf* (2010) presented the label's key artists responding to and reinforcing the mystique of Berghain, presenting techno tracks made purely from field recordings of the space's sonic ambience. While the label also releases more house and even dubstep-oriented material, Ostgut producers Ben Klock and Marcel Dettmann present an extremely tight and sometimes almost clinical version of functionalist Berlin techno.

Despite the new competition, to many techno listeners in Germany and beyond, Tresor as a club and a label retains its position as 'the Vatican of Techno'.[23] Now relocated to the far more modern and imposing Kraftwerk complex, the unique atmosphere of the Tresor vault has been recreated in its basement. The

---

23 Aleksandra Dröner, in *SubBerlin: The Story of Tresor* (dir. Tilmann Kunzel, 2008).

club and label are now entirely professionalized and it continues to expand. Tresor is the most venerable member of Berlin's *Club-Meile* [Club Mile], a cluster of the most important clubs, some of which now find themselves under threat from property developers attracted by their regeneration of the area. As America's NPR Radio describes it, techno is the driving force behind the renewal of the city, but while techno can be renewing, commercialized renewal can often be antithetical to the urban ecology that techno develops. Such threats have created strange alliances between normally apolitical clubbers and some local anti-fascists determined to resist gentrification for more ideological reasons.[24]

Cologne – The Rhineland Variations

Of the early regional centres of German techno and electronica production, Cologne is arguably Berlin's last surviving serious competitor, successfully asserting its regional identity and creative history. This is epitomized by Kompakt, a shop, record label and distribution network as synonymous with the city as Tresor is with Berlin. Kompakt grew out of a trance-oriented predecessor, Delirium, which from 1992 to 1998 released material ranging from trance to (at an early stage) happy (pop-oriented) hardcore techno. Its four founders, brothers Wolfgang and Reinhard Voigt, Jörg Burger and Jürgen Paape became key figures in the history of German techno and electronica. Today, Kompakt is an industry in its own right, operating on a vast scale thanks to a considerable number of sub-labels and releasing an ever-wider range of music, some of which is scarcely connected to its origins.

It was initially most associated with minimal techno and so-called micro-house sounds and the pop/modernist visual aesthetic documented on the *Kompakt Total* compilation series. These were later augmented by the *Pop Ambient series*, which allowed regular Kompakt producers to produce (even) more lush and romantic soundscapes, far from the underground dance productions for which some of the artists are known. Over time, Kompakt's earlier flirtations with pop and indie have become central and the label now also releases lifestyle indie-pop artists. Kompakt's minimalist corporate logo and use of pop art techniques of reproduction and self-mythologization express a bourgeois Rhineland art sensibility which is more playful and eclectic than underground. The hedonistic drive of much 1990s dance music has matured (or decayed) into a cool, self-celebratory (if ironic) narcissism. The film *20 Years Of Kompakt – The Pop Docu-*

---

24 Lessour, *Berlin Sampler*, p. 365.

mentary shows a series of 'pop-up' Kompakt events, including at the Art Cologne fair.

This conceptual artistic sensibility is clear in the work of Wolfgang Voigt, not least his GAS project. Originally released on Mille Plateaux during the 1990s, the four albums Voigt produced under this name stretched the German techno form into new shapes, incorporating extensive samples from modernist composers and a gauzy, muffled aesthetic that nevertheless had great power. The album *Königsforst* [King's Forest] (1999) was inspired by Voigt's transcendent experiences and memories of the forest outside Cologne and was an epic example of symphonic contemporary landscape music.

In 2008, Kompakt reissued the GAS albums as a boxset, *Nah und Fern* [Near and Far], reclaiming this local music for Cologne. The range of music Kompakt releases is now so wide and contradictory that it's in danger of diluting its sonic identity, yet it still asserts its corporate visual identity strongly, as seen in the video for label veteran Wassermann's 'Eisen Mein Herz' [literally Iron My Heart, probably best understood as Iron: My Heart]. Here the self-mythologized Kompakt identity is re-produced via the device of a badge-making machine stamping badges with the words of the title. Kompakt's influence as a distributor is arguably even greater. It handles dozens of labels, including Berlin's Ostgut Ton. In this way it undoubtedly helped shape the minimal aesthetic of the 2000s, which in turn provoked a return to industrial techno, a shift that Kompakt's aesthetic principles don't allow it to follow.

The 'Munich Machine'

Like Frankfurt, Munich also had a (more indirect) house and techno pre-history via the Eurodisco sound associated with Giorgio Moroder.[25] The two main Munich labels, Disko B (short for Disko Bombs) and its sub-label International Deejay Gigolos (referred to hereafter as Gigolo), played on the 1970s Munich sound and the way in which it fed into house and from there into techno. In 1983, the local library music label Sonoton (Germany's largest) released an album by Vee Dee U entitled *Technopop*. Produced by Jean Claude Madonne and John Epping (an alias of German producer Gerhard Narholz), it is a functional and not particularly significant example of computer-themed library music, but it acted as a (commercialized) marker of Munich's already-developed electronic pop tradition. It can also be seen as a precedent for the often blatantly ironic and hedonistic

---

25 Robb, 'Techno in Germany', p. 133.

1990s Munich sound Disko B and Gigolo promoted. The dominant mode of Munich sound was indulgently postmodern and informed by the filtering of house and techno aesthetics into the local context.

Like many other key labels, Disko B emerged in 1991, yet its first release was a re-release from 1981 of the American new wave/disco act Silicon Soul. This illustrated the importance of retro influences on the Munich scene and its drive to unearth obscure classics. It gained momentum during 1993 with releases by producers such as DJ Good Groove and Caesar. The release of DJ Hell's *Red Bull from Hell* EP (1993) took Disko B in a harder and more serious direction. Hell (Helmut Geier), a Munich DJ, was one of the label's key artists and would found Gigolo, which became even better known than its parent. His techno formula blended harsh energy, reversed loops, smeared beats and allusions to Chicago House music.

While early graphics and track titles of Disko B expressed an unapologetic rave functionalism, the music (from local and other producers) was as urgently innovative as Berlin techno releases. R Görl (DAF veteran Robert Görl) produced several percussion-led releases for Disko B. The compilation *Supermarkt* (1994) is a key document of the early phase of the label and of German techno, featuring artists such as Acid Scout (Richard Bartz who also released under his own name on Disko B) and Kotai.

The label gradually became more eclectic, retaining a techno core but branching out into electro, drum n' bass, ambient and conceptual/pop releases, some of which violently contradicted the aesthetics of early techno. Its CDs featured elaborate booklets with retro aesthetics referencing 1970s children's books or comic strips. Arguably, the overtly sleazy visuals sometimes misrepresented the serious music they packaged. This trash aesthetic made Disko B a distinctive presence on the scene, and its excesses sparked the creation of the knowingly named Gigolo by Hell in 1996.

Gigolo was very much a vehicle for the expression of Hell's eclectic personal tastes. Its releases included electro, house, techno and some defiantly bizarre hybrids of them. As well as incorporating 1980s influences from synth-pop and EBM, he reissued the work of 1980s icons such as Tuxedomoon, with label artists remixing their work.

After relatively tasteful initial releases by local producer D.J. Naughty, Detroit legend Jeff Mills, French neo-EBM producer David Carretta and Tresor-affiliated Berliners Rok & Jonzon, Gigolo moved into overt kitsch on its fourth release, the Austrian Christopher Just's ultra-hedonistic 'I'm A Disco Dancer (and A Sweet Romancer)' (1998), which was later licenced to two British labels and became a major hit. In 1999, Gigolo released an eponymous EP by the electro-oriented German duo Zombie Nation. The computer game-sampling track 'Kernkraft

400' [Atomic Power 400] went on to become a major hit, reaching No. 1 in the UK in 2000. The sixth release inaugurated the tradition of using a homoerotic image of Arnold Schwarzenegger as a young bodybuilder on the inner vinyl labels and the front covers of Gigolo CD compilations. Schwarzenegger's image was used without authorization for four years as a pop art style ready-made that helped define the label's aesthetic. That image was then replaced by one of Sid Vicious, then by a transgender model posing Schwarzenegger-style and a version of Vivienne Westwood's use of homoerotic Tom of Finland graphics. Gigolo's aesthetic was often defiantly tasteless and even vulgar, a form of self-distancing from asexual or puritanical forms of dance music. The drawback of this was that more minimally packaged releases featuring less or un-ironic music came to look like an exception to the Gigolo rule.

Although Gigolo was highly successful in Munich, unlike its parent label it could not resist the lure of Berlin and relocated to the capital in 2000. Hell set out his personal style manifesto on the compilation *Electronicbody-Housemusic* (2002), which returned strongly to EBM, including Bigod20 and Belgian Gigolo producer Terence Fixmer. Yet, alongside the second EBM disc, he presented house and electro tracks in a typically idiosyncratic (but influential) way, contributing to the revival of interest in EBM and its infiltration of mainstream dance-floors for the first time since the late 1980s. The label is currently inactive, and has left a mixed but important musical legacy. It also exerted a negative influence, sparking others to respond creatively to their rejection of the frivolity of what Hell called the 'Munich Machine'.

Conclusion – Electronic Germany

Regarding the link between techno and the cultural and political history of Germany, Lessour concludes: 'German techno invented a non-place, a sort of atopia of the spirit. It was envisioned simply as a form of electronic architecture. It might all have been down to Germany's desire to renounce all links to history.'[26] Despite severe ideological criticism and the best efforts of some of its producers, German techno is only partly atopian, and its contested Germanness is an animating force which some have tried to subvert from within, others have rejected entirely and with which still others have formed an artistically and critically productive relationship. Given the types of critique that emerged in the 1990s when techno went mainstream, some artists' continued use of German titles and his-

---

26 Lessour, *Berlin Sampler*, p. 327.

torical references could be seen as a defeat of those arguing for absolute de-Germanization. This approach resists such pressure without lapsing into an openly assertive Germanism.

In 2009, Hell collaborated with German electro producer Anthony Rother on the album *Teufelswerk* [Devil's Work]. The track 'Electronic Germany' was a conceptual update of Kraftwerk's 1977 *Trans Europa Express*. It lists some of the German centres of techno and electronic production – 'München, Frankfurt, Düsseldorf, Berlin' – and presents a slightly kitsch but technically effective celebration of Germany based on rhythm, melody and electronics – 'Rhythmus, Melodie, Klangbaustein, Elektronik Symphonie, Electronic Germany' [Rhythm, Melody. Sonic Components/Building Blocks, Electronic Symphony, Electronic Germany]. The history of techno in Germany reveals just how electronic the country is. In Britain, and especially America, techno remained more of a specialist, underground niche phenomenon, whereas in Germany it gained more mainstream media exposure than anywhere else.

In this light it is interesting to imagine what the sometimes mutually contradictory components of a description of 'techno Germany' might be. German techno's key words might include: collapse, space, construction, destruction, expansion, force, speed, hope, dystopia, freedom, utopia, conformism, self-rejection, self-acceptance, innovation, and dynamism. Germany has initiated some of the form's most distinctive variants, from Berlin dub techno to Harthouse-style trance to Headquarters-style Berlin minimal techno (to name a few). Assigning a 'German' or even 'Germanic' quality to abstract electronic music may seem implausible (and to some undesirable), but, although many German techno sounds had international equivalents, specialist listeners are able to perceive tracks as 'German sounding', even if it may be hard to explain why in strict musicological terms.

Quite apart from the use of German language titles or concepts, the cold, futuristic sheen of the electronic textures used by Thomas P. Heckmann and the urgent sparseness of 3 Phase, can be understood as specifically German sonic variants of the form. They expressed the 1990s German zeitgeist in which techno emerged: the exhilaration of developing a new form and the acceleration of technical and genre development, the euphoria of post-unification Berlin and an attempt to start again, to leave behind recent history through the production of new narratives and sonic archetypes. For better and worse, Germany's history and its self- and international image since 1989 is bound up with techno (through its rejection as well as its acceptance). Ideological debates around German identity have surfaced in and been expressed in German techno and even with the partly techno-generated internationalization visible in Berlin since the year 2000, German techno production still exerts huge influence on the form globally (sometimes precisely through its incorporation of foreign influences). In this sense, it can express and reinforce cosmopolitanism, illustrating the productive potential of intercultural exchange.

The final normalization of techno may come in 2016. Following the successful resumption of the Berlin Atonal festival in 2013, Dimitri Hegemann plans to mark the twenty-fifth anniversary of Tresor by opening The Living Archive of Electronica, which is already being described as a 'techno museum'. Here an old rivalry reappears, as this project associated with Tresor operations is due to open before the previously-announced Museum of Modern Electronic Music due to open in Frankfurt in 2017.

Marissa Kristina Munderloh

Rap in Germany – Multicultural Narratives of the Berlin Republic

'Rap geht zurück bis Aristoteles, die Griechen kannten Cypher schon auf der Ak-
ropolis' [Rap goes back to Aristotle, the Greeks already knew what cyphers were
on the acropolis']: these are the words that Max Herre of the Stuttgarter rap
group Freundeskreis uses to describe rap in his song 'Rap ist' [Rap is] (2012). According to Herre, this means that the creation of 'cyphers', which are small cir-
cular arenas formed by people in which two people battle each other with
rhymes, existed in ancient Greece centuries before becoming an inherent element of hip-hop culture. Indeed, this ancient human tradition of competitive
yet entertaining storytelling in rhyme form has been discovered in various oral
cultures.[1] In medieval Scotland, for instance, a form of insulting one's opponent
in verse, which often occurred in pubs, was called 'flyting'.[2] However, in more
recent times, specific social and cultural developments in the Bronx, a borough
of New York City, were responsible for the reappearance of this narrative tradition which has become globally known as 'rap'.[3]

   This chapter will serve to highlight the role and adaptation of rap in Germany. In particular, it will highlight certain rappers and lyrical examples that reveal
a variety of different multicultural discourses in Germany's society. The following
section will start with a brief introduction on the emergence of rap in the Bronx,
while the predominant part of the chapter aims to shed light on the ways in
which rap has established itself in a German cultural context. In order to identify
the cultural discourses embedded in rap lyrics, rap will be treated as an oral tradition, and hence as a tradition that transfers knowledge through speech. Ex-

---

1 See Sascha Verlan, 'Hip-Hop als schöne Kunst betrachtet – oder: die kulturellen Wurzeln des
Rap', in *Hip-Hop: Globale Kultur – lokale Praktiken*, ed. by Jannis Androutsopoulos (Bielefeld:
Transcript, 2003), pp. 138–146 (p. 141).
2 See Simon Johnson, 'Rap Music Originated in Medieval Scottish Pubs, Claims American Professor', *The Telegraph,* 28 December 2008 (http://www.telegraph.co.uk/culture/music/3998862/
Rap-music-originated-in-medieval-Scottish-pubs-claims-American-professor.html).
3 See Tricia Rose, *Black Noise – Rap Music and Black Culture in Contemporary America* (Middleton, CT: Wesleyan University Press, 1994), p. 30; see Mark Katz, *Groove Music – The Art and Culture of the Hip-Hop DJ* (New York: OUP, 2012), p. 17.

DOI 10.1515/9783110425727-010

cerpts from songs will therefore be analyzed according to the four main categories of rap's oral features as defined by linguists Androutsopoulos and Scholz.[4]

The first category comprises 'song themes' and refers to the topics of the rapped messages. The second category focuses on 'ritualized speech acts' that commonly appear in rapped messages, such as boasting, dissing (insulting) or the popular act of representing one's place of belonging. The third category of 'rap specific rhetoric' concerns the use of metaphors, similes or cultural references, while 'linguistic orientation' comprises the final category in which rap lyrics are identified by their form of language or register. These four categories will facilitate the identification of rap's significance in a new cultural as well as linguistic context pertaining to Germany.

The Beginning of Rap

In the early 1970s, when hip-hop started to evolve as a form of music, many areas in the Bronx were multicultural urban neighbourhoods defined by financial instability and social segregation from the white, middle-class American mainstream majority.[5] Yet, hip-hop music scholar Mark Katz also states that the cultural and ethnic amalgamation of African American, Caribbean and Latino heritages in the Bronx created the existence of 'funk godfathers, soul queens, and disco DJs; street corner 'salseros' and Jamaican sound system makers'[6] and that 'early hip-hop DJs felt genuine affection for their city, taking deep pride in being a Bronxite rather than protesting its harsh conditions'.[7] In fostering this pride, DJs[8] began to employ the musical knowledge that surrounded them, creating live, local open-air dance events, known as neighbourhood 'block parties'.

As these dance parties became more successful over time, the local DJs became more creative. They began using two turntables on which to play two records simultaneously and to mix and match different segments of sound, such as a 'fraction of a waveform, a single note from an instrument or voice, a rhythm,

---

4 See Jannis Androutsopoulos, 'HipHop und Sprache: Vertikale Intertextualität und die drei Sphären der Popkultur', in *HipHop: Globale Kultur*, ed. by Androutsopoulos, pp. 111–136 (p. 116).
5 See Murray Forman, *The 'hood Comes First: Race, Space, and Place in Rap and Hip-Hop* (Middletown, CT: Wesleyan University Press, 2002), p. 87.
6 Katz, *Groove Music*, p. 42.
7 Ibid., p. 40.
8 The first DJs to do so were African American DJs Grandmaster Flash and DJ Afrika Bambaataa, as well as Jamaican DJ Kool Herc.

a melody, a harmony, or an entire work or album'.[9] This practice became known as 'sampling'.

The initial success of sampling as a new style of dance music succeeded because the beats were danceable and because they related to the everyday musical knowledge of the local inhabitants. However, the live sampling techniques eventually became more sophisticated through various cutting and scratching skills. This resulted in the audience beginning to watch the DJs' manual acrobatics, instead of dancing to their beats.[10] In order to counteract this development, a new element was introduced to the block party scene. Hosts or 'masters of ceremony' (MCs) went on stage and 'filled a void – one created by the DJs – by bringing vocals and songs back into the spotlight'.[11] These MCs specifically reconnected to the audience again by shouting 'little phrases and words from the neighbourhood that [they] used on the corner'.[12] What began as an improvised practice of aural and visual entertainment that rested on shared cultural codes quickly evolved into a 'form of rhymed storytelling accompanied by highly rhythmic, electronically based music'.[13] This form of storytelling became the first form of 'rap'.

From a cultural-historical perspective, hip-hop scholar Tricia Rose especially locates the art of rapping in an African American derived tradition, as it comprises the 'improvisational elements of jazz with the narrative sense of place in the blues; it has the oratory power of the black preacher and the emotional vulnerability of Southern soul music'.[14] Yet, beyond the African American cultures found in the Bronx, rappers were also of Caribbean, Latino or Native American descent and this fact continued to reflect the 'multi-ethnic nature of the founding community of hip-hop'.[15] However, US-American hip-hop scholar Jeffrey Ogbar observes that, eventually, only 'African American working-class, urban males emerged as the art's central representatives'.[16] This specifically occurred when rap became detached from the DJ's stage.

---

9 Justin A. Williams, *Musical Borrowing in Hip-hop Music: Theoretical Frameworks and Case Studies* (Nottingham: University of Nottingham, 2009), p. 14.
10 Katz, *Groove Music*, p. 75.
11 Ibid.
12 DJ Kool Herc in Nelson George, 'The Founding Fathers Speak the Truth', in *That's the Joint! The Hip-Hop Studies Reader*, ed. by Murray Forman and Anthony Neal, 2nd ed. (New York: Routledge, 2012), pp. 43–55 (p. 51).
13 Rose, *Black Noise*, p. 2.
14 Ibid., pp. 184–185.
15 Jeffrey O.G. Ogbar, *Hip-Hop Revolution: The Culture and Politics of Rap* (Lawrence, KA: University Press of Kansas, 2007), p. 39.
16 Ibid.

In the early 1980s, rappers started rhyming about 'the pleasures and problems of black urban life in contemporary America'[17] and to record these narratives. Rappers thus shifted from being live entertainers to becoming 'producers of representational space and fictional narratives envisioned within actual environments and experiences'.[18] Most notably, the song 'The Message' (1982) set the cornerstone for the rise of commercially recorded rap, in which rapper Melle Mel, who is of African Cherokee descent, raps about the daily struggle for survival in the urban jungle of New York City.[19]

With recorded rap being easily disseminated via tape, vinyl or airwaves, the need to rhyme about harsh urban conditions as a prerequisite for rap rapidly spread to other urban communities in the United States. In so doing, the conditions of the South Bronx in particular remained paradigmatic for the overall conditions that defined the urban ghetto in its lyrical manifestation. Hence, specifically 'using the ghetto as a source of identity'[20] became the standardized urban perspective and social discourse in commercial rap productions.

This urban scenario also set the scene for new feature-length hip-hop film productions in the early 1980s. The impact of these cinematic hip-hop narratives went far beyond New York City and it led to a new hip-hop generation in East and West Germany.

The Introduction of Hip-Hop into West and East Germany

Rap music had already reached parts of West Germany by the late 1970s and early 1980s through American soldiers stationed across the country. Here, hip-hop was either played in specific dance clubs that catered to Americans or aired on the American Forces Network radio station (AFN).[21] However, the main source through which rap music reached its German audience was US-American hip-hop movies, including Charlie Ahearn's *Wild Style* (1983), Tony Silver's and Henry Chalfant's *Style Wars* (1983) and Stan Lathan's *Beat Street* (1984).

---

17 Rose, *Black Noise*, p. 2.

18 Forman, *The 'hood Comes First*, p. 93.

19 See Mark Anthony Neal, 'Post-industrial Soul: Black Popular Music at the Crossroads', in *That's the Joint!*, pp. 476–502 (p. 486).

20 Rose, *Black Noise*, p. 12.

21 See D-Flame, interviewed by the author, 26 July 2012, and DJ Stylewarz, interviewed by the author, 12 June 2012.

The breakthrough success of hip-hop in Germany via movies was, however, also influenced by the visual effect of the rappers depicted in the films. German American rapper D-Flame, who is of Polish, Jamaican and Cherokee descent, explains that

> the Puerto Ricans (on screen) reminded me of my Turkish friends back then and the blacks were me! And I watched the film together with Turks, with two Turks, and we looked at each other like: 'Wow! They look like us!' You know? 'That's us!'[22]

Here the visual element on screen prompted migrant youth in Germany to compare their own ethnic identity with those of the Bronx. While the actors on screen and the viewers in Germany appeared to be equals in terms of skin and hair colour, D-Flame's observation exposes the ambivalence of ethnic signifiers when translated into another culture.

While hip-hop artists from the United States depicted on film spurred a form of proud identification for West Germany's migrant youth, hip-hop nevertheless also spoke to ethnic German youth. Hip-hop allowed young middle-class white Germans to break free from parental pressures.[23] Graffiti artist Moe from West Berlin, for example, explains that graffiti art offered a new approach to painting in which his father, an art teacher, 'could not butt in. Where he couldn't constantly criticize me. So, comic and graffiti art were the only two art disciplines where I could move freely. [...] Where I could even be in opposition to him'.[24] Thus, the different hip-hop art forms mobilized kids from all ethnic backgrounds to participate in this new cultural and artistic movement together. Furthermore, German hip-hop scholars and activists Hannes Loh and Murat Güngör emphasize that

> the cultural and social force of integration that hip-hop had in the 80s and early 90s cannot be overestimated. [...] Hip-hop culture provided a cultural framework in which German children and migrants could meet and swap ideas, whereby the common prejudices and racisms of mainstream society became irrelevant.[25]

While hip-hop established itself as a new art form in West Germany, it was also gradually introduced into East Germany, where it was marketed as an anti-capitalist statement against the US-American enemy. The hip-hop narratives on

---

22 D-Flame, interviewed by the author, 26 July 2012.
23 See Hannes Loh and Murat Güngör, *Fear of a Kanak Planet – Zwischen Nazi-Rap und Weltkultur* (Höfen: Hannibal, 2002), p. 96 and see Moe, interviewed by the author, 11 March 2012.
24 Moe, interviewed by the author, 11 March 2012 (translated by the author).
25 Loh and Güngör, *Fear of a Kanak Planet*, p. 22.

screen clearly demonstrated the 'bad sides' of living in such a political system.[26] Michael Putnam and Juliane Schicker explain that the new forms of dance and hip-hop music introduced in the film 'Beat Street' were reframed as a socialist cultural activity by the GDR government and hence officially offered as a pastime activity at the *FDJ-Klubs und Kulturhäuser* [Free German Youth clubs and arts centres].[27]

It is also striking to note that, at the time, rap music initially remained an English language phenomenon in both countries. German youth used this foreign language to express affiliation with their US-American rap role models and deemed English the only authentic hip-hop language. Moe, for example, remembers listening to Turkish German rapper Kool Savas' first attempts at rapping in German in the early 1980s and admits that his graffiti crew was

> impressed by his skills but thought it was outrageous that he was doing it in German. It was like breaking a taboo. We said: 'Dude, learn English! Do it in English and you will have a great future. Forget the German. It's shit. It just sounds like crap.'[28]

While Moe's dogmatic perspective on rap's anglicized form of delivery relates to the fact that German youth were only familiar with English as the language of rap due to the nationality of their idols, Sabine von Dirke links the initial importance of the English language to a wider German national discourse. According to von Dirke, the popularity of US-American rap in Germany was primarily based on the fact that it was performed in English. In so doing, rap denied

> German history, namely, that there were no untainted German folk traditions left after Nazism on which alternative popular music and youth culture could have been built. U.S. popular culture, especially those examples originating from African-American musical traditions, was the only valid tune that held the promise of liberation. In this context, the predominance of English within popular culture makes sense as a distancing device from the Nazi past.[29]

---

26 See ibid. and Hannes Loh and Sascha Verlan, *25 Jahre Hip-Hop in Deutschland* (Höfen: Hannibal, 2006), p. 299.

27 Michael Putnam and Juliane Schicker, 'Straight outta Marzahn: (Re)Constructing Communicative Memory in East Germany through Hip Hop', *Popular Music and Society*, 37/1 (2014), 85 – 100 (p. 88).

28 Moe, interviewed by the author, 11 March 2012.

29 Sabine von Dirke, 'Hip-Hop Made in Germany: From Old School to the Kanaksta Movement', in *German Popular Culture – How "American" is It?*, ed. by Agnes C. Mueller (Ann Arbor: The University of Michigan Press, 2004), pp. 96 – 112 (p. 99).

The dissociation from the German language was thus a refusal to value anything German since 'it is in and through language that the values of places are produced'.[30]

This aspect was also reflected in the samples that early German hip-hop artists used, for they favoured funk and soul songs rather than familiar German tunes.[31] The reason for this, as rapper and music producer Samy Deluxe explains, was that

> we did not have a music culture to which we could look back with pride. Like, when you grow up in America and you just know: 'My parents always listened to James Brown and that was our thing back then. I still have childhood memories of when they danced to his music in the living room and that's why I sample it.' That is a completely different association than saying: 'Oh, I too listened to James Brown when I was young. But samples...' We just don't have the German equivalent to that.[32]

If, according to Samy Deluxe, German youth did not have any memory of experiencing music that was sung in the German language, how could hip-hop music evolve into a German cultural product via the use of the German language and the practice of sampling?

German Rap or Rap in Germany?

The answer to this query seems to haunt rap artists from Germany even today, making rap a complex, yet fascinating music genre to explore. In 2002, Loh and Güngör claimed that 'it is still not clear what German rap actually is. German language rap? Rap by German citizens? Rap by ethnic Germans? Rap with German content? And the other important question: What is not German rap?'[33]

Often, the first clue in identifying rap from Germany is, however, rooted in the German language – a factor that became apparent in the early 1990s. The reason for the linguistic shift is twofold. On the one hand, Sabine von Dirke explains that German rappers' 'insufficient knowledge of English'[34] inhibited their achievement of lyrical sophistication. On the other hand, she claims that the 'switch to German made sense since rap wants to communicate with its au-

---

30 Forman, *The 'hood Comes First*, p. 30.
31 See Samy Deluxe, interviewed by the author, 29 July 2012 and Sleepwalker, interviewed by the author, 5 June 2012.
32 Samy Deluxe, interviewed by the author, 29 July 2012 (translated by the author).
33 Loh and Güngör, *Fear of a Kanak Planet*, p. 13.
34 Dirke, 'Hip-Hop Made in Germany', p. 102.

dience. The desire to be understood by the audience, in terms of conveying a message and showing off one's rhetorical skills, became the primary motivating factor'.[35] Indeed, rap's emphasis on verbal aesthetics and lyrical content had the ability to outweigh the negative historical semantics previously attached to the German language by resignifying it as a contemporary symbol of popular Germanness for its artists. According to Hamburg hip-hop DJ Mirko Machine, this meant that

> hip-hop has normalized the German language for the people in Germany so that they don't have to be ashamed of it. That, to sing in German, or whatever you would call it, is not like immediately 'Schlager'. Or that German words and music equal 'Schlager'.[36]

In other words, Mirko Machine, and supposedly other hip-hop artists, understood *Schlager* as being the only (and distasteful, in their opinion) popular music genre sung in German in Germany prior to hip-hop. Thus, this successful mainstream German language music genre, which is still enjoyed by many today, initially distorted the positive relation between the German language in popular music for others, namely for some of Germany's future hip-hop artists.

The new linguistic shift in rap further changed the type of music used in German rap productions. The DJs' aforementioned sampling techniques enabled rappers to discover Germany's musical past beyond *Schlager*, as they began to look for different sounds to mix and match into their musical collages. Rapper Jan Delay from Hamburg, for example, listened to German singer and songwriter Udo Lindenberg during his childhood. Thus, Lindenberg was sampled at the end of the song 'Nie Nett' [Never Kind] (1998) by Delay's rap group Absolute Beginner which in fact echoes Samy Deluxe's previous explanation on the meaning of sampling childhood memories.[37] Similarly, DJ Mirko Machine mentions that he has sampled Hildegard Knef and a drum track from a Lindenberg song in his DJ sets, while German rapper Aphroe sampled Sandra Haas' song 'Kleiner Mann' [Little Man] (1973) in his eponymous track from 2010.[38]

Through such acts of musical mixture and referencing, previous German popular music slowly became consumable for German hip-hop artists as it reappeared in the guise of hip-hop. This created what cultural theorist Homi K. Bhabha calls a

---

35 Ibid.
36 Mirko Machine, interviewed by the author, 10 May 2012 (translated by the author).
37 See Oliver Fuchs and Hannes Ross, 'Udo Lindenberg und Jan Delay: "Wir haben den Nasensound"', *Stern*, 28 March 2008) and Samy Deluxe, interviewed by the author, 29 July 2012.
38 See Mirko Machine, interviewed by the author, 10 May 2012.

'newness' that is not part of the continuum of the past and present. It creates a sense of the new as an insurgent act of cultural translation. Such art does not merely recall the past as a social cause or aesthetic precedent: it renews the past, refiguring it as a contingent 'in-between' space, that innovates and interrupts the performance of the present.[39]

This 'in-between space' remained firmly grounded in a German cultural context since the newness of German hip-hop music was understood and accepted as a German cultural product despite the fusion of US-American musical traditions and German cultural symbols such as language and music.

The Germanness of rap, as mentioned by von Dirke, was also represented in the choice of song topics. The Heidelberg rap trio Advanced Chemistry followed the same socio-political footsteps as their hip-hop idols from the United States when they released 'Fremd im eigenen Land' [Stranger in One's Own Country] in 1992. The Haitian German Torch, Italian German Toni L and Afro-German Linguist addressed the growing problem of racism and xenophobia in Germany, rapping that they were 'kein Ausländer, aber doch ein Fremder' [not a foreigner but still a stranger]. Their song theme proposes a solution to this problem by promoting a 'multicultural type of "Germanness"'[40] as a way to be socially accepted as German citizens with foreign cultural backgrounds. On a similar note, the multicultural rap group Fresh Familee rapped about the struggles for social acceptance for first and second-generation Turkish migrants in Germany in their track 'Ahmet Gündüz' (1992).

Although the first commercial German-language rap songs were thus often recorded by migrants or by descendants of migrants in the early 1990s, most mainstream attention was given to the ethnic German rap group Die Fantastischen Vier. In contrast to the aforementioned song topics, the four rappers from the suburbs of Stuttgart did not address broader social issues in their lyrics. According to German cultural scholar Priscilla Layne, their

first national success came with their nonpolitical, pop-influenced single 'Die Da' [Her Over There] in 1992 – the first number one hip hop single in Germany. Die Fantastischen Vier

---

39 Homi K. Bhabha, *The Location of Culture* (London: Routledge, 1994), p. 10.
40 Timothy S. Brown, '(African-)Americanization and Hip Hop in Germany', in *The Vinyl ain't Final – Hip Hop and the Globalization of Black Culture*, ed. by Dipannita Basu and Sidney J. Lemelle (London: Pluto Press, 2006), pp. 137–150 (p. 142); for more information on the content and impact of 'Fremd im eigenen Land' in Germany see Ayla Güler Saied, *Rap in Deutschland – Musik als Interaktionsmedium zwischen Partykultur und urbanen Anerkennungskämpfen* (Bielefeld: Transcript, 2012), pp. 62–73.

have since been celebrated in the press as pioneers of mainstream hip-hop who helped pave the way for German-language rap.[41]

Their success has nevertheless often been criticized by other German hip-hop artists who claim that the Fantastischen Vier (ab)used the skill of German language rhymes over a musical beat because their rap narratives did not reflect the socio-critical hip-hop spirit.[42] However, Loh and Güngör note that the group's success supported the acceptance of a new national music genre, namely that of German language rap, in the music industry.[43] In so doing, the Fantastischen Vier began to change the image of rap made in Germany, with Loh and Güngör writing that

> most of [the artists], who made hip-hop big in Germany, soon did not fit into the new image of German rap. Their faces were not German anymore, and their social background was not middle-class. Moreover, they could not relate to the new topics in German rap.[44]

One example of these 'new topics' in 'ethnic German rap', for the lack of a better term, can be found in the track 'MfG' (1999) by the Fantastischen Vier. As the title already reveals, the song theme consists of stanzas filled with abbreviations of, mostly, Germany-related contexts. 'MfG', an abbreviation used to end emails or text messages, only appears in the chorus in its full signification '*Mit freundlichen Grüßen*' [Yours Sincerely]. The entire song exhibits the same structure, in which every verse is replete with more or less categorically matching items, institutions and codes. Occasional German phrases or expressions frame the end of a verse, as demonstrated in the following excerpt from 'MfG' (1999):

> ADAC, DLRG – Oh jemine!
> EKZ, RTL und DFB
> ABS, TÜV und BMW
> KMH, ICE und Eschede.

The first verse is based completely in a German cultural context referencing the German automobile club *Allgemeiner Deutscher Automobil-Club e.V.* and the German lifeguard association *Deutsche Lebens-Rettungs-Gesellschaft e.V.*, which is

---

41 Priscilla Layne, 'One Like No Other? Blaxploitation in the Performance of Afro-German Rapper Lisi', *Journal of Popular Music Studies*, 25/2 (2013), 198–221.
42 See Sleepwalker, interviewed by the author, 5 June 2012 and Dietmar Elflein, 'From Krauts with Attitudes to Turks with Attitudes: Some Aspects of Hip-Hop History in Germany', *Popular Music*, 17/3 (1998), 255–265 (p. 259).
43 See Loh and Güngör, *Fear of a Kanak Planet*, p. 119.
44 Ibid., p. 308.

rhymed with the German expression 'Oh jemine!' [Oh, My Goodness!]. The second verse starts with the abbreviation for shopping mall, *Einkaufszentrum*, and ends its consumer-entertainment topic with Radio Television Luxemburg and the German football association, *Deutscher Fußballbund*. This line is then followed by a car-themed verse comprising the *Anti-Blockiersystem* [anti-skid braking system], the German *Technischer Überwachungsverein* [association for technical inspection] and the famous Bavarian car brand *Bayerische Motorenwerke*. Shifting from an automobile to a railway context, the final verse of the example then pairs 'kilometres per hour' with the German speed train Intercity Express (ICE) before ending with the name of the German city Eschede in which an ICE train derailed and fatally crashed in 1998.

The text is thus a clever and creative use of abbreviations in the German language. While the Fantastischen Vier may not represent the socio-political power and tradition of rap narratives, as is made clear by their lack of rap-specific rhetoric and ritualized speech acts, this example demonstrates how rap can nevertheless achieve a German identity. The group creates a unique approach to rap in that the song theme and linguistic orientation cannot be understood without an inherent knowledge of German culture, language and history.

Yet despite releasing 'MfG', a rap song that can be understood as stemming from a German cultural sphere, rapper Linguist of Advanced Chemistry still claims:

> Stylistically speaking there is no German rap. Musically speaking there is also nothing that would give 'German rap' an identity. The only thing that I somewhat accept is the oriental stuff. That's specifically German. That is the only German element in German rap. When the German-Turks take oriental or Turkish pop samples and rap about their existence as German-Turks in German – that's German.[45]

Linguist touches upon a short-lived yet successful rap movement initiated in Germany in 1995 when Turkish Germans sampled Turkish arabesque music. Most notably, the Turkish German rap project Cartel made 'Oriental hip-hop' famous – both in Germany and in Turkey, where they played sold-out concerts and sold over 300,000 albums.[46] The content of their songs was based on the everyday experiences of migrants living in Germany.[47] These narratives were, however, rapped mainly in Turkish, not in German. Nevertheless, what Linguist refers to as being German in oriental rap is the fact that this genre indeed represents an 'in-

---

45 Linguist in Loh and Güngör, *Fear of a Kanak Planet*, p. 146.
46 See Tom Cheesman, 'Polyglot Pop Politics – Hip Hop in Germany', *Debatte*, 6/2, (1998), 191–214 (p. 201).
47 See ibid and Loh and Güngör, *Fear of a Kanak Planet*, p. 182.

between' space, as previously described by Bhabha. Oriental rap was a completely new genre as it took Turkish folkloric music and remixed it according to US-American hip-hop traditions in order to disseminate narratives about the 'in-between' Turkish German lifestyles in Germany. Thus, this new rap sound and lyrical content took on a new name: oriental rap.

What oriental rap also showed was that the German language was not always an indicator of 'rap made in Germany'. Some rap groups from Germany even show global awareness by employing multiple languages in one track. Rappers such as Max Herre, who was mentioned in the beginning of the chapter, engage in rap in order to produce 'transcultural art that promotes unity, diversity, and tolerance'.[48] Hip-hop researcher Terence Kumpf's observation stems from his own analysis of the song theme of 'Esperanto' (1998) by Freundeskreis. In this track the group raps in a mixture of German, Esperanto, French, Spanish, Italian and Yiddish.[49] This linguistic orientation reflects the uniting power of cultures, which is especially emphasized by the language Esperanto.

It is also interesting that standard German was used in the early German-language rap productions of the 1990s. This is specifically striking in comparison to African American and Latino rappers who denoted their socio-racial identity not only through their song themes but also through their linguistic orientation, namely African American Vernacular English (AAVE) and black slang.[50] In Germany, however, Samy Deluxe explains that 'in the beginning, there was a bit of an expectation that you should definitely speak "proper", in quotation marks, German as a German rapper'.[51] Hence, despite the fact that tracks such as 'Fremd im eigenen Land' were written by ethnically 'foreign' rappers who narrated about internal socio-political topics of racism and social segregation, Samy Deluxe elaborates that 'the first Turkish rapper who rapped in German was Boulevard Bou from Heidelberg, who was so eloquent and actually quite German really'.[52]

Similarly, Tom Cheesman, a scholar of German culture, notes in his analysis of Fresh Familee's German lyrics that lead rapper Tachiles

---

48 Terence Kumpf, 'The Transculturating Potential of Hip-Hop in Germany' in *Hip-Hop in Europe – Cultural Identities and Transnational Flows*, ed. by Sina A. Nietzsche and Walter Grünzweig (Zurich: LIT, 2013), pp. 207–226 (p. 222).
49 See ibid.
50 See Rose, *Black Noise*, p. 3.
51 Samy Deluxe, interviewed by the author, 29 July 2012.
52 Ibid.

> exemplifies a delight in linguistic play which characterizes the best contemporary German rap. And this kind of text conveys at least as effectively as any explicit message that 'typical Turks', regardless of their legal status, are full participants in contemporary German culture.[53]

In other words, German rap did not, as did other types of rap, choose to express a different cultural heritage through a distinct form of speech. On the contrary, the rappers' ethnic identities were silenced by their use of 'proper' German.

The reason for the lack of this linguistic translation can be deduced by comparing the ghetto-centric urban space often represented in US-American rap narratives to German ones. Hip-hop scholar Murray Forman notes that, in US-American rap, 'the ghetto is elevated as the source of black authenticity'.[54] In other words, rappers emphasize their dark skin colour as a sign of coming from a socially stigmatized urban ghetto, whereby their language use helped authenticate this socio-racial status. Yet, as Afro-German rapper K-Four explains,

> we don't have no ghetto in Germany, man. Everybody gets money from the welfare [sic]. [...] So, you cannot talk about a ghetto like: 'It's necessary for me to hustle to survive.' You might be greedy like: 'I'm not satisfied with these 300 euros[55] or whatever they give me. I want more. That is why I sell drugs.' You might say that. But it's not necessary for you to survive. So, it's just one sort of luxury. Gangster by choice![56]

Thus, since social outcasts in Germany did not live in ghettos, there was no need for German rappers to establish a linguistic link between ethnic heritage, social class and a specific urban space. However, K-Four's observation would seem to be contradicted by a new form of rap which appeared on the German music scene at the turn of the millenium.

Germany's Gangsta Rappers

On 'Hallo Welt!' [Hello World!] (2012), Berlin rapper Megaloh describes rap as 'unter all den Schafen das Schwarze, die Saat uns'rer Rage, das Sprachrohr der Straße' [amongst all the sheep the black one, the seed of our rage, the voice of the street]. This portrayal may seem familiar to many mainstream

---

53 Cheesman, 'Polyglot Pop Politics', p. 213.
54 Murray, *The 'hood Comes First*, p. 94.
55 The 300 euros mentioned by K-Four refer to the monthly state benefit that can be claimed by unemployed citizens in Germany.
56 K-Four, interviewed by the author, 9 February 2012.

music listeners since the image of the African American male rapping about the hard life on the streets is the status quo in US-American commercial rap music.[57] While some German rappers had engaged in gangstaresque or battle rap narratives in the 1990s, such as Konkret Finn with their rap track 'Ich diss Dich' [I am dissing you] (1994)[58] or Rödelheim Hartreim Projekt (1994–1996), both from Frankfurt, these acts only represented one facet of the overall emerging rap scene in Germany.

However, by 2001, German gangsta and battle rap were slowly taking over the national rap scene and becoming the dominant genres in commercial German rap productions. Specifically, the establishment of the rap label Aggro Berlin in 2001 created a new aggressive hip-hop sound over which rappers rhymed about their deviant and violent lifestyles.[59] What was new, however, was that their lives and hence narratives unfolded in Germany's purported ghettos. This new socio-spatial orientation in rap was especially advanced through rapper Sido's song 'Mein Block' [My Housing Block] (2004), which was set in the 'Märkisches Viertel' of the West Berlin district Reinickendorf:

> Meine Stadt, mein Bezirk, mein Viertel, meine Gegend,
> meine Straße, mein Zuhause, mein Block,
> meine Gedanken, mein Herz, mein Leben, meine Welt
> reicht vom ersten bis zum sechzehnten Stock
>
> [My city, my district, my 'hood, my area,
> my street, my home, my housing block,
> my thoughts, my heart, my life, my world,
> reaches from the first to the 16th floor]

The chorus of his track summarizes the overall theme of living in a socially stigmatized neighbourhood. The '*Block*' in question is a complex of high-rise apartment buildings erected between 1963 and 1974 on the site of a former poor neighbourhood in northwestern West Berlin. Sido, who was born in East Berlin but raised in 'MV', as he refers to his 'hood later in the song, employs the common rap rhetoric of proudly belonging to this, in his perspective, poor and dangerous urban environment. In so doing, he refers to actual physical places in the first two lines and then transitions to identifying his feelings and worldview in the last two lines. This fusion of the physical and emotional elements of his German home culminates in the last line of the chorus. For Sido, his high-rise building

---

57 See Ogbar, *Hip-Hop Revolution*, p. 42.
58 See Loh and Güngör, *Fear of a Kanak Planet*, p. 299.
59 See Maria Stehle, *Ghetto Voices in Contemporary German Culture* (New York: Camden House, 2012), pp. 129–52.

symbolizes both his financially deprived status as a rapper at the bottom and his success as a rapper who has reached the top – the 16th floor by 2004. Even though he no longer lived in the MV when the song was released, this reference serves to show that Sido still has roots in his '*Block*' which further adds necessary authenticity to his gangsta image.

A similar narrative has been promoted by the most successful German gangsta rapper to-date, the Tunisian German artist Bushido. His attitude as a rapper can be surmised from the names of his albums. His breakthrough success came with 'Carlo Cokxxx Nutten' (2002), released together with ethnic German rapper Fler, followed by 'Vom Bordstein bis zum Skyline' [From the Kerbstone to the Skyline] (2003). His next albums, which were released on the major record label Universal, included 'Electro Ghetto' (2004), 'Staatsfeind Nr. 1' [Enemy of the State No. 1] (2006), as well as 'Carlo Cokxxx Nutten 2' (2009) and 'Carlo Cokxxx Nutten 3' (2015). While representing himself as the Carlo Carlucci-wearing, cocaine consuming and prostitute-procuring state enemy no. 1, Bushido also sees himself as having gone from rags to riches, starting out on the street and ending up on the German skyline.

This emphasis on social class and upward mobility (through architectural metaphors) has indeed turned into a new German gangsta rap identifier. In contrast to rap productions of the 1990s, Samy Deluxe explains that 'the social spectrum has opened up. [Rap in Germany] has now become less middle class and somehow an official voice of the lower class – it is no longer only for consumption since everyone now thinks they can participate'.[60] Fittingly, on his track 'Gangsta, Gangsta' (2015), Bushido claims '2015, Rap braucht immer noch kein Abitur' [2015, rap still doesn't need an 'Abitur' (higher education entrance qualification)].

On the other hand, Canadian German gangsta rapper Kollegah, who has won the German music award 'Echo' in 2015 and 2016 as best 'hip-hop/urban national' artist, received his 'Abitur' and spent a further three years pursuing a law degree at university.[61] Nonetheless, he has enjoyed international success as a gangsta rapper by selling himself as a deviant criminal 'boss' or 'pimp' in his song themes,[62] thus creating an image similar to Bushido's. In the track 'John Gotti'

---

60 Samy Deluxe, interviewed by the author, 29 July 2012.

61 'Charterfolg für Kollegah und Farid Bang: Der deutsche Gangster-Rap ist Zurück', *SPIEGEL ONLINE*, 19 Februar 2013 (http://www.spiegel.de/kultur/musik/kollegah-und-farid-bang-mit-hiphop-album-jbh-2-auf-platz-eins-a-884272.html).

62 Gerrit Bartels, 'Doch noch Jugendkultur – Kollegah ist Deutschlands erfolgreichster Musiker', *Der Tagesspiegel*, 20 December 2015 (http://www.tagesspiegel.de/kultur/kollegah-ist-deutschlands-erfolgreichster-musiker-doch-noch-jugendkultur/12748564.html).

from his newest album to date, *Zuhältertape Volume 4* [Pimp Tape Volume 4] (2015), Kollegah lets his imaginary opponent know:

> Ich lass' dich tot da liegen
> Verbrenn' deine Großfamilie und sie passt in 'ne fuckin' Zwei-Quadratmeter-Bootskajüte
> Und das alles, während meine iPhone-Kopfhörer Mozart spielen
> Der Boss – ich steh' voll in meiner Blüte, so wie 'ne Honigbiene[63]
>
> [I'll leave you lyin' dead
> I'll burn your extended family and they'll fit in a fucking two-square-metre boat cabin
> And all this while my iPhone headphones are playing Mozart
> The boss – I stand full in my bloom, like a honey bee]

Kollegah is known for his imaginative rhymes and fast rap pace, and this excerpt not only portrays the roughness of his typical lyrical content but also highlights the lightness and sense of humor often intertwined in his creative comparisons. Thus, he chooses a '*Kajüte*' – a highly specified German nautical term – as a small space to store away the remains of his dead victims. This space stands in contrast to the urban gangstaresque environment, thus triggering a rather comical narrative effect. Yet, by identifying with former New York mafia boss John Gotti, Kollegah also identifies with a sophisticated gangster milieu, one which listens to classical music while committing crimes. In the final verse of this example, Kollegah's often playful puns come into effect as he claims to be the boss who is at the peak of his (rap) career, which he however expresses by using the German idiom to 'fully stand in my flower' – indeed, just like a honey bee. Thus, gangsta rap narratives do not necessarily reflect the rappers' actual social and educational background as portrayed in the lyrics, which reveals a dichotomy and ambivalence inherent in the German rap scene.

Similarly, although rap was initially a means of creating distance from Germany's national-socialist past, some German gangsta rappers have chosen to identify themselves with precisely that past. In addition to emphasizing their social deviance via identifying with stigmatized urban locations, gangsta rappers have started to include Nazi references in their rhetoric. In their article 'National Socialism with Fler? German Hip Hop from the Right', Putnam and Littlejohn state that 'in [...] songs – especially those recorded by present and former artists of the controversial Aggro Berlin label – artists such as Fler and Bushido have openly included nationalistic references in their music, CD covers, and music

---

63 Kollegah, John Gotti, *Zuhältertape Volume 4*, (Selfmade Records, 2015), CD.

videos'.[64] In so doing, these rappers do not declare themselves as new national socialists or racists but rather 'flirt with these taboo themes'[65] as a provocative marketing strategy. Bushido, for instance, raps in his track 'Wenn dein Kiefer bricht' [When Your Jaw Breaks] (2015):

Mann, ich mach' Rap wieder hart
Und all die Missgeburten heulen rum
Nur die Stärksten überleben Deutschraps Säuberung

[Man, I make rap hard again
And all the freaks are crying
Only the fittest will survive German rap's cleansing]

The song theme refers to the ritualized speech act of boasting about one's skills while dissing one's (imagined) opponent. The provocative aggression of Bushido's lyrics is manifest in his ambivalent Nazi ideological references to social Darwinism – the survival of the fittest – combined with the cleansing of German rap. Yet, since Bushido is half-Tunisian, this act of 'cleansing' takes on a new dimension in a German cultural context that reaches beyond race. With such expressions, rappers thus manifest a menacing attitude and simultaneously claim superior status due to commercial success. In addition, the menace and aggression is expressed via a specific linguistic orientation, namely, as Samy Deluxe explains, a 'street uber-slang that not everyone regards as German'[66] due to its unsophisticated form of articulation.

However, in German as opposed to US-American rap, this type of linguistic orientation is not a sign of belonging to an ethnic minority. Rather, it is a means for ethnically German rappers such as Sido and Fler to lend socio-economic authenticity to their lyrics and to distinguish their narratives from those of the overall German rap community, which remains as multicultural today as it was in the 1980s.

Beyond the German Gangsta

After nearly a decade of gangsta rap's commercial domination, early German rappers, such as Jan Delay, Max Herre and Samy Deluxe, have begun to make

---

64 Michael T. Putnam and John Littlejohn, 'National Socialism with Fler? German Hip Hop from the Right', *Popular Music and Society*, 30/4 (2008), 453–468 (p. 453).
65 Ibid., p. 459.
66 Samy Deluxe, interviewed by the author, 29 July 2012.

successful comebacks on the national music scene. Samy Deluxe, for instance, uses his lyrics to criticize the state of commercial rap, which has tainted the overall picture of rap's integrative power and social usefulness. On his comeback album *SchwarzWeiß* [BlackWhite] (2011) he raps:

> Aber ich komme nicht klar auf diese ganzen Rapper,
> die scheinbar nix wissen über diese Kunstform.
> Und deshalb muss ich die Massen von Neuem bekehren,
> und so das Verständnis für unsere Kunst form'.
>
> [But I can't cope with all these rappers,
> who apparently don't know anything about this art form.
> And that's why I need to convince the masses anew,
> and form their appreciation of our art.]

While playing with the ambivalence of the meaning of German words and syntax, this excerpt reveals the impact gangsta rap has had on Germany's understanding of rap. In order to counteract the common image, which is that commercial German rap consists only of gangsta rap, Samy Deluxe deliberately fosters a poetic feeling in his rap lyrics. The word choices and syntax are more complex than in previous gangsta rap narratives and the rap-specific rhetoric even plays with homonymic sentence structures by rhyming 'Kunstform' with 'Kunst form(en)'.

As if to highlight his sophisticated use of rhyme in German, Samy Deluxe states in 'Hände hoch' [Hands Up] from the same album: 'Hör, wie elegant ich diese Sprache hier spreche, / als ob ich diese dunkle Hautfarbe nicht hätte' [Listen, how elegantly I speak this language, / as if I didn't have this dark skin colour]. While thus characterizing his rhetoric as elegant, Samy Deluxe also touches upon the supposed relationship between poor command of the German language and stigmatization as a minority or foreigner – a relationship that most likely emanated from the aforementioned German gangsta rap genre.

As the name of his comeback album suggests, Samy Deluxe's leitmotif throughout the album is the black (and white) skin colour and cultural heritage he inherited from his Sudanese father and German mother, which also allows the political side of hip-hop to return to the forefront once again. In the eponymous track 'SchwarzWeiß' [BlackWhite] (2011), Samy Deluxe, for example, asks his listeners: 'Wär' ab morgen in Deutschland hier plötzlich Apartheid, ratet mal würde ich dann weiß oder schwarz sein?' [If Apartheid would suddenly appear tomorrow in Germany, guess whether I would be black or white?] Samy Deluxe thus touches on past racist events, but, in contrast to gangsta rap narratives, he highlights the problematic separatist social consequences of racism. Hence, Samy Deluxe, as well as Advanced Chemistry, have used rap as a powerful tool with which to address socio-racial problems and have attempted to normalize their German Africanness by challenging

> debates on multiculturalism [which] are generally preoccupied with determining the degrees of compatibility or conflict between cultures. What is obscured by this perspective are the porous boundaries between groups, the diffuse notions of identity, the deterritorialized links between members of groups, the globalizing patterns of communication and the hybrid process of cultural transformation.[67]

While multiculturalism is here expressed via the fusion of the familiar German culture with an African one, cultural clashes are also expressed in German rap. These clashes hail from within the country itself in terms of East versus West German culture.

As Putnam and Schicker assert, the unification of East and West Germany meant that rappers from the former GDR had to re-establish themselves in a new and larger national hip-hop scene.[68] Yet, the fall of the Berlin wall not only affected them as hip-hop artists but as German citizens, for according to Putnam and Schicker, 'East Germans since 1990 have not attained full citizenship in this reunified Germany – not in their own eyes and, [...] certainly not in the eyes of all West Germans either'.[69]

In an interview with hip-hop scholar Inez Templeton, East Berlin rapper Joe Rilla, for instance, explains that 'The Wende (German unification) was thirteen years ago, but you still have people walking around talking about "West Berlin Masculine" or "West Berlin is the shit."'[70] Indeed, Berlin, in particular, seems to invite discussions on this cultural divide as the division is concentrated within one city. Putnam's and Schicker's lyrical analysis of different songs by East Berlin rappers Joe Rilla and Dissziplin show how these hip-hop artists engage in rap to 'target negative perceptions of East Germans that suggest that they are lazy and willingly accept government support rather than work'[71] and

> to give back the voice that the East Germans believe they lost through the Reunification and the gradual process of both intentional and unintentional marginalization that contempo-

---

67 Nikos Papastergiadis, *The Turbulence of Migration: Globalization, Deterritorialization and Hybridity* (Cambridge: Polity, 2000), p. 105.

68 Putnam and Schicker, 'Straight outta Marzahn', p. 89.

69 Ibid., p. 95.

70 Joe Rilla in Inez H. Templeton, *What's so German about It? Cultural Identity in the Berlin Hip Hop Scene* (Stirling: University of Stirling, 2006), p. 167.

71 Putnam and Schicker, 'Straight outta Marzahn', p. 94.

rary East Germans experience in the cultural, economic, and political sectors of German society today.[72]

Aside from socio-political criticism about the East-West Berlin hip-hop scene, other East German rappers living in Berlin have chosen to tell stories and share their thoughts about more mundane topics rooted in everyday life. Marteria, for example, has profited from this evolution in German rap and has enjoyed commercial success since 2010. His style is defined by social criticism wrapped in light-hearted, witty rhyme patterns on top of funky beats. In so doing, he does not deny his problematic East German childhood – 'Aufgewachsen in der DDR [...] Bin ein Kind, was seinen Papa kaum sieht' [Grew up in the GDR [...] Am a child, who hardly sees his dad] – in 'Endboss' (2010), but also touches upon wider generational changes in Germany. In 'Kids (2 Finger an den Kopf)' [Kids (2 Fingers at My Head)] (2014), he, for example, claims:

> Alle sind jetzt 'Troy', niemand geht mehr raus
> Keiner kämpft mehr bis zum 'Endboss' – alle geben auf
> Jeder geht jetzt joggen, redet über seinen Bauch
> Bevor die 'Lila Wolken' kommen sind alle längst zuhaus
>
> [Everyone is now 'Troy', nobody goes out anymore
> Nobody fights to the 'Endboss' anymore – everyone gives up
> Everyone now goes jogging, talks about his belly
> Everyone is already home before the purple clouds appear]

This excerpt from the second stanza briefly captures Marteria's song theme which is an ironic criticism of the changes in people's lifestyles that are ostensibly triggered by current trends and fashion statements. The rap specific rhetoric with which Marteria states his observations is furthermore linked to a German rap context through his use of metaphors (set in quotation marks) referring to rap song titles.

'Troy' (2004) is a song by the Fantastischen Vier in which they rap about band loyalty. 'Endboss', as already mentioned above, is a song by Marteria about the vigour to achieve something in life. 'Lila Wolken' (2012), meaning purple clouds, is also a track by Marteria featuring Berlin singers Miss Platnum and Yasha. The song is about enjoying every moment in life which includes staying awake until the clouds turn purple at dawn. Thus, while the linguistic orientation of the song is in standard German, its full signification can best be understood if one is familiar with the previous work of Marteria and Fantastischen Vier since

---

72 Ibid., p. 95.

there are references to them in the form of verbal sampling. In the end, the song is another example of the creation of a German cultural product, similar to 'MfG', since both tracks rely on a comprehensive knowledge of the German language and, in this case, of German rap music.

Marteria's success is, however, not only dependent on his ironic, humorous song themes, rap specific rhetoric and linguistic orientation, but also on his beats in the sense of the actual underlying music. In contrast to gangsta rap and previous German rap, this music genre was seldom played on the radio or in mainstream dance clubs.[73] The reason for this was that early German hip-hop music was, according to Hamburg DJ Ben Kenobi, simply not 'fat and, let's say, club-suitable'.[74] Recalling a track by Samy Deluxe's hip-hop crew Dynamite Deluxe in the 1990s, DJ Ben Kenobi described their sound as having been 'a bit meagre. There wasn't any fatness somehow. It just wasn't there yet'.[75] Today German producers are making an effort to change this, with the result that German hip-hop music is becoming more bass-heavy and complex and therefore more danceable. As a result, newer rap productions from Germany are being played more frequently in clubs where their multicultural narratives reach a dancing audience, which is a return to the origins of hip-hop.

Conclusion

After a brief overview of the different rap styles and multicultural narratives within rap that have emerged in Germany over the past 30 years, it can be concluded that one cannot talk about German rap but only about rap in Germany. While linguistic orientations have indeed given rap in Germany a national identity, rappers still choose to rap in English, Turkish or other languages, depending on the song themes. These have therefore served to express very different perspectives on Germany's cultural landscape. While rap-specific rhetoric and ritualized speech acts have mostly appeared in gangsta rap, which is the genre that most closely aims to imitate US-American rap, rap in Germany has found its own multiple voices which express the diversity and complexity of Germany's sociocultural landscape.

The chosen examples have shown that while Advanced Chemistry, Freundeskreis and Samy Deluxe have used rap to propose a multicultural type of Ger-

---

73 See Mirko Machine, interviewed by the author, 10 May 2012.
74 DJ Ben Kenobi, interviewed by the author, 3 July 2012.
75 Ibid.

manness or global unity, the Fantastischen Vier have engaged in rap to distance themselves from socio-political topics. Their early commercial success, in particular, created an awareness of the new emerging genre of German language rap, with their label, Four Music, subsequently signing future rap artists such as Freundeskreis and Marteria. Thus, the Fantastischen Vier provided a platform where political rap could thrive once again.[76]

While political rap often focused on Germany's multiculturalism, this chapter also touched upon the prevailing cultural divide between the East and West of Germany. Having named rappers Disssziplin and Joe Rilla from East Berlin as examples of political activists who give East Germans a voice through rap, Putnam and Schicker conclude that this engagement presents a 'Neo-Ossi identity, one that serves as a "call to arms" for modern Ossis to embrace the positive attributes of their socialist past and to re-establish ownership of their present reality and future'.[77]

Yet, Berlin has been home to other rappers with and without ethnic German backgrounds who turned to rap in order to disseminate their socially stigmatized gangsta narratives. This German gangsta-ism was most notably expressed through their aggressive vocabulary and references to National Socialism. The reason for the latter, as Putnam and Littlejohn explain, is because 'Germans simply do not have a cultural history with gangsters such as Scarface. In their own cultural psyche the figures in their immediate cultural past that personify the ideal gangstas who demanded respect and street cred were Adolf Hitler and his associates'.[78] Therefore, they conclude that German gangsta rap can be seen as the 'articulation of a new German identity constructed through a complex engagement with the German past and American popular culture (i. e. gangsta rap)'.[79]

More recent rap productions have nevertheless started commenting on more globally related changes in society while using beats that encourage dancing. Thus, while early hip-hop artists claimed they did not grow up with German music, rap in German seems to be filling that gap while acting as a musical mirror to reflect the various sociocultural and ever-changing identity discourses in contemporary Germany.

---

76 See Loh and Güngör, *Fear of a Kanak Planet*, p. 119.
77 Putnam and Schicker, 'Straight outta Marzahn', p. 97.
78 Ibid., p. 94.
79 Putnam and Littlejohn, 'National Socialism with Fler?', p. 454.

Christoph Jürgensen and Antonius Weixler
Diskursrock and the 'Hamburg School'. German Pop Music as Art and Intellectual Discourse

A glance at the songs with German lyrics that charted in 1992 reveals a collection characterized primarily by clichéd love songs or nonsensical parody. To name just a few, Münchener Freiheit celebrated 'Liebe auf den ersten Blick' [Love At First Sight] and Die Fantastischen Vier pioneered German rap with a song about 'Die da' [Her Over There], while comedian Hape Kerkeling mocked the avant-garde classical music scene with a single entitled 'Hurz', a word that does not exist in German.

However, the very same year saw an attempt to break with this tradition as performances by bands like Blumfeld and Cpt. Kirk & presented a new sound and a new attitude. Their 1992 albums, which were distributed by the label What's So Funny About, have often been described in terms of a revolution. According to this narrative, when Blumfeld hit the music market with their debut album *Ich-Maschine* [I-Machine] and Cpt. Kirk & released their third album *Reformhölle* [Hell of Reforms], a new era in German-language pop music began.

This, it has often been claimed, was the birth of the so-called *Hamburger Schule* [Hamburg School]. However, as is the case with most myths about beginnings, it is not only impossible to untangle different narratives regarding the origins of this new trend, but also very difficult to specify which came first – the phenomenon or its name. Legend has it that the 'Hamburg School' was first labelled by journalist Thomas Gross, who used it in a combined review of the two albums mentioned above.[1] An alternative version maintains that the phenomenon owes its existence to the programmatic approach that informed the foundation of the label L'Age D'Or by Carol von Rautenkranz and Pascal Fuhlbrügge.[2] And, adding to the spectrum of narratives, Fuhlbrügge argues that Volker Backes coined the term of what was, at the time, an emerging brand in his Bielefeld

---

1 For this and other theories regarding when the School came into being, see Björn Fischer, *Tocotronic, Blumfeld, Die Sterne: Die Texte der Hamburger Schule* (Hamburg: Diplomica, 2015), p. 7–9.
2 This version of the story is told in the online magazine *laut.de* (http://www.laut.de/lautwerk/hamburger_schule).

DOI 10.1515/9783110425727-011

based fanzine *What's that Noise*, claiming that this was the source from which Thomas Gross borrowed it.[3]

No matter which of these accounts one might prefer, the label *Hamburger Schule* proved appealing and served as a point of reference for both the branding and self-portrayal of bands based in or originating from Hamburg. Thus, it is no coincidence that bands like Die Sterne, Kolossale Jugend, Ostzonensuppenwürfelmachenkrebs, Die Erde, Huah! and Die Braut haut ins Auge mostly recorded for the label L'Age D'Or. Even though the members of this 'school' are only very loosely linked and despite differences in detail, they share a common aesthetic and, arguably more importantly, a common conceptual approach: apart from the obvious, conscious use of German lyrics – or as Die Sterne ironically declare in the first track of their album *Posen* [Posing], 'Scheiß auf deutsche Texte' [To Hell with German Lyrics] – they all refer to the *Neue Deutsche Welle* (NDW) of the 1980s, British indie rock and German punk. Moreover, the musicians (re)present a socio-critical attitude, which is encapsulated and articulated with admirable clarity by Die Sterne in the title of their 1992 album *Fickt das System* [Fuck the System].

The term 'Hamburg School' aptly fits this pop cultural phenomenon. By singing about the sentimental desire for a 'right life in the wrong one', the bands evoke the tradition of the 'Frankfurt School' of Theodor W. Adorno and Max Horkheimer. Therefore, it is not surprising that agitprop legends Ton Steine Scherben are a frequent and central point of reference in the Hamburg School's construction of their new tradition. For example, Blumfeld's 'Eine eigene Geschichte' [A Story of its Own] from their 1994 LP *L'Etat Et Moi* transforms Ton Steine Scherben's slogan 'Macht kaputt, was euch kaputt macht' [destroy that which destroys you] – a ubiquitous feature of socio-critical protests and graffiti art – into 'Macht verrückt, was euch verrückt macht' [drive crazy that which drives you crazy].

Above all, these bands share an agenda that uniquely combines a (radical) left-wing socio-critical stance spiked with intellectual irony and self-reflexive references to a universe usually alien to pop music. They quote postmodernist theorists and philosophers of language, such as Jacques Lacan or Gilles Deleuze, and manage to engage with postmodern theory and art in such a manner as to satisfy Leslie Fiedler's demand that the demarcation lines between 'high' and 'low' art and between 'art' and 'mass-production' be transgressed[4] – a de-

---

3 See *Läden, Schuppen, Kaschemmen: Eine Hamburger Popkulturgeschichte*, ed. by Christoph Twickel (Hamburg: Nautilus, 2003), p. 171.

4 Walter Grasskamp, *Das Cover von Sgt. Pepper: Eine Momentaufnahme der Popkultur* (Berlin: Wagenbach, 2004), p. 30.

mand which was notably first published in *Playboy* in 1969.[5] Hence, an alternative label for this approach which understands music as a discursive medium of socio-critical debate is *Diskursrock* [Discourse Rock].

This chapter will focus on two of the most distinguished bands of the 'Hamburg School', Blumfeld and Tocotronic. This duumvirate shaped the 'saddle period'[6] of recent German popular music more than anybody else and has exerted a lasting influence on subsequent 'schools'. This investigation is guided by two main questions: firstly, we probe how the bands tackle the arduous task of maintaining a consistent stance of opposition and, secondly, we explore how this task necessitates the constant challenging of an important aspect of the logic of (popular) culture, namely that being an aesthetic outcast and having widespread success are mutually exclusive.

Or, in the words of sociologist Pierre Bourdieu: What happens if one enters the sociocultural field of pop music as a heretic but ends up achieving prominence and marking an epoch? How can one oppose what Bourdieu calls 'the dialectic of distinction – whereby institutions, schools, works and artists which have "left their mark" are destined to fall into the past, to become *classic* or *outdated*, to see themselves thrown *outside* history or to pass "into history"'?[7]

Blumfeld: From Arty Pop to the Pursuit of Simplicity

While Blumfeld's debut *Ich-Maschine* was greeted with approval, their second album *L'Etat Et Moi*[8] (1994) remains their most celebrated work – it ranks highly amongst the most influential and important German pop music albums.[9] It was

---

5 Leslie Fiedler, 'Cross the Border, Close the Gap', *Playboy*, December 1969, pp. 151, 230 and 252–258. The paper was first presented at a conference in Freiburg in June 1968, recently republished as: Leslie Fielder, 'Überquert die Grenze, schließt den Graben! Über die Postmoderne', in *Wege aus der Moderne. Schlüsseltexte der Postmoderne-Diskussion*, ed. by Wolfgang Welsch (Berlin: Akademieverlag, 1988 [1969]), pp. 57–74.
6 See Reinhart Koselleck, 'Einleitung', in *Geschichtliche Grundbegriffe: Historisches Lexikon zur politisch-sozialen Sprache in Deutschland*, vol. 1, ed. by Reinhart Koselleck and Otto Brunner (Stuttgart: Klett Cotta, 1979), pp. XIII–XVII.
7 Pierre Bourdieu, *The Rules of Art: Genesis and Structure of the Literary Field* (Stanford UP: Stanford, 1996), pp. 154–156.
8 To be precise, the album's title on the cover was written all in capitals: 'L'ETAT ET MOI', while the corresponding song was written 'L'etat et moi'; in both versions without the acute accent.
9 For instance, the album was ranked no. 3 in *Musikexpress'* 2003 ranking of 'the 25 best pop LP's with German lyrics', no. 9 in *Musikexpress'* 2005 'the 50 best LP's of the 90s', no. 37 in *Mu-*

groundbreaking in its unique mixture of distorted guitar sounds that keep the original timbre intact and its at times furious, soft or even purely recitative styles of singing, which resulted in a slightly more punkish version of Brit Pop. This album set the tone and the foundation for what would follow and it made clear what kind of 'school' this was to be, one that was neither working-class nor 'popular' – in the literal sense 'of the common people' – but rather elite. While other pop song lyrics were merely texts, the 'Hamburg School' raised the level of debate to that of a 'discourse', as can readily be seen by looking at the band name and the title and cover of the album *L'Etat Et Moi.*

Jochen Distelmeyer (vocals, guitar and piano), André Rattay (drums) and Eike Bohlken (bass) named themselves after Franz Kafka's short story 'Blumfeld, ein älterer Junggeselle' ['Blumfeld, an Elderly Bachelor' (1915, posthumous)]. Few writers of German literature are as cryptic, as enigmatic and as celebrated by intellectuals as Kafka. By alluding to him, one lays claim to being cool, academic and mysterious (if not rebellious) at the same time. Blumfeld's choice of band name thus did nothing less than introduce an intellectual and philosophical attitude and 'discourse level' into pop culture or, conversely, popularize being sophisticated (or 'nerdy').

The same applies to the title of the album, which is a clear reference to Louis XIV's (in)famous statement 'L'état, c'est moi' [I am the state]. Two aspects are of importance here. Firstly, the slight shift of the phrase to *L'Etat Et Moi* [The State and Me][10] sets the song's persona in opposition to society and therefore represents a rebellious and critical gesture as well as the 'enactment' of a lonely and sensitive individual. In addition, the title could linguistically also be construed as 'the state versus me'. This dichotomy between the song's persona and society is immediately reaffirmed and spelled out in the very first song of the album, 'Draußen auf Kaution' [Out on Bail]:

> Das Stechen im Kopf das Stechen im Herz
> treibt mich nur tiefer in den Kummer rein
> und tiefer ins Alleinesein
> überall sind Menschen in den Straßen
> kenn ich nicht gehöre nicht dazu
> frage mich zu wem ich denn gehöre
> und wenn wer zu mir spricht hör ich nicht zu

---

sikexpress' 2003 ranking of 'the 100 best LP's 1969–2009, no. 47 in *Spex's* 1999 'the 100 best LP's of the century' and no. 263 in the German *Rolling Stone's* 2004 ranking of 'the 500 best LP's of all times'.

10 See *laut.de* (http://www.laut.de/Blumfeld/Alben/LEtat-Et-Moi-17724).

[The stabbing pain in the head the stabbing pain in the heart
just drives me deeper into misery
and deeper into loneliness
everywhere there are people on the streets
I don't know them and I don't belong to them
ask myself to whom I belong
and if someone talks to me I do not listen]

The position of the song's persona in relation to society is, on the one hand, an example of a sentimental and sensitive self in the tradition of the German concept of romanticism, in which an individual departs from society by either withdrawing into the inner self or into nature. On the other hand, the third song on the album, '2 oder 3 Dinge, die ich von Dir weiß' [2 or 3 Things I Know About You] celebrates the act of rebellion – i.e. setting oneself in opposition to society – by thinking differently both in terms of politics and in terms of sexuality ('wir sind politisch und sexuell anders denkend' [we are political and sexual dissidents]).

Secondly, as the album title appears in capital letters on the cover (thus blurring the distinction between 'l'État' or 'l'état'), the title could also be read as a catch-phrase for either existentialism (i.e. the state I am in and me) or a (post)modern deconstruction of subjectivity (the state I am vs. me). The complexities created by the album's ambiguous title, which is both ironic and self-reflective, can be taken to exemplify how the band manages to establish a 'discourse' version of rock music. The frequent quotation of renowned thinkers and writers in Blumfeld's lyrics also adds to this discursive level of complexity.[11]

Yet that ambiguous album title yields further readings: firstly, the allusion to the French king's gesture of arrogance merges a provocative stance quite common in pop culture with a pose of elitist omnipotence. This pose is repeated in several songs, sometimes ironically as in 'Mein System kennt keine Grenzen' [My System Knows No Limits], sometimes rather emphatically. The cover of the subsequent album *Old Nobody* (1999), for example, shows all of the band members looking like well brought-up boys wearing fashionable branded clothes. The band members confidently position themselves, quite non-ironically, as upper middle class intellectuals. Secondly, and arguably more importantly in the case of Blumfeld, the combination of a French pun with an intricate self-reflexive

---

11 For a concise overview of quotes in Blumfeld's lyrics see *Zitat-Maschine* (http://skyeyeliner. endorphin.ch/zitatmasch.html). See Jens Reisloh, *Deutschsprachige Popmusik: Zwischen Morgenrot und Hundekot. Von den Anfängen um 1970 bis ins 21. Jahrhundert. Grundlagenwerk – Neues Deutsches Lied (NDL)* (Münster: Telos, 2011), p. 157.

formula which highlights the processes that determine subjectivity shows a level of sophisticated thought that is not common in the sphere of popular music.

What is remarkable here is that Blumfeld is presenting itself as a group of the intellectual and bourgeois elite entering the sphere of popular culture. Thus, Fiedler's demand to blur the lines between 'high' and 'low' art (in order to 'close the gap' and to value every piece of art within a culture as equally important and noteworthy) is turned around by Blumfeld: Whereas the cultural turn claims that 'low' or popular music, pulp fiction and, say, advertisements, are to be considered as 'art', Blumfeld transfer an elite habitus and content into the sphere of pop culture. The rebellious gesture of non-conformity is therefore also turned around: Blumfeld's provocation is that they embody an elitism which is taking over the sphere of pop, replacing 'being against' (e.g. resistance against the dominant ideology of a given society) with the notion of 'being within' – a system, a discursive formation, an ideological framework.

This elitist, sophisticated position is best illustrated by the album track 'L'etat et moi (Mein Vorgehen in 4, 5 Sätzen)' [L'etat et moi (My Method in 4 to 5 Sentences)]: it is not a song but a recited poem,[12] merging poetry with, as the title suggests, poetics:

> Von einem Blatt das unbeschrieben
> vor mir liegt und Fragen stellt
> wie ich dem Blick derer entkam
> die mich durch ihn für sich erzeugen
> kann ich ohne mich zu beugen in ihm leben
> oder wachs' ich lebenslang in ihn hinein
> [...] I killed nature with a groove
> als ich mich gestern aus ihr sprengte
>
> [About a sheet of paper that is blank
> lying in front of me and asking questions
> how I got away from the gaze of those
> who generate me for themselves with it [i.e. with their gaze]
> can I without bending my will live in it
> or do I grow into it all my life long

---

12 Sascha Seiler, for instance, argues that most songs by Blumfeld resemble poems more than lyrics of pop songs. Furthermore, Seiler shows how 'Eines Tages' [Someday] establishes, on the one hand, an intricate intertextual relationship to Ingeborg Bachmann's poetry (in particular to 'Das dreißigste Jahr' and *Die gestundete Zeit*). On the other hand, the song is also alluding to Paul Celan. Since Bachmann and Celan had a relationship that left its mark on their respective poetry and by evoking all of that in a love-song, 'Eines Tages' sets up a fairly complex network of references. See Sascha Seiler, *"Das einfache wahre Abschreiben der Welt": Pop-Diskurse in der deutschen Literatur nach 1960* (Göttingen: Vandenhoeck & Ruprecht, 2006), pp. 267–273.

[...] I killed nature with a groove
as I burst out of her yesterday]

Explaining one's own method is of course a self-reflexive move. And while talking about the beginning of all writing experiences can be regarded as a meta-discursive irony, it is also a reference to a classic trope of Western art – the *horror vacui* of the empty spaces that need to be filled. Furthermore, the reflection on how the gaze of the other constitutes the self which is subjected to that gaze (hence one does not exist without being perceived by others) is a level of discourse usually associated with a certain kind of published poetry, but not with lyrics of a pop music album. In addition, despite the song's title, its lyrical poetics does not in fact set out a method, which would, by definition, entail reducing the complexity of reality as a technique of acquiring knowledge. Rather, this 'poetics' enhances complexity, describes an epistemological problem in an abstract way and, in a symbolic act of liberation, raises more questions than it answers.

On Blumfeld's subsequent album *Old Nobody*, this strategy of artification is carried on and reinforced since the poem 'Eines Tages' [Someday] is strategically made the first track on the album. The heightened lyrical character of both the form and content of this poem is part of an elaborate and successful strategy to make Blumfeld the most intellectual of German bands.[13] Against this background, it is fitting that Eike Bohlken became a lecturer in philosophy after he left the band in 1996 (and was replaced by Peter Thiessen, also a member of Kante). It is striking that both poems repeatedly quote from popular culture: *Kill the Nation with a Groove*, for instance, is a 1992 hip-hop sampler released by the Hamburg label Buback Tonträger, which also featured Die Goldenen Zitronen and Die Türen. Yet despite such quotations, this strategy can be regarded as the deliberate creation of a refined and 'arty' version of pop music rather than a blurring of the threshold between 'high' and 'low' culture in Fiedler's terms.

The album cover of *L'Etat Et Moi* displays a further dimension of an increased awareness of the intricate relationship between 'high' and 'low' culture and the potential that resides in that relationship. The cover picture is another allusion to a king, this time not a historical or political figure, but the 'king' of pop music himself, Elvis Presley. The cover is an almost exact copy of Presley's

---

13 See Reisloh, *Deutschsprachige Popmusik*, p. 157; Dirk Weissmann, '"Es könnte viel bedeuten ...": Ein hermeneutisch-philologisches Experiment mit einem Song der Gruppe Blumfeld (Tausend Tränen tief)', *Das Populäre: Untersuchungen zu Interaktionen und Differenzierungsstrategien in Literatur, Kultur und Sprache*, ed. by Olivier Agard, Christian Helmreich and Hélène Vinckel-Roisin (Göttingen: Vandenhoeck & Ruprecht 2010), pp. 253–264 (p. 256).

50,000,000 Elvis Fans Can't Be Wrong (1959), but with the faces replaced (the centre figure shows the face of Jochen Distelmeyer). While the content of the album *L'Etat Et Moi* arguably offers an artification of pop, the cover illustrates how such an artification can playfully engage with a reference to one of pop's biggest icons as it presents a pop cultural stance as a quotation.

Blumfeld's third album, *Old Nobody*, marks a shift by setting a different tone which paves the way for the albums to come, both in terms of musical style and intellectual and ideological content. Apart from 'Mein System kennt keine Grenzen', all the songs on this album are crooned over a soft bed of guitars and atmospheric lounge drums. The rebellious rock sound is replaced with an easy-listening format and simple melodic hooks. Furthermore, most of the songs are purely and simply about love. In 'Tausend Tränen tief' [A Thousand Tears Deep], for instance, one can identify allusions to poems by German writers such as Heinrich Heine, Else Lasker-Schüler, Rolf Dieter Brinkmann and Ingeborg Bachmann, as well as the notorious concept of romantic desire symbolized by the blue flower:[14]

> Mit dir
> in ein anderes Blau
> wir teilen einen Traum
> ein Bild aus anderen Zeiten
>
> [With you
> into a different shade of blue
> we share one dream
> an image from another time]

This time, however, in contrast to the songs on *L'Etat Et Moi*, these references merge into a simple overall sound and level of 'discourse'. Interestingly, the chorus is an almost verbatim quote of a popular 1939 *Schlager* song, 'Komm zu mir heut' Nacht'[15] [Come To Me Tonight].

This pursuit of simplicity both in sound and lyrics set the tone for all of Blumfeld's subsequent albums. On *Testament der Angst* [Testament of Anxiety] (2001) and *Jenseits von Jedem* [Beyond Everybody] (2003), this process was continued and enhanced, culminating in *Verbotene Früchte* [Forbidden Fruits] (2006). The lyrics on *Verbotene Früchte* again centre on the theme of love, but what becomes particularly dominant on this album is a Rousseau-esque retreat of the song's persona to nature. In fact, almost all aspects of nature are celebrat-

---

14 See Weissmann, "'Es könnte viel bedeuten …'", pp. 253–264.
15 Ibid., p. 257.

ed on this album – animals ('Tiere um uns' [Animals Around Us]), rivers ('Der Fluß' [The River]), birds ('Ich fliege mit Raben' [I Fly With Ravens]), insects ('Schmetterlings Gang' [The Route of the Butterfly]), gardens and fruits ('Der Apfelmann' [The Apple Man]) and seasons ('April').

Blumfeld thus ceased to sing about the confrontation between the individual and society, matching their new harmony with tender, soft and sometimes even cheesy tones. These songs are sometimes closer to *Schlager* than to the origins of their own group history or to what one expects of a *Diskursrock* band. However, one might ask whether this was in itself a subversive romantic move. Perhaps the only way to be provocative in postmodern times is to reject what has become a stereotypical pose in pop culture, that is, reject the very act of outright rebellion and withdraw into nature and privacy instead. One might call this strategy a subversion of a second order.

In other words, Blumfeld was rebelling against the pop system itself. 'Being against' the logic of pop music was Blumfeld's provocative stance. The reviews of *Verbotene Früchte* arguably confirm that this strategy was successful, as most music critics were annoyed with the album. Be that as it may, this strategy of (romantic) simplification arguably reached its peak on this last album. Consequently, after the *Verbotene Früchte* tour in January 2007, Jochen Distelmeyer announced the band's dissolution. In 2014, Blumfeld reunited very briefly for a critically acclaimed tour to celebrate the twentieth anniversary of the groundbreaking *L'Etat Et Moi*.

After Blumfeld split, Distelmeyer started a solo career, but his 2009 album *Heavy* did not match the success of his former work. His debut novel *Otis* (2015), though highly anticipated, was equally met with considerable disdain by critics. His second solo album, *Songs from the Bottom Vol. 1*, published in early 2016, however, has the potential to start a new chapter in Distelmeyer's career. The album title is a reference to Bob Dylan and The Band's *The Basement Tapes* (1975) – and arguably, in the way the album title is phrased, to their *Music from Big Pink* (1968).

Another influential model can be seen in Johnny Cash's *American Recordings* (1994). The 'Vol. 1' adjunct suggests that Distelmeyer intends to start a series as Cash did and the underlying concept of both consists in covers of well-known hits. While Cash transforms American hits into folk music covers, Distelmeyer creates singer-songwriter versions of songs like The Byrds' 'Turn! Turn! Turn! (To Everything There is a Season)', Nick Lowe's 'I Read a Lot' and Joni Mitchell's 'Just Like This Train', Brit Pop classics like The Verve's 'Bittersweet Symphony' or Radiohead's 'Pyramid Song', as well as current pop 'smashers' like Britney Spears' 'Toxic' and Lana Del Rey's 'Video Games'. The 'live and unplugged' performances of this album emphasize musical craftsmanship but still stage the songs as pieces of art. Furthermore, from time to time, Distelmeyer alters lines in the lyrics in a way that makes the songs more abstract and undetermined and therefore – intriguingly – more complex on the discourse level.[16] However, it is not yet clear whether this album will mark a return to Distelmeyer's (and Blumfeld's) arty roots.

Tocotronic: From Popular Art to Arty Pop

The next *Diskursrock* band commonly associated with the Hamburg School – closely following Blumfeld both in time as well as being most frequently linked with them – was Tocotronic, who were quick to self-reflexively refer to their arrival in the song 'Ich bin neu in der Hamburger Schule' [I Am New to the Hamburg School]:

> Ich bin gerade in die erste Klasse gekommen [...]
> Die Klassenzimmer sind angenehm dunkel.
> Es gibt Bier als Pausenbrot.
> Ich bin neu in der Hamburger Schule,
> und lern' kein Griechisch und kein Latein.
> Und trotzdem scheint mir die Hamburger Schule
> 'Ne Eliteschule zu sein.
>
> [I've just entered first form [...]
> The class room is nicely dimmed.
> There is beer for break-time.
> I am new to the Hamburg School.
> There's no need to learn Greek or Latin.
> And nevertheless the Hamburg School seems to be
> a school for the elite.]

What becomes apparent in this quote is the specific intertwining of irony and self-reflection which is quite characteristic of Tocotronic. Self-reflection was the foundation-stone of the band, or to put it another way: theory came first and the practical side of playing music, second. As such, Tocotronic's work can be deemed concept art. In 1993, Dirk von Lowtzow (vocals and guitar), Jan

---

16 For example Distelmeyer changed the last lines of *Toxic*. Spears makes it quite clear in the original that by the end of the song, the song's persona is ready for sexual intercourse after all: 'Intoxicate me now / With your lovin' now / I think I'm ready now'. Distelmeyer, however, alters this line to 'I better go now / Don't want trouble', which not only completely changes the end of this love story, but brings an new level of meaning to the eponymic 'toxicity' and therefore to the whole concept of being in love.

Müller (bass) and Arne Zank (drums and keyboard) came together, named themselves after a Nintendo handheld electronic game called Tricotronic and drew a doodle that they branded as a 'structuralist diagram'.[17] There is no way this scribbled diagram can be understood and it is not meant to be understood since it is a rejection of the myth of authenticity that still plays a prominent role in pop culture.

Central to the Tocotronic concept is the question of how to continue being rebellious in post-rebellious times. The pure and somewhat naive act of rebellion was for years, if not decades, the last sphere untouched by irony – and in a postmodern world of ('high') culture, the last refuge of pathos. It is this very rebelliousness that Tocotronic ironically enacts. To put it in the terms of Friedrich Schiller: the 'sentimental' answer to the realization of the irretrievable loss of *naivetè* is an explicitly anti-rock and ostensibly dilettantish band concept, a concept which becomes obvious in their style of both music and fashion. Their program of non-conformity consisted of wearing corduroy trousers, retro training jackets and quirky second hand T-shirts which they wore in deliberately blurred Polaroid photos on their first album cover. This distinctive fashion code is matched lyrically by a persona that, like Holden Caulfield, is distanced from everything that appears bourgeois and stuffy to an early-20-something.

'Freiburg', for instance – the first song on the debut album *Digital ist besser* [Digital Is Better] (1995), which was recorded in just three days – begins as follows:

> Ich weiß nicht, warum ich euch so hasse,
> Fahrradfahrer dieser Stadt.
> Ich bin alleine und ich weiß es.
> Und ich find es sogar cool,
> und ihr demonstriert Verbrüderung.
>
> [I don't know why I hate you so much,
> you cyclists of this town.
> I am alone and know it.
> And I even think it's cool,
> and you are fraternizing.]

In the subsequent verses the cyclists are replaced by ballet artists and backgammon players, reaffirming the radical alienation between the song's persona and society. This opposition also explains the album title: the stance of the outsider is metonymically explained as the gap between the colourful Swatch chrono-

---

17 See Tocotronic, 'Freiburg', *Digital ist besser*, L'age d'or 1995.

meters which were trendy in the 1990s and the silver Casio digital watch which the lyrical self prefers for reasons of distinction on 'Digital ist besser':

> In einer Gesellschaft
> in der man bunte Uhren trägt,
> in einer Gesellschaft wie dieser
> bin ich nur im Weg.
> Aber Digital ist besser.
>
> [In a society
> in which colourful watches are worn,
> in a society like this
> I am only in the way.
> But digital is better.]

Further rejections include Saturdays ('Samstag ist Selbstmord' [Saturday Is Suicide]), guitar dealers ('Hamburg rockt' [Hamburg Rocks]) and Eric Rohmer's movies, which one nevertheless needs sometimes in order to understand this complicated life.[18]

The most potent and influential song on the first album is without doubt 'Ich möchte Teil einer Jugendbewegung sein' [I Want to Be a Part of a Youth Movement]. This tagline title articulates the outsider's desire to be integrated into a community: 'Ich möchte mich auf euch verlassen können / Lärmend mit euch durch die Straßen rennen.' [I want to be able to rely on you / running and ranting through the streets]. Furthermore, this song imagines a communicative code that creates a communal bond:

> Jede unserer Handbewegungen
> hat einen besonderen Sinn,
> weil wir eine Bewegung sind,
> weil wir eine Jugendbewegung sind.
>
> [Every gesture with our hands
> has a specific meaning,
> 'cause we are a movement,
> 'cause we are a youth movement.]

---

18 The lament in 'Meine Freundin und ihr Freund' [My Girlfriend and Her (Boy-)Friend] goes: 'Und im Leben geht's oft her / Wie in 'nem Film von Rohmer / Und um das alles zu begreifen, / Wird man was man furchtbar haßt / Nämlich Cineast / Zum Kenner dieser fürchterlichen Streifen' [Sometimes life's just like / a Rohmer movie / And in order to grasp it all / one turns into what one hates the most / namely a cineaste / an expert in these dreadful flicks]. Tocotronic, 'Meine Freundin und ihr Freund', *Digital ist besser* (1995).

Nevertheless, the desire to belong is mocked in a distinctive way by the deliberately awkward adaptation of a 'party-official's speech'.[19] And by the end of the song, the lyrical persona is even mumbling

> Jetzt müssen wir wieder in den Übungsraum.
> Oh Mann, ich habe überhaupt kein' Bock.
> Oh Mann, ich hab schon was Besseres vor.
>
> [Now we need to rehearse again.
> Oh man, I don't feel like it.
> Oh man, I have better plans.]

This is pure irony, but ironic speech is predicated on the mutual understanding between sender and receiver. Soon Tocotronic were facing usurpation by a youth culture that took their style and lyrics literally and non-ironically, i. e. as a straightforward statement of a subject identified with singer Dirk von Lowtzow himself. This, in turn, was ironic in itself, epitomized in the 'Toco-clones' which could be seen wandering around in T-shirts displaying their best-known song titles on the front. The anti-fashion had become fashionable.

After several albums in quick succession – *Nach der verlorenen Zeit* [After The Lost Time] (1995), *Wir kommen um uns zu beschweren* [We Come to Complain] (1996), *Es ist egal, aber* [It Doesn't Matter, But] (1997) – which offered only a slight variation of the *Digital ist besser* formula, Tocotronic began to turn their popular art into arty pop in order to re-establish their position as an outsider which had been compromised by their success. They no longer wore training-jackets and awkward T-shirts but rather cultivated their musical concept by abandoning (even ironic) I-messages and by developing their musical complexity. In doing so, they set foot on a career-path established by the Beatles.

This development first emerged on the 1999 album *K.O.O.K* which featured jazz-like piano parts, integrated keyboards into their sound and offered occasional excursions into electro pop, while the vocals reached a new breadth of tone. *K.O.O.K* could be described as Tocotronic's *Revolver*. The self-titled album *Tocotronic* (2002) underscores this pop-historical allusion as it is – just like the Beatles' eponymous album – a 'white album' with a monochrome cover. In line with this iconic tradition and a drift into more fantastical and abstract realms, the song 'Neues vom Trickser' [News From the Trickster] offers an explicit

---

19 See Christian Schlösser, 'Neu in der Hamburger Schule? Schule, Archiv und Markt in deutschsprachiger Popmusik der 1990er Jahre', in: *Deutsches Lied, vol. II: Vom Niedergang der Diseusenkultur bis zu Aggro Berlin*, ed. by Gregor Ackermann, Walter Delabar and Carsten Würmann (Bielefeld: Aisthesis, 2007), pp. 503–511.

rejection of subjective sensitivity and problems of everyday life that character-ized earlier songs: 'Eines ist jetzt sicher / Eins zu eins ist jetzt vorbei' [One thing is for sure now / One to one is over now] – thus, the band eschews simple ascriptions of meaning and offers a growing number of quotations and allusions from pop music history, most notably from Sisters of Mercy ('This Boy Is Toco-tronic'), David Bowie, Roxy Music, Soft Machine, Prefab Sprout, and the writer H.P Lovecraft.

Tocotronic was followed in 2005 by *Pure Vernunft darf niemals siegen* [Pure Reason Shall Never Prevail]. That year, Tocotronic had also expanded their line-up with the addition of guitarist Rick McPhail, who has distinctively shaped their sound ever since. On this album, the band further developed their new art of mystification and enigma, as the following lines demonstrate:

> Pure Vernunft darf niemals siegen
> Wir brauchen dringend neue Lügen
> Die uns durchs Universum leiten
> Und uns das Fest der Welt bereiten
>
> [Pure reason shall never prevail
> We are desperate for new lies
> To guide us through the universe
> And serve the world up for us].

Two years later, Tocotronic's strategy of 'artifying' themselves was decisively en-hanced with *Kapitulation* [Capitulation]. In a way this was their equivalent to *Sgt. Pepper* and therefore deserves a more detailed discussion here. Just like The Beatles' model, *Kapitulation* is not an arbitrary collection of songs but a concept album which adapts the very form that has symbolized the enactment of pop as 'art' ever since the release of *Sgt. Pepper*. The claim to be an ambitious and, in its conception, self-reflective piece of art was articulated by a manifesto published two weeks before *Kapitulation* was released.

This manifesto, published online as an audio file on their webpage, com-mences with a comment on the album title: 'Kapitulation. Das schönste Wort in deutscher Sprache [...] Wie die Töne die Tonleiter hinauf, so gleiten die Silben hinab' [Capitulation. The most beautiful word in the German language. [...] Just as notes climb the musical scale, its syllables glide down]. This onomatopoeic prelude is followed by a semantic reinterpretation of the title's catch-word 'capit-ulation', a reinterpretation organized and designed as a montage of song lines. Art history offers precedents for this kind of manifesto, such as the Dadaist anti-manifestos which match it in both subversion and ironic abstraction.

The album's cover, showing Thomas Eakins' 1889 *Portrait of Douglas Morgan Hall* (Philadelphia Museum of Art), is a reference to high culture. This is of interest here in three main respects: firstly, it is remarkable that a piece of art, a painting, is shown on a pop group's album cover; secondly, since the large majority of the pop music audience are likely to have been unfamiliar with this painting, this cover provides the band with pronounced distinction; and thirdly, the depicted figure epitomizes the entire album's attitude: reddened eyes staring into the void, symbolizing a man full of ennui desolately waiting for the sands of life to run out.

The first song on the album then spells out in detail 'the most beautiful word in the German language' by offering different kinds of 'capitulations' and finally emphatically shouting: 'fuck it all'. This song opposes a zeitgeist of optimistic self-improvement. Despite objecting to such external constraints of the performance-oriented society, there is no call for revolt. This song is not a classic protest song in that it does not advocate a position of individual or collective strength, the exertion of violence or any other variation of the rock phrase 'fuck the system'.

Instead, paradoxically, the very principle of 'capitulation' is turned into a brave last stand, because all attempts at appropriation grasp at nothing after the capitulation of the individual. The vocals are of particular importance here. In this song, the lyrics are not furiously shouted but rather sung in a bright and maddeningly relaxed manner, resulting in an apparent discrepancy between song and text: the more dire the message, the more cheerful the singing. This ironic tension between lyrics and sound culminates in the slogan 'fuck it all' – most graciously sung in what can be described as a heightened '*art*ificiality'. All in all, since the proclamation dovetails with denial, *Kapitulation* can be regarded as a romantic version of punk; or, conversely, as a punk version of romanticism or romantic irony.

The other songs on the album build on this strategy, not by establishing a coherent narrative with a beginning, middle and an end, but rather by matching thematically. The remaining songs offer variations of the uprising of the tired, referring to slackers – as in Ivan Goncharov's novel *Oblomov* (1859) – as well as to a dandy's style of nonchalance. Above all, Herman Melville's *Bartley, the Scrivener* (1853) and its 'I would prefer not to' appears to be the basic sub-text of all of the album's songs. The first song, 'Mein Ruin' [My Ruin], celebrates self-abandonment, fragility and irrationality accompanied by a stoic middle-paced beat, an anthemnic wall of guitars and a mantra-like structure.

The song 'Aus meiner Festung' [From My Fortress] then seems to provide a romantic escape back to nature. Yet this escape to nature is, in a dialectic move, immediately negated: 'In Wahrheit war ich / nie verreist / wie das Protokoll / beweist' [In truth I was / never gone / as the record / shows]. While Lowtzow croons this song as though he was acting in a musical, he uninhibitedly shouts out his dismissal of social constraints in the song 'Sag alles ab' [Call Off Everything] while the band plays furious punk rock. Towards the end of the album, the song 'Luft' [Air] praises uselessness: the chorus 'Ich atme nur' [I'm only breathing] is accompanied by the following lines:

> Das Nutzlose wird siegen.
> Das Nutzlose bleibt liegen.
> Also züchte ich mir Staub.
> Entschuldigung,
> das habe ich mir erlaubt.
>
> [What is useless will prevail.
> What is useless remains undone.
> Hence I gather dust.
> Sorry,
> I allowed myself that.]

The combination and/or contrast between the last two lines can be read as an enactment of Fiedler's demand as it denies the distinction between 'high' and 'low' culture. The reference to conceptual artist Marcel Duchamps, who collected dust in glasses, is followed by a direct quote from the comic band Die Prinzen's song 'Alles nur geklaut' [Everything Is Stolen]. Finally, in the song 'Explosion' [Explosion], high and low culture fade and burn out in a 'tender and innocent but consoling guitar breeze'[20]: 'Alles gehört dir / Eine Welt aus Papier / Alles explodiert / Kein Wille triumphiert' [Everything is yours / A world made of paper / Everything explodes / No will triumphs].

To follow the band's further progress briefly: *Kapitulation* was succeeded three years later by the album *Schall und Wahn* (2010) which, like its predecessor, highlights the method of artification in its design. The cover shows a painting of a flower bouquet by contemporary Dutch artists Jeroen de Rijke and Willem de Rooij named *Bouquet IV* (2005) and the album title is the German translation of William Faulkner's novel *The Sound and the Fury* (1929), which in turn is an adapted quotation from Shakespeare's *Macbeth* (1623). Following this, Tocotronic's 2013 album *Wie wir leben wollen* [How We Aim to Live] represents their – to use another Beatles analogy – *Let it be*. Just as the Fab Four tried (unsuccessfully) to save their band by returning to the simplicity of their early days, *Wie wir leben wollen* is a return not only to Tocotronic's roots, but also to earlier technology in that the album was recorded on a Telefunken four-

---

20 See Jan Wigger (www.spiegel.de/kultur/musik/abgehoert-die-wichtigsten-cds-der-woche-a-490546.html).

track tape machine dating back to 1958 in a studio at Berlin's former Tempelhof airport. In keeping with this approach, the band revealed – describing the time spent recording *Wie wir leben wollen* – that they 'examined their Beatles and Beach Boys LPs for their psychedelic pop appeal'.[21]

In contrast to the old-fashioned and simple equipment, however, the lyrics are more complex and enigmatic than ever. For instance, the opening track begins thus:

> Ich bin hier nur Tourist
> Ich bin nicht integriert
> Das Dasein das ich friste
> hat ein anderer inszeniert
>
> Here I'm just a tourist
> I am not integrated
> The existence that I've led here
> Was a member of someone else's review]

As the song proceeds, the complexity increases: the lyrical persona's body is 'nur eine Hülle / die uns beide trennt / er produziert in aller Stille / was man Liebe nennt' (only a husk / that separates us / it produces in total silence / that which is known as love). And how does the refrain answer the lyrics of the verses?

> Das ist keine Erzählung
> Das ist nur ein Protokoll
> Doch wir können davon lernen
> Wie wir leben wollen
>
> [This isn't some kind of story
> it's only a report
> But from it we can learn
> how we aim to live]

Tocotronic are reluctant to answer the question of how to lead a 'right life' while being stuck in a 'wrong one'. And they do not need to answer it – *Wie wir leben wollen* is a rock album and not a guide book. The question they do attempt to answer, however, is how much art pop music can accommodate.

Unlike the Beatles, Tocotronic did not split up after their *Let it be* but continued with the process of artifying themselves. Tocotronic's eleventh album was released in May 2015. Again, it is a concept album, but one that appears to be

---

21 See Tocotronic's biography on the German website of Universal Music (http://www.universal-music.de/tocotronic/biografie).

more concrete and more grounded in everyday life than its predecessors, since it addresses love in a crystal clear pop sound reminiscent of 1980s legends like The Smiths or Aztec Camera. As usual, the lyrics defy straightforward and unequivocal interpretation, but there is a new attempt at clarity.

An example can be found in the following line from 'Chaos' [Chaos]: 'Unter deiner Decke / Ein freundlicher Empfang [...] / Jetzt will ich bei dir bleiben / Bis der Tag anbricht' [Under your blanket / A friendly welcome [...] / Now I want to stay with you / Until the break of day]. This, however, should not be regarded as a return to naivety, as it is still embedded in a process of predominantly self-reflexive artification. For example, the 2015 album is again untitled, but since the cover is a red monochrome, it is commonly referred to as 'the Red Album'. Thematically, the colour is connected to the album's subjet. However, at the same time, the abstract monochrome calls into question whether 'love' can be represented in pop music.

There are also two recognizable references to the Beatles: this album echoes the monochrome cover style of the Beatles' *White Album* and it also invokes *The Beatles: 1962–66* collection known to fans as the 'red album' for its red-framed cover. Tellingly, this compilation comprises songs before the Beatles went 'arty' and still favoured singing mostly about love. The 'blue album' (officially *The Beatles: 1967–70*) on the other hand is a collection of their more 'arty' work. Further references to art can be found in Tocotronic's 'red album'. For example, the cover is not just printed in red but depicts Kazimir Malevich's *Red Quadrangle* (1915) which dates back exactly a century.

This context suggests that Tocotronic's lyrics are not to be read as naive and/ or romantic poetry, as they might appear to be at first glance, but rather as an ironic version of art songs in the manner of Franz Schubert. Tocotronic's 'Date mit Dirk' [Date with Dirk] commences with birds twittering and waters burbling:

> Wir streunen durch die Wälder
> und sehen unsere Spiegelungen in tiefen Brunnen,
> und im feuchten, modrigen, vom Tau liebkosten Wiesengrund[22]
>
> [We wander through woods
> and see our reflections in deep wells
> and in the moist, mouldy meadow caressed by dew]

Against such a background, Tocotronic have managed to transform their pop music into arty pop.

---

22 Although rather far-stretched given the context of the text, one might argue that an allusion to Theodor W. Adorno can be found here, as his second name was 'Wiesengrund'.

Ja, Panik, or 'Faraway, So Close'

In light of the success of Blumfeld and Tocotronic, it is not surprising that there were soon so many followers that people started to refer to *Diskursrock* as a 'school'. After the 'graduation' of Blumfeld and Tocotronic's promotion to 'higher education', a multitude of bands in the late 1990s proved to be eager students. This resulted in a veritable boom in guitar music with German lyrics in which one could discern the influence of the role models to varying degrees. The class of 2002/03, with bands like Kettcar and Tomte, was particularly successful. Tomte's singer and frontman Thees Uhlmann, for instance, started as a Tocotronic roadie who published his touring experiences in a book called *Wir könnten Freunde werden: Die Tocotronic-Tourtagebücher* [We Could Become Friends: The Tocotronic Tour Diaries] in 2002.

Along with his band, Tomte, he paid homage to his idols with lines like 'Ich rauche, so lange Rick McPhail raucht' [I'll smoke for as long as Rick McPhail does] from the 'Rick McPhail Song'. Such references, however, remained marginal and were not characteristic of the musical project, or to be more precise, were not characteristic of Tomte's lyrics. Indeed, the sound was distinctively *Diskursrock*, but the lyrics did not have the same intellectual brilliance and socio-critical, rebellious attitude since the quotations and references were limited to a level usually associated with more generic pop.

Expressed in prototypical structuralist dichotomies: Tomte – and to some extent this can be said generally about the bands in this 'class' – was more like Oasis than Tocotronic, was more emotional than rational and had more pathos than irony. Ever since Tomte broke up in 2010, Thees Uhlmann has presented himself as a 'German Bruce Springsteen'. For example, he named his 2011 album, *Lat: 53.7 Lon: 9.11667*, after the geographical coordinates of his place of birth and in the track of the same name on that album he praises the simple rural life. Kettcar, for their part, place slightly more emphasis on social problems, but they still consider themselves less eloquent enlighteners than sensitive storytellers. Kettcar's frontman Marcus Wiebusch and Tomte's Thees Uhlmann also founded their own Hamburg label called Grand Hotel van Cleef.

These bands, then, along with others who originated in or are strongly associated with Hamburg, followed the *Diskursrock* path of the 'Hamburg School' rather loosely. A more emphatic and dignified successor, however, can be found geographically much further afield: Ja, Panik (founded in late 2005), from the Burgenland region of Austria. Admittedly, the Burgenland is so far away from Hamburg that clear links between Ja, Panik and Blumfeld or Tocotronic seem unlikely. More important than geography, however, is a stylistic affinity that takes the form of a shared overarching aesthetic approach. By alluding to the enormous archive of popular culture in a virtuoso manner, Ja, Panik prove to be the most notable followers of erstwhile *Diskursrock*:

> Und du kommst schrecklich ins Schwärmen
> In deinen Worten ist Exzess
> All die Sinne in dir lärmen,
> Es ist ein wahrlich großes Fest
>
> [And you start to rave enthusiastically
> Your words convey excess
> All your senses bluster,
> It is like a truly great celebration]

These lines from the song 'Mr. Jones & Norma Desmond' self-reflexively enact the deconstructive polyphonic technique. Two further examples are worth mentioning: in 'A Roadmovie', a track on their second album *The Taste and the Money* (2007), Ja, Panik use lines from a mafia movie and replace names of film characters with the names of band members. Furthermore, this song explicitly declares that this reference is not a 'sentimental' (in Schiller's sense of the term) way of invoking cinematic memories, but rather a deconstructively reflected set of references: 'Erzähl mir nichts von deiner Unschuld / du beleidigst meinen Intellekt' [Spare me stories about your innocence / you are offending my intellect].

Additionally, 'Mr. Jones & Norma Desmond' makes a direct reference to Bob Dylan and a structural reference to Blumfeld. 'Something is happening / but you don't know what it is, / do you, Mr. Jones?', is a question raised by Dylan in 'Ballad of a Thin Man'. 'Mr. Jones & Norma Desmond' varies this slightly: 'Irgendwas ist da im Gange, / du bist nicht sicher, / doch du schreibst' [Something is going on, / you are not sure, / but yet you write].

Blumfeld also borrowed figures from Dylan's 'Desolation Row' in 'Jenseits von Jedem'. Yet it is also possible that Ja, Panik are directly referring to Dylan, who masterfully developed an aesthetic of quotations and revolutionized the language of pop music. Aesthetically, it seems quite logical for Ja, Panik to no longer sing in German if their conceptual approach entails the blurring of reference areas. Singer and songwriter Andreas Spechtl creates an idiosyncratic form by merging German and English with an Austrian accent and occasionally also borrowing from French and Italian.

In addition to a wide range of techniques that set up intertextual relations, Ja, Panik bring politics back into pop music. In 2011, their album *DMD KIU LIDT*, released on the Berlin label Staatsakt (State Occasion) founded by Maurice Summen, caused quite a furore. What stands out on this album is the title song, which sums up the current political situation with the assertion 'Die Manifestation des Kapitalismus in unserem Leben ist die Traurigkeit' [the manifestation of capitalism in our lives is sadness], with the initials of each word creating the acronym of the title *DMD KIU LIDT*.

On the eponymous track of the album, Ja, Panik combines great epics by Bob Dylan like 'Sad Eyed Lady of the Lowlands' and 'Joey' with Falco's 'Jeannie' to tell a 14-minute story of someone who sets forth and only finds the same old Adornoesque world everywhere he goes: 'Letztendlich hab' ich meine Koffer gepackt, / Hab' ein Ticket gelöst und bin weit gefahren' [In the end, I packed my suitcases, / Booked a ticket and went far away]. This sounds familiar and evokes strategies already employed by Blumfeld and Tocotronic. In a way, it can be understood as a reformulation of the most famous dictum of the Frankfurt School: 'Denn nicht Du bist in der Krise, / sondern die Form die man dir aufzwingt' [Because it is not you that is in a crisis / it is the form imposed on you].

For instance, Spechtl transmutes Adorno's concise formula 'Fun ist ein Stahlbad'[23] [fun is a medicinal bath] into the lines:

Unser Schmerz, der darf nicht abfallen,
Allein er fällt mit dieser Ordnung,
Die sich verschwört, uns aufzupäppeln,
Uns gesund zu amputieren

[Our pain must not decrease,
but it declines with this social order,
That is plotting to feed us up
Amputate us until we are healthy]

The diagnosis is that the entertainment industry's objective is to keep us properly functioning by showing us how we *should* live in order to keep us from living how we *would like*. Ja, Panik do not limit themselves to such a negative and resigned account of the condition of society, however, and instead proclaim a new solidarity amongst all excluded groups. Thus, in the last four minutes, the song rises in anger against social conditions and the singer asks the audience to be aware of the daily struggle, finally uttering the following hope:

Die kommende Gemeinschaft liegt hinter unseren Depressionen,
Denn was und wie man uns kaputt macht, ist auch etwas, das uns eint,
Es sind die Ränder einer Zone, die wir im Stillen alle bewohnen

---

23 Theodor W. Adorno and Max Horkheimer, *Dialektik der Aufklärung*. (Frankfurt: Suhrkamp, 2003), p. 162.

[The future society lies beyond our depressions,
Because what destroys us also unites us, as does the way in which we are destroyed
It is the borders of a zone, which we all silently inhabit]

The 'right life in the wrong one' seems to be possible at last, an ascent born from the spirit of depression. Of course the song is not answering the question of what this life should look like. Instead, it uses a surprisingly different technique to articulate its protest message: at the very end, the singer announces that the next verses are the most important ones – 'an denen mir mehr als an allen anderen liegt' [the ones I treasure more than all the others] – but what follows are six minutes of silence.

In early 2014 Ja, Panik released their highly anticipated follow-up *Libertatia*. The album offers the continuation of socially committed *Diskursrock* by other means and provides clear contours to the consequent development of their program. The main new element is the band's sound, which incorporates swing, funk and soul elements and offers – instead of post punk – a variety of licks reminiscent of The Smiths guitar player Johnny Marr. It is a peculiar combination that at times evokes Talking Heads.

The album sounds as if *DMD KIU LIDT* had been a cathartic experience and as if raging anger and infinite sadness had given way to serenity and an old insight: revolution is no fun[24] if you cannot dance to it. Part of this pop attitude can be seen, for instance, in the reinterpretation of the slogan 'ACAB' (All Cops Are Bastards) as 'All Cats Are Beautiful'. The song 'Dance the ECB'[25] expands on the political implications of such an attitude:

Take a step to the side to sing the song of the beast
shake the government, shake its police
dance the ECB, swing die Staatsfinanzen [...the public finances]
sing ihnen ihre Melodien, zwing sie zum Tanzen
[sing their melodies to them, force them to dance]

But popular culture did not invent this insight. Karl Marx spoke about the ability to 'make petrified conditions dance by singing their own melody back at them'. Correspondingly, post-Adornoesque seriousness is not lost in the fun of pop music and the idea of a 'counter-cultural' utopia has not been given up, it has just been expressed differently. This becomes particularly clear in the title track, 'Libertatia', where Ja, Panik imagines themselves in the Indian Ocean of the seventeenth century.

---

24 See Karl Marx, *Marx-Engels-Werke*, vol 1 (Berlin: Dietz, 1976), p. 381.
25 ECB is short for European Central Bank.

According to *A General History of the Robberies and Murders of the Most Notorious Pyrates* (1724), which was written by Captain Charles Johnson (possibly a pseudonym of Daniel Defoe, the author of *Robinson Crusoe*), a colony called Libertatia was situated on the East coast of Madagascar. This colony was inhabited by proto-anarchist individuals whose community enjoyed civil rights and liberties only implemented in Europe after the French Revolution. Of course, such a utopia did not, and does not, exist in reality. It can only be reached via detours, or rather, it can only be reached by overcoming discursive, semantic and metaphoric boundaries.

Ja, Panik's attempt to realize utopia mirrors this. Not only do they merge musical styles, but they also switch intertextually between German, English and occasionally French and Italian, thus overcoming the boundaries between languages and codes and in *Libertatia*, this is accompanied by the dissolution of spatial and temporal categories. 'Ich wünsch mich dahin zurück, wo's nach vorne geht' [I want to go back to where I can move forwards], runs the first line of the album. And then the clock is set to 'back to the future'. Somewhere there, in the future of the past, the very contemporary music of yesterday by Ja, Panik unfolds its utopian potential.

Heinrich Deisl

Saying 'Yes!' While Meaning 'No!' – A Conversation with Diedrich Diederichsen

The theorization of pop music in the German-speaking world developed somewhat later than in Anglophone and Francophone countries. Beginning in the 1980s, magazines like *Spex* and, since 1995, the quasi-academic journal *testcard: Beiträge zur Popgeschichte* [testcard: Contributions to Pop History] helped ignite an interdisciplinary conversation between music journalists and academics influenced by cultural studies, film theory and criticism and sociomusicology.

Diedrich Diederichsen is one of the key players in this debate. Particularly in his roles as a contributor to and Editor-in-Chief of *Spex* (1985–2000) and, since 1998, as a professor, he has made an enduring contribution to the critical understanding of pop music. Since 2006 he has taught at the Institute of Art Theory and Cultural Studies of the Academy of Fine Arts in Vienna. He has never approached pop music in isolation but rather always regarded it as an expression of broader political, social and aesthetic phenomena.

With *Über Pop-Musik* [On Pop Music] (2014), Diederichsen has put forward a comprehensive study of over 470 pages. This book, which was shortlisted for the 2014 Leipzig Book Fair Prize, consolidates his previous work both as an author and editor, including *Musikzimmer* [Music Chamber] (2005), *Eigenblutdoping* [Autologous Blood Doping] (2008) and *Utopia of Sound: Immediacy and Non-Simultaneity* (2010).[1]

Über Pop-Musik is the starting point of the following conversation with Diederichsen.[2] The present chapter comprises three sections, each beginning with a brief introduction followed by excerpts from the interview. At the outset, the conversation turns on the conceptual and critical semantics of the study of pop music. The second part situates this lexicon in the context of Diederichsen's personal development, the theorization of pop in German and the role played by

---

1 Diedrich Diederichsen, *Musikzimmer: Avantgarde und Alltag* (Cologne: Kiepenheuer & Witsch, 2005); *Eigenblutdoping: Selbstverwertung, Künstlerromantik, Partizipation* (Cologne: Kiepenheuer & Witsch, 2008); *Utopia of Sound: Immediacy and Non-Simultaneity. Publications of the University of Fine Arts Vienna*, vol. 10, ed. by Diedrich Diederichsen and Constanze Ruhm (Vienna: Schlebrügge Editor, 2010). As of 2016, most of Diederichsen's books are only available in German. The author would like to thank Brita Pohl and Sina Rahmani for their translation work and Sophie Unterweger for additional feedback.
2 The interview was conducted by the author on 22 April 2015 in Diederichsen's office at the Academy of Fine Arts in Vienna.

DOI 10.1515/9783110425727-012

group-dynamic processes in this debate. The third section focuses on the connections between pop music and Germany since the 1970s.

Über Pop-Musik develops two central theses. Firstly, it argues that it is the recipient (*Rezipient*) who renders pop music possible as both an object and a subject matter and secondly, that the recording studio is an essential site of production of pop music. These theses lead to reception- and technology-based assumptions under which 'the same sign can always signify something different'.[3] Accordingly, 'pop music is not interesting for the sonic combination of voices and instruments, but rather the reality effect (*Wirklichkeitseffekt*) of its playback'.[4] A more precise critical lens makes clear that, in pop music, affirmation reveals itself as criticism. In other words, while nodding its head in agreement, pop music defiantly stands in opposition.

Pop ≠ Popular

At the outset, it must be made clear that this chapter regards pop music and not necessarily popular music. *Über Pop-Musik* outlines how pop music is at once a facet of popular music while retaining an array of its own

> images, performances, (mostly popular) music, texts and narratives tied to real people. This context came into being in the mid-twentieth century. Its elements are not linked by a consistent medium, even though sound recording is an essential technology for pop music. The necessary connection between its different elements is provided by the audience, the fans, the consumers of pop music themselves.[5]

Über Pop-Musik navigates between genres from jazz to musique concrète to black metal, explores *Maschinenmusik* [machine music][6] and the emancipation of low-

---

3 Diedrich Diederichsen, *Über Pop-Musik* (Cologne: KiWi, 2014), p. 114.
4 Ibid., p. 62.
5 Ibid., p. XI.
6 A literal translation of this term would read 'machine music' or 'music made by machines'. It signifies various musical and sociocultural developments emerging in the early years of the twentieth century. The sonic experiments by Luigi Russolo or Lev Termen and their respective innovations, the 'intonarumori' and the 'theremin', can be regarded as a starting point for the relationship between machines (tape recording, synthesizer, computer, effects etc.) and the composer. In German, *Maschinenmusik* is an umbrella term for electro-acoustic, analogue and electronic music, ranging from tape music to digitally-generated genres. For more, see: *Musik und Technik: Veröffentlichungen des Instituts für Neue Musik und Musikerziehung Darmstadt*, vol. 36, ed. by Helga De la Motte-Haber and Rudolf Frisius (Mainz: Schott, 1996); Douglas Kahn, *Noise, Water, Meat: A History of Sound in the Arts* (Cambridge, MA: MIT Press, 1999),

frequency bass sounds, analyses music videos and takes up the theories of Sergei Eisenstein and Roland Barthes. Its aim is certainly not to offer a global history of pop music, but rather to formulate terminologies, classifications and interdependencies and then, with the assistance of Charles S. Peirce's pragmatic semiotics, examine their diverse aesthetic, formal, sociological and music-historical constellations.

But if pop music is not a specific form of popular music, what is it? What is its purpose? Diederichsen provides a simple, yet far-reaching, answer: 'the improvement of promises'.[7] According to him, pop music is a projection onto a backdrop of industrially-fabricated products that can only emerge through active creation (listening, re-listening, remembering, classifying, exchange).

Heinrich Deisl: There seems to be an obvious connection between the title of your book and Adorno's essays 'Über Jazz' ['On Jazz'] and 'On Popular Music'.[8] What were your intentions in *Über Pop-Musik*?

Diedrich Diederichsen: I decided to write this book since I had repeatedly noticed that nearly all academic examinations of pop music were first and foremost about popular music, which reduces many aspects of pop music to secondary phenomena. I wanted to use approaches from cultural studies and sociology to make connections. I thought it important to point out a third way, i.e. to address pop music as an independent form of music and a subject in its own right that could be described via its public and a sociology of its reception or its sociological composition. In other words, I didn't want to address only the musical aspect. The title of the book is reminiscent of Adorno, which was a late, but welcome development. The main reason is that, during a visit to the Sigmund Freud Museum in Vienna, I saw one of his essays on exhibition, namely 'On Cocaine'.[9]

Heinrich Deisl: This means that pop music does not really refer to music per se but rather to the network of media, art, attitudes, sociologies, narratives and products in which it is embedded. How is this network formed?

---

pp. 45–67; Kodwo Eshun, 'Operating System for the Redesign of Sonic Reality', in *The Sound Studies Reader*, ed. by Jonathan Sterne (London/New York: Routledge, 2012), pp. 449–53.

7 Diederichsen, *Über Pop-Musik*, p. 410.

8 Cf. Theodor W. Adorno, *Gesammelte Schriften. Vol. 17: Musikalische Schriften IV: Moments musiceaux/Impromptus*, ed. by Rolf Tiedemann (Frankfurt: Suhrkamp, 2003), pp. 74–108; Theodor W. Adorno and George Simpson, 'On Popular Music', *Studies in Philosophy and Social Science*, IX (1941), 17–48.

9 Sigmund Freud, 'Über Coca', in *Centralblatt für die gesamte Therapie*, 1884, pp. 289–314.

Diedrich Diederichsen: I argue that the musical component, however we define it, is not the decisive factor for the creation and production of pop music. There are many passages in *Über Pop-Musik* where I try to clarify that pop music lacks a centre and I reject the common refrain that music itself necessarily be the focus of the debate. Of course, it's an integral part of the discussion; you cannot completely disregard music. One of the central arguments of the book is that the phenomenon of pop music is generated primarily by the combination of different elements assembled and accumulated by the consumer. This combination might be described as a pop music object rendered manifest. Pop music, therefore, does not exist a priori. Rather, its components are delivered via different channels or media and then – and this is the crux of the matter – compiled by the recipient. While we can for example clearly define the specific site of the experience of cinema[10] – the dark auditorium – pop music can occur in your own living room as well as at a festival. It is crucial, however, that it occurs in at least two, socially-different places and the recipient connects these experiences.

Heinrich Deisl: You postulate a 'third culture industry', taking us back to Adorno. In *Über Pop-Musik,* you do not define a culture industry according to historical stages, but rather the development of media and its convergence with social formations. What are their respective characteristics?

Diedrich Diederichsen: Pop music is the second of the three culture industries.[11] This three-part model tries to address the fundamental problem of the category of cultural industries insofar as, in its original conception, no component of the culture industry is based in the past or in media history. Horkheimer and Adorno[12] are constructing it exclusively from the perspective of a capitalism that remains strangely ahistorical in their account: the only obvious fact is that the cultural industry is conceived as its highest stage. Their argument, in my view, is similar to Althusser's conceptualization of ideology as a form of knowledge without history. I think that, on the contrary, there are historical caesuras linked to new media formations and the resulting media technologies and modes of production. Consequently, they become manifest as historical eras – though this does not rule out the validity of the critique of ideology as a phenomenon that appears to be without history.

---

10 See for instance Jean Mitry, *Semiotics and the Analysis of Film* (Bloomington: Indiana University Press, 2000), pp. 24–108; Michel Chion, *Audio-Vision: Sound on Screen.* Ed. by Claudia Gorbman (New York: Columbia University Press, 1994), pp. 25–34.

11 For a matrix of the three culture industries, see Diederichsen, *Über Pop-Musik,* p. XXII.

12 See Max Horkheimer and Theodor W. Adorno, *Dialectic of Enlightenment: Philosophical Fragments,* ed. by Gunzelin Schmid Noerr (Stanford: Stanford University Press, 2002), pp. 94–136.

We need to distinguish three *dispositifs* that regulate the model of interconnection between the public and the private. The first one is the traditional culture industry of Horkheimer and Adorno constituted by radio and cinema. With radio, the public speaks to me when I am at home, whereas cinema is a place of private dreams that is paradoxically public. In the second stage, these inputs are optimized by television and pop music. The public invades our homes while we can enjoy privacy outside. Especially the first stage has often been criticized for its sedative and politically-neutralizing effects even by more friendly critics. At the second stage, however, we can detect a vitalization of consumers through pop music as they actively seek out specific products. From a culture industry perspective, this may be regarded as a success, not only because it understood that a fanaticized rock aficionado is a better customer than the silent devotee of some film diva, but also from a perspective of mobilization and even politicization. The third culture industry emerges with digitalization. The World Wide Web as well as the computers we use integrate the public and the private in one interface. Here we can see a kind of totality materializing, expressed in part through digital control mechanisms and the enthusiastic 'prosumer' constantly busy liking, sharing, endorsing – the commodity he or she is consuming and in effect adding to it.

Heinrich Deisl: You identify pop music as an indexical form of art. Where do you locate indexical signs in pop music?

Diedrich Diederichsen: Pop music cannot exist if it is not recorded at some point in the chain. A pop music object merely based in musical tradition is impossible. During a live concert, I need to establish a connection to the recorded version of a track, or at least be able to imagine its recorded version. This form of transference is key. In this sense, pop music is related to photography, where it is essential that an actual body has been positioned in front of the camera and light has fallen onto this situation.

This kind of transference is used in diverse ways in pop music's economy of desire: the recorded voice is staged as 'sexy' and certain machine-generated, or instrumental sounds, or sound effects are exposed as specific signifiers. Alternatively, and this is often the case, minute effects augment these arrangements and bring these signifiers to the surface. These effects may be caused, for instance, by knowledge of details of the artists' biographies or by specific technical limitations. The constitution of a pop music whole consists in the combination of such an indexical effect with an iconic one, i.e. linking a musical or other sonic effects to an image. A live concert is a good example of this process: a musician is visible, present and recognizable as such. Simultaneously, one hears a voice or sonic presentation that recalls that on the recording.

Heinrich Deisl: In your book you mention that pop music may be understood in the sense of a denotation. What do you mean by that?

Diedrich Diederichsen: The difference between music and pop music is that the former may be denotative in its self-conception, but never entirely so in all of its communicative execution. Of course, a specific note may denote a tone, and clearly there are certain agreements and conventions, for example that a drum-roll refers to a military execution or a hunting horn indicates that we are to imagine a forest. However, the aesthetic self-conception of music does not allow a musical sign to denote an object in reality.

In pop music, on the other hand, sounds may refer to something specific. These sounds often stand for social signs, representing a specific group or a certain sensory orientation and are thus understood as distinctive signs. However, this is always temporary, for they become less attractive as soon as they are recognized as the denotative component of a pop music signifier. This happens because they are social signs that have been defined unto themselves and also mark a connection to or a disconnection from a group. Besides more collage-like sounds like soundbites from newscasts or samples of police sirens, there are much simpler denotative signs like guitar distortion. When such sound effects were still new, they denoted for example that someone liked riding motorcycles, staying out in the open and drinking beer from a can.

Heinrich Deisl: Does this also apply to drum machines like the 'TR-808' and synthesizers like the 'TB-303', the 'MS-20' or the 'Minimoog', whose specific sounds decisively influenced genres like hip-hop, acid house and techno? Or, to take an earlier example, Jimi Hendrix's 'Cry Baby' wah-wah pedal?[13]

Diedrich Diederichsen: Yes, these are the best examples.

Heinrich Deisl: You are writing about what Roland Barthes calls 'the mastery of the punctum'[14]. How can we adapt this concept from the theory of photography to pop music?

Diedrich Diederichsen: The mastery of the punctum is technically impossible. I concur with Barthes when he says that photography is not really an art because one cannot master the punctum effect. Pop music, however, always tries to mas-

---

13 Examples: Roland 'TR-808': Afrika Bambaataa & The Soulsonic Force, 'Planet Rock' (1982); Roland 'TB-303': Phuture, 'Acid Tracks' (1987). Korg's 'MS-20' was prominently used by the band DAF; and Kraftwerk was one of the first German bands to play a 'Minimoog'. Hendrix used this wah-wah effect device e.g. on 'Voodoo Child (Slight Return)' (1970).

14 See Roland Barthes, *Camera Lucida: Reflections on Photography* (New York: Farrar Straus & Giroux, 1981), pp. 25–46 (p. 27).

ter this effect. Its means to achieve this are primarily performative. These means may be positioned so as to give rise to side effects – for instance special sounds or indexical signs – which may be unintentional. Most obviously, its regulation is attempted through the performative gesture of the pose. A performative frame is created in which something might very well happen to your body that may be perceived as a punctum. However, this contingent event is convenient but not intentional, since this would contradict the logic of the punctum.

Heinrich Deisl: With regard to your concept of the pose, you emphasize that it must always remain unclear whether the performer on stage is speaking for him- or herself or for someone else. This intersects with different critical approaches to stage production and questions of authenticity. One might argue that pop music is only good as long as it does not cash in on its own utopian nature, thus remaining an authentic refuge amidst the inauthentic. Where does this insistence on authenticity come from? Can a musician be him- or herself on stage?

Diedrich Diederichsen: The fundamental aspect of a pose is that you cannot rehearse it. It is a modus that allows something to take place. We are talking about a cultural technology in which pop music has played an important role and has been appropriated by other popular cultures. You cannot be forced into a pose, nor are you allowed to simply master it. A mastered pose – for instance the propeller-like rotating arm of a heavy metal guitarist – functions more as a distinctive marker. It is about the relationship between playing a role and being one's authentic self. If you wanted to be yourself on stage – as a certain authenticism has demanded far too often –, this would be tantamount to ethical masochism. A pop musician would torture him- or herself about lying whenever he or she develops routines or does the same thing he or she did the night before. In the theatre, the opposite is true in that the actors' roles already exist as a finished script and so, by definition, they cannot be played authentically.

In pop music, both extremes – authenticity and pure acting – have been tested again and again, though they cannot but fail. A productive position would be one that plays with these extremes but does not adopt either. People in theatre studies tell me that it is the exact same: it is not about the actor 'being' King Lear, but about the tension the actor establishes between himself and the character. I would disagree, as the existing script of *King Lear* grants the actor an exoneration for his actions; he is only the medium for a role. In the scripts of pop music – i.e. the imagined role of the pop musician – you may end up being called to account as a real person. While theatrical characters may commit all sorts of crimes on stage without being punished, Jim Morrison was arrested after exposing his penis on stage.

Heinrich Deisl: Let us move on to the question of recording. You discuss at some length the English producer Joe Meek, who, among others, produced the band The Tornados in the early 1960s. You state that Meek was the first to 'discover the studio as a variable – or, as people began saying in the 1970s, as 'an instrument', and call him 'one of the first auteurs of pop music'.[15] Later, producers like King Tubby, Conny Plank or Steve Albini played decisive roles in developing the 'sound' of dub, Krautrock or independent rock. Where do you situate the producer in pop music?

Diedrich Diederichsen: At first, I thought the producer was the centre of pop music. However, I later came to think that this would rather resemble the theory of the auteur employed by the group around the *Cahiers du cinéma* in the 1950s. This well-known model of the film director as an auteur could be grafted to pop music too. Naturally, you can identify the signature styles of certain producers which, as your examples show, may be described as a component of artistic skill. From my point of view, however, the producer is at least a candidate for the central role since he decisively influences the character of pop music by introducing a mode of production in which music is no longer produced linearly but rather via a multi-track process on recording tape. These methods are basically sculptural, three-dimensional practices, which no longer take place over time but in space. In summary, we may say that the producer, next to the recipient, constitutes the most important interface in the manufacture of pop music – but he or she is not or is rarely involved in performance styles, image politics, song writing, decisions about social loyalties, etc.

Everyday Pop Music

This section explores the crucial role of music magazines in the early institutionalizations of pop music in Germany. Through their close proximity to current events (e. g. concert reviews), as well as the ensuing interest in pop music in sociology and cultural studies, these periodicals contributed to a corpus that gradually led to a convergence of these approaches. While the period between the 1970s and the early 1990s was marked by a close interconnection of pop cultural codes (habitus, style, identification, etc.), from the 1990s onwards, the coming of the internet age, *Mille Plateaux* [*A Thousand Plateaus*] (1980/92)[16] by Deleuze/

---

15 Diederichsen, *Über Pop-Musik*, p. 53 resp. p. 57.
16 Gilles Deleuze and Félix Guattari, *A Thousand Plateaus: Capitalism and Schizophrenia* (Minneapolis: University of Minnesota Press, 1987). Originally published in 1980, this book, the Ger-

Guattari and the consolidation of electronic dance music (i. e. techno with its numerous sub-genres) – to name only three formative impulses – signalled new nodes within the network of pop music.

The mid- and late 1990s represent a caesura in the analysis of pop music. With publications like *Mainstream der Minderheiten* [Mainstream of Minorities] (1996)[17] and *Politische Korrekturen* [Political Adjustments] (1996)[18], the *testcard* book series and the magazine *de:bug – Elektronische Lebensaspekte* [Electronic Aspects of Life], founded in 1997, pop music theory developed across a wide spectrum. In his essay 'Ist was Pop?' [Is Anything Pop?] (1999), Diederichsen sketched a two-stage model consisting of Pop I (1960s to 1980s; specific pop) and Pop II (1990s; general pop): 'In Pop I, a transparent commitment to the community was dominant; in Pop II, superimpositions prevailed.'[19] The 2014 conference 'Pop III' in Vienna[20] extended this model with aspects of academization, museumization and retro, which have been key issues in pop music debates in recent years.[21]

Heinrich Deisl: In addition to cultural studies-related work, the last three decades have witnessed a number of publications that combine journalistic and academic approaches and have helped shape pop theory. How are we to imagine the 1970s and 1980s from a German perspective?

Diedrich Diederichsen: Naturally, 'classics' like *Rap Attack* (1984), *Lipstick Traces* (1989) or *England's Dreaming* (1991) were important to my thinking.[22] However, an even more important sources of inspiration were the German theo-

man translation of which was published by Merve Verlag in 1992, may be regarded as one of the most important texts in the debates within German language pop culture theory of those years.

17 *Mainstream der Minderheiten: Pop in der Kontrollgesellschaft*, ed. by Tom Holert and Mark Terkessidis (Berlin: Ed. ID-Archiv, 1996).

18 Diedrich Diederichsen, *Politische Korrekturen* (Cologne: KiWi, 1996).

19 Diedrich Diederichsen, *Der lange Weg nach Mitte: Der Sound und die Stadt* (Cologne: KiWi, 1999), pp. 272–86 (p. 278).

20 This conference, organized by Moritz Baßler, Diedrich Diederichsen and Heinz Drügh, took place in mid-October 2014 at the Internationales Forschungszentrum für Kulturwissenschaften IFK in Vienna.

21 See e.g.: Simon Reynolds, *Retromania: Pop Culture's Addiction to its Own Past* (London: Faber & Faber, 2011); Mark Fisher, *Ghosts of My Life: Writings on Depression, Hauntology and Lost Futures* (Winchester: Zero Books, 2014); Thomas Edlinger, *Der wunde Punkt: Vom Unbehagen der Kritik* (Berlin: Suhrkamp, 2015).

22 David Toop, *Rap Attack: African Jive to New York HipHop* (London: Pluto Press, 1984); Greil Marcus, *Lipstick Traces: A Secret History of the 20th Century* (Cambridge, MA: Harvard University Press, 1989); Jon Savage, *England's Dreaming: Anarchy, Sex Pistols, Punk Rock, and Beyond* (London: Faber & Faber, 1991).

retical debates on film of the 1960s and 1970s. Among those connected to *Spex*, people were much more likely to be influenced by *Filmkritik* or *Cahiers du cinéma*. These magazines attempted to advocate for film as a particular phenomenon, against the classical critical theory position that only ever saw it as a by-product of the culture industry. However, they also opposed a film theory derived from drama and literary studies. Their aim was to establish film as a genuine object of inquiry. What I found interesting at the time was how German authors like Frieda Grafe, Uwe Nettelbeck, Enno Patalas and Harun Farocki and theorists like Roland Barthes and Gilles Deleuze, developed a specific terminology of cinematic knowledge practically before my very eyes. I was once asked to name a text that has influenced me and I chose an essay by Frieda Grafe on Howard Hawks. It was in fact *Filmkritik* that inspired me to try and establish similar approaches, concepts and structures for pop music.

Heinrich Deisl: What are the parallels or divergences between pop journalism and pop theory?

Diedrich Diederichsen: Back then, there was no German pop theory in a strict sense. In addition, I never even asked myself whether what I was doing was pop journalism or pop theory. In magazines like *Sounds* and *Spex,* everything was thrown together: reviews of the latest shows next to theoretical considerations.[23] At the time, none of us could have foreseen that these practices would eventually clear the path to pop music theory being taught at universities. We also need to remember that academic music theory was in a completely different place then. The only academics working on pop music were in sociology. Other fields with an early interest in pop as a subject were the visual arts and design. Maybe this is why I had a more intimate connection to the visual arts, because they had been part of my personal development for a long time. In any case, the design theorists connected to the International Design Centre in Berlin were the first to invite me and others to join their conversations.

Heinrich Deisl: How could we define terms associated historically with pop music like popular music, pop and pop- or subculture?

Diedrich Diederichsen: In the book, I address pop music precisely in order to avoid speaking about pop in general. The only time I am willing to speak about pop culture – and even then I am not really happy to do so – is when

---

23 For an historical overview of *Spex*, see André Doehring, *Musikkommunikatoren: Berufsrollen, Organisationsstrukturen und Handlungsspielräume im Popmusikjournalismus.* ASPM Texte zur populären Musik 7 (Bielefeld: Transcript, 2011), pp. 71–76.

pop music-specific modes of production emerge in other cultural phenomena. For example, when an actual person, a performer, is staged in a way that is derived from pop music, as happens in certain forms of reality TV. There I can see links. Otherwise I think the term pop culture is too vague. Criteria for distinguishing between popular and pop music are discussed throughout the book and pop as such is a term I do not really use. And subculture – even though it is often associated with pop music – is also a completely different matter. I do use different approaches or definitions of subculture, but only in relation to the issue at stake at the time. Pop music cannot be explained by subculture; there are many subcultures that have nothing to do with it. Pop music makes its appearance in mainstream as well as in subcultural phenomena.

Heinrich Deisl: In *Über Pop-Musik* you describe pop music as a communicative model that generates ambiguities through both aesthetic and sociological processes. It is true that anyone can participate in pop music and that it is aimed at everyone, and thus involves an emancipatory gesture. However, as regards definitions and perceptions of pop music scenes, pop music has a very exclusionary quality. How does pop music contribute to hegemonic borders or attributions becoming more fluid, or how does it strengthen them?

Diedrich Diederichsen: It is true that the self-definition of pop music is comprised of equal measures of inclusion and exclusion. Exclusion, when it is aimed at everybody, is interesting. What makes pop music so compelling is that it allows a particular group to define itself as special, more or less for everyone to see. It is not true that these mechanisms necessarily have to develop along class barriers. On the contrary, the opposite may very well be the case: it is possible for an excluded group to define itself as elite through pop music. We have seen this phenomenon often. The dialectic we are alluding to here is that, while pop music is aimed at everyone, it can only be successful when it does not reach everyone. This social game is an important part of pop music.

The formative or heroic years of pop music were when – not exclusively but mostly – proletarian young men found their voices. This new confidence was often linked to sexual or sexual-political concepts of liberation that quite frequently turned into sexism. This has permanently poisoned many genres of pop music. The problems in this context are most likely structural. For example, the fact that 99.9% of black metal musicians are male is probably due to that genre's original message. It would therefore be pointless to wait for a woman to make good black metal. I think that this male dominance is not due to social factors inherent to pop music but rather to pre-existing societal forces that have always tended to confirm the status quo.

Heinrich Deisl: For a long time, pop music was closely linked to affiliations with groups or scenes: mod, punk, skinhead, etc. Since the mid-1990s and the techno movement, there are hardly any scenes left and, at the moment, it seems that a collage of styles prevails. In this context, we might see social conditions as a re-alization of rhizome-like dynamics, insofar as the old peer pressure towards a certain preference seems to have vanished. On the other hand, we might take a pessimistic stance and bemoan a hedonistic 'anything goes'. Have codes or af-filiations become redundant or less easily identifiable to the observer?[24]

Diedrich Diederichsen: It used to be necessary to establish scenes, understood as stable systems of reference. Therefore, the connection between sartorial styles, a panorama of world-views and a taste in music were more closely drawn. A scene needed to constitute itself in front of an audience, the public, who did not look too closely and to whom the respective internal group codes did not mean any-thing. In order to allow for a deliberate differentiation or the signalling of a cer-tain affiliation, these codes and signs needed to be clearly delimited and con-trasted.

We have a similar situation today. In their style choices, young people still pay close attention to internal coherence, i.e. to ensuring the codes they send match. Regarding the dynamics of group affiliations, the situation today obvi-ously is more sophisticated and complex. The difference is that pop musical signs no longer designate the task of one particular group, but have, if you like, arrived among the general public. Therefore, you can work with a much broader stylistic palette. A collective background is less and less manifest. Nowa-days, it only becomes visible at mass events like concerts or festivals, if at all.

Heinrich Deisl: As a member of the editorial board of Transcript publisher's 'Sound Studies' series, you were part of the group of German-language theorists interested in sound more or less from the beginning. In *Über Pop-Musik*, sound plays a very prominent role. What is the relation between music and sound?

Diedrich Diederichsen: In the interim, a research group has been formed around this series, which was largely the responsibility of Holger Schulze, and these the-orists are developing a kind of encyclopaedia of sound in media cultures. I had written an article for the first edited volume in the series that addressed the re-lationship between music and sound, rather than sound as such. Generally

---

24 On techno-specific aspects of transformation, see Gabriele Klein, *Electronic Vibration: Pop Kultur Theorie* (Wiesbaden: VS Verlag für Sozialwissenschaften, 2004), pp. 22–32; Michaela Pfa-denhauer, 'Lernort Techno-Szene: Über Kompetenzentwicklung in Jugendszenen', in *'They Say I'm Different …' Popularmusik, Szenen und ihre Akteur_innen*, ed. by Rosa Reitsamer and Wolf-gang Fichna (Vienna: Löcker, 2011), pp. 195–207 (pp. 195–96).

speaking, sound has always been an integral part of pop music. Sound is the unpredictable, indexical component that does not submit to a grammar or other rules. Music, on the other hand, shares many characteristics with other types of semiotic signs: clearly symbolic signs define a convention. And you might refer to chords as somewhat iconic signs. Viewed pragmatically, music may be understood as a speech act. A subject's speech is expressed in parallel to the chrono-politics of biographies or narratives unfolding in time.

Sound lacks these dimensions. Whether a sound event lasts for three seconds or a minute is irrelevant: nothing changes with regard to its sonic characteristics. Consequently, with sound an excessive duration is possible. This is impossible in music that understands itself as sound speech, i.e. in relation with a subject playing the music. The differentiation between music and sound is at the moment questionable to the extent that digital technology facilitates the creation of sound. Putting aside the defining characteristics of sound, we can now achieve results with sound that were only possible with music before.

Heinrich Deisl: To quote John Cage, 'everything we do is music'. Is it possible to hear music as sound, or sound as music?[25]

Diedrich Diederichsen: As soon as there are sound waves, we have sound. Therefore, all music is sound, too. Inverting this question is interesting. The great challenge of sound art is to try and compose sound as music. However, in historical terms, there is an objection. As early as the 1960s, Pierre Boulez criticized Cage's aleatory music – correctly, I think – arguing that it is impossible to compose chance. Chance can only occur. If Cage had insisted on the music of pure chance, he probably would not have been regarded as a serious composer for long. In regards to composition methods and reception behaviour, the situation has radically changed since Cage. Today, aleatory composition is computerized and the authors of such pieces are definitely regarded as serious artists. We are now able to compose with sound, as many creative people are currently proving.

Heinrich Deisl: Pop music is often criticized for promoting emotionality and hedonistic escape. Do you agree?

Diedrich Diederichsen: All art harbours an ideological prejudice against reflection. Applied to pop music, this means that legitimating a reflection about it is as easy or as difficult as, for instance, thinking about football. I suspect the

---

25 In his famous essay, 'The Future of Music: Credo', Cage writes: 'If this word "music" is sacred and reserved for eighteenth- and nineteenth-century instruments, we can substitute a more meaningful term: organization of sound.' John Cage, *Silence: Lectures and Writings* (Middleton, CT: Wesleyan University Press, 1961), pp. 3–7 (p. 3).

problem – or rather the accusation – is based on the fact that pop music is a phenomenon that often comes with a degree of affective and emotional commitment. More than that, it seems to involve an imperative that resists any kind of reflection. Of course, pop music toys with such commitments. But I believe it is counterproductive to claim that an emotional reaction precludes contemplation. Affect, after all, does not only occur in pop music, but also in mass demonstrations or fascism. I don't think anybody would discourage a scholar of contemporary history from analyzing fascist mass phenomena because the people involved were emotionally engaged. Why, then, put a ban on pop music research?

The German Dimension

In general, Krautrock and the 'German Invasion'[26] it was bound up with – the best known examples being bands like Amon Düül, Can, Faust,[27] Harmonia, early Kraftwerk, Neu! And Tangerine Dream – can be regarded as one of the most powerful catalysts of popular German post-war music.[28] Krautrock defines Germany's specific situation in terms of the country's National Socialist past, the Cold War and the links between art universities and experimental music. In recent years, we have witnessed a renewed interest in Krautrock, both in pop music and academic research. Record labels like Bureau B from Hamburg or Berlin's Groenland have reissued the back catalogues of many bands and artists related to Krautrock.

The second music genre Germany is often associated with in an international context is techno. Reunified Berlin in particular reverberated with the electronically-generated vibrations of the post-1989 generation after the fall of the Wall.[29]

---

26 See Mark Jenkins, 'The German Invasion: British one got better press, but the Teutonic influence endures', *The Washington Post*, 21. January 1996.

27 Heinrich Deisl, 'Im Faust'schen Maelstrom: Hans-Joachim Irmler zu *Faust Is Last*', *skug – Journal für Musik*, 83/7–9 (2010), 18–21.

28 Biba Kopf writes: 'The only country to successfully challenge American road mythology is pre-unification West Germany, where the Autobahn has superseded Route 66 in the roadmap of rock history.' Biba Kopf, 'The Autobahn goes on forever: Kings of the road: The Motorik Pulse of Kraftwerk and Neu!', in *Undercurrents: The Hidden Wiring of Modern Music*, ed. by Rob Young and *The Wire* (London: Continuum, 2002), pp. 141–152 (p. 143). See also David Stubbs, *Future Days: Krautrock and the Building of Modern Germany* (London: Faber & Faber, 2014).

29 See Anja Schwanhäußer, *Kosmonauten des Underground: Ethnografie einer Berliner Szene*, Interdisziplinäre Stadtforschung (Frankfurt: Campus, 2010); Ingo Bader and Albert Scharenberg, 'The Sound of Berlin: Subculture and Global Music Industry', in *The Berlin Reader: A Compen-*

Through an integration of sound art and updates of electronic music since the 1960s,[30] the experimental branches of techno (ambient, Detroit techno, electronica/'glitch', 'intelligent dance music', post-industrial/noise music) inaugurated shifts in approaches to pop music. Many debates on the logics of composition, production and utilization of purely electronic as well as predominately lyric-free music bourgeoned in this context, sparking a more precise denotation of sounds and sound duration: 'For the first time, *Maschinenmusik* made it possible to envisage art without human authors.'[31]

Heinrich Deisl: To what extent did German bands and Germany as a site of music production influence you?

Diedrich Diederichsen: I was born and raised in Germany. Many of my acquaintances and friends made German pop music and of course I enjoyed some of it. I was interested in German pop music when it tried to imitate something or someone. My favourite example, which I also mention in *Über Pop-Musik*, is the band 39 Clocks, who played psychedelic 1960s music in the 1980s inflected in a Hanover accent. I always detested German pop music that purported to be 'German'.

Heinrich Deisl: Krautrock as genuinely 'German' music[32] has attracted much attention of late as a result of both various re-issues of albums as well as academic assessments. What is your perspective on this development?

Diedrich Diederichsen: I still remember all the countless Krautrock concerts I attended in the 1970s. But, to be honest, you didn't go to see the local Krautrock band that was opening, but rather the British or American headliner. Of course, there were many Krautrock bands I really liked. There was a time when I was a really devoted fan of early Can.

My hypothesis about Krautrock is that there was as much strange music in Britain as there was in Germany. However, in Britain, its nonconformist edge was always quickly subdued by the record companies in order to make it sell. British progressive rock was as crazy and weird as Krautrock, but prog rock existed in an

---

dium on Urban Change and Activism. Urban Studies, ed. by Matthias Bernt, Britta Grell and Andrej Holm (Bielefeld: Transcript, 2013), pp. 239–60.

30 See Tim Caspar Boehme, 'The Echo of the Wall Fades: Reflections on the "Berlin School" in the early 1970s', in *The Acoustic City*, ed. by Matthew Gandy and BJ Nilsen (Berlin: Jovis, 2014), pp. 84–90.

31 Diederichsen, *Über Pop-Musik*, p. 334.

32 For a discussion on the characteristics of 'typically' German popular music, see *Typisch Deutsch. (Eigen-)Sichten auf populäre Musik in diesem unserem Land*, ed. by Dietrich Helms and Thomas Phleps (Bielefeld: Transcript, 2014).

environment in which you were able to make money from it. In Germany this was not a viable option. Firstly, the recording industry was not as organized as in the UK. Secondly, the relationship between 'traditional' experimental music and the arts was different in Germany, since it was not established through art schools, as in the UK, but rather through art institutions or well-known individuals. I am thinking of the connection between Uwe Nettelbeck and Faust, or between Can and Schloss Nörvenich.[33]

Apart from that, I don't think Krautrock was something specifically 'German'. Music like that simply happened in the 1970s when you left long-haired, bearded and drug-consuming people alone. This was also the case in France as well as in Uruguay, in Turkey or in Hungary. However, there may have been no other place where so many such people were left so alone to do their thing without anybody caring, as in Germany.

Heinrich Deisl: Germany is regarded as one of the most important places for techno. I am thinking of the Berlin techno scene and of record labels like Basic Channel, BPitch Control, Disko B, Mille Plateaux, Kompakt and Tresor. Why might that be?

Diedrich Diederichsen: Techno has a lot to do with an international post-1989 atmosphere. The fall of the Berlin Wall was crucial: it was the spark for German techno culture. Even though there are other techno centres, like Cologne for instance, techno in Germany has a special connection to Berlin and its history. Techno is very much alive in Berlin and many tourists come to the capital for this reason. On a less euphoric note, we might say that techno was just a further step in the successful development of the city as a hot spot, which it had already been in the 1980s.[34] The well-established Berlin subculture of the time reinitialized itself with techno in 1989, a kind of ground zero, so to speak. You were instantly able to get on board with a pop music that was not, as German pop music had long been, full of tributes to the past and burdened with Western post-war

---

33 Former *Filmkritik* and *Die Zeit* author and producer Nettelbeck had facilitated the deal between Faust and the label Polydor as well as their studio in Wümme (near Hamburg), and produced the first two Faust albums. From 1968 to 1971, Can recorded their first three albums in this manor in North Rhine-Westphalia that sculptor Ulrich Rückriem had converted into a studio for them.

34 See Wolfgang Müller, *Subkultur Westberlin 1979–1989*. Freizeit. Fundus vol. 203, 4th rev. edn (Hamburg: Philo Fine Arts, 2014).

history and its unresolved catastrophes. The world of the 1990s with its techno scenes was a determined new beginning with an international orientation.[35]

---

35 For an early evaluation of these topics, see Diedrich Diederichsen, 'Digital Electronic Music: Between Pop and Pure Mediality. Paradoxical Strategies for a Refusal of Semantics', in *Sonic Process: A New Geography of Sounds,* Exhibition catalogue, ed. by Mela Dávila and Christine Van Assche (Barcelona: Museu d'Art Contemporani de Barcelona/Actar, 2002), pp. 31–37.

Contributors

Alexander Carpenter is an Associate Professor and Director of Music at the University of Alberta, Augustana campus. His research interests include the music of Arnold Schönberg, the musical, cultural and intellectual history of Vienna, music and psychoanalysis and popular music. His research has recently appeared in *Popular Music and Society, Journal of Popular Culture, Musical Quarterly* and the *Grove Dictionary of American Music*. He is currently working on a monograph on the history of gothic rock for Lexington Press.

Heinrich Deisl is a cultural theorist, music journalist and radio producer based in Vienna. He is a doctoral candidate at the Vienna Academy of Fine Arts, analysing the sound topography of Viennese popular culture since the mid-1990s. He is director of the arts and culture department of Campus & City Radio 94.4 at the University of Applied Sciences St. Pölten and a regular contributor to the series 'Zeit-Ton' for the Austrian state radio station Ö1. From 2013 to 2015, he was editor-in-chief of the periodical *Skug – Journal für Musik*. Latest publications include *Im Puls der Nacht: Sub- und Populärkultur in Wien 1955–1976* (Vienna: Turia + Kant, 2013) and with Katharina Gsöllpointner (eds), *Peter Weibel* (Vienna: Der Konterfei, 2015).

Diedrich Diederichsen is widely regarded as one of the leading German pop music theoreticians, building up important links between journalistic and academic approaches on pop music. From the mid-1980s to 2000, he was mainly associated with the magazine *Spex*, of which he was editor and later publisher. Since 2006, Diederichsen holds a chair at the Institute for Art Theory and Cultural Studies at the Academy of Fine Arts Vienna. There are some 25 books on pop music, cinema and contemporary arts he authored or edited, addressing these topics as symptoms of wider political, social and aesthetic phenomena. His latest major publication, *Über Pop-Musik* (Cologne: KiWi, 2014), presents a comprehensive and ground-breaking theory of pop music.

Christian Jäger is Privatdozent at the department of German at the Humboldt Universität zu Berlin, a former Max-Kade-Professor at Duke University and UNC at Chapel Hill in 2008, as well as Visiting Scholar at Cornell University in 2006. His publications focus on contemporary literature, popular music and culture, the Weimar Republic, GDR literature, literature of the Goethe era, literary theory and aesthetics. He is the author of 'Wiederkehr der Neuen Sachlichkeit? Eine Obduktion der neuen deutschen Pop-Literatur', in *Berlin – Kultur und Metropole in den 20er und seit den 90er Jahren*, ed. by Godela Sussex-Weiss and Ulrike Zitzlsperger (Munich: Iudicium, 2007), pp. 62–77 and 'Die "härteste Band von allen": Terrorismus in der gegenwärtigen Literatur und Populär-Kultur', *Jahrbuch Literatur und Politik* 1 (2006), pp. 117–127.

Christoph Jürgensen is Akademischer Rat at the Bergische Universität Wuppertal. His research and teaching focus on cultural studies, particularly popular culture. He has written a number of articles on German pop literature and cinema. With Ingo Irsigler he co-edited *Nine Eleven: Ästhetische Verarbeitungen des 11. September 2001* (Heidelberg: Winter, [2]2011); with Gerhard Kaiser he co-edited *Schriftstellerische Inszenierungspraktiken – Typologie und Geschichte*

(Heidelberg: Winter, 2011). He is currently working on an extensive study dealing with propagandistic writing during the Napoleonic Wars.

John Littlejohn is Visiting Assistant Professor of German at Randolph-Macon College in Virginia. His research and teaching interests include German cinema and popular music. In the latter of these areas, he has written several articles and book chapters focusing on Rammstein, Kraftwerk and German hip-hop. In 2009 he served as a guest editor for a special Krautrock edition of the journal *Popular Music and Society*. He co-edited *Rammstein on Fire: New Perspectives on the Music and Performances* (Jefferson: Mcfarland, 2013). His current projects examine East German rock music and silent film.

Julio Mendívil is a professor of ethnomusicology at the Johann Wolfgang Goethe University in Frankfurt. He was director of the Center for World Music at the University of Hildesheim (2013–2015) and Chair of IASPM Latin American Branch (2012–2016). He specializes in the area of musical sociology and Andean music. He is an acknowledged expert on German *Schlager* and has published *Schlager, Ein musikalisches Stück Heimat: Ethnologische Beobachtungen zum deutschen Schlager* (Bielefeld: Transcript, 2008).

Alexei Monroe is a London-based cultural theorist with a PhD in Communication and Image Studies from the University of Kent. His work *Interrogation Machine: Laibach and NSK* (Cambridge: MIT Press, 2005) has also been published in Slovenia, France and Germany. He was programme director of the *First NSK Citizens' Congress* and editor of the Congress book *State of Emergence* (Leipzig: Ploettner /Poison Cabinet, 2011). He is one of the organizers of the *2nd NSK Folk Art Biennale* to be held in Ireland in summer 2016 and the co-editor of *Total State Machine* (Bristol: PC Press, 2015), a major anthology on the British industrial group Test Dept. Research interests include techno, electronic and industrial music, monumentalism and architecture and the cultural history of the stag. He is the founder of the electronic music label VEB89 and active as a reviewer and DJ.

Marissa Munderloh received her Ph.D. in 2015 from the University of St Andrews. Her research interests comprise national identity, cultural hybridity and pop culture. Her thesis has appeared as *The Emergence of Post-Hybrid Identities: A Comparative Analysis of National Identity Formations in Germany's Hip-Hop Culture* (London: IMLR, 2016). Further publications include '"Heb' die Fahne hoch, Santa Pauli Patriot": A Case Study of Place-Making in German Rap Music', in *Place-Making in urbanen Diskursen*, ed. by Beatrix Busse and Ingo Warnke (Berlin: De Gruyter, 2014).

David Robb s a Senior Lecturer in the School of Creative Arts at Queen's University Belfast. His research specialism is the history of German political song. Publications include *Zwei Clowns im Lande des verlorenen Lachens: Das Liedertheater Wenzel & Mensching* (Berlin: Links, 1998) and *Protest Song in East and West Germany since the 1960s* (Rochester/NY: Camden House, 2007). Since 2008 he has been involved in a research collaboration with the Zentrum für populäre Kultur und Musik at the University of Freiburg on the history of the reception of the songs of the 1848 Revolution.

Uwe Schütte is Reader in German at Aston University, Birmingham/UK. He gained his PhD in 1997 from the University of East Anglia in Norwich. His *Basis-Diskothek Pop & Rock* (Stuttgart:

Reclam, 2011) is currently in its third edition and he regularly contributes to German newspapers and magazines such as *Spex*, *Der Freitag*, *Wiener Zeitung* and *Volltext*. He is the author of more than thirteen monographs and has edited six volumes. His latest publications include, *GODSTAR – Der verquere Weg des Genesis P-Orridge* (Vienna: Der Konterfei, 2015), *Interventionen: Literaturkritik als Widerspruch bei W.G. Sebald* (Munich: Edition Text & Kritik, 2014), *Unterwelten: Zu Leben und Werk von Gerhard Roth* (St. Pölten: Residenz, 2013), *Urzeit, Traumzeit, Endzeit – Versuch über Heiner Müller* (Vienna: Passagen, 2012).

Cyrus Shahan is Assistant Professor of German at Colby College. He gained his Ph.D. (2008) in German Literature from the University of North Carolina at Chapel Hill and is the author of *Punk Rock and German Crises: Adaptation and Resistance After 1977* (London: Palgrave, 2013) and co-editor of *Beyond No Future: Cultures of German Punk* (London: Bloomsbury, 2016). His additional research focuses on the aesthetics and politics of twentieth- and twenty-first century literature and culture, literary and cultural theory, media studies, modern European intellectual history and terrorism. He has published on terrorism and punk, Elfriede Jelinek and September 11, 2001, Alexander Kluge and is writing on the birth of Autotune and a monograph on globalization titled *Containment*.

Antonius Weixler is Wissenschaftlicher Mitarbeiter at Bergische Universität Wuppertal. His research and teaching focus on narratology, cultural studies and the European avant-garde. He has written a number of articles on the phenomenon of authenticity in contemporary German Literature and edited *Authentisches Erzählen: Produktion, Narration und Rezeption eines Zuschreibungsphänomens* (Berlin: De Gruyter, 2012). He recently published a monograph on the avant-garde writer and critic Carl Einstein (*Poetik des Transvisuellen: Carl Einsteins "écriture visionnaire"* (Berlin: De Gruyter, 2016). He is currently executive editor of *DIEGESIS: Interdisciplinary E-Journal for Narrative Research*.

Bibliography

Adelt, Ulrich, *Krautrock: German Music in the Seventies* (Ann Arbor: University of Michigan Press, 2016).

Adelt, Ulrich, 'Machines with a Heart: German Identity in the Music of Can and Kraftwerk', *Popular Music and Society*, 35/3 (2012), 359–374.

Adorno, Theodor W. and Max Horkheimer, *Dialektik der Aufklärung* (Frankfurt: Suhrkamp, 1988).

Agard, Olivier, Christian Helmreich and Hélène Vinckel-Roisin, eds, *Das Populäre: Untersuchungen zu Interaktionen und Differenzierungsstrategien in Literatur, Kultur und Sprache* (Göttingen: Vandenhoeck & Ruprecht, 2010).

Albiez, Sean and David Pattie, eds, *Kraftwerk: Music Non-Stop* (New York: Continuum, 2011).

Androutsopoulos, Jannis, ed., *Hip-Hop: Globale Kultur – lokale Praktiken* (Bielefeld: Transcript, 2003).

Applegate, Celia and Pamela Potter, eds, *Music and German National Identity* (Chicago: University of Chicago Press, 2002).

Arnold, Heinz Ludwig, ed., *Franz-Josef Degenhardt: Politische Lieder 1964–1972* (Munich: Edition Text & Kritik, 1972).

Baacke, Dieter, *Beat: Die sprachlose Opposition* (Munich: Juventa Verlag, 1970).

Bardong, Matthias, Hermann Demmler and Christian Pfarr, *Das Lexikon des deutschen Schlagers* (Mainz, Munich: Schott & Piper, 1993).

Bargeld, Blixa, *Stimme frisst Feuer* (Berlin: Merve, 1988).

Barr, Tim, *Kraftwerk: From Dusseldorf to the Future With Love* (London: Ebury, 1998).

Brown, Timothy S., '(African-)Americanization and Hip Hop in Germany', in *The Vinyl ain't Final: Hip Hop and the Globalization of Black Culture*, ed. by Dipannita Basu and Sidney J. Lemelle (London: Pluto Press, 2006), pp. 137–150.

Brown, Timothy S., 'Music as a Weapon? Ton Steine Scherben and the Politics of Rock in Cold War Berlin', *German Studies Review*, 32/1 (2009), 1–22.

Buckley, David, *Kraftwerk: Publikation* (London: Omnibus, 2011).

Bundeszentrale für politische Bildung, ed., *Rock! Jugendkultur und Musik in Deutschland* (Berlin: Links, 2005).

Busse, Burkhard, *Der deutsche Schlager: Eine Untersuchung zur Produktion, Distribution und Rezeption von Trivialliteratur* (Wiesbaden: Athenaion, 1976).

Büsser, Martin, *On The Wild Side: Die wahre Geschichte der Popmusik* (Mainz: Ventil, 2013).

Büsser, Martin, *Wie klingt die Neue Mitte? Rechte und reaktionäre Tendenzen in der Popmusik* (Mainz: Ventil, 2001).

Bussy, Pascal, *Kraftwerk: Man, Machine and Music* (London: SAF, 2005).

Bussy, Pascal, *The Can Book* (Harrow: SAF, 1989).

Cheesman, Tom, 'Polyglot Pop Politics: Hip Hop in Germany', *Debatte*, 6/2 (1998), 191–214.

Connell, John and Chris Gibson, *Sound Tracks: Popular Music, Identity, and Place* (London: Routledge, 2003).

Cope, Julian, *Krautrocksampler*, 2nd edn (Great Britain: Head Heritage, 1996).

Czerny, Peter and Heinz Hofmann, *Der Schlager: Ein Panorama der leichten Musik*. Bd. 1. (Berlin: VEB Musikverlag, 1968).

DOI 10.1515/9783110425727-013

Dedekind, Henning, *Krautrock: Underground, LSD und kosmische* Kuriere (Höfen: Hannibal, 2008).

Degenhardt, Franz Josef, *Spiel nicht mit den Schmuddelkindern: Balladen, Chansons, Grotesken, Lieder* (Reinbek: Rowohlt, 1969).

Denk, Felix and Sven von Thülen, *Der Klang der Familie* (Berlin: Suhrkamp, 2014).

Derogatis, Jim, *Kaleidoscope Eyes: Psychedelic Rock from the '60s to the '90s* (Secaucus, NJ: Carol, 1996).

Diederichsen, Diedrich, *Der lange Weg nach Mitte: Der Sound und die Stadt* (Cologne: KiWi, 1999).

Diederichsen, Diedrich, *Eigenblutdoping: Selbstverwertung, Künstlerromantik, Partizipation* (Cologne: KiWi, 2008).

Diederichsen, Diedrich, *Musikzimmer: Avantgarde und Alltag* (Cologne: KiWi, 2005).

Diederichsen, Diedrich, *Politische Korrekturen* (Cologne: KiWi, 1996).

Diederichsen, Diedrich, *Über Pop-Musik* (Cologne: KiWi, 2014).

Dietrich, Wolfgang, *Samba, Samba: Eine politikwissenschaftliche Untersuchung zur fernen Erotik Lateinamerikas in den Schlagern des 20. Jahrhunderts* (Strasshof: Vier-Viertel-Verlag, 2002).

Dirke, Sabine von, 'Hip-Hop Made in Germany: From Old School to the Kanaksta Movement', in *German Popular Culture: How "American" is It?*, ed. by Agnes C. Mueller (Ann Arbor: The University of Michigan Press, 2004), pp. 96–112.

Eisler, Hanns, *Musik und Politik: Schriften 1924–1948* (Leipzig: VEB Deutscher Verlag für Musik, 1973).

Elflein, Dietmar, 'From Krauts with Attitudes to Turks with Attitudes: Some Aspects of Hip-Hop History in Germany', *Popular Music*, 17/3 (1998), 255–265.

Fisher, Mark, *Capitalist Realism: Is there no alternative?* (London: Zero Books, 2009).

Flür, Wolfgang, *Kraftwerk: I Was A Robot* (London: Sanctuary, 2000).

Frith, Simon, *Performing Rites: Evaluating Popular Music* (Oxford and New York: Oxford University Press, 1998).

Grasskamp, Walter, *Das Cover von Sgt. Pepper: Eine Momentaufnahme der Popkultur* (Berlin: Wagenbach, 2004).

Grönholm, Pertti, 'When Tomorrow Began Yesterday: Kraftwerk's nostalgia for the Past Futures', *Popular Music and Society*, 38/3 (2015), 372–388.

Groos, Ulrike and Peter Gorschlüter, *Zurück zum Beton: Die Anfänge von Punk und New Wave in Deutschland 1977–'82: Kunsthalle Düsseldorf, 7. Juli–15. September 2002* (Cologne: König, 2002).

Hagström, Andréas, ed., *Influenser, referenser och plagiat: Om Kraftwerk estetik* (Göteborg: Röhsska Museet, 2015).

Hall, Mirko, Seth Howes and Cyrus Shahan, eds, *Beyond No Future: Cultures of German Punk* (New York and London: Bloomsbury, 2016).

Häusermann, Jürg, *Und dabei liebe ich euch beide: Unterhaltung durch Schlager und Fernsehserien* (Wiesbaden: Breitkopf & Härtel, 1978).

Hebdige, Dick, *Subculture: The Meaning of Style* (London: Methune, 1979).

Helms, Siegfried, ed., *Schlager in Deutschland: Beiträge zur Analyse der Popularmusik und des Musikmarktes* (Wiesbaden: Breitkopf & Härtel, 1972).

Herrwerth, Thommi, *Katzeklo & Caprifischer: Die deutschen Hits aus 50 Jahren* (Berlin: Rütten & Loening, 1998).

Höfig, Eckhart, *Heimat in der Popmusik: Identität oder Kulisse in der deutschsprachigen Popmusikszene vor der Jahrtausendwende* (Gelsenhausen: Triga Verlag, 2000).

Hornberger, Barbara, *Geschichte wird gemacht: Die Neue Deutsche Welle: Eine Epoche deutscher Popmusik* (Würzburg: Königshausen und Neumann, 2011).

Hurley, Andrew Wright, *Into the Groove: Popular Music and Contemporary German Fiction* (Rochester: Camden House, 2015).

Jäger, Christian, 'Wörterflucht oder Die kategoriale Not der Literaturwissenschaft angesichts der Literatur der achtziger Jahre', *Internationales Jahrbuch für Germanistik* 1 (1995), 85–100.

Kaul, Timor, 'Kraftwerk: Die anderen "Krauts"', in *Reflexionen zum Progressive Rock*, ed. by Martin Lücke and Klaus Näumann (Munich: Allitera, 2016), pp. 201–225.

Koch, Albert, *Angriff auf Schlaraffenland: 20 Jahre deutschsprachige Popmusik* (Frankfurt: Ullstein, 1987).

Kotsopoulos, Nikolaos, ed, *Krautrock: Cosmic Rock and its Legacy* (London: Black Dog, 2009).

Kraushaar, Elmar, *Rote Lippen: Die ganze Welt des deutschen Schlagers* (Reinbek: Rowohlt, 1983).

Kreier, Florian Tobias, *Die Band Ton Steine Scherben: Subpolitiker einer Gegenkultur?* (Hamburg: Diplomica, 2012).

Kumpf, Terence, 'The Transculturating Potential of Hip-Hop in Germany', in *Hip-Hop in Europe – Cultural Identities and Transnational Flows*, ed. by Sina A. Nietzsche and Walter Grünzweig (Zurich and Berlin: LIT, 2013), pp. 207–226.

Layne, Priscilla, 'One Like No Other? Blaxploitation in the Performance of Afro-German Rapper Lisi', *Journal of Popular Music Studies*, 25/2 (2013), 198–221.

Lessour, Théo, *Berlin Sampler: From Cabaret to Techno: 1904–2012, A Century of Berlin Music* (Berlin: Ollendorff, 2012).

Lindenberg, Udo, *Rock'n'Roll und Rebellion: Ein Panisches Panorama* (Munich: Heyne, 1984).

Littlejohn, John T. and Michael T. Putnam, 'Rammstein and *Ostalgie*: Longing for Yesteryear', *Popular Music and Society,* 33/1 (2010), 35–44.

Littlejohn, John T. and Michael T. Putnam, eds, *Rammstein on Fire: New Perspectives on the Music and Performance* (Jefferson, NC: McFarland, 2013).

Littlejohn, John T., 'Kraftwerk: Language, Lucre, and Loss of Identity', *Popular Music and Society*, 32/5 (2009), 635–653.

Loh, Hannes and Murat Güngör, *Fear of a Kanak Planet: Hip-Hop zwischen Nazi-Rap und Weltkultur* (Höfen: Hannibal, 2002).

Loh, Hannes and Sascha Verlan, *25 Jahre Hip-Hop in Deutschland* (Höfen: Hannibal, 2006).

Mahnert, Detlev and Harry Stürmer, *Zappa, Zoff und Zwischentöne: Die Internationalen Essener Songtage 1968* (Essen: Klartext, 2008).

Malamud, René, *Zur Psychologie des deutschen Schlagers: Eine Untersuchung anhand seiner Texte* (Winterthur: Keller, 1964).

Mäsker, Mechthild, *Das Frauenbild im Schlager von 1970 bis 1985: Eine repräsentative Textanalyse deutscher Erfolgsschlager* (Phil. Diss.: Westfälische Wilhelms-Universität zu Münster, 1989).

Meinecke, Thomas, *Mode & Verzweiflung* (Frankfurt: Suhrkamp, 1998).

Mellmann, Katja, 'Helden aus der Spielzeugkiste: Zu einem Motiv in den Texten der Neuen Deutschen Welle (NDW)', *Mitteilungen des Deutschen Germanistenverbandes: Songs* 52 (2005), 254–274.

Mendívil, Julio, *Ein musikalisches Stück Heimat: Ethnologische Beobachtungen zum deutschen Schlager* (Bielefeld: Transcript Verlag, 2008).

Mezger, Werner, *Schlager: Versuch einer Gesamtdarstellung unter besonderer Berücksichtigung des Musikmarktes der Bundesrepublik Deutschland* (Tübingen: Tübinger Vereinigung für Volkskunde, 1975).

Munderloh, Marissa K., *The Emergence of Post-Hybrid Identities: A Comparative Analysis of National Identity Formations in Germany's Hip-Hop Culture* (London: MHRA, 2016).

Neumann, Thomas, *Rechtsrock im Wandel: Eine Textanalyse von Rechtsrock-Bands* (Hamburg: Diplomica, 2009).

Nye, Sean, 'Minimal Understandings: The Berlin Decade, The Minimal Continuum, and Debates on the Legacy of German Techno', in *Journal of Popular Music Studies*, 25/2 (2013), 154–184.

Poiger, Uta, *Jazz, Rock, and Rebels: Cold War Politics and American Culture in a Divided Germany* (Berkeley: University of California Press, 2000).

Port le roi, André, *Schlager lügen nicht: Deutscher Schlager und Politik in Ihrer Zeit* (Essen: Klartext, 1998).

Potter, Pamela, 'What is Nazi Music?', *Musical Quarterly*, 88/3 (2005), 428–455.

Putnam, Michael and Juliane Schicker, 'Straight outta Marzahn: (Re)Constructing Communicative Memory in East Germany through Hip Hop', *Popular Music and Society*, 37/1 (2014), 85–100.

Putnam, Michael T. and John Littlejohn, 'National Socialism with Fler? German Hip Hop from the Right', *Popular Music and Society*, 30/4 (2008), 453–468.

Redaktion Musikexpress, *Made in Germany: Die hundert besten deutschen Platten* (Höfen: Hannibal, 2001).

Reed, S. Alexander, *Assimilate: A Critical History of Industrial Music* (Oxford: OUP, 2013).

Reiser, Rio, *König von Deutschland: Erinnerungen an Ton Steine Scherben und mehr* (Berlin: Möbius Rekords, 2001).

Reisloh, Jens, *Deutschsprachige Popmusik: Zwischen Morgenrot und Hundekot: Von den Anfängen um 1970 bis ins 21. Jahrhundert* (Münster: Telos, 2011).

Robb, David, ed, *Protest Song in East and West Germany* (Rochester/ NY: Camden House, 2007).

Saied, Ayla Güler, *Rap in Deutschland: Musik als Interaktionsmedium zwischen Partykultur und urbanen Anerkennungskämpfen* (Bielefeld: Transcript, 2012).

Savage, Jon, *England's Dreaming: Anarchy, Sex Pistols, Punk Rock and Beyond* (New York: St. Martin's Griffen, 2002).

Schär, Christian, *Der Schlager und seine Tänze im Deutschland der 20er Jahre: Sozialgeschichtliche Aspekte zum Wandel in der Musik- und Tanzkultur während der Weimarer Republik* (Zürich: Chronos Verlag, 1991).

Schiller, Melanie, 'Fun Fun Fun on the Autobahn: Kraftwerk Challenging Germanness', *Popular Music and Society*, 37/5 (2014), 618–637.

Schlösser, Christian, 'Neu in der Hamburger Schule? Schule, Archiv und Markt in deutschsprachiger Popmusik der 1990er Jahre', in: *Deutsches Lied, Volume II: Vom Niedergang der Diseusenkultur bis zu Aggro Berlin*, ed. by Gregor Ackermann, Walter Delabar and Carsten Würmann (Bielefeld: Aisthesis, 2007), pp. 503–501.

Schmidt-Joos, Siegfried, *Geschäfte mit Schlagern* (Bremen: Schünemann, 1960).

Schmidt, Hildegard and Wolf Kampmann, *Can Book Box* (Münster: Medium Music, 1998).

Schneider, Frank A., *Als die Welt noch unterging: von Punk zu NDW* (Mainz: Ventil, 2006).

Schneider, Frank A., *Deutschpop halt's Maul! Für eine Ästhetik der Verkrampfung* (Mainz: Ventil, 2015).

Schütte, Uwe, *Basis-Diskothek Rock und Pop* (Stuttgart: Reclam, 2004).

Seidel, Wolfgang, *Scherben: Musik, Politik und Wirkung der Ton Steine Scherben* (Mainz: Ventil Verlag, 2005).

Seiler, Sascha, *"Das einfache wahre Abschreiben der Welt": Pop-Diskurse in der deutschen Literatur nach 1960* (Göttingen: Vandenhoeck & Ruprecht, 2006).

Shahan, Cyrus M., 'The Sounds of Terror: Punk, Post-Punk and the RAF After 1977' in *Popular Music and Society,* 34/3 (2011), 369–386.

Shryane, Jennifer, *Blixa Bargeld and Einstürzende Neubauten: German Experimental Music – 'Evading Do-Re-Mi'* (Farnham: Ashgate, 2011).

Sichtermann, Kai, Jens Johler and Christian Stahl, *Keine Macht für niemand: Die Geschichte der Ton Steine Scherben* (Berlin: Schwarzkopf & Schwarzkopf, 2003).

Sperr, Monika, *Das Große Schlager-Buch: Deutscher Schlager 1800–Heute* (Munich: Rogner & Bernhard, 1978).

Stehle, Maria, *Ghetto Voices in Contemporary German Culture* (New York: Camden House, 2012).

Stubbs, David, *Future Days: Krautrock and the Building of Modern Germany* (London: Faber & Faber, 2014).

Teipel, Jürgen, *Verschwende deine Jugend: Ein Doku-Roman über den deutschen Punk und New Wave* (Frankfurt: Suhrkamp, 2001).

Templeton, Inez H., *What's so German about It? Cultural Identity in the Berlin Hip Hop Scene* (Stirling: University of Stirling, 2006).

Terkessidis, Mark, 'Die Eingeborenen von Schizonesien: Der Schlager als deutscheste aller Popkulturen', in *Mainstream der Minderheiten: Pop in der Kontrollgesellschaft*, ed. by Tom Holert and Mark Terkessidis (Berlin: Edition ID-Archiv, 1996), p. 115–138.

Twickel, Christoph, *Läden, Schuppen, Kaschemmen: Eine Hamburger Popkulturgeschichte* (Hamburg: Nautilus, 2003).

Ungeheuer, Elena, *Wie die elektronische Musik 'erfunden' wurde: Quellenstudien zu Werner Meyer-Epplers Entwurf zwischen 1949 und 1953* (Mainz: Schott, 1992).

Varon, Jermey, *Bringing the War Home: The Weather Underground, the Red Army Faction, and Revolutionary Violence in the 1960s and 1970s* (Berkeley: University of California Press, 2004).

Wagner, Peter, *Pop 2000: 50 Jahre Popmusik und Jugendkultur in Deutschland* (Hamburg: Ideal, 1999).

Wicke, Peter, 'Das Ende: Populäre Musik im faschistischen Deutschland', in *Ich will aber gerade vom Leben singen…: Über populäre Musik vom ausgehenden 18. Jahrhundert bis zum Ende der Weimarer Republik*, ed. by Sabine Schutte. (Reinbek: Rowohlt, 1987), pp. 418–429.

Wicke, Peter, *Vom Umgang mit Musik* (Berlin: Volk und Wissen Verlag, 1993).

Wicke, Peter, *Von Mozart zu Madonna: Eine Kulturgeschichte der Popmusik* (Frankfurt: Suhrkamp, 2001).

Williams, Justin A., *Musical Borrowing in Hip-Hop Music: Theoretical Frameworks and Case Studies* (Nottingham: University of Nottingham, 2009).

Wißmann, Friederike, *Deutsche Musik* (Berlin: Berlin Verlag, 2015).

Worbs, Hans Christoph, *Der Schlager: Bestandsaufnahme, Analyse, Dokumentation* (Bremen: Schünemann, 1960).

Wulf, Joseph, *Musik im Dritten Reich. Eine Dokumentation* (Gütersloh: Sigbert Mohn, 1963).

Index